CAPITALISM WITH CHINESE CHARACTERISTICS

Since 1978, the Chinese economy has grown phenomenally. This is not in dispute. By exactly what mechanisms has China managed to grow so fast? There is more room for debate on this question. A widespread view is that private entrepreneurship, financial liberalization, and political reforms played a minor role in explaining China's economic takeoff. Based on archival research and survey data, this book offers an alternative view: Private entrepreneurship, facilitated by access to capital and microeconomic flexibility, was at the center of China's takeoff in the 1980s. The political system, then as now, was authoritarian, but it was moving in a liberal direction. China lacked well-specified property rights, but it substantially improved security of proprietors. But given this initial success, how then to explain the substantial distortions in the Chinese economy today? The key to getting the China story right is to recognize the existence of two Chinas – an entrepreneurial rural China and a state-controlled urban China. In the 1980s, rural China gained the upper hand, and the result was rapid as well as broad-based growth. In the 1990s, urban China triumphed when the Chinese state reversed many of the productive rural experiments of the previous decade. While this reversal does not show up in the GDP numbers, it shows up in the welfare implications of growth. Since the early 1990s, household income has lagged behind economic growth and the labor share of GDP has fallen. Social performance has deteriorated. The directional liberalism of China in the 1980s and the emerging India miracle today debunk the widespread notion that democracy is automatically anti-growth. As the country marks its 30th anniversary of reforms in 2008, China faces some of its toughest economic challenges and vulnerabilities. The long overdue political reforms are required to improve governance and accountability and to put China on a sustainable path of development.

Professor Yasheng Huang teaches political economy and international management at the Sloan School of Management, Massachusetts Institute of Technology. He previously held faculty positions at the University of Michigan and at the Harvard Business School and as a consultant at the World Bank. He has published *Inflation and Investment Controls in China* (1996), *FDI in China* (1998), and *Selling China* (2003; Chinese version in 2005). His work on FDI in China has been featured in the *Wall Street Journal*, the *Economist*, *Bloomberg*, *Businessworld*, *Le Monde*, *Economic and Political Weekly*, and *Economic Times*, as well as in Chinese publications such as *Nanfang Zhoumo*, *Nanfang Dushibao*, *Economic Observer*, *Global Entrepreneur*, *China Entrepreneur*, *Fortune Weekly*, *21st Century Business Herald*, *Liangwang*, and Xinhuanet. In addition to academic journal articles, he has written for *Financial Times*, *Foreign Policy*, and *New York Times*. In collaboration with other scholars, Professor Huang is conducting research on education and human capital in China and India and non-performing loans, privatization, and entrepreneurship in China. At MIT, Professor Huang runs a "China Lab" and an "India Lab" that help entrepreneurial businesses in China and in India improve their management.

Capitalism with Chinese Characteristics

Entrepreneurship and the State

YASHENG HUANG

Sloan School of Management, Massachusetts Institute
of Technology

CAMBRIDGE
UNIVERSITY PRESS

CAMBRIDGE UNIVERSITY PRESS
Cambridge, New York, Melbourne, Madrid, Cape Town, Singapore,
São Paulo, Delhi, Dubai, Tokyo

Cambridge University Press
32 Avenue of the Americas, New York, NY 10013-2473, USA

www.cambridge.org
Information on this title: www.cambridge.org/9780521898102

First published 2008
Reprinted 2009 (four times), 2010

Printed in the United States of America

A catalog record for this publication is available from the British Library.

Library of Congress Cataloging in Publication Data
Huang, Yasheng.
Capitalism with Chinese characteristics : entrepreneurship and the state /
Yasheng Huang.
p. cm.
Includes bibliographical references and index.
ISBN 978-0-521-89810-2 (hbk.)
1. Capitalism – China.   2. China – Economic policy.   3. Rural industries – China.
4. Entrepreneurship – China.   I. Title.
HC427.92.H8429   2008
330.12'20951–dc22   2008027116

ISBN 978-0-521-89810-2 Hardback

This book is dedicated to Nian Guangjiu, Zheng Lefeng, and Sun Dawu and millions like them who created the true China miracle.

Contents

Preface

In 1998, during my field research in Shanghai for my last book, *Selling China*, I asked a government official whether he could introduce me to some private entrepreneurs. He gave me a quizzical look and asked, "Are you a Harvard professor?" (I was teaching at Harvard then.) "As a Harvard professor," he continued, "why are you interested in those people selling watermelons, tea, and rotten apples on the street?"

Somewhat taken aback by his response, I gently reminded him that companies such as Microsoft and Hewlett-Packard were all founded and run by private entrepreneurs. I then ventured to him that maybe the reason private entrepreneurs in Shanghai were just selling watermelons and tea is because these were the only activities the government allowed them to do.

The comment by that Shanghai official has always stayed with me, and it provided the initial inspiration to write this book. (One chapter in this book is entitled, "What is wrong with Shanghai?") It is striking how his comment contrasts with much of the theorizing about Chinese reforms in the West. A prevailing view among Western academics, especially economists, is that the goal of the Chinese state was to create a market economy based on private ownership, but the reforms were blocked by political obstacles. For political expediency, policy makers then settled for the second-best options to achieve the same goals – such as partially privatizing state-owned enterprises (SOEs), introducing foreign competition, and encouraging new entrepreneurship while retaining SOEs.

The truth is closer to the spirit of the comment by that Shanghai official. As late as 1998 much of the Chinese officialdom held private entrepreneurship in utter contempt. If it is indeed the case that the Chinese state *chose* to repress the private sector, there are some major puzzles. For one, how to explain the undisputed fact that the private sector actually managed to grow over time? I provided an explanation in my last book, *Selling China*, which shows that foreign direct investment (FDI), instead of bringing technology and knowhow, acted as venture capital or private equity by providing some financing to the repressed entrepreneurs. This is the reason why FDI is so prevalent in China, from high-tech to low-tech industries and from rich to poor regions of the country. Several empirical papers have systematically confirmed this hypothesis since the publication of my book.

FDI is not the end of the story. FDI flowed into China in the 1990s, and if FDI explained the growth of the private sector and economic growth in the 1990s, how does one explain the decade of the 1980s? The question of the 1980s exposed my own ignorance of recent Chinese history. I had always assumed, as do many other academics, that the Chinese reforms followed a gradualist trajectory – first beginning with modest, small steps and then accelerating the pace and the intensity of economic transformation over time. For many years, I held the view that the reforms in the 1990s were far more radical and far-reaching than the reforms in the 1980s.

A reader of this book would recognize that the thesis of this book is exactly the opposite. It shows that the true China miracle occurred in the 1980s and that it was a miracle created by the bottom-up entrepreneurship and considerable liberalization on many fronts. In the 1990s, there was in fact a substantial reversal of reforms.

I began to question my own assumption after I had an opportunity to discuss and debate with Dr. Zhang Wei. Zhang, now a lecturer of Chinese economy at Cambridge University, is extremely knowledgeable about the history of reforms. He was a rising star in the Chinese government in the 1980s, heading an important economic development zone in Tianjin at a young age. Zhang Wei, gently but firmly, told me that my gradualist perspective significantly understated the pace of reforms in the 1980s. Since that conversation, I began to notice that quite a few insiders – those who worked in the Chinese system – held a similar view. Li Changping, a rural official whom I quoted in Chapter 3, was most direct about the reversal of reforms in the 1990s.

But an academic treatment of this topic requires more than producing the opinions of insiders. The view has to be substantiated by data. This is the challenge. Few social scientists appreciate just how difficult it is to get accurate Chinese data, especially about the 1980s. The Cultural Revolution completely destroyed the Chinese system of data collection. According to one account, only 46 people worked at the National Bureau of Statistics (NBS) in 1976 and, as late as 1986, 90 percent of the Chinese economic data were handled manually. (In 1985, the NBS conducted an economic census. An American economist inquired about obtaining the raw data of the census, to which the reported response was that the magnetic tape containing the data fell into water and was completely damaged.)

At MIT, I often marvel at and envy some of my colleagues for their ability to generate data for their research – by designing elaborate experiments, sometimes using their students as objects. One of my colleagues designed an experiment in which he would take pictures of students in the dinning hall. (Maybe I would only marvel at them up to a point.) I do not have the similar luxury of generating data experimentally, and it is not easy to retrospectively survey people about their past, especially when the relevant people are former premiers or ministers (including quite a few who are still persona non grata, politically).

I settled on an alternative – researching government documents. China is not short on documents. One particular source of documents proved to be extremely useful to my project – collections of bank documents. For this book project, I examined thousands of pages of bank documents, many going back to the early 1980s. It is on the basis of the cumulative weight of the documentary evidence that I came to reject the gradualist interpretation of Chinese reforms.

A skeptical reader may argue that a conclusion based on documentary evidence is not rigorous enough. (Apart from the documentary evidence, I have also collected a substantial body of survey data.) In leveling this criticism, one should be reminded that the gradualist perspective was never systematically proven in the first place. The most convincing piece of evidence in support of the gradualist perspective is the rising output share by the private sector. In Chapter 1, I went into some detail explaining why this is a problematic indicator of policy evolution.

The question of methodological rigor is most relevant when we try to draw causal inferences, not when we attempt to establish facts. Here is one major difference between researching Chinese economy and researching American economy. In studies of American economy, scholars may debate about the effects of, say, "Reagan tax cuts." In studies of the Chinese economy, the more relevant question would be, Did the government cut taxes in the first place? Much of this book is about documenting facts, including establishing an accurate definition of township and village enterprises (TVEs) and coming up with an analytically appropriate measure of policy evolution toward the private sector.

Two individuals should be singled out for being most helpful in my effort to source documentary evidence on Chinese reforms. One is Jean Hung, who was the librarian at the University Service Centre at the Chinese University of Hong Kong. Jean created an amazing collection of documents on China. One book that I used at her library shows the reach and the depth of her collection: Only 24 copies of that book were ever printed. Her collection goes way back – to the late 1970s and the early 1980s – and was meticulously catalogued. I owe her a huge debt of gratitude.

Nancy Hearst, at Harvard's Fairbank Center Library, was equally instrumental to my project. Her library, unquestionably, is the best place to do research on contemporary China outside of Asia. Nancy has also helped this book project in other ways. She edited and proofread the earlier versions and corrected many of the mistakes I made. I am very grateful to her.

Over the years, I have had a number of capable research assistants. These include Lu Gao, Yu Lu, Heiwai Tang, Yanbo Wang, and Wendi Zhang. Others tracked down and provided crucial data. Professor Yifan Zhang at Lingnan University in Hong Kong generously shared data with me, and Yang Zhi at Hong Kong University assisted me in data analysis. Scott Parris, my editor at Cambridge University Press, and Ken Karpinski, my project manager at Aptara, provided the most efficient assistance in the production process of this book. I am deeply grateful to them.

Let me also thank those individuals and colleagues with whom I have discussed the ideas in the book and those who have provided valuable comments on earlier drafts or presentations of ideas. These include William Baomul, Pranab Bardhan, Suzanne Berger, Kristin Forbes, Jun Fu, Simon Johnson, Devesh Kapur, Tarun Khanna, Nicholas Lardy, Don Lessard, David Li, Rick Locke, Minxin Pei, Guy Pfeffermann, Ed Steinfeld, Lester Thurow, Laura Tyson, Ashutosh Varshney, Eleanor Westney, and Alan White. Four anonymous reviewers at Cambridge University Press provided very helpful comments.

This book would not have been written without the unfailing support and encouragement from my wife, Jean Yang. She endured many of my absences from home while she was taking care of our two young daughters, Kunkun and Nanan, and working as a high-level executive at a health insurance company. She was my first testing ground of the sanity of many of my ideas. My daughters may have improved my work as well, if indirectly, when they took away my laptop and wrote or painted their own expressions over my writings.

Finally, I devote this book to three individuals who, I believe, represent the true China miracle. I referred to them in different parts of the book – Nian Guangjiu in Chapter 2 and Zheng Lefang and Sun Dawu in Chapter 3. All three were rural entrepreneurs, and they met the common unhappy fate of being brought down by the illiberal policies of the 1990s. In my modest way, I am noting their contributions here.

– Yasheng Huang on June 6, 2008, in Delhi, India.

A Detailed Synopsis of the Book

Since 1978, the Chinese economy has grown phenomenally. This is not in dispute. By exactly what mechanisms has China managed to grow so fast? There is more room for debate on this question. The near-consensus view – or the view that has achieved the greatest traction – among economists is that China has grown by relying on unique, context-specific local institutional innovations, such as ownership by the local state of township and village enterprises (TVEs), decentralization, and selective financial controls. The conventional mechanisms of growth, such as private ownership, property rights security, financial liberalization and reforms of political institutions, are not central components of China's growth story.

Much of the economic research on the Chinese reforms revolves around the following question: Given the manifest inefficiencies in the Chinese economy, how do we explain its growth? The answer, often backed up by formal, mathematical models, is that seemingly inefficient policies, practices, and institutions – such as public ownership of TVEs and financial controls – perform underlying efficient *functions* in the specific context of China. The approach is typically inferential – these efficient functions of observably inefficient forms are inferred from China's excellent economic performance.

This book takes a different and factual approach. It starts with the following set of questions: Were TVEs really publicly-owned? Did China implement financial reforms prior to or concurrently with the initial economic takeoff in the early 1980s? The research is based on detailed archival examinations of policy, bureaucratic, and bank documents as well as several waves of household and private-sector firm surveys. The qualitative and quantitative data span the period from 1979 to 2006. This book is factually dense – I have examined thousands of pages of memoranda, directives, operating manuals, and rules of personnel evaluations issued by the presidents of

China's central bank, all the major commercial banks, rural credit cooperatives, and so on. These documents are contained in a 22-volume compilation of bank documents, which, while available at Harvard and in Hong Kong, have never been examined by a Western academic. I have also gone to the raw database on TVEs established by the Ministry of Agriculture. The Ministry of Agriculture was in charge of collecting data on TVEs, and its data have finer ownership breakdowns than the TVE data available in *China Statistical Yearbooks*. Based on this body of research, here are the main findings:

- *Explicitly* private entrepreneurship in the non-farm sectors developed vigorously and rapidly in rural China during the 1980s.
- Financial reforms, again in the rural areas, were substantial in the 1980s, and the Chinese banking system channeled a surprisingly high level of credits to the private sector in the 1980s.
- Conventional property rights security was – and still is – problematic, but the security of the proprietor – the person holding the property – increased substantially at the very onset of the economic reforms.
- The Chinese policy makers in the early 1980s strongly, directly, and self-consciously projected policy credibility and predictability.
- The political system, although absent of the normal institutional constraints associated with good governance, became *directionally liberal* early during the reform era.

This book clarifies the following perspectives/issues and provides new information and illustrative data:

- The Chinese definition of TVEs refers to their *locations* of establishments and registration (i.e., businesses located in the rural areas), not their ownership; Western researchers, on the other hand, have come to understand TVEs in terms of their *ownership* status.
- The cognitive gap is huge: As early as 1985, of the 12 million businesses classified as TVEs, 10 million were *completely* and *manifestly* private.
- Almost every single *net* entrant in the TVE sector between the mid-1980s and the mid-1990s was a private TVE; thus both the static and dynamic TVE phenomena were substantially private.
- Private TVEs were most vibrant in the poorest and the most agricultural provinces of China (and this feature of private TVEs also explains the understatement of their size in the conventional reporting as well as the connections between rural private entrepreneurship and poverty alleviation).

- There are reports of privatization of collective TVEs in the early 1980s and large-scale privatizations in the poor provinces.
- Rural financial reforms – credit provisions to the private sector and allowing a degree of private entry into financial services – in the 1980s were endorsed by the governor of the central bank and the presidents of the major commercial banks.
- Chinese reforms were heavily experimental in nature rather than relying on a blueprint approach, but the outcome of the experimentation was private ownership and financial liberalization.

A good explanation for the Chinese growth experience should be able to account for its well-known successes as well as its equally well-known failings (such as a weak financial sector, rising income disparities, constraints on private-sector development, etc.). The key to our understanding of the China story is that China reversed many of its highly productive rural experiments and policies beginning in the early 1990s. In the 1990s, Chinese policy makers favored the cities in terms of investment and credit allocations and taxed the rural sector heavily in order to finance the state-led urban boom. The policy changes in the 1990s were not experimental; rather they were rooted in a technocratic industrial policy blueprint and a heavy urban bias. This book shows:

- By the measure of private-sector fixed-asset investments, the most liberal policy epoch, by far, was in the 1980s; in the 1990s, the policy was reversed, and many of the productive rural financial experiments were discontinued.
- Rural administrative management was substantially centralized in the 1990s.
- Credit constraints on rural entrepreneurship, including private TVEs, rose substantially in the 1990s.
- Growth of rural household income in the 1990s was less than half of its growth in the 1980s, and the declining growth in the rural business income was especially pronounced.
- The size of government – measured in terms of headcounts of officials and the value of fixed assets it controls – expanded enormously in the 1990s.
- The directionally liberal political reforms of the 1980s were discontinued and reversed.

This book devotes an entire chapter to Shanghai, for two reasons. One is that Shanghai represents the classic urban-bias model – the city restricted the development of small-scale, entrepreneurial, and typically rural businesses while conferring tax benefits on foreign direct investment (FDI) and on businesses closely allied with the government. The other is that at the end of the 1980s Shanghai was among the least reformed of the urban economies in China, and yet its leaders during the second half of the 1980s went on to dominate Chinese politics during the entire decade of the 1990s. This book asks, What is wrong with Shanghai? and proceeds to present the following illustrations:

- Although they are located in the richest market in China, indigenous private-sector businesses in Shanghai are among the smallest in the country, and self-employment business income per capita is about the same in Shanghai as it is in provinces such as Yunnan, where GDP per capita is about 10 to 15 percent of that in Shanghai. (As an illustration of how unusual the above pattern is, imagine finding that self-employment business income per capita in the United States was about the same as that in Turkey.)
- The political, regulatory, and financial restrictions on indigenous private entrepreneurship in Shanghai were extreme, as evidenced by the fact that the fixed asset investments by the indigenous private-sector firms peaked in *1985*.
- The share of labor income – inclusive of proprietor income – to GDP is very low in Shanghai.
- Shanghai's GDP increased massively relative to the national mean, but the household income level relative to the national mean experienced almost no growth.
- Although wage income is high in Shanghai, asset income is among the lowest in the country.
- Since 2000, the poorest segment of Shanghai's population has lost income *absolutely* during a period of double-digit economic growth.
- Although aspiring to be a high-tech hub of China, the number of annual patent grants in Shanghai decreased substantially relative to that in the more entrepreneurial provinces, such as Zhejiang and Guangdong, in the 1990s.
- Shanghai was also corrupt.

Capitalism with Chinese characteristics is a function of a political balance between two Chinas – the entrepreneurial, market-driven rural China vis-à-vis the state-led urban China. In the 1980s, rural China gained the upper hand, but, in the 1990s, urban China gained the upper hand.

Although China made notable progress in the 1990s in terms of FDI liberalization and reforms of state-owned enterprises (SOEs), this book assigns greater weight to the rural developments in determining the overall character and the pace of China's transition to capitalism. When and where rural China has the upper hand, Chinese capitalism is entrepreneurial, politically independent, and vibrantly competitive in its conduct and virtuous in its effects. When and where urban China has the upper hand, Chinese capitalism tends toward political dependency on the state and is corrupt.

Most economists judge China's economic performance by its GDP data. While decadal differences in China's GDP growth are fairly small, the economic and social implications of a more entrepreneurial version of capitalism in the 1980s and the one closer to state-led capitalism in the 1990s in fact differed enormously. There are substantial and real welfare consequences:

- Although GDP growth was rapid during both the 1980s and 1990s, household income growth was much faster in the 1980s.
- The share of labor income to GDP was rising in the 1980s but declining in the 1990s.
- Several studies on total factor productivity (TFP) converged on the finding that TFP growth since the late 1990s has either slowed down from the earlier period or has completely collapsed.
- The majority of the much-touted poverty reduction occurred during the short 8 years of the entrepreneurial era (1980–1988) rather than during the long 13 years of the state-led era (1989–2002).
- Income disparities worsened substantially in the 1990s, while they initially improved in the 1980s.
- Governance problems, such as land grabs and corruption, intensified greatly in the 1990s.
- The heavy taxation on the rural areas led to the withdrawal and rising costs of basic government services.
- Between 2000 and 2005 the number of illiterate Chinese adults increased by 30 million, reversing decades of trend developments; this development has garnered almost no attention in the West.
- The way the Chinese measure adult illiteracy implies that all of this increase was a product of the rural basic education in the 1990s, and this adverse development coincided closely in timing with the intensification of urban bias in the policy model.

ONE

Just How Capitalist Is China?

In 2004, Lenovo, a computer maker based in China, acquired the manufacturing division of IBM. This event, coming off the heels of the news that China had contributed more than the United States to global GDP growth, took the world by storm. Richard McGregor (2004), a reporter for the *Financial Times*, captured a widespread sentiment when he wrote that the purchase was "a symbol of a new economic era, of how a fast-rising China had suddenly grown powerful enough to subsume an iconic American brand." Princeton economist and *New York Times* columnist Paul Krugman (2005) had not been alarmed with Japanese acquisitions in the 1990s but he was about Chinese investments. He believed that the Chinese corporate acquisitions posed a great threat to the United States. There are even those who hailed the Lenovo acquisition as heralding a new world order with China at its center (Shenkar 2006).

Business-school academics are particularly enamored with Lenovo. For them, Lenovo is proof positive of China's fertile entrepreneurial environment and rising competitiveness. In his book, *The Chinese Century*, Oded Shenkar, a professor at Ohio State University, rejects the notion that China lacks its own homegrown corporate giants. Lenovo, he argues, is just as homegrown as the best of the Indian corporations, such as Wipro or Infosys (Shenkar 2005). Lenovo is also featured prominently in *Made in China: What Western Managers Can Learn from Trailblazing Chinese Entrepreneurs*, a book by Donald Sull, a business professor at INSEAD (Sull 2005).

There is one problem with these otherwise perceptive books – Lenovo is not a Chinese company. There is no question Lenovo is a huge success story but it succeeded precisely because it was able to operate outside of the Chinese business environment. The Chinese face of the firm is Lenovo China headquartered in Beijing. This is the original firm founded in 1984 under the Chinese Academy of Sciences (CAS). But the real corporate control

1

and equity holdings of the production and technology development of Lenovo actually reside elsewhere – in Hong Kong. Consider Lenovo (Beijing) and Lenovo (Shanghai), the business units of the firm that run manufacturing, R&D, software development, and customer services. Both of these business units are not only foreign-invested enterprises (FIEs); they are, in fact, wholly owned FIEs – that is, they are 100 percent owned by a legal foreign entity, which is Hong Kong Lenovo. They have no direct equity relationship with Lenovo China. As wholly owned FIEs, the Beijing and Shanghai divisions of Lenovo are more foreign than GM's operation in Shanghai, which is a 50–50 equity joint venture. The foreign operations of Lenovo are so substantial that in 2003, seven of Lenovo's Hong Kong subsidiaries were included on a list compiled by the Chinese government as among China's 500 largest FIEs.

This is a book about this and many other phenomena of the Chinese economy. In the first part of this chapter, I provide a detailed account of Lenovo in order to make a larger point – the Chinese economy is so complicated that what appears to be straightforward and obvious on the surface is not at all so once we dig into the details. To get into these details requires going far beyond the normal empirical basis of much of the economic analysis on China (e.g., data on GDP and foreign exchange reserves). In this book, I have examined numerous government documents, including memoranda and instructions issued by officials of the central bank and by senior bank managers and a large quantity of survey data on households and Chinese firms. The conventional economic data, such as GDP, exports, and FDI, serve as motivations for further research rather than as statements about settled conclusions. (I provide more details on the empirical sources of the book later in this chapter.)

The Lenovo example is not just about getting the facts right about the Chinese economy; it is also about drawing the right analytical and policy implications from China's growth experience. This is another theme running throughout the book. Much of the received wisdom in the academic literature states that entrepreneurship, financial liberalization, and private property rights security are not significant components of Chinese economic growth. (Or, at the very least, to the extent that these components are important, they have very different manifestations from those prevailing elsewhere.) The success of the Chinese economy has inspired the idea that economic growth follows from an adept tailoring of economic policies and institutions to their local contexts rather than from an application of universal economic principles. Let me apply this idea to the experience of Lenovo.

A critical detail of the Lenovo story is its foreign registration status. A reader may wonder, "So what?" What is so significant about the fact that Lenovo is registered as a foreign-owned company in China? Furthermore, isn't it the case that Hong Kong is now a part of China so the designation of Hong Kong Lenovo as a foreign firm is a frivolous legal fiction? The answers to these questions show precisely how important it is to get the details of the Lenovo story right.

Understanding the Hong Kong roots of Lenovo entails significant implications about constructing the right causal attributions. Hong Kong is a laissez-faire economy based on a market-oriented financial system, rule of law, and property rights security. Hong Kong, many would argue, is the closest living case to the textbook version of neoclassical economics in the world. This is why it matters so much to accurately attribute the success of Lenovo. If we believe Lenovo to be a product of China's business environment, then many of those who argue that China has created a unique, country-specific formula for cautious deregulation, state ownership, and selective government intervention in the economy have a point. If we believe Lenovo to be a product of Hong Kong and Hong Kong institutions, the success of Lenovo then becomes a story of rule of law and market-based finance. It is thus worth going into some details about this matter.

Apart from the initial financing from CAS in 1984, it is the market-oriented and conventionally Western Hong Kong capital market that supplied Lenovo with almost all of its subsequent capital during the critical growth period of the firm.[1] In 1988, Lenovo received HK$900,000 from China Technology, a Hong Kong–based firm, to invest in a joint venture in Hong Kong. This investment thereby established Lenovo's legal domicile in Hong Kong. (Originally, the firm was known as Legend.) Here, luck and fortuity played a role. The father of Liu Chuanzhi, the main founder of Lenovo, ran China Patent Agent based in Hong Kong. China Patent Agent was a major shareholder of China Technology. Computer manufacturing is capital-intensive and requires substantial investments. It was the capital market in Hong Kong that met this high level of capital requirements of Lenovo. In 1993, Hong Kong Lenovo went public on the Hong Kong Stock Exchange. The initial public offering (IPO) raised US$12 million, which the firm plowed back into its investments in China. Lenovo is a success story of the market-based finance of Hong Kong, not of China's state-controlled financial system.

Although it is true that the founders of Lenovo all came from CAS, that the firm became a business subsidiary of CAS is a historical artifact. The founding capital was 200,000 yuan, an enormous sum in China in

1984. The money was actually a loan from CAS, not an equity investment. In fact, the arrangement was exceedingly convoluted. According to one account, the 11 founders of Lenovo had secured the money as a bank loan, which they lent to CAS. CAS then turned around and loaned the money back to Lenovo. Under Western law, Lenovo would have been a straightforward private firm with CAS as its creditor, not the equity holder. But the reason why Lenovo incorporated itself this way has nothing to do with the actual share of capital contributions. The reason is that in 1984, there was really no legal vehicle to register an independent private-sector firm of the size of Lenovo and operating in a modern industry such as computer manufacturing. In the 1980s, although private-sector liberalization in rural China went far and deep (a topic I revisit in the next chapter), the urban economy remained almost completely state-controlled. Many of the large-scale otherwise private businesses were incorporated in this way in the 1980s.

Understanding Lenovo's Hong Kong connections also helps us gain the right perspective on the Chinese business environment. The legal status of Lenovo as foreign-owned mattered to Lenovo in a most fundamental way – this was its entry ticket into computer manufacturing in the first place. After its founding, Lenovo was denied a production license in computer manufacturing in China. Instead, the Ministry of Electronics granted a production license to the Great Wall Group, a traditional SOE. Lenovo only began to produce computers in China not as a Chinese company but as an FIE originating in Hong Kong. Every single manufacturing, service, and R&D operation launched by Lenovo in China has followed exactly the same route. They are either wholly owned by Hong Kong Lenovo or they are foreign joint ventures with other Chinese firms. In 1997, Hong Kong Lenovo absorbed the last remaining Chinese operation, its Beijing operation.[2]

As an FIE, Lenovo came under the jurisdiction of the Foreign Equity Joint Venture Law or the Wholly Foreign Equity Law. Chinese laws and regulations provide a more liberal operating space for foreign-registered firms than they do for domestic private firms. In the 1990s, China pursued a highly biased liberalization strategy that conferred substantial tax and policy incentives on FDI while restricting the growth potentials of the indigenous private sector.[3] Until 2005, many of the high-tech and so-called strategic industries were declared off-limits to domestic private entry. Indigenous private entrepreneurs, many highly capable, could grow their businesses only via foreign registration. This is why Lenovo acquired a foreign legal status. As an FIE, Lenovo was able to operate in greater regulatory space and with more autonomy. As an illustration, the firm that bypassed Lenovo and was given the production license in computer manufacturing – the Great Wall Group – operated completely within China's domestic business environment. The firm floundered badly.

Professor Sull chronicles seven other firms in his book: Sina, UTStarcom, AsiaInfo, Haier, Galanz, Wahaha, and Ting Hsin. Every single case Professor Sull discusses is a Lenovo-like story. The firms are all registered as foreign firms in China, or some of their main operations are so registered. Sina, UTStarcom, Ting Hsin, and AsiaInfo are wholly owned FIEs, 100 percent owned by foreign investors, identical to Lenovo (Beijing) and Lenovo (Shanghai). Galanz and Wahaha are joint ventures. (In 2007, Wahaha's founder was involved in a bitter dispute with its foreign business partner, Danone.) Haier itself is not an FIE but its main business and production units are FIEs, including its core areas in refrigerator and washer and dryer production. All of these firms are legally classified as FIEs and they fall under the relatively more liberal purview of China's foreign investment laws and regulations.

It is quite understandable that Sull assumed that all of these firms are Chinese. They are Chinese to the extent that their managers and owners are ethnically Chinese, but their legal status is *foreign*. That corporate success in China requires a combination of Chinese management and foreign legal status is probably the cleanest illustration of the massive distortions in China's business environment – that this is a system that has imposed a straitjacket on the domestic private sector. It is thus not a coincidence that corporate success stories in China all share an underlying commonality with Lenovo and Sina. In 2002, *Forbes* compiled a list of the most dynamic small firms in the world. On that list, four are run by Chinese entrepreneurs and derive most of their revenue from their China operations, but each one of them is actually headquartered in Hong Kong.

The rise of Lenovo has so impressed some foreign analysts that a McKinsey consultant goes so far as to claim that China has the "best of all possible models" (Woetzel 2004). This reasoning holds up the particular policy and institutional path that China has followed as a model for other developing countries. China has inspired Western researchers to argue that microeconomic and macroeconomic successes do not depend on adoption of Western-style financial and legal institutions. This is the argument in an influential finance paper that claims that informal finance is nearly as good as market-based financial institutions in channeling capital to the private sector (Allen, Qian, and Qian 2005).

The story of Lenovo casts doubt on all these postulations. Yes, China lacks efficient legal and financial institutions, *but it has access to them – in*

Hong Kong. Take the view that formal finance does not matter. The management of Lenovo certainly would not agree with this. The firm raised more than US\$12 million from its Hong Kong IPO. Formal finance – and the institutions supplying it – is absolutely essential to the success of Lenovo. Informal finance might be sufficient to start small kiosk businesses or simple production, but it is not adequate for firms to acquire modern production facilities and to move up on the technological ladder.

Lenovo is the most prominent product of what is known as "round-trip" FDI – "foreign" capital that is first exported from China and then imported back into China. The key function of Lenovo's Hong Kong operation has nothing to do with technology. In fact, according to one of the best and most-detailed accounts of Lenovo, the managers and scientists at Lenovo had far superior technical expertise than the Hong Kong firm with which it teamed (Lu 2000). The true contribution of China's open-door policy is not just about allowing foreign entry but also about allowing Chinese exit. It enabled some of China's own indigenous entrepreneurs to find an escape valve from a very bad system. To put it another way, China's success has less to do with creating efficient institutions and more to do with permitting access to efficient institutions outside of China.

This – largely unintended and under-appreciated – effect of China's open-door policy should be explicitly recognized, but recognizing this effect is qualitatively different from stating that China does not need efficient market-based institutions. The story of Lenovo is precisely about the importance of efficient market-based institutions. Lenovo was able to tap into these institutions because China is fortunate enough to have the most laissez-faire economic system at its doorstep. Hong Kong is a safe harbor for some of the talented Chinese entrepreneurs and an alternative to China's poorly functioning financial and legal systems. It is only a slight exaggeration to say that Lenovo benefited as much from the British legacy as from the growth opportunities within China itself.

China is unique in that some of its capable entrepreneurs have the option of accessing one of the most efficient financial markets and legal institutions in the world. But here is an important policy implication. It would be futile for other developing countries to emulate China's domestic financial and legal institutions and practices as a way to achieve economic growth. As successful as Lenovo is, the special circumstance of Hong Kong limits the general applicability of this model. In this connection, McKinsey's exhortation that China has "the best possible" business model is equivalent to urging other poor countries to acquire their own Hong Kong, a piece of advice of dubious utility.

Finally, there is the issue of whether or not getting the story right about Lenovo and about China really matters for China. Maybe the lessons of China cannot be readily extended to other countries, but as long as the China model works for China, this is fine. Isn't it the case that many firms like Lenovo are able to tap into Hong Kong's financial market and legal institutions and are able to emerge as competitive giants on the world stage? As long as there are substitute mechanisms, China's growth can continue.

This is a flawed inference from the success of Lenovo and other Chinese companies. Recall the fact that Lenovo was able to tap into the financial market of Hong Kong surreptitiously – Liu Chuanzhi's father was an executive in Hong Kong. Familial connections enabled Lenovo to escape from the clutches of China's poor institutions, but for each Lenova-type success story, there are untold cases of failure of indigenous entrepreneurs for whom access to Hong Kong is not an option. This is true especially of those would-be entrepreneurs located in China's vast rural and interior regions. One can go even a step farther. China's need for an efficient financial system is greater in the interior regions than it is in the coastal provinces precisely because the interior is so short of other conditions for growth.

Bad institutions are especially detrimental to rural entrepreneurship, the type of entrepreneurship that matters far more to the welfare of the vast majority of the Chinese, as compared with urban, high-tech entrepreneurship. Two chapters of this book delve extensively into this issue. Unlike many countries, the most dynamic, risk-taking, and talented entrepreneurs in China reside in the countryside. These rural entrepreneurs created China's true miracle growth in the 1980s, first by dramatically improving agricultural yields and then by starting many small-scale businesses in food processing and construction materials. The open-door policies alone can do very little – and they did very little – to help these entrepreneurs in the interior regions.

To a large extent, the story of Lenovo mirrors the story of China. What appears to be abundantly obvious on the surface is, in fact, not obvious at all. To get the facts right requires a deep digging into many details. A substantial portion of this book illustrates this point. In part, this is a history book – marshaling facts and data about the evolution of the Chinese economic system over the last three decades. But, as my account of Lenovo shows, getting the China story right is also about constructing the correct explanations about China. The explanation I put forward in this book is simple and even bordering on the mundane: China succeeded where and when bottom-up, private entrepreneurship flourished and it stagnated where and when entrepreneurship was suppressed.

In this chapter, I begin with a basic question, "Just how capitalist is the Chinese economy?" This is a legitimate question, considering the following. First, the year 2008 marks the 30th anniversary of China's economic reforms (1978–2008). By 2008, it will have taken China one year longer to reform its socialist economic system than the duration of the pre-reform central planning system itself (1949–1978). (Indeed, by the account of economic historians, a full-fledged central planning system was not established until the mid-1950s.[4]) The question of the pace at which China is transitioning to capitalism is worth considering. Second, some of the most prominent and authoritative China economists have already declared that China's transition to a market economy is now complete.[5] The remaining challenge, they argue, is economic development. It is legitimate to subject this judgment to an empirical test.

One of the most important – if not the most important – hallmarks of a market economy is the role and magnitude of the private sector. However, as in so many other areas of the Chinese economy, there is no straightforward answer to this seemingly direct question about the size of the Chinese private sector. The reason is that the Chinese style of reforms has spawned a large number of firms that have fundamentally confusing and often deliberately vague ownership structures. After sorting through some definitional complications, I show that the size of the Chinese private economy, especially its indigenous component, is quite small. Using fixed-asset investment as a measure of policy, I show that the policy treatment of the indigenous private sector deteriorated substantially in the 1990s as compared with the 1980s. This policy reversal is the most important reason why China's transition to capitalism remains incomplete 30 years after the reforms began.

The second section of this chapter provides a preview of my account of the Chinese reforms during the last 30 years and concludes with a précis of the remaining four chapters of the book. Three issues are highlighted. First, a good account of the Chinese economy should be able to explain both its many well-known weaknesses – the weak financial system, the underdeveloped private sector, and the deterioration of social performance – as well as many of its considerable achievements, such as its rapid growth and its impressive reduction of poverty. The key factor identified in my account is a reversal of economic policies at the end of the 1980s. In the 1980s, the direction of economic policy was progressively liberal, primarily in the rural areas of the country. Access to finance by the private sector improved rapidly and rural entrepreneurship was vibrant. In the 1990s, the direction of economic policy was reversed, with an increasing emphasis on industrial policy and state-led investment drives. Although GDP growth was rapid during both eras, both the drivers and the effects of the growth differed substantially. In the 1980s, the rapid GDP growth was accompanied by fast personal income growth, an improving income distribution, and a steep decline in poverty. Since the early 1990s, and at an accelerating pace since the late 1990s, the welfare implications of the fast GDP growth turned adverse. In other words, many of the best-known achievements of the Chinese economy owe their origins to the policies of the 1980s and many of the deep-seated problems today are an outgrowth of the policies of the 1990s.

The second part of my account emphasizes the importance of the rural sector. The importance of the rural sector derives not just from its sheer weight in the Chinese economy and society – that China has a large rural population – but also from the institutional perspective. In China, the origins of market-based, entrepreneurial capitalism are heavily rural in character. This observation entails some significant auxiliary implications. One is that the fate of rural entrepreneurship has a disproportionate effect on the character of Chinese capitalism. When small-scale, market-oriented, broad-based, and politically independent rural entrepreneurship is accorded greater operating freedom and supported by policies, entrepreneurial capitalism thrives and produces many of its associated virtuous effects. When rural capitalism is restricted in favor of its urban counterpart, Chinese capitalism is less welfare-improving. In essence, this is the tale of the two decades. In the 1980s, the country was moving directionally toward the virtuous kind of capitalism, or what Baumol, Litan, and Shramm (2007) describe as entrepreneurial capitalism. In the 1990s, the country still moved toward capitalism but of a different and less virtuous kind – the state-led brand of capitalism.

The third part of my account has to do with how to interpret China's growth experience. My purpose here is to present the relevant factual details and to develop the right analytical perspective based on them. I argue that China's growth experience is actually very conventional. Private ownership, financial liberalization, property rights security, and even some degree of constraints on the political rulers are as essential to China's economic success as they are to economic successes elsewhere. The success of Lenovo, which "borrowed" the institutional benefits of Hong Kong, illustrates this point. On the other hand, many of China's failings are a direct result of the country's poor and underdeveloped economic and political institutions and, more important, a consequence of the fact that the country reversed its policies and practices from the directional liberalism of the 1980s to the directional illiberalism of the 1990s.

1 Just How Capitalist Is China?

A hallmark of a market economy is the size and the vitality of its private sector. There are two standard perspectives on this question as related to China. One is the view that growth happened in China despite the absence of sizable private ownership. Advocates of this view point to TVEs – the growth engines in the 1980s and the first half of the 1990s – as an illustration. The other standard perspective is that China's private sector was not substantial *ex ante* but became substantial *ex post*. This perspective is rooted in the gradualist framework on the Chinese economy. According to the gradualist perspective, China did not actively privatize its SOEs, but it successfully created a hospitable business environment for the entry and the organic growth of private entrepreneurship. Over time, the private sector grew to overshadow the state sector. Market economy developed by evolution rather than by revolution.

I provide an alternative perspective in this book. Later in this chapter and in Chapter 2, I delve extensively into the TVE phenomenon; the gist of the finding is that TVEs, upon a microscopic examination, were in fact a substantially private phenomenon. In this section, I look into the gradualist perspective on China's private sector. The issue here is not so much whether the gradualist perspective is directionally accurate about the growth of China's private sector. There is little question that the size of China's private sector today is much larger than that in 1978. (In 1978, it was zero.) The issue is just how successful is China's evolution toward a market economy. Scholars schooled in the gradualist perspective declared a huge success. The analysis I present in the following paragraphs reached a far more tempered judgment on this question.

As almost with any other aspects of the Chinese economy, the issue comes down to data as well as perspectives. Let me use the example of Huawei Technology Corporation, one of the largest private-sector firms in China, to illustrate the myriad complexities of the Chinese economy. By most accounts, Huawei, with sales revenue of about US$5.7 billion and operating in more than 90 countries, is China's most successful private-sector firm. But our knowledge of its actual ownership structure is almost non-existent. Huawei is a microcosm of China's private sector – we know that it is there but we do not know its actual size and its boundaries. The convoluted ownership structure of China's private sector – and of Huawei in particular – makes it very difficult to answer the question, "Just how capitalist is China?" Huawei, like Lenovo, is an apt case study of the enormous complexities of the Chinese economy.

We came to know a bit more about Huawei as a result of a lawsuit against the firm in 2002. The lawsuit itself reveals little about the ownership structure of the company, but it reveals some of the reasons why there is so little outside knowledge about it.[6] The case was filed by Mr. Liu Ping, one of the earliest employees of the company. Upon leaving the company, Mr. Liu, who had accumulated substantial shares in the company, was told that Huawei would redeem his shares only at the original 1-to-1 ratio. Mr. Liu contended that this was unfair. The assets of Huawei had increased several-fold since he joined the firm in the early 1990s.

The lawsuit reveals some fascinating details about this otherwise very secretive company. For example, Huawei mandated that all of its employees purchase shares, which suggests that its employees own at least a portion of the firm. But the company has never issued any share certificates explicitly recognizing their ownership. The employees were required to sign share certificates upon purchasing the shares, but Huawei kept all the copies. Because there is no information about how many shares were issued, we do not know whether Huawei is an employee-owned company. Even if we assume this to be the case, there is no paperwork actually documenting it as such. For a firm that even Cisco views as its main technological rival in the 21st century, it has some of the world's most medieval recordkeeping practices.

It is not unreasonable to assume that Huawei has gone out of its way to purposely obfuscate its ownership structure. The reason is not hard to understand. The firm was established in 1988 and, until very recently, the telecommunications sector was declared off-limits to private-sector firms in China. In addition, Chinese financial regulations have stringent restrictions about issuing shares to employees. It is all but certain that Huawei, by virtue of the fact that it is a private-sector firm, is in technical violation of many of these regulations. This hypothesis also dovetails with the widely held knowledge that Huawei has backing from the Chinese military. It is inconceivable that a politically naïve private entrepreneur could have gone as far as this firm has.

The lawsuit also shows that a number of state-owned telecommunication firms in Shenzhen were granted shares by Huawei, although, again, there is no information about the amount of the shares. It is possible that Huawei has some state share capital on its balance sheet, but we can safely rule out the possibility that Huawei is a state-owned firm. One telling clue is that its general manager, Ren Zhenfei, has been in his position since the founding of the firm in 1988. The longevity of the general manager is the most reliable way to distinguish a true private-sector firm from an SOE. The government frequently shuffles the management of SOEs and, therefore, SOE managers typically have very short tenures.

Obviously, it is impracticable to determine the size of China's private sector by examining the tenure of general management. The information simply is not available. In this section, I present two measurements, each with its advantages and disadvantages. But the common advantage is that they are relatively systematic and they are derived on the basis of explicit assumptions and judgments about the workings of the Chinese economy. They are thus "falsifiable."

We distinguish between two types of measurements – output-based and input-based measures of the size of China's private sector. The output-based measure is often used by academics to gauge both the size of China's private sector and the evolving policy environment for the private sector. I show that this is the correct measure to assess the size of the private sector in China, but it is deeply problematic as a measure of the evolving policy environment. The basic problem is that this measure confounds the effects of two factors – the policy changes and the firm-level efficiency differentials between SOEs and private-sector firms. A rising ratio of private-sector output to the output of the state sector can be a result of policy changes toward the private sector or can be a result of the fact that private-sector firms are simply more efficient than SOEs. We do not know which factor is driving the change in this ratio.

Let me illustrate this point with an extreme example. No one would accuse Leonid Brezhnev for being pro-private sector, but actually under his leadership, private plots contributed to roughly one half of agricultural household income in the Soviet Union (Gregory and Stuart 1981, p. 230). This was so because private farming was so much more efficient than the state farming so its contributions to income were disproportionate to the inputs allocated to it. Private plots only accounted for 1.4 percent of cultivable land in the Soviet Union (Hewett 1988, p. 117).

The minuscule share of private plots in the Soviet Union suggests that a better measure of the changes in the policy environment should be based on an input allocated to private sector rather than its share of the output. The most appropriate input-based measure is the fixed-asset investment capital. Fixed-asset investments are equivalent to purchases of plants, property, and equipment in the Western accounting system. There are two reasons why this is a better measure of policy. One is that fixed-asset investments remain substantially controlled by the state; thus, changes in the patterns of fixed-asset investments are a more accurate reflection of the policy preferences of the Chinese state. The second reason is that in a poor country, capital is scarce relative to labor. So capital allocation is more indicative than labor allocations of the fundamental orientation of the economic system.

In the following sections, I assess these two questions. First, how large is China's private sector? Second, has the policy environment improved over time for China's private entrepreneurs? Unfortunately, these weighty questions do not have straightforward answers. I elaborate on various measures and approaches and on the assumptions and definitions behind them. The treatment is quite detailed (and even tedious), but the only way to get at these issues is to sort out many of the complications in the Chinese data.

1.1 How Large Is the Chinese Private Sector?

Defining China's private sector is fiendishly difficult. Some scholars have used the state and non-state categories of firms as a way to assess private-sector development in China (Bai, Li, and Wang 2003). The state-sector firms are traditional SOEs, whereas the non-state-sector firms encompass a huge variety of firms, including collective enterprises, truly private firms, shareholding enterprises, domestic joint-ownership firms, and FIEs. In some studies, SOEs that have issued shares on the stock exchanges are also counted as part of the non-state sector.

Information on state and non-state firms is easily available but it is not very useful. Depending on the definition that is used, there are vastly different estimates of the size of the non-state sector. Based on one definition, the share of the non-state sector in industrial output value was 68.4 percent in 1997 (Wang 2002).[7] Based on the definition of the National Bureau of Statistics (NBS), the non-state sector accounted for only 21.2 percent of industrial value-added in the same year (NBS 1999a). Equating the non-state sector with the private sector is problematic.[8] Local governments control collective firms to varying degrees.[9] The vast majority of the SOEs that have issued shares on China's stock exchanges are technically classified as non-state firms but they are still tightly controlled by the state.

In the following paragraphs, I present estimates based on a superior approach that gets at the core issue about firm ownership. An accurate definition of a private-sector firm should be based on how its control rights are assigned. Control rights mean the rights to appoint management, dispose of assets, and set the strategic direction of the firm. On this count, SOEs that issued shares on the stock exchanges are not private because they are still tightly controlled by the government. The difficulty, however, is that it is not easy to know whether a firm in China has private or governmental control rights. To arrive at an estimate of the size of China's private sector, an analyst would have to make certain assumptions about which types of firms in China have private control rights.

A study by two Organisation for Economic Co-operation and Development (OECD) economists, Sean Dougherty and Richard Herd (2005), represents the most systematic and comprehensive attempt.[10] Their paper is based on a very unique dataset compiled by the NBS. The dataset covers more than 160,000 industrial firms in China between 1998 and 2003. (The Appendix to this chapter provides further details on this dataset.) I first summarize their findings and then present my own estimates. My own estimates, which reveal a far smaller indigenous private sector as compared with the OECD study, are based on the same methodology as the OECD study but on different assumptions about what types of firms have private control rights.

The advantage of the NBS dataset is that its data are disaggregated at the firm level and cover a wide range of firm activities. One critical piece of information in the dataset is the shareholding structure of the firms. This is a solution to the uncertainty over the ownership boundaries of Chinese firms. The OECD economists use the shareholding structure as the basis for their definition. One caveat, however, is that the NBS dataset is biased toward large firms – defined as those with at least 5 million yuan in sales. So the estimates here reflect the private share of the industrial value-added produced by the largest firms in China, not the private share of the entire industry. (The 2004 economic census has data on private businesses below the 5-million-yuan threshold. However, NBS does not publish the shareholding information.)

The Appendix to this chapter explains their classification methodology in greater detail. The most critical assumption in their methodology is that a category of firms known as legal-person shareholding firms are privately owned. They conclude that the private economy accounted for 52.3 percent of industrial value-added in 2003, compared with 27.9 percent in 1998.

I examined the dataset used by the OECD economists and checked their findings. I used exactly the same ownership classification methodology they used and was able to reproduce findings broadly similar to theirs.[11] I also extended their methodology to the 2005 data. The results are presented in Table 1.1.

Table 1.1. *Estimates of private-sector shares of industrial firms above scale in Chinese industrial value-added/profits, 1998, 2001, and 2005 (%)*

OECD Definition of the Private Sector				Definition of the Private Sector Based on the Guangdong Statistical Manual			
	(1a)	(1b)	(1c)		(2a)	(2b)	(2c)
Definition/Year	1998	2001	2005	Definition/Year	1998	2001	2005
Indigenous:	**17.2**	**27.8**	**50.5**	**Indigenous:**	**7.9**	**9.65**	**22.0**
(1) Individual share capital >50.0	5.9	10.6	19.1	(1) Registered	2.4	5.97	16.3
(2) Legal-person share capital >50.0	11.3	17.2	31.4	(2) Individual share capital >50.0	5.5	3.68	5.7
Foreign:	**11.7**	**16.9**	**20.7**	**Foreign:**	**23.9**	**29.1**	**28.8**
(1) Foreign share capital >50.0	11.7	16.9	20.7	(1) Registered	21.8	26.4	28.3
				(2) Foreign share capital >50.0	2.1	2.74	0.48
Sum of indigenous and foreign	**28.9**	**44.7**	**71.2**	**Sum of indigenous and foreign**	**31.8**	**38.8**	**50.8**

Notes: I follow the classification methodology used by Dougherty and Herd (2005). Their methodology involves two steps. First, they divide the firms into state and non-state firms. State firms, in turn, comprise two types of firms: SOEs and collective firms in which the collective share capital exceeds 50 percent. The second step is to classify all those firms in the non-state category as those with more than 50 percent of share capital held by legal persons, individual investors, and foreign firms. The Guangdong definition includes all the firms explicitly registered as private-sector firms (*siyin qiye*) and those non-state firms in which private share capital is substantial. I set the "substantial" threshold at 50 percent. The non-state firms in the Guangdong definition refer to shareholding cooperatives, other alliance firms, and other shareholding firms with limited liabilities.

Source: NBS database of industrial firms above 5 million yuan in sales. See the Appendix to this chapter for an explanation.

I separate data on indigenous and foreign private-sector firms rather than reporting them together. In the OECD definition, indigenous private-sector firms are defined as those firms with substantial individual share capital and legal-person share capital (i.e., exceeding 50 percent of the total share capital). The foreign private-sector firms are those with foreign share capital exceeding 50 percent. By the OECD definition, the sum of the indigenous and foreign private-sector firms in China's industrial profits is 28.9 percent in 1998, 44.7 percent in 2001, and 71.2 percent in 2005, respectively.[12]

The OECD economists assign the entire output by legal-person shareholding firms to the private sector.[13] Is this a reasonable approach? Getting this question right is critical. In 1998, legal-person shareholding firms accounted for 40 percent (11.3/28.9) of the purported private sector. Excluding these firms would reduce the share of the private sector in industrial value-added from 28.9 percent in 1998 to only 17.6 percent (i.e., 28.9 percent minus 11.3 percent). For 2005, the private sector exclusive of legal-person shareholding firms would be 39.8 percent rather than 71.2 percent (i.e., 71.2 percent minus 31.4 percent). This is another illustration of a common refrain in this book – getting the details right matters.

Legal-person shareholding refers to cross-shareholding by firms. Probably because of the connotations of this term, the OECD economists might have assumed that legal-person shareholding implies that China has a *keiretsu* arrangement similar to that in Japan where firms own each others' stocks. The difference with Japan, however, is that in China much of the legal-person share capital originates in the state sector, via SOEs establishing or holding significant equity stakes in other firms. These firms then become affiliates or subsidiaries of the SOEs. The subsidiaries of the SOEs, on account of their final ownership, are still SOEs.

One way to learn more about these legal-person shareholding firms classified by the OECD study as private is to check their names. Even a casual glance at the data reveals that many of these legal-person shareholding firms are among the best-known and quintessential SOEs in China. They include subsidiaries of Daqing and Dagang oilfields, owned and operated by two of China's largest SOEs. Daqing is owned by PetroChina and Dagang is owned by China National Petroleum Corporation (CNPC). The list also includes subsidiaries of NORINCO, a large defense-product firm. PetroChina, CNPC, and NORINCO are not only SOEs; they also are known as central SOEs directly supervised by the State Council. In fact, some of these firms have the word "state-owned" in their names.

Another well-known SOE on the list classified by the OECD study as private is SAIC Motor Corporation Limited (SAIC Motor). In the NBS dataset, the state share of SAIC Motor's share capital structure is 0 percent; it is 70 percent legal-person shareholding and 30 percent individual shareholding. So this firm qualifies as a private firm in the OECD definition. But SAIC Motor is not even remotely a private firm. SAIC Motor was established in 1997; its predecessor was Shanghai Gear Factory. In 1997, 30 percent of the share capital was issued on the Shanghai Stock Exchange and the rest of the share capital was held by Shanghai Automotive Industry Corporation (SAIC), which is 100 percent owned by the Shanghai government. Because the Shanghai government owns SAIC Motor via SAIC – a legal-person shareholder – the state share capital is reduced to zero; however, from a control perspective, there is little question about who controls this firm.[14]

The example of SAIC Motor also illustrates the nature of the SOE reforms in the 1990s. Much of the reform effort had nothing to do with actually changing the owners of the firms but rather it was directed at securitizing the full but previously implicit equity holdings of the state in the SOEs. Although these reform measures copy the superficial forms of a capitalistic market economy, none of them has anything to do with its essence – transferring corporate control from government to private investors.

The high concentration of the ownership structure of the legal-person shareholding firms is another sign that these firms are not private at all. In the NBS dataset, SAIC Motor has the most dispersed shareholding structure among the legal-person shareholding firms because 30 percent of its shares are held by individual shareholders. (This is because the firm is listed.) In contrast, of 16,871 legal-person shareholding firms in the NBS dataset for 1998, 75 percent have zero individual share capital. The average individual share capital is only 3.7 percent. This is entirely expected given the heavily accounting nature of the SOE reforms. As evidence, 7,612 of these so-called legal-person shareholding firms are actually factories – they are simply production subsidiaries of other SOEs. This explains the extraordinary concentration of ownership and control of these firms.

Table 1.1 breaks down the private sector into indigenous and foreign components. There is a substantive reason for doing this. It is well documented by now that in the 1990s the Chinese state systematically favored foreign firms at the expense of indigenous private-sector firms.[15] Although this policy bias can be evaded in various ways (Lenovo being a successful example), it cannot be evaded completely. The brunt of the policy bias is borne by those indigenous private entrepreneurs who do not have the option to convert their businesses into legal foreign firms. These types of firms show up as indigenous private-sector firms in the NBS dataset.

According to the OECD definition, indigenous private-sector firms are those with individual share capital of more than 50 percent. Another definition is suggested by a statistical manual prepared by the Guangdong Bureau of Statistics.[16] The Guangdong definition of indigenous private-sector firms includes registered private-sector firms and non-state firms in which individual share capital is substantial. (The non-state firms in the Guangdong definition refer to shareholding cooperatives, other alliance firms, and other shareholding firms with limited liabilities.) I set that threshold at 50 percent of the private share of the equity. These two definitions lead to similar estimates. Under the OECD definition (excluding the legal-person shareholding firms), indigenous private-sector firms produced 5.9 percent of profits in 1998, 10.6 percent in 2001, and 19.1 percent in 2005.

According to the Guangdong definition, these three figures are 7.9, 9.7, and 22 percent.

It is striking how small the indigenous private-sector firms were as recently as 2001. Let me use the average of the OECD and Guangdong estimates, which comes to 6.9 percent for 1998 and 10.2 percent for 2001. To be sure, because the NBS dataset covers only the largest industrial firms, this finding reflects the position of China's indigenous private sector at the top of the corporate chain, rather than at the bottom. But, we still reach the same inescapable sobering conclusion: At the end of the twentieth century, the size of the indigenous private sector in China was minuscule. By 2005, however, the indigenous private sector did become sizable (at 22 percent of the industrial value-added). The flourishing of the indigenous private-sector firms is a very recent development.

Let us also compare indigenous private-sector firms with FIEs. There are two definitions of FIEs. The OECD study adopts a conservative definition, covering only those firms with foreign share capital exceeding 50 percent. This definition is too narrow because under Chinese law, any firm with 25 percent of foreign share capital is classified as an FIE and an FIE is subject to the regulatory regime of the foreign sector. The prevailing Chinese definition classifies FIEs by their registration status because it is the registration status that determines the basis of their legal and regulatory treatments. I adopt this definition here under columns (2a), (2b), and (2c) of Table 1.1. In addition, I include firms not registered as foreign firms but whose foreign share capital exceeded 50 percent.

Based on the OECD definition, the percentage shares of FIEs were about 1.6 to 2 times the percentage shares of indigenous private-sector firms (excluding the legal-person shareholding firms), although the two came much closer by 2005. Based on the Guangdong definition, the differences are larger. In fact, the data on aggregate size obscure the extent to which indigenous private-sector firms are undersized. This is because there are far more indigenous private-sector firms than there are FIEs. Let me illustrate this point using the OECD definition. The 5.9 percent share of indigenous private-sector firms in 1998 was spread among 19,322 firms, whereas the 11.7 percent share of FIEs was produced by 15,934 FIEs. The aggregate size of the indigenous private-sector firms is less than half the size of the foreign private-sector firms, and their individual sizes are even smaller. Even the latest data for 2005 show a larger foreign sector – at 28.8 percent – than the indigenous private sector at 22 percent.

To the extent that the Chinese economy is capitalistic, it is based on foreign capital, not on indigenous private capital. This is *prima facie* evidence of the severity of the policy biases in China. The system privileges one type of firm – FIEs – at the expense of another type, indigenous private firms. This is not to imply that China has not made progress in its economic transition. It has, but let us keep an appropriate perspective. Between 1978 and 2001, the size of the indigenous and foreign private sector among the largest firms grew from 0 to 38.8 percent. This implies an annual growth rate of the size of the private sector of about 1.7 percent a year. It is commonly alleged that China adopted a gradualist pace of reforms, and here is a concrete illustration of this gradualism. Economist Jagdish Bhagwati once described India's embrace of Fabian socialism under Nehru as a "measured and slowly paced ascent up the Marxist mountain."[17] What happened in China since 1978 can be described as a very measured and slowly paced descent from the same mountain.

1.2 Has the Policy Environment Improved for China's Private Sector?

The industrial value-added is the right measure of the size of the private sector in China today (provided that the assumptions of what constitutes the private sector are correct). However, many economists have used the output-based measure for a different purpose – to show the evolution of China's policy environment over time. This is problematic.

Recall the example of the Soviet agriculture in which private farming contributed substantially to agricultural income despite the massive restrictions placed on the private sector. An output-based measure incorporates two very different effects. One is the "policy effect": the increase in the private-sector share that results from a more favorable policy environment. But this measure also incorporates what might be called an "efficiency effect." The private firms are more efficient than the SOEs and, therefore, even given a very narrow business space, they can out-compete the SOEs. This suggests, at least theoretically, that the ratio of the private to the state sector can rise without any improvement in the policy environment for private-sector firms and with rising inefficiencies of SOEs. Indeed, one can think of a situation in which the private output share rises *because of* policy constraints on the private sector. Credit-constrained private-sector firms have few options to grow other than to increase their efficiency. SOEs, lavished with resources, have no such incentives. Thus, the efficiency differential can be very large precisely because of the policy discrimination.

There is an easy way to expose the flaw with the output-based policy measure. Let us choose a period we know for sure to be adverse for private-sector firms. That way, we cannot attribute any increase in private-sector output during that period to policy improvements. This is the 1989–1990 period when the post-Tiananmen leadership launched a systematic crackdown on the private sector. Private-sector employment fell during this period and many private firms were closed down. Credit was tightened. Yet, despite the adversity in the policy environment, the gross output value of the industrial private sector, as a ratio to the SOEs, increased from 7.6 percent in 1988 to 8.6 percent in 1989 and to 9.9 percent in 1990.[18]

Apart from the empirical inaccuracy of using the output of the private sector as a policy measure, there is also the issue of correctly attributing credit for the growth of the private sector. Treating output increases as a measure of policy implicitly assigns credit to the government. On the other hand, if we view the output increase as an efficiency measure, credit would then go to the Chinese entrepreneurs. The fact that the private sector was still able to grow in an enormously difficult environment after the Tiananmen crackdown is a tribute to the agility and acumen of Chinese entrepreneurs, not to the wisdom of the policy of the Chinese government.

I advocate using a different indicator to measure the policy evolution. This is an input-based measure of policy evolution. The input we focus on is capital allocated for fixed-asset investments (FAIs). There are several advantages to using fixed-asset investment data as a measure of China's evolving policy environment. First, by Chinese standards of statistical reporting, the data are remarkably consistent across different reporting sources. The standard source of data used by scholars is the annual *China Statistical Yearbook* (CSY) published by the NBS. I have cross-checked the CSY with a number of publications specializing in reporting fixed-asset investment data and found few variances among the sources.

Another advantage is that the coverage of the private sector in the area of investment activities goes back to the earliest years of the reforms. This may be because fixed-asset investment activities went through a government scrutiny process that required a bureaucratic paper trail. The third reason we focus on fixed-asset investments is that they are heavily controlled by the government, as compared to other activities in the Chinese economy. (The Appendix to this chapter provides more details related to fixed-asset investment data.) Because this measure directly tracks government policy preferences and practices, it is superior to the output measure. It does not involve the kind of confounding problems of distinguishing between the effect of policy and the effect of firm-level efficiency differentials that cloud the output measures of private-sector development.

Table 1.2 presents a number of private-sector development indicators based on fixed-asset investments. The reform era is broken down into four

Table 1.2. *Fixed-asset investment measures of private-sector development:*
Period averages (%)

	1981–1989	1990–1992	1993–2001	2002–2005
Panel (A) Share/ratio indicators: Registered private sector				
1) Private share of total FAI:				
a) All private	21.4	19.8	13.3	14.7
b) Rural private	19.2	17.1	9.5	5.5
2) Private-to-state % ratio of FAI:				
a) All private	34.6	28.8	25.9	39.9
b) Rural private	29.6	25.9	17.8	14.5
3) Rural private/collective % ratio of FAI:	214.3	183.8	80.3	48.7
4) Private share of equipment purchases:				
a) All private	11.3	5.1	4.7	9.3[c]
b) Rural private	11.3	5.1	4.3	5.9[c]
c) Rural private/rural collective ratio	118.5	38.9	28.8	30.8[d]
Panel (B) Share indicators: Alternative definitions of the private sector				
5) Private share of total FAI:				
a) Registered + unclassified[b]	n/a	n/a	14.1	15.6
b) Guangdong definition[a]	n/a	n/a	17.2 (1998)	27.6 (2002) 33.5 (2005)
Panel (C) Share indicators: Indigenous firms only (excluding FIEs from total)				
6) Share of FAIs by indigenous firms:				
a) All private	n/a	n/a	15.1	16.2
b) Rural private	n/a	n/a	10.4	5.8
Panel (D) Real annual growth (deflated to 1978 prices)				
7) FAI:				
a) All private	19.9	2.6	12.4	26.0
b) Rural private	19.1	1.1	7.5	6.8
c) SOEs	8.1	23.8	9.1	13.4
8) Equipment purchases:				
a) Rural private	25.4	1.4	20.8	15.3[c]
b) Rural collective	26.0	42.8	29.6	23.7[c]
9) Nonresidential installations:				
a) Rural private	84.2	19.7	−3.9	−3.1
b) Rural collective	13.9	38.3	12.9	19.7[d]

[a] The Guangdong definition includes registered private-sector firms as well.

[b] Unclassified refers to units outside the state, collective, and private sectors, as well as FIEs and various mixed-ownership firms.

[c] 2002–2003 only.

[d] 2002–2004 only.

Note: FAI stands for fixed-asset investment. In 1996, the government raised the reporting threshold from 50,000 to 500,000 yuan for the state and collective sectors.

Sources: Based on various sources on fixed-asset investments compiled by the NBS. See the Appendix to this chapter for a detailed explanation.

periods in the table: (1) 1981–1989, (2) 1990–1992, (3) 1993–2001, and (4) 2002–2005. This represents a political periodization of the reform era. The 1981–1989 period was the era of Hu Yaobang and Zhao Ziyang. The 1990–1992 period is often described as the "Tiananmen interlude," when central planners exerted control over economic policy after the Tiananmen crackdown. The 1993–2001 period carries the unmistakable policy stamp of Jiang Zemin and Zhu Rongji. During the 2002–2005 period, a new leadership, headed by Hu Jintao and Wen Jiabao, established its rule. It is only natural to ask what the private-sector policies were under these four distinct leadership periods.

Panel (A) of the table presents statistics on fixed-asset investments in the *registered* private sector. The registered private sector includes two types of entities – self-employed household businesses (*getihu*) and what are known as privately run enterprises (*siying qiye*). For both types of entities, the control and revenue rights are unquestionably private. The difference between the two stems from a historical policy of registering small household businesses and large private enterprises separately. The regulatory definition of the former is an entity with seven or fewer employees and the definition of the latter is an entity with more than seven employees. (Throughout this book, unless otherwise noted, "private sector" refers to the indigenous private sector and excludes the FIEs.)

This is admittedly a narrow definition of the private sector. In the Appendix to this chapter, I address various definitional and measurement complications that may surround the indicators presented in the table. (These dynamics include the declining importance of agriculture, the existence of hybrid ownership firms, and the effect of including housing investments in the data.) None of these issues detracts from the following central point – the most liberal policy toward the private sector was in the 1980s under the leadership of Hu Yaobang and Zhao Ziyang, not in the 1990s. The primary difference between the two decades is the private-sector policies in rural China: In the 1980s, the policies were liberal, but in the 1990s, they became restrictive. In Chapters 2 and 3, I examine numerous government documents and household survey data to illustrate the specific policy developments that explain this pattern of fixed-asset investments.

Table 1.2 presents two types of indicators – indicators based on percentage shares and indicators based on annual growth statistics. Row (1) presents percentage shares of the registered private sector in China's fixed-asset investments. The private sector claimed the highest share of China's fixed-asset investments at the very start of the reform period; its share then lost to other firms throughout the 1990s and began to recover somewhat only during the 2002–2005 period. During the 1981–1989 period, the share of the private sector was 21.4 percent; during the Tiananmen interlude, the share declined modestly, to 19.8 percent, and then sharply to 13.3 percent during the 1993–2001 period. During the 2002–2005 period, the share rose slightly to 14.7 percent.

The most important development in the 1990s is that the contraction of the rural private investments. What China economists understatedly call a "Tiananmen interlude," in fact, was both severe in its effect and long-lasting in its duration. The growth rates of private investments slowed down dramatically during the 1990–1992 period. The rural private investment rate after the Tiananmen interlude never recovered to the levels prevailing before.

The most revealing effect of the 1989 Tiananmen crackdown is the contrast between the growth rates of the private sector and the growth rates of the state and rural collective sectors. This is shown in Panel (D) of Table 1.2. The growth of the private sector virtually collapsed during the Tiananmen interlude and recovered only during the 2002–2005 period. Row (7a) shows that the annual growth rate was 19.9 percent in the 1980s, 2.6 percent during the 1990–1992 period, 12.4 percent during the 1993–2001 period, and 26 percent during the 2002–2005 period. Rural private sector investments, however, never regained their momentum of the 1980s. The growth rate in this critical sector of the economy in the 1990s and 2000s was a fraction of the growth rate during the 1980s (Row [7b]).

By contrast, the investment growth of the state and collective sectors accelerated sharply in the aftermath of Tiananmen. The growth rate of SOEs during the 1990–1992 period tripled over that in the 1980s. Contrary to the view that the state was divesting from the SOEs in the 1990s, the investment growth rate of the state sector in the 1990s and 2000s accelerated over the growth rate in the 1980s. Row (7c) shows that the growth rate of the state sector averaged 8.1 percent in the 1980s. But, during the 1990–1992 period, growth accelerated to 23.8 percent and then 9.1 percent during the 1993–2001 period and 13.4 percent during the 2002–2005 period. Data on equipment purchases and nonresidential installations in the rural collective sector exhibit exactly the same trends (Rows [8b] and [9b]).

The Appendix illustrates that broadening the definition of the private sector does not change qualitatively the point that the private-sector policy environment became illiberal in the 1990s. (The only revision is that the broadest definition of the private sector does show the policy environment during the 2002–2005 period to be more liberal than that in the 1980s.) We also have some independent verifications that our measure accurately tracks private-sector policies. It is not in dispute that the Chinese government implemented a crackdown against the private sector after the 1989 Tiananmen crackdown. This shows up in our fixed-asset investment measure. All indicators in the table during this period contracted. (It should be noted that a measure based on output would show an *improvement* in the policy environment immediately following Tiananmen.) We also know that since 2002 there have been a number of liberalization measures aimed at the indigenous private sector. There was a more explicit political affirmation of the private sector at the Sixteenth Party Congress in 2002, a constitutional amendment in 2004 aimed at enhancing property rights, and a fairly sweeping sectoral liberalization measure in 2005 (the so-called 22 articles). Our fixed-asset investment measure tracks very well these policy developments during this period.

2 Getting the China Story Right

The previous portrayal of the state of the private sector and the uneven pace of policy evolution is not as positive as much of the received wisdom on the Chinese economy. But, let me state the following point explicitly and strongly: China's economic achievements have been both substantial and real. A good, parsimonious account has to be minimally consistent with and hopefully explanatory of both the real successes of the country as well as its many obvious failings. The key component in the explanation is suggested by the fixed-asset investment data presented previously: Private-sector development in the rural areas was rigorous and broad-based in the 1980s but it languished in the 1990s. In the remainder of this chapter, I provide an outline of my account.

As the Lenovo story shows, getting the details right matters both for analysis and for drawing the right policy implications. But here is the difficulty about researching the Chinese economy: We have abundant data on macroeconomic outcomes, such as statistics on GDP, exports, FDI, and so forth, but there is an acute shortage of data on what I call microeconomic processes – referring to policies, institutions, and the nature, behavior, and conditions of the economic agents. All things considered, it is relatively easy to get the facts right about Lenovo. After all, it is a Hong Kong–incorporated and listed firm and, as such, it is required to disclose a lot of information about its operations. Yet, some still get it wrong. Now try to arrive at an accurate estimate of the size of China's private sector when we do not even have available the basic information that one takes for granted in a market economy – such as who owns what – about the most prominent private-sector firms such as Huawei.

In this section, I first present a number of perspectives on Chinese economic policies and institutions in Western academic literature. In the formulation of their views on the Chinese economy, many of these academics were heavily influenced by observations of the easily available outcome data. They then proceeded to make inferences about Chinese policies and institutions. I call this approach an inference-based approach. Although this approach has some merits, its accuracy critically depends on the accuracy and comprehensiveness of the outcome data. Often, Western academics work with and accept at face value a narrow set of data, such as GDP per capita. In this book, I show that in certain circumstances, there is no guarantee that GDP per capita truthfully reflects the welfare of the average Chinese person.

My own approach is primarily based on making direct observations of Chinese policies and institutions. This approach first formulates a view of these policies and institutions and then renders a judgment on their economic outcomes. A view produced by this approach would argue that the most important factors in China's growth experience are private ownership, security of property rights, financial liberalization, and deregulation. The welfare of the Chinese population improves along with the growth of its GDP when and where these institutional conditions are becoming stronger. The welfare of the Chinese population improves less or even declines when and where these institutional conditions are being attenuated. But, this perspective requires a massive amount of empirical documentation about China's microeconomic processes and practices on the one hand and policy developments on the other. Much of this book focuses on this empirical task.

2.1 Making Inferences vis-à-vis Making Direct Observations about Policies and Institutions

In 2004, the *Wall Street Journal* published an article based on a survey on and subsequent interviews with a number of Nobel laureates in economics (Wessel and Walker 2004). China featured prominently in the Nobelists' views of the world and of the future. Most of the Nobel winners in the survey believed that China will overtake the United States or the European Union in 75 years. When asked which country in the world has the best economic policies, the answers were "a tie between Norway and the United

States – with China the runner-up." Professor Harry Markowitz of the University of California in San Diego picked the United States as his top choice because it has the most free market. But, in his estimation, China was a close second to the United States. Professor Robert Mundell of Columbia University argued that Deng Xiaoping did more than anyone in the 20th century to improve the living standards of hundreds of millions of people because he "opened the country to foreign investment." Professor Joseph Stiglitz, also of Columbia University, ranked China very highly in terms of its economic management. The *Wall Street Journal* article describes Professor Kenneth Arrow of Stanford University as having "grudging respect" for China's performance.

By the OECD's methodology, the private sector produced 71.2 percent of China's industrial output as of 2005, the most recent data available. This figure can be considered as the upper-bound estimate of the size of China's private sector. Irrespective of its many problems, let me take this claim at its face value and compare China with a number of other countries. It turns out that the private sector's share of industrial output in China in 2005 was broadly similar to that of the India of Indira Gandhi, not that of Manmohan Singh – India during the early 1980s. (Chapter 5 presents more details of the China/India comparison.) It is extremely difficult to reconcile this microeconomic observation with the view that China is a close second to the United States in terms of *market freedoms*. Although Deng Xiaoping probably did contribute more than anyone else in the 20th century to poverty reduction, as Professor Mundell points out, it is questionable to assign the full credit to his FDI policies. The most impressive poverty reduction in China occurred at a time when China had no FDI – in the early 1980s – and, in fact, after China became a member of the World Trade Organization (WTO) in 2001, the emerging evidence is that China's poverty level increased. (I return to this issue in Chapter 5.)

The most likely reason for the highly laudatory views held by these eminent economists is that their judgment calls were heavily influenced by the easily available and highly visible achievements in terms of GDP growth. Because its GDP performance has been so phenomenal, it must be the case that the country has rational economic policies and institutions. This is one example of the inference-based approach in the study of the Chinese economy. For these eminent economists, the Chinese economy presents no analytical challenges: Excellent economic performance must be the result of excellent economic policies.

In Chapter 5, I show that this single fixation on GDP data is a mistake. My view here is not rooted in the common criticisms of GDP statistics – that GDP data may not sufficiently reflect resource costs, the extent of environmental degradation, or the subjective sense of well-being. I leave aside all these universal complications of GDP data. The argument is that China had rapid GDP growth during both the 1980s and the 1990s but the welfare implications for the Chinese people during these two periods have been very different. During the entrepreneurial decade of the 1980s, fast GDP growth was accompanied by equally fast household income growth. During the state-led 1990s, fast GDP growth diverged from household income growth. In particular, rural income – the best measure of the welfare of the majority of the Chinese population – sharply declined in terms of its growth rates compared with the 1980s. Other indicators such as education and health in the rural areas also showed some significant problems in the 1990s.

A second variant of the inference-based approach reasons that China's economic policies and institutions provide rational and efficient *functions* even though those policies and institutions may appear, at first glance, to be lacking in conventional economic efficiencies. This is a more sophisticated and nuanced approach, and it is more fact-based than the simple declaration that China has good policies. It recognizes a seeming incompatibility – that China has many economic policies and institutions that are overtly inefficient and yet the country has performed well (again in GDP terms). Scholars then propose analytical devices to solve this incompatibility. Although there are different versions of this approach, their commonality is to reason that these manifestly inefficient policies actually have strong underlying efficiency attributes *given* the specific context of China. This is the approach that has traveled very far in mainstream economics, and several papers anchored in this approach have won coveted spots in some of the most prestigious social science journals.

Let me illustrate by a few examples. One of the most profound puzzles in the study of the Chinese economy is the so-called township and village enterprise (TVE) phenomenon. The best articulation of this puzzle – and the broader puzzle about why China grew at all – is by another Nobel laureate, Professor Douglass North. He states (2005):

This system in turn led to the TVEs and sequential development built on their cultural background. But China still does not have well-specified property rights, town-village enterprises hardly resembled the standard firm of economics, and it remains to this day a communist dictatorship.

A huge amount of analytical energy has been invested in trying to explain the TVEs, a corporate form that seems so different from "the standard firm of economics." The view that has gained the most traction is the one that models the normally inefficient public ownership – associated with TVEs by many analysts – as a transitional institution to overcome governance problems.[19] According to this view, local government ownership of firms is a solution to the problem of a lack of rule of law, in several ways. One is that the absence of rule of law makes it possible for private stealing of assets. Public ownership mitigates against information problems and other problems in a transitional context. Second, the absence of rule of law creates a commitment problem for the public sector as well. The Chinese state, unconstrained by any institutional checks and balances, may expropriate private assets at will. TVEs thus command a substantial advantage in such a hostile political environment. They are owned by the local governments and, because of the incentive alignment between the central government and local governments, they are not subject to the expropriation risks that afflict private entrepreneurs.[20]

Some scholars have inferred efficient functions from even the most manifestly inefficient policies and institutions. For example, the widely acknowledged fact that the private sector in China is credit-constrained is reasoned to be not so inefficient in its effects. The financing repression of the private sector has an underlying stronger economic rationale – financing government deficits in a system that has poorly developed public-finance tools. And, the financing repression in the formal sector does not matter anyway because of the availability of informal finance (Allen, Qian, and Qian 2005). Whereas elsewhere in the world the concern is that an unconstrained government is a grabbing hand undermining economic growth (Frye and Shleifer 1997), local governments in China are viewed as helping hands because they are subject to effective constraints in the form of "federalism, Chinese style" (Montinola, Qian, and Weingast 1995).

The analytical attraction of this approach is easy to see. Take, as an example, the missing-institutions explanation of TVEs. The model has the feature of "killing two birds with one stone." It identifies two attributes of the Chinese economic system otherwise viewed as inefficient when each is analyzed separately – lack of political self-constraints and public ownership. Combining the two, an efficiency function emerges. This approach seems to be well suited to China, a country associated with good growth but also with many manifestations of microeconomic inefficiencies.

This functional-efficiency perspective on China – often formalized with mathematical models and proofs – is extremely influential in economics. Papers advocating this perspective were published in top journals and are widely cited by general economists who otherwise may not have detailed country expertise on China. In this book, I adopt a different approach and it is one based on direct observations of institutions and policies. This approach will lead to a depiction of Chinese reforms considerably at odds with the stylizations summarized previously. Instead of devising elaborate analytical tools to solve the supposed incompatibilities, I ask whether these incompatibilities actually exist in the first place. These are the types of questions this book explores:

- "China has experienced rapid GDP growth since the late 1970s, but has that growth always promoted welfare to the same degree?"
- "Are TVEs really publicly owned?"
- "Did China undertake financial reforms in the 1980s?"
- "Did these reforms continue in the 1990s?"
- "Did the Chinese political system always lack self-constraint?"

The devil is in the empirical details. Constructing direct observations, as opposed to making inferences, about the Chinese economy requires a massive amount of information and data. To that end, I have conducted detailed and wide-ranging archival research on government and bank documents, edicts, and directives. The details and the sources of these documents/data and the citation information are presented in the relevant parts of the book, but let me highlight one source of documentary data to illustrate the depth of this research. To ascertain China's financial policies toward the private sector, I have examined thousands of pages in a 22-volume compilation of internal documents of the central bank, all major state-owned commercial banks, and the rural credit cooperatives (RCCs). These bank documents, issued between 1982 and 2004, range from speeches given by bank presidents to their employees, operating instructions issued from headquarters to regional bank branches, internal regulations governing human resource screening and evaluations, lending criteria and rules, and so forth. Although this compilation of bank documents is accessible at libraries at Harvard University and the Chinese University of Hong Kong, as far as I know they have never been examined by a Western academic.

To ascertain the ownership meaning of TVEs, I have tracked down the original government document that provides a detailed definition of TVEs, as well as many other government documents and regulations bearing on the ownership status of TVEs. I have also resorted to different data series from the familiar GDP and output data. As I have already shown, using fixed-asset investment data series suggests a different dynamic regarding private-sector policy evolution as compared with a dynamic based on output data. Instead of simply relying on the *Chinese Statistical Yearbook,* a standard source of economic data, I have looked at the database on TVEs compiled by the Ministry of Agriculture. The Ministry of Agriculture was in charge of collecting data on TVEs and its database provides a far more detailed breakdown of the ownership categories of TVEs than the *Chinese Statistical Yearbook*.

For this book, China's GDP and output performance are the beginning of the analysis, not its end. I have used extensively the household income surveys conducted by the NBS on urban and rural areas to examine the growth of personal income – a closer measure of economic well-being of the average Chinese person than the crude measure of per capita GDP. In addition, I have looked into several waves of surveys on Chinese private-sector businesses. The totality of this qualitative and quantitative evidence, as I show throughout this book, conveys an alternative picture of the Chinese reforms compared with the familiar stylizations in Western economics research on China.

2.2 Getting the China Story Right

As far as the leadership and cadre systems of our Party and state are concerned, the major problems are bureaucracy, over-concentration of power, patriarchal methods, life tenure in leading posts and privileges of various kinds.
– Deng Xiaoping, August 18, 1980

In this section, I develop and elaborate on the main argument that I put forward in the book. Let me state the central idea of this argument as explicitly and as directly as possible: The successes of the Chinese economy are a function of conventional sources – private-sector development, financial liberalization, and property rights security. In regions and periods when Chinese economic growth has faltered *and/or* Chinese economic growth has failed to improve the welfare of the average Chinese, it has been the result of governmental interventions, illiberal financial policies and practices, and property rights insecurity. A second and related idea in this argument is that Chinese economic success is a result of a movement toward *manifestly and explicitly* efficient policies and institutions, not just a result of *functionally* efficient policies and institutions. This is probably the stronger of the two ideas that run through this book and it is the one I concentrate on developing empirically.

The social science literature against which I benchmark China is that on the connections between institutions and economic development. This book focuses on the institutional sources of economic growth. I mention but do not go into details about the role of education and human capital in the concluding chapter (mainly as a way to differentiate between China and India). I take for granted the assumption that education, especially basic education, contributes substantially to economic growth.

This book is concerned with three economic institutions and their effects in China – the organization of firms (e.g., TVEs), the orientation of providers of finance, and property rights security. By necessity, we cannot study these three institutions in isolation from politics and from China's political system. Political institutions structure, organize, and order economic institutions and, in this respect, China is no exception. The bulk of the empirical coverage in this book concerns the three economic institutions mentioned previously. However, I offer conjectures – plausible postulations – about the workings of Chinese politics to contextualize the economics and policy discussions.

Ownership, Finance, and Property Rights Security in China. It is no exaggeration to say that the importance of private ownership is a fundamental, core principle of neoclassical economics. Private actors, consumers, or firms, acting in their self-interests and maximizing their own payoffs in the ways they understand them, promote both private and social welfare. This is a central tenet of economics, going back to Adam Smith. Although there are circumstances in which private and public welfare may diverge in a privately owned economy, it is safe to say that the majority of economists accept the general claim that private ownership is more efficient on average as compared with state ownership.

It is in this sense that the TVE phenomenon is viewed as a puzzle. TVEs are believed to be owned publicly, although at lower levels of the government, such as townships and villages. Yet, they have performed superbly. I resolve this puzzle in Chapter 2 where I present detailed documentary evidence that shows a huge gap between the Chinese definition of TVEs and the Western understanding of TVEs. The Chinese define TVEs as a *geographic* phenomenon – that TVEs are businesses *located* in rural areas. The Western academic literature has an *ownership* understanding of TVEs – that TVEs are *owned* by townships and villages. How substantial is this gap in these two understandings of TVEs? Data from the Ministry of Agriculture show that as early as 1985, out of 12 million businesses classified as TVEs, more than 10 million were purely private. If we get the facts right, TVEs, as it turns out, are a huge private-sector success story.

In recent years, social scientists, especially economists, have substantially advanced our understanding of the effects of financial and legal institutions on economic growth as well as the specific channels whereby these institutions exert such effects. Much of the work in this area is not only theoretical but also deeply empirical, showing strong empirical correlations between good institutions and economic growth. Another characteristic of this body of work is that it identifies fairly specific mechanisms linking institutional quality with growth. It is not an exaggeration to say that the idea that good institutions – understood in a conventional and straightforward sense – are important for growth is based on a solid empirical foundation.[21]

Against this large and cumulative backdrop of the solid empirical demonstration of the virtuous effects of efficient financial and legal institutions, China appears to be a staggering anomaly, as the previous quote from Douglass North suggests. This book argues that once we look a bit closer, China is not an anomaly. I have already shown that in the case of Lenovo, the microeconomic development of the firm was critically contingent on the presence and operations of conventionally efficient financial and legal institutions – in Hong Kong. Is there any reason to think that the general economic success of China has been a result of institutional forces dramatically different from those that have favored growth elsewhere?

I take on this issue in Chapters 2 and 3. Going through thousands of pages of bank documents, I have uncovered evidence that China implemented financial reforms very early in the reform era – beginning in the early 1980s. These financial reforms encompassed two areas – improving access to finance for the private sector and allowing or even encouraging some private entry into the financial services sector. The documentary evidence also shows, directly and explicitly, that these reforms were initiated at the very top of the Chinese financial system. There were directives and instructions supportive of private-sector lending issued by the governor of the People's Bank of China (PBoC), China's central bank, and presidents of the Bank of China and the Agricultural Bank of China. In the 1980s, China's financial system was moving *directionally* toward liberalism at a time and at a speed that previous scholarship on China may have under-estimated.

There is an important caveat to this interpretation of China's financial development. Almost all financial liberalization took place in the rural part of the country. In the 1980s, urban China was virtually unaffected by the financial reforms. This raises the issue of the relative economic and institutional importance of rural China vis-à-vis that of urban China. This issue, presented in great detail in Chapters 2 and 3, is at the heart of understanding China. The essence of the argument I put forward in these chapters is that rural China matters for the country not just economically but also *institutionally*. The economic importance of rural China derives from the fact that China – even today – is deeply rural. The institutional importance of rural China is that rural China was always more predisposed toward capitalism and entrepreneurship.[22]

Recognizing the extant rural disposition toward capitalism entails important analytical implications. One is that it partially resolves a puzzle why seemingly modest policy changes nevertheless enlisted huge entrepreneurial responses. Economists characterize a critical piece of rural reforms – the dual-track system at which farmers sold their crop at the market prices after they fulfilled their obligations to the state at price points set by the state – as a modest policy departure from the *status quo ante* (Lau, Qian, and Roland 2000; Rodrik 2007). I come back to this issue later and discuss whether this characterization of the dual-track system is accurate, but for now let me take the claim at its face value. The dual-track system was operationally simple and straightforward, but it required economic agents to have a basic concept of residual claims. As of the late 1970s, rural China still retained some rudimentary capitalistic practices that operated on the principle of residual claims.

Even at the height of the commune system, Chinese peasants still possessed what is known as "private plots" – the land that was owned by the collectives but worked by the peasants themselves.[23] The land was not tradable but the revenue rights were private. The production on private plots was not taxed and the returns accrued to the peasants with the assignment rights to the land. Of course, the degree of private appropriability varied substantially in the 1960s and 1970s and depended heavily on the twists and turns of the Chinese politics, which had swung in unpredictable fashions during the Cultural Revolution.

Sachs and Woo (1994) also emphasized the "ruralness" as a determinant in economic transition, similar to the view laid out here. A rural economy, being poorer and simpler, could grow even with partial reforms, they argued. My reasoning, although reaching the same conclusion, postulates an entirely different causal mechanism. It was the pre-existence of entrepreneurship that mattered. "Ruralness" can be thought of as a proxy of entrepreneurship. To illustrate this point, consider a situation in which any residues of entrepreneurship were completely absent. This was in the industrialized Soviet Union. Gorbachev copied the Chinese dual-track system but the experiment failed completely. By contrast, the same reforms produced stunning results in a country similarly rural as China – Vietnam.

The second analytical implication has to do with the effects of *ex ante* rural entrepreneurship. Financial reforms, even though limited to the rural areas, had a disproportionately contributory effect on the overall entrepreneurial and market development because rural China was already predisposed toward capitalism in the first place. This is why the supply response – surging private-sector investments and rural entrepreneurship – was so elastic with respect to seemingly modest policy changes. By the same token, financial under-development and urban biases in economic policies also had a disproportionate effect on the overall entrepreneurial and market development *in the opposite direction.* As I show later in this section and in Chapter 3, in the 1990s China moved away from the policy direction of the 1980s. Many of the productive financial experiments in rural China were reversed and the government favored the cities in its investment allocations. This reversal greatly stunted the development of broad-based, entrepreneurial capitalism in China.

Did China grow without a conventional version of property rights security? This is the subject of Chapter 2. Documentary research uncovers internal as well as public policy deliberations in the early 1980s that explicitly sought to enhance policy and political commitments to reforms and liberalization. In the early 1980s, Chinese leaders chose to word their policy announcements very carefully, with the objective of conveying the stability and predictability of their policy actions. They also took proactive and highly symbolic acts, such as returning assets to former capitalists, direct and public meetings between some of the top leaders of the country and private entrepreneurs, and, in some of the local cases, publicly apologizing to those private entrepreneurs who had been wrongly treated by the government in the past.

Directional Liberalism. But, surely this is not the final story. A deeper question is why these policy promises made by the Chinese leaders, however well intentioned and explicitly worded, should have been viewed as at all credible. The political system, then as now, imposes no institutional constraints on the rulers to renege on their promises. The commitment problem, as political economists know very well, is massive in an unconstrained political system. The fundamental dilemma, as stated by Weingast (1995, p. 1), is as follows: "A government strong enough to protect property rights and enforce contracts is also strong enough to confiscate the wealth of its citizens." This commitment problem, on top of a holdup problem whereby the political elites confiscate wealth *ex post*, normally would have deterred investments of energy, effort, and capital by would-be entrepreneurs.[24]

One of the deepest puzzles in the history of Chinese economic reforms is why the supply response of rural entrepreneurship was so massive in the early 1980s. The economic policy change is believed to be "modest," for one thing. For the other, millions of rural entrepreneurs took upon themselves considerable risks. They put up a significant amount of capital, as we saw in Table 1.2. They needed to feel reasonably confident about the security and the predictability of the investment and political environments. They needed to trust the Chinese state not to renege on reforms. Keep in mind that China was just four years away from the Cultural Revolution. Up to that point, the record of the Chinese state in keeping its promises and delivering on its commitments was not outstanding, to put it mildly.

The political economy question – how China managed to create a *prima facie* sense of policy credibility and political predictability so soon after the Cultural Revolution – is the crux of the matter. But, arguably, it is the least understood aspect of Chinese economic success. Consider the view that dual-track reforms were a "modest" change. The mechanics of the reforms were simple and straightforward. This is true, but for the system to work as designed, it was critical for the Chinese peasants – numbering in the hundreds of millions – to trust that the grain quotas would not be instantaneously ratcheted up each time they were exceeded. The economics of the dual-track system might be modest; the political economy of it was not.

I offer a conjecture here. It is a conjecture, not a settled claim, because there are simply no data to directly demonstrate my hypothesis. Yet, the question is so monumentally important that any account of the Chinese reforms is incomplete without at least an attempt to explain this question. This conjecture rests on two exercises. The first is trying to come up with a reasonable approximation of the perspective with which a potential Chinese entrepreneur viewed his political milieu. The second exercise is to postulate that a potential Chinese entrepreneur had the ease of knowledge that Chinese politics of the 1980 vintage was objectively different from the Cultural Revolution.

The key to an understanding of the explosive entrepreneurship in the early 1980s is to specify the right baseline benchmark with which the would-be Chinese entrepreneurs viewed their political world of the 1980s. That baseline is not a Westministerian system of checks and balances, which would have shown the Chinese system in a poor light indeed. That baseline is China of the Cultural Revolution from 1966 to 1976, a period during which Chinese politics can be safely described as "nasty, brutish and short" in the Hobbesian sense. The Chinese political system circa 1980, as arbitrary and as absent of self-constraints as it was, marked a substantial *marginal* change from the *status quo ante* of the Cultural Revolution. The incentive effects – that the would-be private entrepreneurs felt increasingly assured of the safety of their assets – came from this dynamic development. This is what I call "directional liberalism."

The next question to consider is whether this marginal change from the *status quo ante* was substantial. There are two ways to think about this question. First, it is important to highlight the extreme ideological antagonism toward capitalism during the Cultural Revolution era. Private businesses were strictly forbidden and in urban China, all vestiges of capitalism were completely eliminated. (There was more leeway in rural China.) Anyone who went into private business faced instantaneous risks of being arrested and of being severely persecuted.

Entrepreneurs in China of the early 1980s no longer faced this imprisonment risk. Imagine the incentive effect changing from an equilibrium in which a would-be entrepreneur faced instantaneous arrest to one in which this was no longer an automatic risk. This gets to the distinction between the security of the proprietor – the person holding the property – and the security of the property itself. The security of the proprietor is the necessary condition for the security of his or her property. China then and now does not have well-specified property rights security. But, China in the early 1980s moved very far and fast toward establishing security of the proprietor. One should never underestimate the incentive effect of not getting arrested.

A second way we consider this issue is that there were objective – and objectively large – differences between China of the 1970s and China of the 1980s. This gets to the question of whether the potential entrepreneurs in the early 1980s viewed the political and policy signals that they would not be imprisoned as credible. This is not an idle question because the standard political indicators do not show any difference between Chinese politics in the 1970s and Chinese politics in the 1980s. The issue is whether the would-be entrepreneurs themselves had a *prima facie* reason to believe that there was a great difference. The surging entrepreneurship in the early 1980s was a function of the incentives and the mindset of those going into entrepreneurship. It was not a function of an exact match or lack thereof between the Chinese political system circa 1980 and the textbook version of good political governance.

Quantitative indicators used by social scientists are unable to show any meaningful differences between China under Mao and China under Deng. One widely used political database is the Polity IV database developed by political scientists at the University of Maryland and other universities. The polity score for China in both 1976 and 1980 was −7, with −10 referring to the most autocratic and 0 most democratic. (In fact, China had a score of −7 throughout the reform era.)[25] This political ranking implies that the nature of Chinese politics under Deng Xiaoping was identical to that during the waning years of Mao Zedong as well as that in the Soviet Union in 1953, the year Stalin died.

If the Chinese peasants had relied on the Polity IV to judge their property rights security, none of them would have gone into entrepreneurship. The political risks would have been prohibitively high. But, equating Deng's China with the Soviet Union under Nikita Khrushchev and with the last year of Mao Zedong would strike anyone with even rudimentary knowledge of China as incredulous. The political science work on China demonstrates clear and sharp differences between China under Mao and China under Deng in terms of the predictability of the political rules of the game and the degree of institutionalization. Mao, as Shirk (1993) notes, launched mass campaigns such as the Great Leap Forward and the Cultural Revolution to stem the trend of institutionalization. From the very beginning of his rule, Deng Xiaoping "proposed a system governed by rules, clear lines of authority, and collective decision-making institutions to replace the over-concentration of power and patriarchal rule that had characterized China under Mao" (Shirk 1993, p. 9).

The quote printed at the beginning of this section from Deng Xiaoping is the single most incisive analysis of the problems of the Chinese political system. Notice the date of the speech: It was given in 1980, at the very beginning of rural reforms. Every single important political reform, as noted by Pei (2006, p. 11), such as the mandatory retirement of government officials, the strengthening of the National People's Congress, legal reforms, experiments in rural self-government, and loosening control of civil society groups, was instituted in the 1980s. The timing here is critical. The institutional literature stresses the institutional conditions as preconditions for and as antecedents of growth. China met this test. China began to implement these political reforms either prior to or concurrently with its economic takeoff. Although these efforts to institutionalize Chinese politics and to implement incremental reforms may not show up in the Polity IV rankings, they might have contributed to the rising and cumulative sense that the reforms were irreversible and that proprietors and property grew more secure. This dynamic story seems to be able to account for the substantial supply of entrepreneurship at a time when a political commitment problem was theoretically present and realistically massive.

However, the relevant question is not whether China specialists know that there is a difference in Chinese politics between the 1970s and the 1980s. The relevant question is whether the would-be rural entrepreneurs in China noticed the directional liberalism being postulated here. In

Chapter 2, I speculate that it is not implausible that the Chinese peasants sensed a change in the political climate in the late 1970s. Admittedly, the evidence I can provide is casual and scant. A stronger statement, however, is that the Chinese rural entrepreneurs had *reasons* to know that the Chinese politics had changed. This is the Deng Xiaoping effect.

The almost instantaneous credibility of the Chinese reforms owes in no small measure to the fact that Deng Xiaoping, not somebody else, presided at the helm of the Chinese politics. It is the conventional wisdom – both among academics and practitioners – that Deng was the architect of Chinese reforms.[26] My account stresses not his reformist inclinations or his political power but rather his credibility vis-à-vis the would-be entrepreneurs. He might have prevailed over his conservative opponents to push forward his reforms, but none of this would have mattered from the point of view of peasants' incentives and their sense of property rights security if he was not viewed credible. The importance of Deng is that he was *observably different* from Mao. (And I am not just talking about their difference in physique.) The key word here is "observable" – Deng had a set of credentials that were not obtuse but commonly known. The ease of knowledge is important. The entrepreneurial response originated not from a select group of urban elites but from hundreds of millions of Chinese peasants scattered in far-flung places. They had to believe that the policy change under Deng was permanent rather than cyclical and that Deng's China was objectively different from Mao's China. Here is why Deng mattered: He was purged *three times* by Mao and one of his sons was crippled by Mao's red guards during the Cultural Revolution. No other Chinese leaders commanded the kind of automatic credibility that he did.[27]

This book ends with a view that many current problems in China are due to the lack of genuine institutional reforms – reforms of the political system itself rather than a simple shift within the system. Is there a contradiction with the notion of directional liberalism proposed here? Not at all. I go into this issue in more detail herein but suffice it to say here that in the 1990s, China reversed much of the directional liberalism of the 1980s. The policy and political reversals weakened the virtuous incentive effects associated with the directional liberalism and may have irrevocably undermined the hard-won credibility that the Communist Party had acquired in the 1980s. Another factor is that directional liberalism works in a time-varying way – the strength of its effect is a diminishing function of time. The reason for this is straightforward: In 2008, the Cultural Revolution does not loom as large as a baseline benchmark as it did in 1978. Marginal changes, however substantial, may no longer be sufficient to establish confidence in and a sense of property rights security. Institutional convergence with democracy, clean government, and quality governance may now be necessary to move the Chinese economy to the next stage because both the private-asset stakes and the value of political predation have increased substantially.

Reversal of Fortunes. The conjectures and some of the factual details presented in the previous sections are descriptively consistent with the story of surging and vibrant entrepreneurial development and the general economic success of the country in the 1980s. However, the empirical account of the Chinese economy as of the first decade of the 21st century has another side – a relatively small indigenous private sector, severe financing constraints, increasingly investment-driven growth, and massive governance problems. A reasonable reader may ask, "How does one account for all these problems as well as China's well-known successes?"

The fixed-asset investment data presented earlier illustrate a phenomenon few China economists seem to have noticed: Private-sector policies, especially in the rural areas most predisposed to capitalism, became illiberal in the 1990s. Chapters 3 and 4 offer empirical support for this view of the Chinese economy on the basis of documentary and survey evidence. The most substantial reversal occurred in the area of rural finance. Private-sector access to capital to engage in nonfarm activities became very difficult in the 1990s. The embryonic rural financial liberalization – decentralization of management of local savings and loans organizations and a permissive stance toward private entry into the financial services sector – was completely stopped. Rural political and fiscal management was centralized. In more recent years, lease holdings of land have become increasingly insecure as local officials have grabbed land on a massive scale. Directional liberalism turned into directional illiberalism. Not a single new political reform initiative was proposed in the 1990s and many of the political reform initiatives of the 1980s were discontinued (Pei 2006, p. 11).

This portrayal of China in the 1990s is at sharp variance with the received wisdom in the economic research on China, much of which argues that China in the 1990s not only continued but also deepened the reform program of the 1980s. Let us put to a plausibility test the idea that the three generations of Chinese leaders since 1978 have continued with and have deepened the same policy programs. The leadership of the 1990s put Zhao Ziyang – premier and Party general secretary in the 1980s – under what amounted to house arrest from 1989 to 2005. (He died in 2005.) The relationship between the current generation of leaders – Hu Jintao and Wen Jiabao – and their predecessors from the 1990s is no more congenial. An article in the Singapore press summarizes the situation in the five years since

Hu Jintao succeeded Jiang Zemin as follows: "[Hu] wrested control of the military from Mr Jiang, co-opted rivals who could be persuaded to switch sides, and ruthlessly sacked those who failed to toe the line, such as former Shanghai party boss Chen Liangyu."[28] The starting presumption – until proven otherwise – ought to be that there were significant policy differences among leaders so at political odds with one another.

The three generations of Chinese leaders do share one thing in common: They do not want to return to central planning. At this level of aggregation, the received wisdom is correct, but this is surely too sweeping a statement to be analytically useful. (It amounts to saying that both Bill Clinton and George W. Bush want to preserve capitalism and, therefore, their economic policies are identical.) We have enough information and data to probe into the specifics of the policies and the policy orientations of the three generations of Chinese leaders. Their rural policies are at the front and center of their policy differences.

Just as rural China illustrates the extent of the directional liberalism in the 1980s, rural China in the 1990s is a case study of policy and political developments in the opposite direction. This is the subject of Chapter 3. (The book focuses on the 1980s and 1990s. In Chapter 5, I take a look at the leadership of Hu Jintao and Wen Jiabao. All indications show that the current leadership is returning to a version of the policy model of the 1980s.) In the 1990s, China did move forward in FDI liberalization and in the area of restructuring urban SOEs. In this book, I assign a greater weight to rural developments than to these other developments in my explanation of the pace and the character of China's transition toward capitalism. The argument is that FDI and SOE reforms are fundamentally urban and, to the extent that entrepreneurial capitalism is rural in origin, rural policies matter more for China's economic transition. One may wish to disagree with how I weight different components of reforms, but it is not the case that I "ignored" FDI liberalization and the SOE restructuring in the 1990s.

What triggered these policy reversals? I leave this issue to future historians, who may have better access to government archives to resolve the issue more definitively. Let me propose a conjecture based on both the timing of the turning points detected in the economic data and the observable characteristics of Chinese leaders in the 1980s and the 1990s.

We have already seen in the data on the fixed-asset investments that the turning point occurred during the 1989–1990 period. Chapter 3 presents data on the growth of rural income and on the changing composition of the sources of rural income. Those data also show that there was a turning point during this period. Documentary research on bank documents shows that the policy reversals became apparent a few years later, during 1993 or 1994.

A reasonable conjecture is that the political and policy turning point was the 1989 Tiananmen turmoil. It is well known that the post-Tiananmen leadership sought to crack down on the private sector, mainly on ideological grounds. The ideological assault was quickly halted, as is well known by China scholars, but a longer-lasting effect of Tiananmen was a substantial change in the composition of the Chinese leadership. Suffice it to mention that the pre-Tiananmen and the post-Tiananmen leaderships differed in one critical aspect – their rural vis-à-vis urban credentials. Before Tiananmen, many of the top Chinese leaders charged with day-to-day economic management – Zhao Ziyang, Wan Li, and Tian Jiyun – hailed from rural provinces that had pioneered in agricultural reforms. They built their economic credentials by having succeeded in the management of agriculture. After Tiananmen, the top Chinese leaders in charge of the economy – Jiang Zemin and Zhu Rongji – came from the most urban and the least reformed region of China – Shanghai. We cannot know for sure whether these observable characteristics of the Chinese leaders explain their policy orientations, but they are not inconsistent with the view that there was a rural policy bias in the 1980s and that there was an urban policy bias in the 1990s.

3 The Outline of the Book

The key to getting the China story right is to understand its rural entrepreneurship. This is why the decade of the 1980s is so important in our efforts to explain China. I devote all of Chapter 2 and a portion of Chapter 3 to this topic. I show that rural entrepreneurship was not only vibrant but also virtuous. Rural entrepreneurs built businesses of a substantial scale in some of China's poorest provinces and, after only a few years into the first decade of the reforms, the private portions of the TVEs were extraordinarily high.

An important theme of this book is that capitalism in rural China is broad-based and vigorously entrepreneurial. Chapter 3 documents the policy reversals that led to financing repression and other restrictions on this virtuous form of capitalism. In the 1990s, China did not revert back to central planning. Far from it. But China began to adopt policies and practices that favored the more state-controlled urban areas. During this period, China made notable progress in reducing the ideological stigma associated with the private sector (much of which was actually revived during the Tiananmen period). But, financial policies became adverse in the rural areas and fiscal and economic affairs in the rural areas were centralized. The power and the reach of the state expanded even when the ownership role of the state declined in the 1990s.

Chapter 4 focuses on a pivotal region of the country – Shanghai. Shanghai is a large economy in its own right but the main reason I focus on Shanghai is political. Shanghai dominated Chinese politics and policy making in the 1990s. In many ways, the Shanghai model is the apex of the development model of the 1990s: The Shanghai leaders designed and presided over this policy model in the late 1980s and in the 1990s expanded this model to the rest of the country in their capacity as national leaders. The Shanghai model possesses the following central elements: an urban bias, heavy-handed interventionism by the state, an investment-intensive growth strategy, and a biased liberalization that privileges FDI over indigenous – especially small-scale – private entrepreneurship.

Chapter 5 takes stock of all these findings and asks the question of whether the policy developments documented in Chapters 2 through 4 really mattered. This is a legitimate question. From the GDP data, one cannot identify a meaningful difference between the 1980s and 1990s. This is why this book treats GDP data as the beginning of the analysis rather than the end. Surveys on household incomes show a dramatic difference between the 1980s and the 1990s. Rural income slowed down considerably in the 1990s. Also, in the 1990s, national income accounting data – that is, GDP data – began to diverge from household income survey data. To put it briefly, household income as a ratio to GDP (all on a per capita basis) declined substantially in the 1990s compared with the 1980s.

In fact, national income accounting data show a substantial difference between the 1980s and the 1990s if one is willing to go one level down in the data disaggregation. In the 1980s, the labor share of GDP was rising and in the 1990s it was declining. In the 1990s, China was producing output at an impressive rate but this output production began to benefit its citizens less and less. This is a cautionary note that we should rely on empirical details other than GDP growth, exports, and FDI to formulate a view of the Chinese economy. Other indicators such as acute income inequalities, social tensions, rising illiteracy, and so forth all show adverse developments in the 1990s. In other words, although GDP growth was fast in the 1980s and the 1990s, the welfare implications were quite different.

A central mechanism of the growth model of the 1990s was to finance state-led, urban China by heavily taxing entrepreneurial rural China. The result was the urban boom – the skyscrapers and urban amenities in Beijing and Shanghai – that many take as a sign of China's economic success.

Very few observers have asked the obvious question, "What financed these expensive projects in a poor country like China?" The second obvious question is, "If China spent precious resources on such projects, what other projects had to be given up to finance these projects?" The first question gets to the actual costs of these projects; the second question gets to the opportunity costs. These are especially pertinent questions because such urban projects are nonproductive and state-led urban China is less efficient.

The answer is that entrepreneurial rural China paid the price. Chapter 5 provides some details. In the 1990s, rural tax burdens were high and increased substantially. In addition, the state increased charges for providing basic services, such as education and health. In some parts of the country, local governments began to charge for administering immunization shots. The number of primary schools, as well as the number of medical facilities, fell in the rural areas.

The magnitude of these costly resource-allocation decisions is only beginning to show up now. A little-known fact is that China experienced a sharp rise in adult illiteracy between 2000 and 2005, all of which took place in the rural areas. According to the official data, there was an increase of 30 million illiterates. In Chapter 5, I look into this development in some detail. The way adult illiteracy is measured in China implies that all the new illiteracy was a product of the basic education in the 1990s. Under some highly realistic assumptions, we can show that an increase of illiteracy by 30 million people suggests that China's basic education failed about 30 percent of the rural school-age children in the second half of the 1990s. This estimate is within a close range of the dropout ratios reported by Chinese analysts based on their field research. The rising illiteracy is probably the most long-lasting and the most damaging legacy of the 1990s. The simple GDP data, upon which Western economists have been fixated, do not capture this development at all.

Chapter 5 also places the state of the private sector in China against a broader perspective. It shows that even as China is about to enter the fourth decade of reforms, the size of its indigenous private sector is conspicuously small. The best way to characterize the Chinese economy today is that it is broadly similar to many of the commanding-heights economies of the 1970s. It is capitalistic to be sure, but it is a version of the state-led capitalism that, as Baumol, Litan, and Shramm (2007) argue, characterized Latin America. Today China has other attributes that also put the country closer to the Latin American end of capitalism rather than to the East Asian end – the rising income disparities and the contraction in social opportunities available to the population to attain education and health.

A country that was habitually written off in comparison with China is showing increasing economic vitality and strength – India. Chapter 5 presents a stylized comparison of the two countries. Understanding the emerging Indian miracle is both analytically meaningful and relevant to policies. As China begins to ponder the question of political reforms, it is worth revisiting the supposed tradeoff between growth and political freedom. Many held the view that such a tradeoff existed when India was growing at 2 to 3 percent a year, but this belief was increasingly untenable when India began to grow at an East Asian level. The rise of India, when explicitly benchmarked against China, also raises questions about the importance of "soft infrastructures" – financial and legal institutions – vis-à-vis the importance of "hard infrastructures," such as bridges and buildings. I delve into some of these issues in Chapter 5.

I conclude the book with some speculative comments about China's prospects in the short to medium run. To get at this issue, one has to start with an assessment of the current leadership of Hu Jintao and Wen Jiabao. At the time of this writing, it is clear that the current leadership is rethinking the policy model of the 1990s and has signaled, if obliquely, an intention to return to the directional liberalism of the 1980s. In the past five years, despite significant political baggage from the 1990s, Chinese leaders have revived the policy emphasis on the rural areas, begun to address the massive problems in the social sector, introduced some financial reforms, and revived at least discussions of political reforms. The policy platform unveiled at the Seventeenth Party Congress in October 2007 is probably the most liberal and progressive one since the Thirteenth Party Congress exactly 20 years earlier. These events bode well for China.

There are, however, monumental odds. The political system today is manifestly and substantially more self-serving than the system in the 1980s. The size of the Chinese bureaucracy has roughly doubled in the last two decades and there are powerful vested interests in the status quo. Corruption has intensified greatly in scope and scale. It is a legitimate question to ask whether the top-down policy adjustments, although raising expectations, can actually deliver the desired results on the ground. There are also significant economic risk factors such as the enormous challenge of managing asset bubbles, rising cost pressures, and stagnant microeconomic performances (e.g., the sharp reduction in productivity growth since the late 1990s).

Although there are no easy choices and there are substantial transitional or transitory risks associated with this strategy, this book ends with a prescriptive note that political reforms – reforms of political governance – will help China return to a sustained and welfare-improving growth trajectory. Directional liberalism worked well in the 1980s because of the special historical and political configurations at the time. This time around, however, a fundamental reorientation toward institutional liberalism is needed.

APPENDIX

A.1 NBS Datasets on Industrial Enterprises

Dougherty and Herd (2005) provide detailed information on the NBS datasets. In the NBS industrial dataset, the shareholders are classified in the following categories: (1) state (direct or indirect), (2) collective (i.e., local governments), (3) individuals, (4) domestic legal persons, and (5) foreign companies. The definition of private sector used by the OECD economists includes firms owned by individuals, domestic legal persons, and foreign companies. The NBS datasets cover all industrial enterprises above 5 million yuan in sales. The number of firms range from 160,000 to 180,000 per year. I thank Professor Yifan Zhang at Hong Kong Polytechnic Institute for making the 1998 to 2001 datasets available to me for analysis and Professors Tao Zhigang and Yang Zhi at Hong Kong University for providing the 2005 data.

A.2 China's Fixed-Asset Investments

The Chinese government has published a series of specialized publications on fixed-asset investments. These are NBS (1987), NBS (1991), NBS (1992), NBS (1993a), NBS (1997a), NBS (1998), NBS (1999b), NBS (2002), NBS (2003a), NBS (2004b), and NBS (2005c). The data in the text and in Table 1.2 come from these sources. In addition, the CSY has a section on fixed-asset investments and our data are complemented by these sources. See, for example, NBS (2005b). Data on rural collective installation investments are partially available. For 1981–1983, 1986, 1988, 1989, 1991–1995, and 1999–2001, there are data on the entire collective sector but not on the rural component. For these years, I have estimated the rural installation investments by using the rural shares of collective investments.

Fixed-asset investments are subject to heavy government controls. A telling piece of evidence, as marshaled by Rawski (2001a), is that China's seasonal investment cycles, as recently as during the 1999–2001 period, matched almost perfectly those prevailing during the centrally planned era. Because fixed-asset investment is a large component of China's GDP, fluctuations in investment levels have a substantial impact on GDP. Here, Rawski shows that China's quarterly GDP growth patterns differed substantially from those in South Korea, Taiwan, and Hong Kong, an indication that factors such as weather or traditional Chinese holidays are not the principal determinants of the seasonal rhythm of China's GDP. Rawski quotes a Chinese economist's overall assessment of the Chinese investment process as follows:

Many basic components of a pure market economy are still in their incipient stage in China, although market-oriented reform started two decades ago. Government-guided investment mechanisms, a state-controlled banking system and dominant state-owned enterprises . . . still run in a framework molded primarily on the previous planned economy.

A.3 Ownership Classifications

In the 1990s, according to Chinese statistics, a new category of firms, the "other" ownership, increased from zero in the second half of the 1980s to 11 percent during the 1991–1995 period and then to 18.7 percent during the 1996–2000 period. To what extent are these "other" ownership forms effectively capturing domestic private investment?

The "other" ownership category consists of four types of firms: (1) joint-ownership firms, (2) shareholding firms, (3) FIEs, and (4) unclassified firms. Shareholding firms and FIEs dominate this category. During the 1996–2000 period, shareholding firms accounted for 42 percent of the fixed-asset investments of firms in the "other" ownership category and FIEs accounted for 53.2 percent. Since then, shareholding firms have become dominant, accounting for 70.1 percent in 2003, whereas FIEs have accounted for about 27 percent.[29]

Some of these shareholding firms are private-sector firms. For example, a category of firms known as "shareholding cooperatives" can be viewed as private-sector firms. Many of them are majority-owned by their employees; however, shareholding cooperatives represent only a small portion of the shareholding firms. As of 2002, shareholding cooperatives accounted for only 2.89 percent of China's industrial output by value, as compared with 11.7 percent for privately run enterprises (*siying qiye*).[30] The majority of the shareholding firms, especially the large ones, are still state-controlled. (I revisit this issue in Chapter 4.) So, excluding the "other" ownership category of firms in our definition is empirically defensible.

A.4 Complications and Definitional Issues in the Fixed-Asset Investment Data

Let me address a number of complications involved in the definitions and measurements used in Table 1.2. One potential concern is that the dynamics of the Chinese economy may have affected our findings. For example, the decline of rural private investments may result from the declining importance of agriculture in the Chinese economy, not the decline of the private sector. Agriculture did decline, from around 30 percent of GDP in the early 1980s to about 12 percent in 2005. (It should be noted that rural employment is still very large even today.) Also in the 1990s, the ownership structure of the Chinese economy proliferated with the entry of foreign firms and the rise of firms with mixed ownership. The private share could be pushed down – mathematically – by the entry of new firms. Let me address these concerns here and show that these complications do not fundamentally alter the qualitative nature of our assessment.

The urbanization hypothesis predicts a decline of the rural private sector, not an across-the-board decline of the private sector in the fixed-asset investment share. It is noteworthy that the rural private share declined in the 1990s *in conjunction with* an overall decline of the private share of fixed-asset investments. If urbanization converted rural capitalists into urban capitalists, then the logical consequence should be a substitution of rural private-sector investments with urban private-sector investments, rather than an across-the-board decrease in the overall private share. This is not what happened. As shown in Table 1.2, the overall private share in the 1990s and 2000s was nowhere near the level prevailing in the 1980s and the rural private share was a fraction of its level in the 1980s. There is no evidence of a rural-to-urban switch.

A more straightforward way to dispel the urbanization hypothesis is to focus only on rural China. In this way, we avoid bundling the two developments together in the data – urbanization and changes in the composition of investment ownership. Row (3) of Table 1.2 presents the percentage ratios of the rural private sector to the rural collective sector. The private sector declined sharply relative to the collective sector in the 1990s. In the 1980s, the rural private sector invested twice as much as the rural collective sector; in the 1990s and 2000s, the rural private sector invested between 50 and 80 percent of what the collective sector invested.

A second potential concern with our findings is our definition of the private sector. Our definition in Panel (A) of Table 1.2 includes only the registered private-sector businesses. This may introduce a downward bias because the decade of the 1990s experienced a proliferation of mixed-ownership firms, such as shareholding firms and FIEs. These new ownership firms are included in the denominator of the ratio calculations but not in the numerator. Is it then possible that the private share was diluted over time by the entry of new types of firms? Let us consider this possibility in a number of ways.[31] There is no evidence that FDI diluted the share of the registered private sector. Panel (C) removes the fixed-asset investments by FIEs from the denominator and presents the private investment shares of only indigenous firms. The private investment share in the 1990s and 2000s is still smaller than that in the 1980s when the FIEs were minuscule (under Rows [1] and [6]).

The rise of mixed-ownership firms also does not affect the substance of our findings, but it is more complicated to explain why. First, it is important to stress that the share of the registered private sector *declined* rather than remaining constant since the early 1990s. Thus, even if it is true that mixed-ownership firms became more important in the 1990s, their rising importance was achieved at the expense of the registered private sector, not at the expense of the state sector. This is a finding worth emphasizing. Many of the reforms touted by economists as ownership reforms have nothing to do with privatization. They are designed as alternative funding devices to supplement a massive investment program organized by the state.

Even if we use a more encompassing definition of the private sector incorporating the mixed-ownership firms, our measure still shows a declining share of the private sector in fixed-asset investments in the 1990s. However, our measure does show some improvement in the 2000s. To illustrate this point, I applied the Guangdong definition to my calculation and included other shareholding firms, domestic joint ventures with non-state firms, and shareholding cooperatives, in addition to the registered private sector. The results are shown in Row (5b). As recently as 1998, based on this broad definition of the private sector, the investment share of the private sector was only 17.2 percent, smaller than that in the 1980s (21.4 percent). Since then, the share went up to 27.6 percent in 2002 and 33.5 percent in 2005. Thus, based on this broad definition of the private sector, all we can claim is that the ownership policies since the late 1990s seem to have become more liberal than those in the 1980s. By the same token, the policy environment during much of the 1990s was more restrictive toward the private sector.

Another way to address the concern of this definitional under-counting of the private sector is to benchmark firms that have clear, straightforward ownership rights at the two extreme ends of the ownership spectrum. This exercise helps us assess two common views in economics research on

China. One is that private-sector policies became more liberal over time; the other is that the Chinese state embarked on an increasingly aggressive privatization program vis-à-vis SOEs. The combination of these two alleged developments would have led to rising private-to-state sector ratios of their respective investment shares. Row (2) presents the private-to-state ratios.

In Row (2a), which includes both urban and rural data, the private-to-state ratio declined sharply during the Tiananmen interlude (28.8 percent) and during the 1993–2001 period (25.9 percent). During the 1980s, the ratio was as high as 34.6 percent. The ratio rose above the level of the 1980s to 39.9 percent only during the most recent period (2002–2005). If we confine ourselves only to the rural private sector, the ratio declined continuously since 1990, including during the most recent period, as shown in Row (2b). This is *prima facie* evidence that the policy treatment of the explicit private sector did not improve relative to the policy treatment of the explicit state sector. In fact, our evidence points to a substantial deterioration of the relative policy treatment of these two types of firms in the 1990s.

Another definitional concern has to do with the inclusion of households in the definition of the private sector. As mentioned earlier, the concept of the individual economy includes household businesses. Households may invest in machines or equipment to run businesses, but they may also invest in housing. The fixed-asset investments recorded under the private sector in Table 1.2 incorporate both types of investments. The issue here is whether if we strip the data of their housing component, we still will see the same declining share of the private sector over the course of the 1990s.

The answer is an unambiguous yes. Rows (8) and (9) of Table 1.2 include only the nonhousing components of the fixed-asset investments. One component is equipment purchases; the other is expenses for nonresidential installations (e.g., factory buildings). The figures in these two rows show the real annual growth rates (deflated to 1978 prices) averaged over the years during the different periods. In both categories of nonhousing fixed-asset investments, the growth rates of the rural private sector are the fastest during the 1981–1989 period, with the growth rates moderating substantially in the later periods. Interestingly, the rural collective sector exhibits the opposite pattern: Its growth rates accelerated by a huge margin in the 1990s. These trends are entirely consistent with the other indicators on fixed-asset investments.

TWO

The Entrepreneurial Decade

In 1982, there was a commercial sensation in Shanghai – sunflower seeds. Sunflower seeds, stir-fried and salted, are one of the most popular snack foods in China. People munch on them when watching TV or playing cards, not unlike the way potato chips are consumed in the United States. But this sensation in Shanghai had a distinct flavor as well as a distinct brand-name – Idiot's Seeds. Idiot's Seeds was the invention of Nian Guangjiu, a farmer in the agricultural and impoverished province of Anhui. Nian held a rather low opinion of himself. He thought that he was good at nothing but making sunflower seeds, hence the brand-name.[1]

Nian's sunflower seeds caught on, not just in Shanghai but also nation-wide. This is a fascinating story about how a humble rural entrepreneur succeeded within a few years of the reforms. First, Mr. Nian came up with a brand-name. Whether conscious or not, he introduced the most rudimentary idea of marketing to China. Until Mr. Nian, sunflower seeds had been viewed as an undifferentiated product. The labeling in Chinese stores was by product – sunflower seeds, peanuts, walnuts, and so forth. There was no recognition that the same products might have been made differently. (Nian's brand-name was not always helpful. In 1987, he was considering setting up a scholarship fund at a local school. The teachers balked at the idea of awarding students with an "Idiot's scholarship.")

Second, Mr. Nian was a poor farmer in what was a poor province at the time. Anhui province in 1980 had a per capita GDP of 291 yuan, ranking 27th in the country out of 29 provinces. The province was heavily agricultural, and 88 percent of its population resided in the rural areas.[2] Yet, with a good product, Mr. Nian was able to access the state-controlled distribution system. His Idiot's Seeds were sold in many major cities, including Beijing, Shanghai, and Dalian.

Third, the scale of Mr. Nian's operations was phenomenal. He hired hundreds of workers at a time when private-sector employment was supposedly capped at seven workers per firm. In 1981, he started with four employees and in 1983 he had 103. By 1986, his business was netting 1 million yuan in profits. To put this number in perspective, in 1985, the average profit per SOE – the largest of the businesses in the country at the time – was only 1.1 million yuan.[3] There is another way to illustrate just how substantial Mr. Nian's operations were in 1986: 1 million yuan in 1986 is roughly equivalent to 3.14 million yuan in 2003. We have profit data on about 3,000 large private-sector firms as of 2003 from a private-sector survey conducted in 2004. (The survey is hereafter referred to as PSS2004. The Appendix to this chapter contains more details about PSS2004.) With 3.14 million yuan in profit, Mr. Nian's business would have been considered a corporate giant in 2003 and it would have been larger than 90 percent of the firms covered in the survey. (In PSS2004, a firm in the 90th percentile had a profit of 2.45 million yuan.) Considering that 1986 was only a few years into the reform decade and that China in 1986 was much poorer than China in 2003, this is a remarkable achievement indeed.

Mr. Nian was not alone. The idea of this chapter is to present a perspective on the China of the 1980s that is largely missing in economic research on China. China in the 1980s witnessed an explosion of indigenous, completely private entrepreneurship, but almost all of this entrepreneurship occurred in the rural areas of the country (which might explain its relative obscurity in scholarly research). Although it was a largely rural phenomenon, entrepreneurship in the 1980s was not an agricultural phenomenon. This is an important insight. As the case of Mr. Nian shows, the entrepreneurs were rural residents but they engaged in industrial production and service provision activities. This has important implications for how China managed to rapidly reduce poverty and how the country achieved a virtuous cycle between economic growth and social performance in the 1980s.

The decade of the 1980s deserves far more analytical attention than it has received. Economic research on China is heavily colored by the developments in the 1990s. This is because the Chinese economy became sufficiently important in the 1990s to attract considerable analytical attention. Conducting in-depth economic research was feasible in the 1990s. With better and more data, we know vastly more about China in the 1990s than we do about China in the 1980s. Furthermore, our views of the 1980s are often based on inferences rather than on direct empirical observations. Here, the gradualist framework – that China moved to a market economy progressively and steadily over time – exerted a powerful influence on how scholars framed the issue. Whatever progress China was supposed to have made during the reform era, there are still substantial distortions in the economy today. If so, it must be the case, as the gradualist reasoning would suggest, that the distortions in the 1980s were more severe.

In this chapter and the following chapter, I offer a direct and detailed account of one of the most remarkable phenomena in Chinese economic history – the rapid rise of rural entrepreneurship in the 1980s. In the 1980s, small and impoverished rural entrepreneurs such as Mr. Nian started businesses easily, operated their stalls in urban areas with freedom, accessed bank credits, and had growing confidence in the security of their assets. There was also financial liberalization and even some privatization. I return to this issue in greater detail in the next chapter, but suffice it to say here that some of the rural reforms in the 1980s were quite far-reaching and that in the 1990s there was a reversal of some of the key elements of the reforms that had allowed for a flourishing of rural entrepreneurship in the 1980s.

Another aspect of China of the 1980s is worth mentioning. Private entrepreneurship was developing most vibrantly in the poorest and the most agricultural regions of the country. Yes, the entrepreneurship of the 1980s was exclusively a rural phenomenon, but keep in mind that China in the 1980s was a predominantly rural society, with 80 percent of the population living in the rural areas. Thus, private entrepreneurship had a huge impact on the largest segment and the poorest of the population.

Although the agricultural success is widely believed to have been the result of private-sector development, such as the household contract responsibility system, the consensus among academics is that township and village governments spearheaded China's massive rural industrialization. This is the famous TVE phenomenon. I would argue that this is an incomplete perspective. I show in this chapter that purely private entrepreneurship contributed substantially to the *nonagricultural* success of rural China in the 1980s. One indication of this is the increasing importance of nonagricultural business income for Chinese rural households. Business income refers to the profits derived from owning and operating a business. It corresponds roughly to the returns from entrepreneurship. In the 1980s, business income was the fastest growing segment of rural household income. As a share of total rural household income, business income rose from 8.1 percent in 1983 to 14.9 percent in 1988, a level that was exceeded only in 1998 and 2000. Rural entrepreneurship thus played an enormous role in contributing to the rapid income gains during the 1980s.

There are two important analytical reasons for why we should get the story right about the 1980s. One is that the gradualist view of the Chinese reforms leads to the logical conclusion that the reforms in the 1990s were more radical. This assumption tilts research attention to those policy developments that were the hallmarks of the 1990s. In the 1990s, China experienced a rapid growth in FDI and international trade. In part because globalization fits well with mainstream economics, many came to view globalization as a critical factor in China's broad economic success. World Bank economists are the most vocal in touting the benefits of globalization. David Dollar, the director of development policy for the World Bank, has referred to China as a hugely successful globalization story. The World Bank cited from official Chinese sources that the number of rural poor in China fell from 250 million in 1978 to 34 million in 1999.[4]

As in all aspects of the Chinese economy, details matter. The two data points cited by the Bank convey the impression that poverty reduction was a smooth, continuous process between 1978 and 1999. Nothing is further from the truth. Let's look at the same official data used by David Dollar.[5] In 1978, the number of rural poor stood at 250 million (as defined by the Chinese poverty line) but, in the first 10 years of reforms, this number already declined to 96 million in 1988. The poverty headcount declined by 154 million. In the next 10 years of reforms from 1989 to 1999, the poverty headcount declined by only 62 million. This was a fraction of what China achieved in the 1980s.

One may argue that poverty reduction in the 1980s was faster because it was easier. It was a case of "picking the lowest-hanging fruits," one may say. In the 1990s, by contrast, the residual poverty was entrenched and permanent. A standard explanation is that the currently poor people are ethnic minorities living in mountainous regions. The poverty in China now is structural and therefore persistent. It is very resistant to the effects of policies and of economic growth.

There is some truth to this structural explanation but it cannot be the entire truth. One indication is that the Chinese poverty figures are highly sensitive to the definition of poverty line. At the poverty line of US$1 per day, in 2002, 7 percent of the Chinese population lived in absolute poverty, but when the poverty line was redrawn at US$2 a day, this fraction increased to 45 percent (World Bank 2003). The ethnic and geographic explanation is unable to explain this high level and wide spread of poverty incidence. Also, the structural explanation oddly assumes that it was easier to tackle poverty in the 1980s than in the 1990s. In the 1990s, the Chinese government commanded substantially more resources than in the 1980s.

I return to this question in more detail in Chapters 3 and 5 but suffice it to mention here that the policy model of the 1990s may have contributed to the persistent poverty in rural China. The essence of the policy model of the 1990s was to tax the poorer rural China to benefit the richer urban China and to restrict rather than expand the opportunities for small-scale and humble entrepreneurs like Mr. Nian. There is another facet about the poverty reduction record of the 1990s – it was partially a result of statistical manipulations. In 1998, 1999, and again in 2002, the Chinese authorities *lowered* the official poverty line, making it easier for a *statistical* reduction of poverty. In 1997, the rural poverty line was drawn at 640 yuan per person; by 2002, it was 627 yuan per person (NBS 2007b). (I return to this issue in Chapter 5 but let me note here that during the same period, the Chinese state increased the salaries of its civil servants five times, each time by a double-digit rate.)

The record of FDI and globalization in poverty reduction does not even come close to matching the record of rural reforms.[6] This is not a criticism of globalization but rather a matter of framing the issue with the right perspective. Globalization is the story of the 1990s, not of the 1980s. In the 1980s, FDI and international trade were minuscule. In 1988, China received just 3 billion dollars in FDI, half of what India – widely viewed as an FDI laggard – receives today. And yet, China's record in poverty reduction in the 1980s is substantially more impressive than its record in the 1990s. Other social indicators, such as literacy performance, also show the 1990s in a poor light. By loosely referring to China's poverty reduction during the entire reform era, the World Bank economists vastly understate the achievements of the 1980s and overstate the achievements of the 1990s by the same margin. They also exaggerate the effects of FDI and trade on poverty reduction and completely neglect the role of indigenous private entrepreneurship.

The second analytical reason to get the story right about the 1980s is to resolve what can be described as the "China puzzle." The "China puzzle" is that China's economic development does not seem to fit with a standard economic framework. Qian (1999) succinctly summarizes the sense of this puzzle: "[T]he Chinese path of reform and its associated rapid growth seemed to defy the necessity part of the conventional wisdom: Although China has adopted many of the policies advocated by economists, such as being open to trade and foreign investment and macroeconomic stability, violations of the standard policy prescriptions are also striking." The World Bank's 1996 annual report – devoted to economic transition – proposes a number of analytical categories, such as economic liberalization, private-sector development, and political transition, for all transition economies.

Unable to categorize China, the report placed China in a geographic grouping. China was a part of the "East Asian group" along with Vietnam, and the report made no attempt to explicitly benchmark China against the various liberalization measures.[7]

There is no China puzzle at all. The true China miracle is a classic and conventional one – the country grew because of private-sector dynamism, a relatively supporting financial environment, and increasing property rights security. These are the three institutional conditions that mainstream economists hold to be critical to economic growth, as summarized in Chapter 1. (The present chapter focuses on private ownership and security of property rights. I take on the third institution – finance – in the next chapter.) In the 1980s, directional liberalism reached far and wide. I formulated this view of the 1980s based on direct, empirical, and – as much as possible – systematic observations of the 1980s.

This chapter begins with an account of what I call the true China miracle – the vibrant rural entrepreneurship and its virtuous effect in the 1980s. In the second section, I analyze an institution that has fascinated and puzzled many Western social scientists – the township and village enterprises (TVEs). TVEs are widely believed to be a public-sector institution. Not so. On the basis of detailed archival research of government documents and contemporaneous accounts, I show that the vast majority of TVEs in the 1980s were completely private. I close with a concluding section on a few broad implications of this new perspective on the 1980s.

1 The True China Miracle

As is clear to everyone, the spontaneous forces of capitalism have been steadily growing in the countryside in recent years, with new rich peasants springing up everywhere and many well-to-do middle class peasants striving to become rich peasants.

– Mao Zedong, 1955

The countryside has a vast number of skillful craftsmen and capable producers, educated youth and retired soldiers. Their expertise should be put to full use and [we] should support their efforts to establish technical-service organizations and allow any rural economic organizations to recruit them into their workforce. . . .

– Central Committee of the Chinese Communist Party
– (Central Committee 1992 <1983>, p. 176)

Mao Zedong and the leadership of the 1980s had something in common: They both recognized the huge entrepreneurial potential of China's rural residents. Mao went to great lengths – through the commune system and the

Great Leap Forward – to destroy those potentials because he understood the political ramifications of unleashing them. In 1955, as quoted previously, Mao recognized two fundamental attributes of the Chinese peasantry. One is that Chinese peasants are very entrepreneurial – "spontaneous" – and that they stand ready to be providers of capital and business capabilities as business owners and operators. The second attribute is that Chinese peasants are very motivated – "many well-to-do middle class peasants striving to become rich peasants."

In a political system laden with urban biases, the Chinese reformers in the 1980s recognized these same potentials and created a policy environment to permit and to encourage their realization. The result was that the 1980s was a decade of vibrant, grassroots, bottom-up entrepreneurship in China's massive countryside.

The speed of entrepreneurial development was breathtaking. Because the Chinese statistical system in the early 1980s was not well equipped to track the output production in the private sector, we instead use tax data as an indicator. According to the Ministry of Finance (1989, pp. 23–24), the tax receipts from self-employment businesses – most of which were rural – increased from 884 million yuan in 1981 to 3.5 billion yuan in 1982, a more than fourfold increase in just one year.

In the 1980s, Chinese peasants experienced the most rapid income gains in history. Per capita rural income between 1978 and 1981 grew at a real rate of 11.4 percent; the urban/rural ratio of the purchase of consumer goods fell from 10 to 1 in 1978 to 6 to 1 in 1981. According to a rural survey, rural per capita income more than doubled between 1978 and 1984, and real rural per capita consumption increased by 51 percent between 1978 and 1983 (Riskin 1987, p. 292). Rural poverty also declined dramatically in the 1980s, as indicated before.

China scholars have researched this phenomenon extensively. The consensus view is that the rural reforms accounted for the largest segment of the income gains. Administrative measures, such as price increases, played a smaller role. According to one analysis, one-fifth of the increase was due to price increases; the rest, by implication, came from improving allocative efficiencies (Riskin 1987, p. 293). These include improving labor productivities, as evidenced by the fast growth of per capita production of food grains and edible oil, and income diversification opportunities to become involved in nonagricultural activities. Let me add another factor – the flourishing of rural entrepreneurship.

Chinese capitalism is heavily rural in origin. The reasons are complex but one hypothesis is that central planning was always weaker in the countryside than it was in the cities. As I show in this section, even at the height of the Cultural Revolution, rural residents engaged in private commerce and industry in ways that would have been unimaginable in the cities. This may explain the explosion of rural entrepreneurship just a few years into the reform era as the policy and business environment became more permissive. Rural entrepreneurship was also virtuous because it emerged first and developed fastest in the poorer regions of China.

1.1 The Rural Origins of Chinese Capitalism

Today, we can still observe one lasting legacy of the rural origins of Chinese capitalism: Many of the largest manufacturing private-sector firms hail from the backward, predominantly agricultural provinces of China. This is a striking empirical regularity. Kelon Group, until 2005 China's largest refrigerator maker, was founded by Wang Guoduan, an entrepreneur in rural Shunde county in southern Guangdong province. Huanyuan, China's largest air-conditioner maker, is based in the agricultural province of Hunan. China's first automobile exports will not come from Shanghai but more likely from the agricultural hinterland of Anhui province where Chery is located. The Hope Group is even more interesting. The four brothers who started a business in quail eggs abandoned their urban residency and founded their company in a rural part of Sichuan province. Today, it is China's largest agribusiness firm.

Very few of China's successful corporate giants in the competitive manufacturing industries are based in the metropolitan, industrial centers such as Beijing, Shanghai, and Tianjin. (Firms in politically connected sectors such as real estate are another story altogether.) This is puzzling. One would have thought that these urban centers possessed ample and propitious conditions for the growth and development of businesses. They have human capital, agglomeration economics, export market linkages, and high incomes. But none comes close to producing the microeconomic success stories that have come out of some of the initially poorer agricultural provinces. The reason is that the economic policies in rural China were far more liberal than those in urban China.

Zhejiang province is widely acknowledged to be a huge economic success. The province, located south of Shanghai, is home to half of China's largest private-sector firms. It is also rich, especially as measured in asset terms. In 2004, an average urban Zhejiang resident earned an income from owning stocks and bank deposits that was multiples of what an average Shanghai resident earned. But what is often lost in the Zhejiang story is that the province was poor and deeply agrarian in the 1970s. It was ranked No. 13 in per capita GDP in the late 1970s. In 1978, 32.2 million out of a population of 37.5 million resided in the rural areas.

Wenzhou region of Zhejiang province is typical of the province. Today, Wenzhou is the bastion of Chinese capitalism. Its businesses dominate European markets in garments, shirts, and cigarette lighters and the region has begun to venture into electronics and petrochemical products. Wealthy individuals from Wenzhou export a massive amount of capital to the rest of the country, making or breaking real estate markets in Shanghai, Beijing, and Guangzhou. In the entire country, only in Wenzhou have the highways and airports been financed by private capital. All of this private wealth was built on a rural foundation. Of 5.6 million Wenzhou residents, only 550,980 had an urban registration in 1978, just below 10 percent. The region was poor and inconvenienced by high mountains on three sides and ocean on the fourth. For years, Wenzhou lacked basic transportation infrastructures such as a seaport, an airport, and highways to nearby locations.

A universally accepted definition of entrepreneurship is self-employment business. Self-employment businesses are single proprietorships, and in China they are formally known as individual businesses (*geti hu*) or individual economy entities (*geti jingji*) in the Chinese statistical reporting system. By this measure, rural China in the 1980s was extraordinarily entrepreneurial.

We go first to the business registration data maintained by the Bureau of Industry and Commerce Administration (BICA). We then go to two large-scale surveys on private businesses conducted in the early 1990s. The first is a self-employment business survey conducted in 1991 (SEBS1991). Although it was conducted in 1991, it was sufficiently close to the decade of the 1980s to reflect the dynamics of that era. Also, the survey includes retrospective questions about the 1980s. Altogether, 13,259 self-employment business people participated in SEBS1991. It is the only large-scale survey that I know of that was conducted on these self-employment businesses.

We then supplement our findings from a private-sector survey conducted in 1993 (PSS1993). This survey was administered on the larger and more established private-sector firms. These are known formally as the private-run firms in the Chinese system (*siying qiye*). The formal difference between the self-employment businesses and the private-run firms is that the former employ seven or fewer than seven workers, whereas the latter employ more than seven. PSS1993 sampled 1,421 private-sector firms. Like SEBS1991, PSS1993 also contains retrospective questions about the 1980s. We use these questions to gauge the situation prevailing in the 1980s. The Appendix to this chapter contains more details on these two surveys.

According to the BICA registration data, in 1981 there were comparable numbers of registered rural and urban self-employment establishments: 868,000 in the urban areas and 961,000 in the rural areas.[8] Thereafter, the rural number increased rapidly. By 1986, there were 9.2 million registered rural self-employment businesses as compared with 2.9 million urban ones, a rural/urban ratio of 3.2. By 1988, the rural self-employment businesses numbered 10.7 million compared with 3.8 million in the urban areas (a ratio of 2.8). In terms of employment size, the ratios were even more skewed in favor of the rural areas. The rural-to-urban employment ratios for these self-employment businesses were 3.6 in 1986 and 4.5 in 1988.

But is this surprising? After all, China was predominantly rural in the 1980s and there should have been more rural entrepreneurs. However, a more meaningful fact is that the rural entrepreneurs in the 1980s no longer operated in the agricultural sector, not that the absolute number of rural entrepreneurs was large. In the BICA registration data for 1988, commerce claimed the largest share, about 50 percent, followed by industry (13 percent). Altogether, 17 million people were engaged in these nonagricultural activities. This is not a trivial number; it is about 5 percent of China's very large agricultural workforce. There is nothing automatic or natural about such an arrangement. Rural residents did not have an automatic advantage over urban residents in terms of expertise or market access in these nonagricultural activities.

SEBS1991 and PSS1993 also confirm the heavily rural origins of Chinese capitalism. One advantage of these two surveys over the BICA registration data is that we have information about whether the rural entrepreneurs operated in cities or in rural areas. The BICA data tell us only where the business was registered, not the location of its operations. Arguably, it is more meaningful to know that many rural entrepreneurs operated in the cities as opposed to the fact that there were more registered rural entrepreneurs. Here, SEBS1991 and PSS1993 are especially helpful because they targeted private businesses located in the cities.

Both SEBS1991 and PSS1993 contain questions about the prior residential status of the respondents. I thus classify those entrepreneurs who had a rural residential status as rural entrepreneurs. Both surveys give the years in which the business was founded. For those businesses founded between 1979 and 1990, in SEBS1991, 59 percent were rural entrepreneurs. Certain years had an extraordinarily high rural entry; for example, 1980 (63.6 percent),

1984 (65.5 percent), and 1986 (63.9 percent). The figures in PSS1993 are lower. Of those surveyed firms founded before 1990 in PSS1993, 30 percent were run by rural entrepreneurs. It should be emphasized that this finding means that 30 percent of the private-sector firms *based in the urban areas* were run by rural entrepreneurs, not that only 30 percent of the private entrepreneurs in China were rural. In fact, based on the registration data, a Ministry of Agriculture report estimates that private-run firms in the rural areas accounted for 81 percent in terms of establishments, 83 percent in terms of employment, and 84 percent in terms of registered capital (Editorial Committee of TVE Yearbook 1989a, p. 138). At both the small and large ends of the spectrum, capitalism was an overwhelmingly rural phenomenon.

PSS1993 reveals another intriguing finding. Those private-sector firms run by rural entrepreneurs were substantially larger than those run by urban entrepreneurs. For example, their average employment per firm in the first year of business was 22, as compared with 17 for firms run by urban entrepreneurs. (All the data here refer to those firms founded before 1990.) They also had more investors per firm (2.4 compared with 1.8). In the first year of operations, they had more registered capital (208,900 yuan per firm compared with 120,500 yuan per firm) and larger fixed assets (133,800 yuan compared with 87,330 yuan). These figures may be a result of a survivor-of-the-fittest dynamic. The urban areas must have been a tougher environment for rural entrepreneurs and, thus, only the best of the rural entrepreneurs were able to maintain operations there.

Readers may wonder why capitalism in China was rooted in the rural areas. There is a demand-side dynamic – rapid income growth in rural China creating the derived demand for more consumer goods and services (Naughton 2007). The more interesting explanation is on the supply side – why rural entrepreneurs were able to respond to the market changes so quickly and on such a massive scale. One important reason is the radical and market-conforming nature of the reforms initiated by the Chinese leadership in the 1980s. I go into more detail about this later in this chapter. Let me offer two other postulations here. Economic research on entrepreneurship consistently shows that education is a key factor in explaining who becomes an entrepreneur. In this respect, rural China was well positioned in the early 1980s. For whatever its faults, the Maoist leadership invested heavily in the health and educational sectors of rural China. Here, a comparison with India is illustrative. As early as the mid-1960s, China led India across a host of social indicators, including life expectancy, school enrollment, and literacy.[9] The greatest contrast with India is that in China, rural entrepreneurship was able to grow out of the traditional agricultural sector on a massive scale. The rural Indians, in contrast, hampered by a poor endowment of human capital, were not able to start entrepreneurial ventures remotely on the scale of the Chinese. (I revisit this theme in Chapter 5.)

Micro data show that the first generation of Chinese rural entrepreneurs was very well educated. In SEBS1991, few of the rural entrepreneurs – 8 percent – said that they were illiterate; 85 percent of them reported having finished at least middle school (and 14 percent of them finished high school.) Interestingly, there is not much difference in the educational levels of the rural and urban entrepreneurs in SEBS1991. Because educational attainments were higher in the cities than in the countryside, this finding suggests that the rural entrepreneurs came from a better-educated group in their own cohort.

The second reason is that even at the height of the Cultural Revolution, there was still some residual capitalism in rural China. This is, in part, due to a structural factor – agriculture is much harder for the government to plan as compared with industry. Soil conditions vary substantially, even within the same geographic region, and weather changes can be very unpredictable. For this reason, the agricultural sector in some of the centrally planned economies (e.g., Poland and Hungary) was only partially nationalized and limited private plots were allowed in the Soviet Union.

There was also a political factor. The Cultural Revolution, however sweeping and penetrating, was largely an urban affair and it may have undermined the urban political control of the countryside. In a planned economy, the urban centers are always more state-owned than the rural areas and thus a diminution of urban control would inadvertently allow for some breathing ground for capitalism. The Cultural Revolution also inflicted a severe political shock on China's urban economy, seriously constraining the supply side of the economy. The massive supply constraints, in turn, created shortages that the rural entrepreneurs rose to fulfill. Thus, ironically, the Cultural Revolution, however disruptive to the Chinese economy as a whole, might have laid the foundation for the post-reform takeoff of rural entrepreneurship. This dynamic explains an otherwise puzzling phenomenon noted by a number of scholars – even at the height of the Cultural Revolution, some rural residents were engaged in fairly large-scale private-sector activities.

By its very nature, we do not have systematic evidence of the aggregate scale of the private economy during the Cultural Revolution period.[10]

However, Chinese academics have assembled some very interesting accounts of the informal economy in the 1960s and 1970s. In one notorious case, Shishi (Stone Lion) township of Fujian province boasted a vibrant private market consisting of more than 600 merchants during the most feverish years of the Cultural Revolution – the second half of the 1960s. The market was closed down in 1971. The authorities discovered that one entrepreneur, Wu Xiayun, was making an income of 7,000 yuan a year, an enormous amount of money at that time. Another entrepreneur in the same township had raised 6,000 yuan from 36 investors and had started 30 small factories producing Mao Zedong pins (for which a market of considerable size existed during the Cultural Revolution).[11]

Another famous case concerns a village leader of Huaxi village in Jiangsu province. The village leader, while featured in a 1975 article in the *People's Daily* as a model, revolutionary Dachai-type cadre,[12] operated a clandestine hardware-tool factory. He pooled 20 investors and ran a highly profitable business. By 1978, Huaxi village had accumulated fixed assets worth some 1 million yuan and another 1 million yuan in bank deposits. The agricultural output of the entire village was only 240,000 yuan.[13]

1.2 The Scale of Rural Entrepreneurship

We know from the previous section that entrepreneurship in the 1980s was heavily rural in nature. But how substantial was the rural entrepreneurship phenomenon? And how large were the household businesses as individual units? A common measure in economics literature of the size of individual business units is employment. This is an appropriate measure here. We want to know whether the rural entrepreneurial businesses were mainly single proprietorships without any hired labor or whether they were of a size sufficient to have recruited and hired outside employees.

This is an important question from both a political and an economic perspective. Politically, it is widely believed that China in the 1980s imposed employment restrictions on private businesses. This is the so-called seven-employee rule.[14] We want to know how exacting and binding these restrictions were. From an economic perspective, it is important to know how substantial the rural entrepreneurship was in terms of creating employment opportunities outside of agriculture. As agricultural productivity improved, there was a greater pool of rural labor available for nonagricultural activities. From a welfare point of view, it is important to know whether rural businesses generated employment opportunities in nonagricultural sectors for the rural surplus labor.

We have several sources of information that indicate the substantial scale of rural entrepreneurial businesses only a few years into the 1980s. I first provide the findings based on government reports. Apart from the insight and data that we get from them, the very fact that they were recorded in the government reports means that the Chinese government was fully aware of the scale of such entrepreneurial ventures. In other words, these were not back-alley businesses operating in the shadow of an informal sector.

Despite the nominal restrictions of seven persons employed per firm, some of the rural businesses – such as that operated by Mr. Nian – were very large in scale. According to official sources, which might very well have under-counted them, some of the largest rural household businesses in the mid-1980s employed more than 1,000 workers each (State Council 1986, p. 6). The Jiangsu Statistical Bureau has compiled data on the largest private operations in the province. In 1986, for example, the largest employer was Mr. Qian Taiping, who hired 210 workers and earned an income of 600,000 yuan. (Mr. Qian apparently was not the richest person in Jiangsu; that title went to Chen Yubing, who operated a paint business. His income for 1986 was 1.3 million yuan.) In 1987, the largest employer in the province was Chen Tongyin, who employed 270 workers and earned an income of 2.75 million yuan.[15]

These anecdotal stories show that the ceiling effect of the employment restrictions was not as stringent as the seven-employee rule suggests. There were numerous cases of private businesses employing far more than seven persons.[16] An entrepreneur in Shaanxi, Chen Changshi ("a man who can make everything except babies") started a construction-material business in 1986 by employing 50 workers. Song Taiping of Hubei province started a bra production line in the early 1980s. He lined up a sales contract worth some 200,000 yuan in 1983 (an enormous amount of money at the time) and was able to sell in the Shanghai market, as well as landing an export license to sell to the European market. In 1983, he hired 50 workers, but by 1988, his workforce had increased to 700 workers. In addition, he outsourced work to 300 additional workers.

More systematic data based on PSS1993 confirm that rural China had some very large private employers. PSS1993 provides data on the number of investors and workers in the founding year of the business; we use these data to assess the size of rural private-sector firms in the 1980s. Of all firms founded between 1980 and 1990 by rural entrepreneurs, only one year, 1980, had an average size of private-sector firms close to the seven-employee rule. In that year, the average number of employees was 8.89. The largest average employment was 37 persons in 1983, and it was 30 persons in 1985.

Another way to illustrate the large employment size of rural private businesses is to look at those firms in the top tier. After all, if the seven-employee rule was truly binding, it should have been most binding on the largest firms. Again, the year 1983 had the largest firms. The firm at the top 10th percentile employed 106 persons in that year. The fewest employees were in 1981 when the firm at the top 10th percentile had only 21 workers. In most other years, the number ranges from 50 to 100 persons. These findings are not meant to suggest that there were no ceiling effects as a result of the seven-employee rule. Without the seven-employee rule, China doubtlessly would have had private firms employing thousands of employees in the 1980s. So, the ceiling effect was there but its restrictiveness was not nearly as crippling as the letter of the rule suggests.

The aggregate size of rural private entrepreneurship was also substantial. This is our second measure of the scale of rural entrepreneurship. Chapter 1 shows that the private share of fixed-asset investments was already more than 20 percent in the first few years of the 1980s. There is other supporting evidence as well. A carefully designed study based on surveys on 37,422 rural households (supplemented by interviews) shows that those rural households primarily engaged in nonagricultural activities comprised 11 percent of the total rural households as of the mid-1980s.[17] This translates into 21 million rural households nationwide. The entire number of urban households at that time was 50 million. This thus gives an idea of the magnitude of rural entrepreneurship only five years into the reform decade.

1.3 Rural but not Agricultural

Rural entrepreneurship was a method of choice on the part of rural residents to transition out of agriculture in the 1980s. (I show in the next chapter that paid employment at decreasing returns became a dominant option in the 1990s.) We saw in the BICA registration data more than 50 percent of the rural self-employment businesses were engaged in commerce. In SEBS1991, 72 percent of the surveyed entrepreneurs with a rural background were in manufacturing. In the construction business, for example, rural construction firms – not just rural construction workers – began to bid successfully for some large projects in the major cities. In Beijing, the International Hotel and the Bank of China buildings were awarded to a rural construction company based in Henan province (Zhang Houyi and Ming Lizhi 1999, pp. 180–181). As early as 1986, private entrepreneurship had already gained a substantial foothold in the transport sector. Outside the traditional state sector, in 1986, private businesses accounted for 67.6 percent of shipments and 77.6 percent of sales (Editorial Committee of TVE Yearbook 1989b, p. 84).[18] Rural entrepreneurs from Evergreen township in Beijing even began a direct flight from Beijing to Shantou of Guangdong province (Editorial Committee of TVE Yearbook 1989b, p. 84).

All of these developments reveal an important dynamic of the era – there was a great deal of arbitrage activities intermediated by the rural entrepreneurs. One indication is that many of the rural entrepreneurs operated a business in the urban areas. The SEBS1991 asked respondents whether they operated in the urban areas. Of those who answered in the affirmative, 55 percent came from a rural background. Also, many of the rural entrepreneurs with an urban operation appeared to have established a permanent base there. When asked whether or not they "owned" their facilities, 41 percent of the rural entrepreneurs with an urban establishment said yes.

The SEBS1991 data suggest that barriers to rural/urban mobility may have come down in the 1980s, earlier than many Western academics have assumed. Based on SEBS1991, the earlier years of the 1980s had a surprisingly higher rural entry in urban areas than the later years of the 1980s. In 1980, for example, of those entrepreneurs operating in urban areas, 55.6 percent were rural. However, the reason that Western academics assume that rural/urban mobility was greater in the 1990s than in the 1980s is that there were more labor migrants from the rural areas in the 1990s. But here is a critical difference between the two decades. In the 1980s, as SEBS1991 shows, it was the rural entrepreneurs who came to the cities and established operations there. In the 1990s, it was mainly the rural laborers who flooded the cities in search of jobs. Both were engaged in arbitraging activity between the rural and urban areas, but the underlying activities were very different. In the 1980s, the rural entrepreneurs were engaged in arbitraging the rural/urban differences in the returns to their investments, whereas the rural laborers of the 1990s were arbitraging the rural/urban differences in the returns to their labor.

1.4 Rags-to-Riches Entrepreneurship

We saw earlier that the rural income gains were substantial following the reforms and that there was a reduction in rural/urban income inequalities during the first half of the 1980s. Did rural entrepreneurship play a role in the huge poverty reduction of the 1980s?[19] A particularly virtuous aspect of the rural entrepreneurship in the 1980s is that it occurred among the low socioeconomic groups of the society. SEBS1991 shows that only 12.3 percent of the rural respondents had held a prior village or enterprise leadership position before becoming an entrepreneur. SEBS1991 asked about motivations for going into entrepreneurship. In response to this question, 62 percent of the rural entrepreneurs cited "to make a living" as their motivation for going into business, compared with 19.8 percent who answered "to make additional money." Thus, their entrepreneurial motivations were grounded on subsistence needs.

In the 1980s, there were two cross-cutting dynamics in the income distribution trends. One was a rise of within-rural inequality; the other was a decrease in rural/urban inequality.[20] The case of Mr. Nian of Idiot's Seeds illustrates why this was happening. Nian came from a very poor region and yet he was able to develop a sizeable business by the mid-1980s. Relative to others in his village, his income gains were substantial, but relative to urban residents, Mr. Nian brought down the income gap. In the 1980s, especially in the first half of the decade, the overall income disparity lessened because the improvement of rural/urban income distribution sufficiently offset the deterioration in the rural income distribution.

This is a little-known fact but one with monumental significance: In the 1980s, private-sector development and entrepreneurship were growing fastest and most vibrantly in the poorest parts of the country. Entrepreneurship was a poor man's affair. Let me use Guizhou, China's land-locked and poorest province with a large rural population, as an example. We go to SEBS1991 for a more detailed look. We use the amount of registered capital as a measure of the size of the entrepreneurial ventures. Surprisingly, the size of the entrepreneurial ventures in Guizhou was very large compared with those in the more developed regions of the country. During the 1979–1983 period, the average amount of registered capital of self-employment businesses was 1,717 yuan in Guizhou, compared with 2,145 yuan in the city of Shanghai and 1,813 yuan in the city of Chengdu. Guizhou had exactly the same median registered capital as these two much richer cities (500 yuan).

Given how poor Guizhou was, the scale of private businesses in Guizhou was considerable. We can demonstrate this point by calculating the ratio of the registered capital of these entrepreneurial ventures to the per capita GDP of the region. This is a proxy for the state of private-sector development in a province relative to the general level of economic development. By this measure, the private sector in Guizhou was "over-developed." We compare the average value of the registered capital for the 1984–1989 period with the per capita GDP for 1988. In 1988, Shanghai's per capita GDP was 3,471 yuan, the highest in the country. Guizhou's 406 yuan per capita GDP was the lowest in the country. The ratio of the average registered capital to the per capita GDP was 8.31 for Guizhou and only 1.27 for Shanghai. Interestingly, Guizhou's ratio was quite similar to that of Guangdong (8.55), a province that is widely acknowledged to be a pioneer of the reforms in China (Vogel 1989).

This is another lesser known story: Some of the poorest provinces in China undertook far-reaching reforms in the 1980s.[21] In Guizhou, agricultural household contracting was adopted at a faster pace than in the country as a whole. According to one source, by the end of 1981, 98.2 percent of households were already operating on a contracting system. (China as a whole reached this ratio by 1984.) Guizhou had a very liberal private-sector policy. In Guizhou, almost the entire TVE sector was private. In 1987, there were more than 405,000 TVEs in the province, of which 395,000 were completely private. These were labeled as "household" TVEs and, as of 1987, the household TVEs in Guizhou accounted for more than 97 percent of the total number of TVEs, 77.4 percent of the TVE employment, and 66.2 percent of the output value. The few remaining collective firms were put on performance contracts and, in effect, were rendered private in terms of their control rights. As of 1988, according to a survey of seven regions in Guizhou, 1,033 out of 1,516 collective TVEs were leased to either managers or outsiders. The provincial government openly sanctioned the conversion of the "official sponsorship" of firms to "civilian sponsorship" (Editorial Committee of Ten Years of Reforms in Guizhou 1989, p. 262). This was a code word for privatization.

The liberal policy enabled private businesses in the province to scale up their operations. By the mid-1980s, private TVEs had already developed to a level whereby they began to source capital and technology from other regions. In 1984 and 1985, Guizhou's TVEs imported 100 million yuan, entered into 300 technology licensing agreements, and recruited 3,000 technicians and managers from other provinces (Editorial Committee of Contemporary China Series 1989, p. 206). According to a detailed province-by-province study, some of the rural businesses in Guizhou reached a substantial scale.[22] One family founded an agricultural service business and contracted with the local government to run an agricultural machinery station. From that base, the family branched out into manufacturing and established seven factories, producing everything from alcohol to vinegar. The family business employed some 342 workers and realized sales of 51,000 yuan in 1984. It accumulated 200,000 yuan in fixed assets.

What is interesting is that this business was located in the poorer part of Guizhou – in Zunyi county. Zunyi county's per capita annual income was even smaller than that in Guizhou as a whole, about 200 yuan. To appreciate how substantial fixed assets valued at 200,000 yuan were, let me point out that in 1984, the entire fixed-asset investment credit line of Zunyi's banking system was slightly more than 3 million yuan.[23] It is quite impressive that this one household was able to accumulate such a large quantity of capital equipment so soon after the reforms began and this household was not alone. Some rural entrepreneurs, even in this most impoverished province, had already begun to venture into capital-intensive businesses. An entrepreneur in Zunyi county ran a trucking operation. His long-distance trade netted some 20,000 yuan per year, a huge sum of money in a province where the average rural income was 260 yuan (NBS 1986). Another rural entrepreneur operated a flour mill and earned an annual income of 10,000 yuan.

In this poor province, the purchase of capital equipment, such as a milling machine or a long-haul truck, necessarily required external financing. This gets to one of the least known stories about rural China in the 1980s – private-sector financing from the Chinese banks was sizeable. (I provide more details on this issue in the next chapter.) In Zunyi county, the rural credit cooperatives (RCCs) – a critical financing vehicle for private-sector development in the 1980s – increased their lending by 65 times in just three years between 1979 and 1982. In 1979, lending to rural households was 4.53 percent of that to collectives. In 1982, the lending to rural households was 3.5 times of that to collectives. Between 1982 and 1988, lending to households rose sharply, from 14.6 million yuan to 22.8 million yuan, while lending to collectives – including collectively run firms – remained roughly constant during this period.

There was also some nascent financial liberalization. The provincial branch of the People's Bank of China – an institution that in the 1990s would crack down harshly on informal rural finance – described an increasingly diverse financial scene in Guizhou in very positive terms: "A large number of shareholding and collectively owned financial institutions emerged, while informal finance and individual borrowing and lending developed rapidly."[24] The rapid rise and the scaling up of the private economy in Guizhou provide one answer to the question of why rural poverty declined so rapidly and so substantially in the first five years of the 1980s – this was not just an agricultural success but also a broad veritable entrepreneurial revolution.

2 What Exactly Is a TVE?

Nobel laureate in economics, Joseph E. Stiglitz, an eminent professor at Columbia University and a former chief economist of the World Bank, is probably one of the most prominent proponents of China's development strategy. In particular, Professor Stiglitz is enamored with the corporate organization known as township and village enterprises. TVEs, he argues, are a unique form of public enterprise that can solve what he views as an extremely serious problem afflicting transitional economies – the stealing of assets by private investors. Monitoring institutions are under-developed, he goes on, and therefore public ownership is needed to minimize stealing. TVEs seem to have the best of two worlds – they prevent asset stripping and they mimic the efficiency of private enterprise.[25]

Professor Stiglitz apparently formed this impression of TVEs during a field trip to Guangdong in 1992. In Shunde county of Guangdong province, Stiglitz – accompanied by Yingyi Qian, then a professor at Stanford – visited what was described to him as a TVE – the Pearl River Refrigerator Factory. He was deeply impressed by this firm. According to Stiglitz, this TVE had only 2 percent of the market share in 1985 but it was able to capture 10 percent in 1991, becoming the largest refrigerator maker in China (Qian and Stiglitz 1996). For Stiglitz, this TVE represented the virtues of local government ownership in a transitional context.

Just as in the case of Lenovo in the last chapter, the devil is in the details. The details about the Pearl River Refrigerator Factory, better known as the Kelon Group in China, directly contradict the postulations by Stiglitz. Exactly contrary to the idea that TVEs prevented asset stripping, as a collective TVE, Kelon actually represented a massive expropriation of what would have been straightforward private assets in any market economy. Kelon performed well as long as the township treated the firm as *de facto* private. It collapsed immediately after the township began to exercise its control rights.

First, Kelon was not started by the township government of Rongqi (where Kelon was based).[26] The idea of going into refrigerator production came from a rural entrepreneur by the name of Wang Guoduan. Wang was running a transistor radio factory at the time. Pushed by the competition, he began to look for other products to produce. He observed many Hong Kong people carrying refrigerators to their relatives across the border. This gave him the idea to go into refrigerator production. He asked his Hong Kong relatives to bring him two refrigerators from which he built a prototype.

The start-up equity capital did not come directly from the government. As was common among the large entrepreneurial businesses in the 1980s, financing by the government took the form of a loan. The Rongqi township provided Mr. Wang with a 90,000-yuan technical assistance loan and arranged for a credit line of 4 million yuan for his firm. In return, the township took over nominal control of the firm and assigned an official, Pan Ning, to be the general manager. The loan was quickly repaid to the township, but the firm remained registered as a collective TVE.

The point of the story is that Kelon would have been registered as a straightforward private business in any market economy. But China at that time did not have a legal framework to accommodate a private enterprise the size of Kelon and a firm operating in what was viewed then as a modern industry.[27] Township and village governments assumed controls of these firms as a matter of political prerogative rather than on the basis of their share of capital contributions. The logic of township control had nothing to do with economics; it was deeply political.

Stiglitz was correct that Kelon performed impressively. The firm won market shares not only from state-owned refrigerator producers (e.g., Snowflakes in Beijing) but also held its own against Whirlpool, the huge US home appliance company. In 1997, Whirlpool announced that it would exit the China market after having lost some 100 million dollars there.[28] The reason for Kelon's success is precisely because Rongqi township understood the private origins of this firm and for a long period of time it entrusted the control rights of the firm to its private founders. The first group of employees of this firm was later given the title of founders and they stayed on as top managers from 1984 to 2000, an usually long tenure in a country where the average tenure at a SOE was 5.5 years.[29] As an implicit acknowledgment of the private origins of this firm, the Rongqi township yielded 20 percent of the shares of the firm to the founders and employees in 1992.

But, the entire arrangement that gave rise to the private control rights of Kelon was completely tacit and without any legal foundation. Kelon prospered as long as Rongqi township was benevolent, but this benevolence was not to last forever. In December 1998, Rongqi township, without any advance warning, announced the resignation of Pan Ning. In effect, Rongqi chose to exercise its legal control right over Kelon and abruptly dismissed the entrepreneur who had single-handedly created the Kelon miracle. The background to this decision remains murky to this day. But, apparently, Pan had resisted an order by Rongqi to take over a loss-making air-conditioner firm, Huabao, and might have provoked the township that was eager to shed a poorly performing asset.[30]

The exercise of legal control rights by Rongqi was the beginning of the rapid demise of Kelon. In 2000, Rongqi township replaced all the founding members of the firm. The head of Rongqi township was dispatched to run the firm and he promptly implemented strategic changes that proved to be destructive. Kelon departed from its previous core competence of producing energy-efficient refrigerators and embarked on fanciful and ultimately unfruitful ventures, such as home appliances with artificial intelligence, driverless vehicles, home security, and educational software for online research. None of these turned into anything useful (Huang and Lane 2002).

Even more troubling is that there might have been a massive plundering of Kelon's assets by the state-owned holding company under Rongqi. Kelon, which issued shares on the Hong Kong Stock Exchange and the Shenzhen Stock Exchange, was itself majority controlled by a state-owned holding company 100 percent owned by Rongqi township. Between 1984 and 1998, Pan Ning had built up a formidable Kelon brand and, by the late 1990s, Kelon controlled 25 percent of the world's second-largest refrigerator market. One estimate put the worth of the Kelon brand at 5.5 billion yuan (Leung 1999). But neither Pan nor Kelon itself owned the Kelon brand. The Kelon brand was registered with Kelon's state-owned holding company. That all the business value was located in Kelon but all the corporate control was located in the state-owned holding company created an opportunity to expropriate Kelon's assets. As soon as Pan Ning exited the scene, Kelon suddenly began to record massive payables to its holding company (most likely due to engaging in overpriced related transactions). Net cash flows plunged from a positive 804 million yuan in 1998 to a negative 545 million yuan in 1999. In an interview years later, a former consultant working at Kelon during this period made an oblique reference, "I could turn a bad thing such as losses into a good thing and I could turn a bad thing such as frequent management changes into a good thing. But I was not able to turn a bad thing such as the stealing of money into a good thing" (quoted in Wu Xiaobo 2007, p. 43).

The bleeding continued until 2002 when a little-known Hong Kong–listed firm, Greencool, acquired Kelon. This transaction would begin another tangled saga for the firm. Amid charges of plundering state-owned assets, the head of Greencool, Gu Chujun, was arrested in 2005. In his prison cell, Gu signed the paperwork transferring Kelon to a firm based in Qingdao. In 2006, it was determined that Kelon had incurred losses of 3.7 billion yuan in 2005, it had −1.09 billion yuan in net assets, and there were 93 pending lawsuits against the firm (Wu Xiaobo 2007, pp. 56–58). An excellent business, built by Pan Ning from scrap metals into a 5.6 billion yuan refrigerator empire, was completely destroyed.

Just as in the examples of Lenovo and Huawei, it is hazardous to form a view of this firm without detailed factual knowledge. Kelon was financed by private share capital and built by smart entrepreneurs such as Pan Ning and Wang Guoduan. It succeeded as a *de facto* private firm and it collapsed almost immediately after the township decided to exercise its control right. The story of Kelon turns on its head the theory that TVEs prevented private plundering of public assets. Exactly the opposite was the case. Through the TVE mechanism, Rongqi township or its subsidiary tunneled the assets out of Kelon and robbed what ought to have belonged to Pan Ning and the other founders. (After he left Kelon, Pan, who now lives in Canada, would visit Rongqi only once every year to sweep his ancestors' tomb. He has never visited or talked about Kelon.) Stiglitz's high praise of the township government is miles away from Pan Ning's own view. In a private conversation with a Peking University professor, Pan Ning remarked that he never had to cultivate ties with government officials in Hong Kong so he devoted 100 percent of his time to marketing and management. In China, he was resigned to an untold amount of obligatory time with the government (Wu Xiaobo 2007, p. 58).

The story of Kelon suggests that we need to examine the entire TVE phenomenon carefully rather than accepting the received wisdom among Western economists. Because the TVEs drove much of China's economic dynamism in the 1980s and the early 1990s, an understanding of the true ownership nature of the TVEs entails important analytical implications for how we interpret the role of the private sector in China's growth experience. Many have hailed the TVEs as a tremendous public-sector success story.[31] I show in this chapter that this is far from the case. The TVE story can plausibly be shown to be a substantial private-sector success story.

Understanding the real ownership nature of the TVEs also helps us interpret the policy developments in the 1990s. In the 1990s, the TVEs began to fail. Conventional wisdom holds that the TVEs failed because their public-sector ownership became a liability in the more competitive environment of the 1990s. Thus, their failure in the 1990s was taken as a sign that the Chinese reforms were working. I again disagree. Chapter 3 details the facts and the argument, but suffice it to mention here that in the 1990s the TVEs were almost completely private. The very reason for their failure is that the business environment for rural entrepreneurship turned dramatically adverse in the 1990s. The successes of the TVEs in the 1980s and their failures in the 1990s reflect not firm characteristics but rather policy differences between the two decades. This is the tale of the two decades.

As Professor Stiglitz's writings and views on TVEs show, the TVE phenomenon has powerfully shaped Western economists' interpretation of China's growth experience. In the following paragraphs, let me first summarize how TVEs are commonly portrayed by Western economists. I then present documentary evidence – based on a close reading of numerous government reports and data going back to the early 1980s – that shows that this view of TVEs bears very little resemblance to the real TVE phenomenon.

2.1 What Is a TVE?

Many China economists and other social scientists believe that TVEs have a distinct ownership structure. This consensus view is summarized by Naughton (2007, p. 271) in his textbook on Chinese economy: "TVEs had a special distinction during this period [1978–1996] because of their unusual ownership and corporate governance setup. Originating under the rural communes, most TVEs were collectively-owned...." This view is widely accepted by other scholars.[32]

This special feature of TVEs, according to Roland (2000), poses a challenge to researchers because, given their public ownership, they are not supposed to perform well. The strong theoretical priors of mainstream economists are that private ownership rights motivate entrepreneurs to invest and to take risks. The lack of this incentive device as embedded in a public ownership structure is why the TVE phenomenon was so puzzling.

Elaborate theories – some backed up by mathematically derived formal proofs – have been proposed to explain the performance of TVEs as public-sector businesses. One prominent theoretical strand models TVEs as an efficient substitute in a weak environment.[33] In particular, the public ownership of TVEs is supposed to perform two economically useful functions. One is that it aligns the interests of the central government with those of the local governments.[34] The second function of TVEs, supposedly, is that they are an effective mechanism to prevent private stealing of public assets (Stiglitz 2006). Roland (2000, p. 282) hails this explanation of TVEs as an important application of the path-breaking work in economics on the incomplete contracting framework. This is high praise indeed. The TVE research not only enhances our understanding of China, but it may also represent an advance in economic theory.

All of these theoretical conceptualizations about TVEs are predicated on one empirical detail – that TVEs are public. Let me step back and ask a question that economists should have asked before they began to model: Are the TVEs really public?

The TVE label owes its origins to the commune and brigade enterprises created during the Great Leap Forward. In part because of this lineage, some Western scholars came to believe that the Great Leap Forward laid the foundation for the TVEs in the 1980s.[35] This is not really the case. In 1978, there were only about 1.5 million commune and brigade enterprises (Zhang Yi 1990, p. 25), but by 1985, there were already 12 million businesses labeled as TVEs (Ministry of Agriculture 2003). Clearly, the vast majority of TVEs had nothing to do with the Great Leap Forward. As a product of the reforms, they were completely new entrants during the first half of the 1980s. This is an important observation because the supposed Great Leap Forward lineage of the TVEs implicitly reinforced the view that the TVEs were a collective institution.

The term *TVE* first appeared in a policy document issued by the State Council on March 1, 1984. (There is a semantic issue involving the term. The details need not detain us here except to note that the English usage of the term is actually quite different from its Chinese usage. The English term lumps together two very different types of rural firm. I provide an explanation of this issue in the Appendix.) The full title of this document is "Report on creating a new situation for commune and brigade enterprises." The document coined the term *TVE*. This coinage was to replace the previous term, "commune and brigade enterprise." The new term was necessary, as this historic document pointed out, because many new forms of rural businesses had arisen in the first half of the 1980s. This was not just a semantic change. The label, "commune and brigade enterprise," was used to refer to the collective rural firms from the Great Leap Forward era. But, only a few years into the reform era, a large number of private businesses entered into China's rural corporate landscape. This raised two complications. First, the TVEs began to compete with SOEs on the product and factor markets, which created a sense of unease on the part of planning bureaucrats. The 1984 document was to affirm the high-level political support for the new entrants.

The second complication is that the old label was no longer accurate. So, the 1984 document dropped the old label of commune and brigade enterprises and provided a concise working definition of TVEs. The second paragraph of the document – known famously in China as document No. 4 – defined TVEs as follows (Ministry of Agriculture 1985, p. 450): "TVEs include enterprises sponsored by townships and villages, the alliance enterprises formed by peasants, other alliance enterprises and individual enterprises."[36]

Enterprises sponsored by townships and villages are the collective TVEs, the kind the Western economists assume to represent the entire TVE sector. The rest of the firms under the TVE label are all private businesses or entities. Individual enterprises refer to household businesses that typically have fewer than seven employees. The alliance enterprises – in Chinese, *lianying* – are a 1980s euphemism referring to larger private-sector enterprises. These are private-sector firms with multiple investors and with more than seven employees. In the official documents adopted in the late 1980s, references to alliance enterprises were gradually replaced by the term *private-run enterprises, siying qiye,* after a major 1987 Politburo document began to explicitly use the term *private-sector firms* (Editorial Committee of TVE Yearbook 1989a, p. 138). (*Siying qiye* is the standard term for large private-sector firms employing seven or more employees.)

Let me stress that the private TVEs discussed here are not "red-hat" firms. Red-hat firms are typically those very large private-sector firms that are registered falsely as collective firms. Kelon is a classic example. When it began operations, it recruited 4,000 workers. Even though there was more employment flexibility than suggested by the seven-employee rule, in the 1980s it would have been difficult to register a firm with thousands of workers explicitly as a private-sector firm. The private TVEs were fully private and their private ownership identity was fully known to the government. The issue here is one of definition: The official definition and the official data include both TVEs controlled by townships and villages and TVEs controlled by private entrepreneurs.

Let me quote from Chinese officials, policy documents, and references to show that the official definition of TVEs has been remarkably consistent in its inclusion of private businesses. The following excerpts are extensive and detailed because I want to illustrate just how consistent this definition is across different and multiple sources and to underscore the authenticity of the TVE definition inclusive of rural private-sector businesses. Excerpts follow:

- Wan Li, the reformist vice premier in charge of agriculture in the 1980s, criticized those officials whom he said had "an incomplete understanding of TVEs." Following is an excerpt from a speech he gave in 1984: "[Some officials] only include the original collectively-owned enterprises of townships and villages started by the masses as TVEs, but do not include those businesses later established by peasants on their own or those alliance enterprises financed from pooled capital as TVEs. [They] even discriminate against them. This is not correct."[37]
- An official from the Ministry of Agriculture provides the following assessment, "In the 1980s, Chinese peasants finally broke free from the long-standing straitjacket that restricted enterprise sponsorship at two levels (township and village). . . . Their own alliance enterprises and household businesses sprung up like mushrooms and they became an important part of the TVEs" (Editorial Committee of TVE Yearbook 1989b, p. 29).
- A manual prepared by the Shanxi TVE Management Bureau (1985, p. 1) defines a TVE as follows, "[A TVE] belongs to collective ownership *or* individual ownership" (italics added by the author for emphasis).

- A 1989 Ministry of Agriculture report to the State Council summarizing the state of TVE development: "Nowadays a large portion of TVEs comprises individual businesses and alliance enterprises. . . . Currently, individual businesses and alliance enterprises account for a large share of the TVEs in the northwest, southwest, and other economically backward regions" (Editorial Committee of TVE Yearbook 1990, p. 4).
- A 1987 document by the Agricultural Bank of China instructing its regional branches not only to lend to enterprises at the township and village level but also to pay attention to alliance enterprises and household businesses in their TVE loan programs (Editorial Committee of TVE Yearbook 1989b, p. 524).
- The following is from a report by the Ministry of Agriculture: "In 1996, the total profits of TVEs amounted to 388.6 billion yuan, an increase of 63.5 billion from the year before and a growth rate of 19.53 percent. Of this amount, 173.1 billion yuan was in the collective *xiangcun* [township and village] enterprises" (Ministry of Agriculture 1997, p. 3).
- This is how an analysis in the *China TVE Yearbook (1978–1987)* portrays the TVEs: "Compared with an SOE, a TVE has the following characteristics. First, it is a collective-ownership and individual-ownership enterprise with a lot of autonomy and able to make decisions concerning its own fate" (Editorial Committee of TVE Yearbook 1989b, p. 3).

Because the default definition of TVEs automatically covers rural private businesses as well as collective TVEs and because there are policies that treat collective and private firms differently, some of the official documents and regulations always delineate their applicable scope. This is another way to illustrate the same point – that the Chinese TVE definition and, therefore, the TVE data incorporate private-sector activities in rural China. Consider the following examples:

- Compare the 1990 "PRC Township and Village Collective Enterprise Regulation" with the 1997 "PRC Township and Village Enterprise Law."[38] Provision 2 of the 1990 law, which specifically covers collective TVEs, states that the law only applies to "rural enterprises sponsored by townships and villages." However, the 1997 law, which is meant for all TVEs, defines its applicable scope as "rural collective enterprises or enterprises with the main investments by peasants located in townships and villages."

- In 1986, the Ministry of Finance and Ministry of Agriculture promulgated a "TVE Accounting Regulation." It was designed only for
  collective TVEs, not for private TVEs. Thus, Provision 2 of the regulation states that regulations for rural alliance enterprises and household
  businesses "will be promulgated separately" (Editorial Committee of
  TVE Yearbook 1989b, p. 513).
- As a way of contrast with the previous, the TVE labor and TVE health
  regulations cover both collective and private TVEs. Provision 2 of each
  of these two regulations stipulates its applicable scope as "all" TVEs
  (Editorial Committee of TVE Yearbook 1989b, pp. 530–532).
- Mindful of the ownership differences between collective and private
  TVEs, the Chinese state adopted different profit-retention regulations
  for these two types of TVEs. For collective TVEs, the regulations are
  quite specific and stringent. For example, 60 percent of the after-
  tax profits of the collective TVEs cannot be distributed as dividends
  and must be retained by the enterprise (Editorial Committee of TVE
  Yearbook 1990, p. 12). In comparison, a 1988 policy document on
  private TVEs does not specify a profit-retention target even though it
  states a preference for profit reinvestments by these firms (Editorial
  Committee of TVE Yearbook 1989a, p. 139).

2.2 How Large Were Private TVEs?

TVEs, as used by the Chinese, are a *locational* concept – enterprises *located*
in the townships and villages. Western economists, on the other hand,
understand the term from an ownership perspective – that they are *owned*
by townships and villages. This huge gulf between the two understandings
of TVEs has contributed to massive confusion in writings about TVEs.

There is confusion even about some basic facts; for example, how many
TVEs there were. Brandt, Li, and Roberts (2005, p. 524) remark that by the
early 1990s, "there were more than 1.25 million of these local government-
owned and run enterprises, employing 135.1 million individuals. . . . " The
data the three economists refer to are for 1996. In that year, there were
actually 23.4 million TVEs, of which 1.5 million were collective. (The 1.25
million figure cited by the three economists apparently refers to collective
TVEs at the village level only.) It was the *entire* TVE sector of 23.4 million firms that employed 135.1 million individuals. The collective TVEs
employed only 59.5 million individuals.[39]

In terms of establishments, the overwhelming majority of TVEs, even at
the early stage of the reforms, were actually private TVEs. In 1985, according

to Ministry of Agriculture data, there were more than 12 million TVEs, of which 10.5 million were private. (A careful and well-versed reader may point out that the data from the Ministry of Agriculture reported here seem to be different from the data reported by the NBS. There is no inconsistency, but the two data series are organized differently. I explain this in the Appendix.) In addition, a huge portion of the collective TVEs were concentrated in a few rich, coastal provinces. In many other provinces, the private TVEs completely dominated the TVE pool.[40]

In this section, I present the data on TVEs according to the Chinese definition. One effect of the No. 4 document is that it changed the statistical reporting procedure by the Ministry of Agriculture,[41] the agency in charge of collecting and reporting on TVE data. The Ministry of Agriculture began to consolidate all the rural firms under the category of TVEs in its statistical reporting starting in 1985. The Ministry of Agriculture data provide detailed ownership breakdowns of the TVEs: (1) collective TVEs, (2) privately run TVEs, and (3) self-employment household businesses. The data on the ownership composition of TVEs in terms of establishments and employment from 1985 to 2002 are presented in Table 2.1.

Even a casual glance at Table 2.1 reveals that private TVEs absolutely dominated the total pool of TVEs. The highest number of collective TVEs in 1986 is 1.73 million. In contrast, the lowest number of household TVEs in 1985 is 10.1 million. It is true that before the mid-1990s, there were more collective TVEs than private-run TVEs. In the four years between 1985 and 1988, the number of private-run TVEs more than doubled, from 530,000 in 1985 to 1.2 million in 1988, whereas there was almost no change in the number of collective TVEs (from 1.57 million in 1985 to 1.59 million in 1988). In 1988, the collective TVEs outnumbered the private-run TVEs by only 300,000. In subsequent years, the number of private-run TVEs would decline, due to the Tiananmen effect. Without the 1989 Tiananmen interlude, the private-run TVEs would have surpassed the collective TVEs within three to four years.

Stiglitz (2006), for example, believes that the rise of TVEs challenges the standard claims of economics. He explains: "Many of the new enterprises were created in the 1980s and early 1990s by township and village enterprises (TVEs). These were public enterprises and the standard ideology would have said that you cannot succeed with public enterprises; but they were enormously successful." His assessment is not even remotely close to reality. In 1985, there were 1.57 million collective TVEs; by 1996, as pointed out before, the number of collective TVEs was still 1.5 million. But, during this period, the total number of TVEs increased from 12 million in 1985 to

Table 2.1. *Ownership composition of TVEs, 1985–2002*

	Number of TVEs, Million Units			Employment in TVEs, Million Persons			
		Private TVEs				Private TVEs	
Year	Total	Collective TVEs	Private-run	Household Businesses	Total	Collective TVEs	Private-run	Household Businesses
1985	12.2	1.57	0.53	10.1	69.8	41.5	4.75	23.5
1986	15.2	1.73	1.09	12.3	79.4	45.4	8.34	25.6
1987	17.5	1.58	1.19	14.7	88.1	47.2	9.23	31.6
1988	18.9	1.59	1.20	16.1	95.5	48.9	9.77	36.8
1989	18.7	1.53	1.07	16.1	93.7	47.2	8.84	37.6
1990	18.7	1.45	0.98	16.3	92.7	45.9	8.14	38.6
1991	19.1	1.44	0.85	16.8	96.1	47.7	7.27	41.2
1992	20.9	1.53	0.90	18.5	106.3	51.8	7.71	46.8
1993	24.5	1.69	1.04	21.8	123.5	57.7	9.14	56.6
1994	24.9	1.64	0.79	22.5	120.2	58.9	7.3	53.9
1995	22.0	1.62	0.96	19.4	128.6	60.6	8.74	59.3
1996	23.4	1.55	2.26	19.6	135.1	59.5	24.6	50.9
1997	20.1	1.29	2.33	16.5	130.5	53.2	26.3	51.0
1998	20.0	1.07	2.22	16.8	125.4	48.3	26.2	50.9
1999	20.7	0.94	2.08	17.7	127.1	43.7	28.5	54.8
2000	20.9	0.8	2.06	18.0	128.2	38.3	32.5	57.3
2001	21.2	0.67	2.01	18.5	130.9	33.7	36.9	60.2
2002	21.3	0.73	2.3	18.3	132.9	38.0	35.0	59.8

Source: Data are from the Ministry of Agriculture (2003).

23.4 million in 1996. Assuming that the entry and exit rates of collective and private TVEs were similar, *every single new entrant during the reform era was a private firm.*

However, as both Oi (1999) and Naughton (2007) stress, the private TVEs were individually smaller than the collective TVEs so their employment and output shares were smaller as well. Household businesses are single proprietorships, with a very small number of employees. Although some private-run TVEs were large, they were fewer in number. Table 2.1 illustrates this point. Employment in the collective TVEs was larger than employment in the private TVEs. In 1985, the collective TVEs employed 41.5 million people as compared with 4.75 million in the private-run TVEs and 23.5 million in household businesses.

There is nothing surprising or unusual about the statically large collective sector. Collective TVEs were founded in the late 1950s and had more than 20 years of development. Private TVEs were a result of rural reforms and began only in the early 1980s. Despite their statically small size, the dynamism was on their side, not on the side of the collective TVEs. Private TVEs were growing rapidly to claim an ever larger share of employment. In 1989, private TVEs accounted for 49 percent of employment, and in 1990, they accounted for 50 percent. In 1989, the private TVEs claimed 58 percent of the after-tax profits and 45 percent of the total wage bill of all TVEs. By the end of the 1980s and just within a single decade of reform, the private TVEs were on the verge of overtaking the collective TVEs across a number of dimensions. The static advantage of the collective TVEs quickly eroded as private TVEs accumulated growth momentum. From a dynamic perspective, the TVE miracle took place *entirely* in the private sector, not in the collective sector.

Some scholars cite the smaller share of private TVEs in industrial output value to support their view that the main source of growth came from collective TVEs. Apart from the static and dynamic stories, there is an inherent data bias in this view. As mentioned before, in the 1980s, private businesses first ventured into the service sector rather than into industry. By definition, the industry data will understate the importance of the private TVEs. By 1987, private TVEs already accounted for 32.1 percent of the gross output value in the entire TVE sector, compared with 23 percent of the industrial output value.[42] Private TVEs were still smaller than collective TVEs by the output measure, but their share was by no means insignificant as of the mid-1980s.

In fact, even the 32 percent of the output value by private TVEs understates the economic importance of private TVEs. The 32 percent is the average of the private shares of TVEs in all provinces implicitly weighted by the economic size of the provinces. This introduces a subtle bias. Private entrepreneurship and private TVEs first started in the poorer provinces, an issue I go into in greater detail next. Poorer provinces have a smaller GDP and, therefore, their economic weight is small in the calculation of the national means. The weighted average shares of private TVEs in the output value reflect the size of the private TVEs but also reflect the size of the provincial economies. Private TVEs would necessarily thus appear small simply because they were clustered in the poorer provinces.

The weighted average figure is the correct statistical measure of private TVEs, but it may not be the correct economic measure. Private TVEs were sizeable in the poor provinces and, if so, we need to know how big they were in those provinces. Because the poor provinces lacked many alternatives as compared with the rich provinces, it is important to examine the role of private TVEs in those provinces. The unweighted average of the private

TVEs' share of gross output value in 1987 is 40 percent, 8 percent higher than the weighted average. This is because the poorer and smaller provinces in the 1980s had a larger private sector.

Table 2.2 presents the percentage of private TVEs in the gross output value of the entire TVE sector across all 29 provinces in China. In addition, the table presents provincial data on per capita GDP, provincial shares of China's GDP, and percentage shares of agricultural population in the provincial population. The data refer to 1987. The table arrays the provinces from high to low according to their shares of private TVEs in the provincial gross output value. The highest share is Hebei, at 70.4 percent; the lowest share is Shanghai, at 6 percent. This is an extraordinary range. At the bottom of the private TVE output shares, three out of the five provinces are cities – Shanghai, Beijing, and Tianjin. The other side of the argument that capitalism is rural in origin is that socialism is urban in China. Another interesting finding is that the province that became a private-sector success story in the 1990s, Zhejiang, in fact had a fairly small private TVE sector in 1987. Its output share of private TVEs was only a bit larger than that of Jiangsu: 16.3 percent in Zhejiang compared with 10.7 percent in Jiangsu. The basic difference between Zhejiang and Jiangsu is that Zhejiang continued with the 1980s' model of incremental and spontaneous private-sector development in the rural areas, whereas in the 1990s, Jiangsu adopted the urban-centric development model.

As of 1987, private TVEs already contributed more than 50 percent of the TVE output in eight provinces. In another 15 provinces, private TVEs accounted for between 30 and 50 percent of the output value. Although we do not have data, in the late 1970s, the private share would have been close to zero. This is indicative of the rapid private-sector development in the 1980s. Within only eight years of the reform era, private TVEs already produced the majority of the rural output in one third of the Chinese provinces and accounted for a sizeable share of the rural output in another half of the Chinese provinces. It is difficult to reconcile this finding with the view that the TVE miracle occurred exclusively in the public-sector domain.

2.3 Virtuous Capitalism

Although it is seldom cited by academic economists writing about TVEs, by far the best study of TVEs in the English language is *China's Rural Industry*, a collaborative research project between World Bank economists and Chinese researchers from the Chinese Academy of Social Sciences (referred to

Table 2.2. *Geographic and economic distributions of private TVEs, 1987*

Province	% of Private TVEs in Gross Output Value	Per Capita GDP (Yuan)	Provincial Share of China's GDP	% of Agricultural Population
Hebei	70.4	921	4.56	85.8
Guizhou	63.9	546	1.45	87.8
Henan	61.3	755.8	5.32	88.2
Guangxi	57.7	607	2.11	87.3
Ningxia	56.3	922	0.35	77.7
Neimenggu	55.9	1025	1.85	70.5
Jilin	52.8	1269	2.60	62.2
Anhui	51.9	842	3.86	85.2
Shaanxi	49.3	796	2.09	81.9
Xizang	48.0	863	0.15	86.1
Heilongjiang	47.3	1335	3.97	58.6
Qinghai	46.9	1018	0.38	70.9
Xinjiang	45.1	1053	1.30	55.2
Sichuan	43.0	721	6.52	85.5
Fujian	41.5	1004	2.44	83.3
Gansu	41.4	764	1.39	84.0
Jiangxi	40.7	729	2.30	81.9
Shanxi	37.8	962	2.25	78.7
Hunan	36.2	818	4.10	85.4
Liaoning	36.0	1917	6.28	58.9
Hubei	34.0	1031	4.52	78.0
Guangdong	33.0	1383	7.05	77.5
Yunnan	31.1	653	2.00	88.1
Shandong	23.2	1131	7.79	86.0
Zhejiang	16.3	1470	5.27	83.8
Tianjin	12.2	2682	1.92	45.1
Beijing	10.9	3338	2.85	39.2
Jiangsu	10.7	1462	8.05	81.5
Shanghai	6.0	4396	4.76	34.2
Average of all provinces	40.0	1256	3.4	74.8
Average of top 10	56.8	855	2.4	81.3
Average of bottom 10	21.4	1946	5.1	67.2
Two-way correlation with private TVE shares	n/a	−0.71	−0.39	0.49

Source: The calculation is based on the data provided by the Ministry of Agriculture (2003).

hereafter as the World Bank TVE study).[43] A key insight from the World Bank TVE study is that collective ownership of TVEs prevailed in a few rich regions of the country whereas private TVEs tended to be dominant in the poorer regions.

This is in part because the poor regions lacked a viable collective alternative and in part because the poorer regions by definition were also more rural. Herein is the connection with the rural origins of Chinese capitalism: More rural regions had a stronger version of residual capitalism. For example, in Jieshou, one of the poorer research sites in the World Bank TVE study, 73 percent of the TVEs were private, despite their TVE designation (Luo 1990, p. 147). As was true elsewhere in the country, private TVEs were individually smaller so their employment share was smaller, at 49.4 percent of the TVE workforce, but still a substantial size.

The aggregate data presented in Table 2.2 corroborate exactly the findings in the World Bank TVE study. The bottom rows of Table 2.2 present summary statistics. The average of the 10 provinces with the largest shares of private TVEs is 56.8 percent, compared with 21.4 percent for the bottom 10 provinces. The 10 provinces with the largest shares of private TVE output were substantially poorer and much more agricultural as compared with those 10 provinces with the smallest shares of private TVE output. The average per capita GDP among the top 10 provinces was 855 yuan in 1987, compared with 1,946 yuan among the bottom 10 provinces.

The provinces in the top 10 also had a smaller GDP, less than half of those of the bottom 10 provinces. They were far more agricultural. The agricultural population accounted for 81.3 percent among the top 10 provinces but only 67.2 percent among the bottom 10 provinces. The last row of the table presents simple two-way correlation statistics between the percentage shares of private TVEs and the various other indicators. The private TVEs are negatively correlated with per capita GDP and with the provincial shares of Chinese GDP and positively correlated with the agricultural share of the population.

These are specific illustrations of a central point in this book – Chinese capitalism is an overwhelmingly rural affair. A related point is that Chinese capitalism – *in the 1980s* – was also a poor man's affair. As the case of Mr. Nian shows, poor people and poor provinces went into the rural entrepreneurship in the 1980s. This is one of the most remarkable and under-rated attributes of rural entrepreneurship in the 1980s. Capitalism in the 1980s was not only vibrant, it was also virtuous. Rural entrepreneurship was one of the few feasible mechanisms to transition out of low value-added agriculture and to move beyond the abject poverty. In this sense, it is much more meaningful to study the development of private TVEs in poor regions of China than to study the development of collective TVEs in the rich regions of the country heavily researched by Western academics, such as Jiangsu and Shandong. The policy implications are far more significant.

Private TVEs also affected a large number of Chinese people. As mentioned before, in 1987 there were nine provinces in which private TVEs accounted for more than 50 percent of output in the TVE sector and another 15 provinces in which they accounted for between 30 and 50 percent of TVE output. Those nine provinces were home to 260.2 million rural Chinese (30 percent of China's rural population); the additional 15 provinces accounted for another 427.8 million rural Chinese and 49.7 percent of the rural population.

This book examines Guizhou at close range. Completely land-locked Guizhou is China's poorest province. Yet, it had many private TVEs. Table 2.2 shows that Guizhou had the second highest private TVE output share in the country, at 63.9 percent in 1987. Guizhou managed to have doubled this share in just three years. In 1984, the private TVEs accounted for 31 percent of the output value in the TVE sector in Guizhou. (In the 1990s, as I show in the next chapter, the private TVEs in Guizhou, relative to the collective TVEs, stagnated.)

By contrast, the richer provinces had far smaller private TVEs. In 1984, Jiangsu, a rich, coastal province, had only 4 percent of the private TVE output value (Zhang Yi 1990, p. 192 and p. 200) and in 1987, the share was 10.7 percent (see Table 2.2). The per capita GDP in Jiangsu was 1,462 yuan in 1987, almost three times that of Guizhou (546 yuan). Another example can be found in Shandong province, also a coastal and relatively well-off province (per capita GDP in 1987 was 1,131 yuan). Shandong also had a much smaller private TVE sector. As shown in Table 2.2, Shandong's private TVEs contributed to 23.2 percent of TVE output value. According to a survey of 84 villages in Shandong, in 1988, township-level enterprises dominated the pool of TVEs across the board – in terms of number of business establishments, employment, size, and so on. There were 350 TVEs among these villages, 283 of which were at the township level. These township-level firms accounted for the vast majority of employment and the stock of fixed assets.[44]

This contrast between Guizhou on the one hand and Jiangsu and Shandong on the other is deeply meaningful. In general, the developed parts of China – such as its urban centers and industrialized provinces – were more state-owned. The under-developed and agricultural parts of the country were more privately owned. If we accept the premise that welfare gains of GDP growth are greater in poor regions than in rich regions, then it is not so much the aggregate size of private TVEs at the national level that is of first-order importance. Rather, it is the size of private TVEs in poor provinces to which we should pay special attention. Private TVEs, more than collective

TVEs, contributed to Guizhou's fast growth in the 1980s. Between 1981 and 1984, Guizhou's per capita GDP grew at a real double-digit rate. In other years of the 1980s, the per capita annual GDP growth was consistently around 7 or 8 percent (NBS 1996, p. 731). This is the true China miracle.

3 "Nothing but Revolutionary Reforms"

I remember that it was in 1978. There was an article in People's Daily about raising cows. I got so excited upon reading it. During the Cultural Revolution, every newspaper article was about revolution and class struggle, non-stop, only editorials. At that time, raising chickens or growing vegetables were viewed as capitalist tails to be cut. Now the People's Daily has an article about raising cows. Things have definitely changed.

– Liu Chuanzhi, founder of Lenovo, in 1998[45]

Recall the puzzle I posed in Chapter 1 – how the pronouncement by a completely unconstrained state to honor its commitments to reforms could have been viewed as credible. The quote from Liu Chuanzhi, the founder of Lenovo, provides a clue. His statement helps establish the appropriate baseline benchmark against which we should assess the policy changes in the 1980s. What would strike anyone in the West as utterly mundane and inconsequential – raising cows – was a signal of deep significance to Mr. Liu. The baseline benchmark in Mr. Liu's mind was "revolution and class struggle." Against this benchmark, publicity about raising cows in the *People's Daily* signaled a monumental change in policy. Deng Xiaoping would agree with Mr. Liu. The title of this section is a quote from a speech by Deng Xiaoping in 1984, "The rural reforms that were carried out in the past few years are nothing but revolutionary reforms."[46]

Chinese economic policies – and its politics – in the early 1980s were a world apart from the standard prescriptions of neoclassical economics. Land was not private, prices were controlled, and the state chose not to privatize SOEs. In a famous paper, Hausmann, Pritchett, and Rodrik (2004) put forward the thesis that the initial triggers of growth can often be "humble" in nature. These reforms amount to nothing more than some relaxation of existing constraints on the private sector. No fundamental institutional reforms – those aiming at property rights protection, for example – are needed. Deng's agricultural reforms, according to these authors, fit with this model.

The Chinese themselves – including Deng and Liu – did not see the agricultural reforms as "humble" at all. The reason for the different perspectives is simple: The baselines are different. To Hausmann, Pritchett, and Rodrik, the baseline is the "Washington Consensus" – the famous template of the necessary conditions for economic growth, ranging from macroeconomic stability to private ownership. China in the 1980s – or China now – looks quite different from the Washington Consensus. But to Deng and Liu, the baseline is China of the 1970s during the radical leftist period of the Cultural Revolution. Relative to the Cultural Revolution, the bubbling rural entrepreneurship, the crowded rural market fairs, and the demise of the commune system represented a remarkable departure from the *status quo ante*. This is the essence of directional liberalism.

It is extremely important to make explicit this huge difference in perspectives for it helps us to identify the sources of Chinese incentives. One reason why standard economic analysis emphasizes the importance of the sanctity of property rights for economic growth has to do with incentives. Economic agents need to be confident that their future gains will be safe in order for them to be motivated to expend efforts and capital today. The security of property rights is an incentive device. It is here that the standard economic analysis finds China puzzling. This is a country without the conventional sources of property rights security, such as a constrained government, an independent judiciary, free media, and political power for the propertied class. Where, then, is the incentive for economic growth in this system?

Deng's perspective provides the answer. Property rights protection in China, now or in the 1980s, is very poor, but *relative to the Cultural Revolution period*, the marginal improvement was huge. Directional liberalism, not an exact match with the Washington Consensus, was the relevant modus operandi and was the source of Chinese incentive to go into entrepreneurship. To illustrate the size of the marginal change from the pre-reform order, keep in mind that an average commune – the decision maker before reforms – was 5,000 households (World Bank 1983, p. 30).[47] Within just a few years after the reforms, it was replaced by a system based on household production. It is difficult to exaggerate both the incentive and economic effects of such a change.

The rapidity with which the household responsibility system (HRS) was adopted illustrates Deng's perspective on rural reforms. In September 1980, only three provincial Party secretaries supported the HRS (Rural Economy Research Team 1998). On the basis of this rather fragile political support, the HRS spread extremely rapidly. According to Naughton (1996, p. 141), at the end of 1979, only 1 percent of rural households had adopted the HRS; by the end of 1982, the percentage had increased to 80 percent. In another two years, in 1984, the percentage share of participating households reached 99 percent.

More recent Chinese estimates provide an even faster rate of adoption: 90 percent by early 1982, according to the Rural Economy Research Team (1998). Rural households claimed a rapidly rising share of production assets. By 1983, just four years after the reforms, 53 percent of plowing equipment and animals and 58 percent of vehicles were privately owned. In 1982, the private purchase of tractors reached 1 million units, equivalent to one third of the existing stock of tractors at that time.[48] It was this type of changes that convinced entrepreneurs such as Lenovo's Liu Chuanzhi to leave the comfort of this job as a scientist and to venture into entrepreneurship. The incentive effect came from how far China departed from the Cultural Revolution of the 1970s, not from the proximity of China to the textbook version of Western economic and political institutions.

Recall from Chapter 1 that private fixed-asset investments (FAIs) grew rapidly in the 1980s. In this section, I provide a direct description of the policy developments that matched the fixed-asset investment data. If directional liberalism is the mechanism that motivated Chinese entrepreneurs, then asking whether China fits with the Washington Consensus is the wrong framing. The right framing is to ask whether China was moving in the right direction and, if so, by how much. Even more precisely, the right way to frame the discussion is to ask how far and at which speed China was moving from the rigid central planning – or a sort of Moscow Consensus, if you will. Within only a few years into the reform era, personal security was enhanced, microeconomic flexibility was increased, and individual incentives were augmented. Furthermore, these achievements were a result of a consistent, deliberate, and progressively liberal policy framework.

3.1 Moving Away from the Status Quo Ante

The reforms in China are often described as having occurred during the post-Mao era. Strictly speaking, this is incorrect. The reforms occurred in post-Hua China. Hua Guofeng was a faithful Maoist and he relinquished his power only in 1978. The reformist leadership established full control of the economic agenda at the historic Third Plenum of the Eleventh Party Congress concluded on December 22, 1978. The two strongest advocates of the rural reforms, Zhao Ziyang and Wan Li, were appointed premier and vice premier, respectively, in 1980. (Sichuan and Anhui, led by Zhao and Wan, respectively, had led the country in the pioneering agricultural reforms in the late 1970s.) It took China just six years between 1979 and 1985 to create a policy environment sufficiently liberal that a rural private sector with 10.5 million businesses strong, with 40 percent nonagricultural employment, had emerged. China may not have embraced the Washington Consensus, but it moved away from the Moscow Consensus at a rapid and purposeful speed.

Some China scholars believe that this development occurred spontaneously without much prodding from the government (Zhou 1996). This is not entirely wrong, but it is incomplete. Even if some of the specific initial reforms were spontaneous, they occurred against the backdrop of a relatively flexible political environment. The most famous example of spontaneous reforms is the household responsibility system. The HRS was not launched by the Chinese leadership from the top down but instead by a group of farmers in the poor village of Xiaogang in Anhui province. According to many accounts, farmers from 18 households in Xiaogang village secretly adopted the HRS on their own at a meeting in December 1978. They entered into a pledge – apparently written in blood – that they would contribute toward the costs of raising the children of the leaders of the reforms if the ringleaders were to be arrested.[49]

But, this action did not take place in a vacuum. The timing of the event – December 1978 – is highly significant. The 18 Anhui farmers entered into this pledge during the middle of the historic Third Plenum of the Eleventh Central Committee that launched the economic reforms. We do not know if the Xiaogang farmers knew about the deliberations at the Third Plenum, but they certainly would have had access to other information that suggested an imminent departure from the orthodox Maoist policy stance of Hua Guofeng. In the second half of 1978, several significant political events preceded the Third Plenum. During the summer, there was a famous debate on "seeking truth from practice" that explicitly challenged Hua's "two-whatevers" position on Mao Zedong. (The "two-whatevers" referred to support for whatever Mao supported and opposition to whatever Mao opposed.) On November 15, 1978, after Hua had repeatedly expressed his opposition, the CCP passed a resolution declaring that the April 5 Movement – during which hundreds of thousands of Beijing residents protested against the Gang of Four and, implicitly, against Mao himself in Tiananmen Square – was legitimate. The Party secretary of Beijing, who had overseen the suppression of the April 5 Movement, was summarily dismissed.[50] If we assume that the Xiaogang farmers calculated the benefits and costs of their action, it is reasonable to argue that they might have rationally believed that the probability of the success of their action became nontrivial in late 1978.

The true implication of the action by the Xiaogang farmers is not that the policies did not matter; rather, the implication is that the policies accommodated the spontaneous actions on the ground.[51] This is a hallmark of the reform policies in the 1980s. Probably the best illustration of this policy openness is a group of five policy documents famously known in China as the five No. 1 documents. Between 1982 and 1986, at the beginning of each year, the Central Committee of the CCP issued a No. 1 policy document about the rural reforms. The label, No. 1 document, was intended to signal that the rural reforms were a top policy priority of the government. Each No. 1 document addressed the questions of private-sector development and liberalization. They did so in a progressive manner: the later No. 1 documents provided solutions to problems and issues raised in earlier ones. These No. 1 documents are the best true example of the sequential, pragmatic, and learning-by-doing reforms.

The 1982 No. 1 document, the first of such documents, addressed private-sector development only in the context of agricultural production and marketing of agricultural products. The 1983 No. 1 document began to touch on the issue of private-sector development in nonagricultural activities, such as long-distance trade, rural processing of agricultural raw materials, access of rural residents to urban markets, and so on. The 1984 No. 1 document addressed the ideologically sensitive issue of employment by private-sector businesses, land contracting, reforms of rural credit cooperatives, deepening reforms of rural supply cooperatives, and rural industrialization. The 1985 No. 1 document abolished compulsory grain purchases by the state and instituted a contract system, permitted some interest-rate flexibility among rural financial institutions, allowed private mining, and opened infrastructural construction to private participation. The 1986 No. 1 document focused on some of the social consequences of the rapid private-sector development in the previous years, such as the rising income inequalities and the persistent rural poverty in some regions.

My claim is not that all the reforms were fully implemented. Rather, the claim is that the reforms moved progressively forward. Given the ideological environment in China so soon after the end of the Cultural Revolution, some of the early reforms were path-breaking. Consider the example of share issues. Many analysts believe that the concept was introduced in the 1990s. In fact, the 1982 No. 1 document already permitted the issuance of individual shares by some public-sector institutions (Central Committee 1992 <1982>). The specific context was the reform of the rural supply cooperatives, a critical institution linking the rural economy to the urban economy by procuring agricultural products from and selling industrial products to the peasants. The 1982 No. 1 document reformed the rural supply cooperatives in two ways. One is that the higher-level cooperatives – for example, at the county level – were decentralized to the "basic level" (township and village). The other is that the basic-level cooperatives were partially privatized by issuing shares to the peasants.

Several of these No. 1 documents explicitly recognized and supported the potential role of rural residents as providers of capital and business knowledge and expertise. The 1982 No. 1 document encouraged the pooling of capital and business formation among individuals and across different geographic boundaries. The 1983 No. 1 document went one step further: It allowed the pooling of capital from individuals not just in the production stages but also in the procurement and marketing stages of the rural economy (Central Committee 1992 <1983>). The 1984 No. 1 document removed the sectoral restrictions – now, rural residents were encouraged to invest in all types of enterprises and to pool their funds to jointly set up enterprises following the principles of voluntary participation and mutual benefit. The document also pledged government protection of the investors' interests (Central Committee 1992 <1984>). The 1985 No. 1 document allowed what in essence amounted to "stock options" – issuing shares to those who contributed knowledge and expertise (Central Committee and State Council 1992 <1985>).

As I showed previously, the distribution sector claimed more than 50 percent of the rural private-sector businesses. This did not occur by chance. Service-sector reforms were launched very early on. Service-sector reforms are important because, by definition, the service sector touches on the rural–urban linkages. The essence of the service-sector reforms was to allow rural residents to directly source their industrial inputs and to directly market their products to urban residents. This was a significant move in a number of ways. One is because of the substantial rural/urban segmentation created by the *hukou* system. The other is because they allowed rural access to urban markets and thus multiplied the size of market opportunities available to rural entrepreneurs by several fold. Mr. Nian, our sunflower-seed entrepreneur from Anhui, was a direct beneficiary of these reforms because he was allowed to sell not only to consumers in Anhui but also to the much richer consumers in Shanghai and Beijing.

The 1982 No. 1 document permitted direct marketing by peasants, essentially breaking the marketing monopoly held by the rural supply cooperatives. This policy was reinforced in all subsequent No. 1 documents. In 1982, Wan Li, a senior vice premier, called for an end to the state monopoly in the distribution channels. Private entry into marketing activities was to be permitted immediately and rural supply cooperatives were to be run by their members, not by the government (Wan Li 1992 <1982>). To entice investments in the rural supply cooperatives, in 1984 the Chinese government authorized the rural supply cooperatives to issue what amounted to convertible bonds – potential rural investors could receive both a fixed-interest payment and a variable dividend payment (State System Reform Commission, Ministry of Commerce, and Ministry of Agriculture 1992 <1984>).

The service-sector liberalization was quickly followed by policies to reduce inter-regional trade. The 1983 No. 1 document endorsed private entry into long-distance trade between different rural areas as well as between rural and urban areas. "Peasants in their private capacity," the document declared, "can engage in trade. They can go into cities and leave their counties and provinces." A State Council circular issued in 1984 specifically authorized rural entrepreneurs to operate stores and service outlets in cities. The 1984 document also called for a reduction in the size of local governments in the rural areas and for instituting caps on fees and taxes levied on the peasants. The document tried to involve the local people's congresses in scrutiny of the enactment of rural fees and taxes.

3.2 Creating Policy Credibility

The reformist leaders made several moves very early on with a clear intention of signaling an improvement in property rights security. In 1979, the Chinese government returned confiscated bank deposits, bonds, gold, and private homes to those people who had been classified as "capitalists." The number of people affected by this policy was around 700,000 (Zhang Houyi and Ming Lizhi 1999, pp. 29–30). Mindful of the frequent political reversals and cycles during the Cultural Revolution, the reformist leaders went out of their way to repeatedly stress the continuity and the durability of the reforms. The wording is strong and explicit. Consider the following paragraph from a major policy document on agriculture (Central Committee 1979):

Those policies that have proven to be effective in practice shall not be changed. Otherwise, credibility with the people will be lost and the incentives of the peasants will be undermined. At the same time, those policies that are harmful to the incentives of the peasants and to agricultural productivity must be resolutely revised and corrected . . .

The Chinese leadership sought to improve the property rights security of private entrepreneurs not through constitutional reforms but rather through enhancing the political status of the entrepreneurs. Many Western analysts believe that the political breakthrough for China's private sector occurred in 2001 with the promulgation of Jiang Zemin's "Three Representations" theory, which endorsed the idea that the CCP could recruit members from among private entrepreneurs. Again, as in so many other issues, this is simply not the case. As early as 1981, a major policy document, "Expanding channels and enlivening the economy, and solving employment problems in cities and townships," already endorsed the idea of recruiting Party members from the private sector. The policy document referred to private entrepreneurs as individual households or individual laborers, which persisted in usage in the 1990s, and called for the same political treatment for individual laborers as for workers in the state sector (Central Committee and State Council 1982 <1981>). The term *private enterprise* (*siying qiye*) first appeared in a major policy document in 1987 (Editorial Committee of TVE Yearbook 1989b, p. 518).

These developments expose another myth – that the ideological stigma against private sector came down only in the 1990s. Yes, it is true that the Chinese leadership began to tone down this ideological stigma since the mid-1990s, but much of this ideological stigma was actually revived by the leadership of the 1990s in the wake of Tiananmen events. The explicit prohibition against recruiting CCP members from the private sector was instituted in 1989, by Jiang Zemin himself. In a speech dated August 21, 1989, Jiang (1991 <1989>, p. 584) remarked, "The document of this conference said that private entrepreneurs were not allowed into the CCP. I agree with this view." (I come back to this topic in the next chapter.) The effect of Jiang Zemin's much-heralded "Three Representations" theory in 2001 was to lift the policy restriction his own leadership had instituted 12 years before.

My archival research uncovers at least five occasions when China's top leaders held public face-to-face meetings with private entrepreneurs in the 1980s. In the still rigid ideological environment of the 1980s, this gesture mattered enormously. In the first instance, in 1980, two vice premiers paid a visit and brought New Year's greetings to Ms. Liu Guixian in her restaurant. Liu was the first private entrepreneur to have been granted a private business license in Beijing (Wu Xiaobo 2006). In the second instance, in August 1983, Hu Yaobang, then CCP general secretary, attended a conference celebrating the employment achievements of collective firms and individual businesses.[52] In the third instance, Zhao Ziyang, the premier at the time, came to the founding meeting of the Association of Individual Laborers. In the fourth instance, Zhao Ziyang visited a private entrepreneur in Hubei province whose bra business was able to enter the European market.[53] In the fifth instance, on September 6, 1987, top Party and State Council officials invited 10 rural entrepreneurs to a meeting in Zhongnanhai (the official residence of the top Chinese leaders). The 10 were selected as the best rural entrepreneurs at what amounted to a business competition event organized by the Chinese Central Television station (Editorial Committee of TVE Yearbook 1989b, p. 359). In the 1990s, while it was customary for China's top leaders to attend forums with the CEOs of MNCs (e.g., the Fortune Global Forum), there is not a single documented case of top Chinese leaders attending similar functions organized by indigenous private entrepreneurs. This is so despite the fact that indigenous private businesses created employment opportunities several multiples that of the opportunities created by foreign firms.

The leaders in the 1980s sought to elevate the political status of private entrepreneurs but also they were harshly critical of the state sector. At the 1983 employment conference of the collective and private sectors, Hu Yaobang coined the term "glory project" (*guancai shiye*). He said that only business activities undertaken by the state sector were traditionally viewed positively – as "glorious" – and that activities undertaken by the private sector were automatically viewed with suspicion. To eradicate the ideological stigma of the private sector, he then went on to proclaim that the economic contributions by the private-sector were "glorious." This was in 1983.

According to a biography, in 1984, Hu Yaobang issued the following instruction in reaction to a complaint by 20 peasants from Hebei about difficulties to enter the transportation business. The tone was remarkably harsh (Chai Hongxia, Shi Bipo, and Gao Qing 1997, p. 127):

There are two issues here. One is that some basic-level cadres and SOE managers took advantage of scarce supplies and engaged in hoarding and monopolistic practices. They jacked up prices and extorted and blackmailed the masses. The other issue is that SOE managers are incompetent and they use the name of SOEs to exclude and attack individual enterprises.

Recent revelations about internal policy deliberations during this period show that maintaining policy credibility and stability was a top concern of the Chinese leaders. Deng Liqun, the head of the Propaganda Department between 1982 and 1985 and a leading CCP theoretician, revealed some fascinating details about this period. One contentious issue at the time was employment by private-sector firms. The Party ideologues challenged the policy of permitting large-scale employment by private-sector businesses. They argued that the policy amounted to allowing exploitation of labor. When Deng Liqun proposed convening a conference to discuss the issue, the reformist leaders, Hu Yaobang, Zhao Ziyang, and Wan Li, vetoed the idea. Hu Yaobang, as quoted by Deng Liqun, said, "If you convene this conference, it is a signal to the people lower down that the policy will change."[54]

3.3 Security of Proprietors vis-à-vis Security of Property

To be sure, none of the policy measures described previously amounted to a genuine institutional guarantee of private property rights. The CCP never allowed itself to be subject to any external constraints. What these documents reveal is that the reformist leaders were showing a degree of self-constraint and were fully cognizant of the reputational effects of their actions. In the early 1980s, such political self-constraint was reasonably credible. Again, the baseline benchmark matters here. Relative to the completely arbitrary behavior of Mao, these straightforward pronouncements of fairly specific policy rules by the top leaders helped establish a sense of confidence and stability on the part of those contemplating going into business in the 1980s.

The area where the policy changes matter the most is the sense of personal security on the part of first-generation entrepreneurs. Here, I draw a distinction between security of proprietors and security of property. The explicit and strong legal protection of private property was not promulgated until the 2004 Constitutional amendment and the 2007 Law of Physical Property. (Even with the passage of these legal documents, there is still a question of how they can be enforced fairly in a top-down, authoritarian system.) But, in the early 1980s, the appropriate benchmark is the baseline of the 1970s. Let me offer an extreme but nevertheless realistic scenario to illustrate this point. Imagine that during the Cultural Revolution, as soon as someone went into private commerce, he would be arrested. (This was especially true in the urban areas.) Now, imagine in the 1980s, a private entrepreneur simply in her capacity as a private entrepreneur no longer feared such a fate. The incentive effect between being arrested and not being arrested must have been massive. The cumulative effects of the policy changes in the 1980s resulted in an increase in the security of proprietors. The security of the proprietor is the necessary condition for the security of the property itself. In the 1980s, China completed the necessary conditions toward establishing property rights security.

The steady changes in policies and the business environment documented in the previous sections really mattered to the first generation of Chinese entrepreneurs who took calculated risks to go into business so soon after the Cultural Revolution. The following short cases show the intimate interactions between policies and the incentive effects of the first generation of Chinese entrepreneurs.

Table 2.2 shows that Hebei province had the highest output share of private TVEs in the country, already 70.4 percent in 1987. Hebei, about average in its economic development level, is a northern province (bordering both Beijing and Tianjin). Our first case comes from Qinhe county of Hebei province. This was a poor region with very few collective assets with which to start. In 1983, the county government launched a number of collective TVEs, but none of them was successful. Because of its poor financial situation, the county government ended up accumulating payroll arrears to its own staff. This experience led the county government to turn to the private sector for economic development. The first policy act by the county government was to rehabilitate more than 100 individuals who had been prosecuted during the "anti-capitalist tail" campaign of the Cultural Revolution. The county government also awarded the title of "model worker" to individuals who grew rich. The strategy seemed to work. By the late 1980s, Qinhe had developed a sizeable cluster of industries (all based on household businesses), and it was a large supplier of motorcycle components (Editorial Committee of TVE Yearbook 1989b, p. 233).

To be sure, there were policy setbacks in the 1980s, but how these policy setbacks were resolved is also telling of the era – some of the local officials publicly and proactively reversed their own mistakes. These quick corrections, rather than stubbornly persisting with policies that clearly did not work, established and consolidated a sense that the liberal policy environment was durable. Two episodes from the severe policy setback in 1982, when the central government cracked down on "speculation," are illustrative of this point.

In 1982, the State Council issued a policy document decrying the poor quality of products produced by the emerging private firms and the price hikes supposedly due to the speculative activities by private traders. The 1982 campaign against market speculation bore the classic symptoms of an ailing state sector using its political power to shut out its more nimble competitors. One of the first victims of the 1982 crackdown was Han Qingsheng in Wuhan, the capital city of Hubei province in interior China.[55] His crime was to have had received 600 yuan for providing technical assistance to a TVE. Mr. Han, an engineer at a SOE, like many engineers, also worked as a consultant for a TVE. Such engineers were known as "Sunday engineers" because they spent their Sundays at the TVEs. But, in 1982, with the adverse change in the environment, Mr. Han was sentenced to 300 days for engaging in "technological speculative activities."

The fate of Mr. Han became a huge media event. (This is another lesser known fact about the 1980s: The Chinese media in the 1980s were quite free and active.) Intellectuals and scientists strongly objected to his treatment. The Wuhan government then backed down, and Mr. Han was released. Not just that: The mayor of Wuhan city, apologizing on behalf of the city, personally delivered the court's verdict and the 600 yuan that the government had confiscated to the home of Mr. Han.

The 1982 crackdown also reached Wenzhou in Zhejiang province. In 1982, the Ministry of Machinery Industry issued a ban prohibiting private firms from producing electric transformers. The official reason was that products made by private enterprises were poor in quality and lacked safety standards. The document singled out Wenzhou for criticism because Wenzhou was emerging as a manufacturing center of electric transformers. Zhejiang province then initiated an investigation into the business activities of the eight richest private entrepreneurs in Wenzhou. (They were known as the "eight big kings" at the time – they each had accumulated wealth in excess of 100,000 yuan.) Seven were arrested and one fled the city.

The economy of Wenzhou crashed immediately. In 1980 and 1981, industry had expanded by 30 percent. But, in 1982, it screeched to a halt, contracting by 1.7 percent (Wu Xiaobo 2006, p. 84). Private fixed-asset investment fell from 280 million yuan in 1981 to 155 million yuan in 1982. The Wenzhou government swiftly reacted to the downturn. In 1984, it released all the imprisoned private entrepreneurs and restituted their assets. Not only that, the Wenzhou government published the decision in local newspapers explaining why it had erred. It was unprecedented – and it is still unprecedented today – for a branch of the Chinese government to openly and so publicly acknowledge its own mistakes. The following is an excerpt from a later account of this event:[56]

The teleconference [announcing the release of the private entrepreneurs] and the rehabilitation of the "eight big kings" were headline news in the local newspapers. Lower-level officials were emboldened and those with previous reservations then began to feel relaxed. The urban and rural areas of Wenzhou economy were greatly stimulated. In the rural area of Wenzhou, commercial activities began to proliferate massively.

Fixed-asset investment data support this qualitative assessment. For the first time after a two-year contraction, fixed-asset investments in 1984 exceeded their 1982 level and then in 1985 they expanded another 42 percent. This marked the beginning of the Wenzhou miracle. The man credited with this policy is Yuan Fanglie, the Party secretary of Wenzhou from 1981 to 1984. Today, many Wenzhou entrepreneurs regard Yuan with respect and gratitude. In a revealing 2001 interview, Yuan recalled why he took such actions. He noted that Wenzhou was poorly endowed with natural resources, but Wenzhou had one asset – its human capital, especially the commercial and trading skills of its entrepreneurs. Unusual for a Chinese official, he knew what was holding back a full utilization of these skills – lack of confidence in the durability of the reforms. Yuan then quoted a popular saying – "The policy of the CCP is like the moon, taking different shapes every fifteen days" – to illustrate his point. He came to the conclusion that it was essential to create a safe environment for the entrepreneurs to go into business. A footnote to the policy directive issued by the Ministry of Machinery Industry is that today Wenzhou is the home of China's largest producer of electric transformers, the Zhengtai Group, also one of China's largest private-sector firms. The SOEs that the Ministry of Machinery Industry had sought to protect have long since gone bankrupt.

Our final case comes from the famous No. 4 document of 1984 that recognizes the legality and status of private TVEs. The document stipulated specific provisions; for example, it entitled private TVEs to the tax incentives previously reserved for collective TVEs. But, it was also a political document. The No. 4 document decreed that TVEs should be granted the same policy treatment as SOEs. This was a policy milestone. Recall our earlier discussion that the No. 4 document defined TVEs in such a way as to include private firms. Thus, in effect, the No. 4 document of 1984 equated private firms notionally with SOEs.

The No. 4 document had a huge psychological impact on potential private entrepreneurs. Contemporaneous accounts recount what happened after the No. 4 document was announced – a massive wave of private placements. Within one month, rural residents in the county of Yiwu in Zhejiang province reportedly raised 10 million yuan and established 500 businesses. (In 1984, the entire agricultural output of Yiwu was just 200 million yuan.)[57] In the city of Shenyang, when a notice went out about raising capital for a private garment factory, peasants formed long lines the night before the shares were to go on sale. The venture raised 100,000 yuan in one day. In the same region, another proposal to raise 110,000 yuan for a food factory was fully subscribed in just 40 minutes. In the Nantong city of Jiangsu, a private commercial building project raised 1 million yuan in three days. In 1984, Zhejiang province created 250,000 private-sector businesses; Shandong, another 700,000. In Yichang of Hubei province, 50,000 peasants created 17,000 businesses. In Huanyuan county of Anhui province, 8,700 peasants pooled capital to form 205 private enterprises (Zhang Yi 1990). Thus, 1984 should be designated the year of embryonic private equity and organized capitalism in China. The entrepreneurial contagions were not confined to rural China. Lenovo, Stone, and Kelon were all founded in 1984; the Hope Group, China's largest agribusiness firm, was founded in 1983.

3.4 Getting the Incentives Right

If you want to bring the initiative of the peasants into play, you should give them the power to make money.

> – Deng Xiaoping comment to *New York Times*
> magazine delegation in October 1985
> – ("Sayings of Deng Xiaoping" 1997)

It is well known that the commune system suppressed the financial incentives of its members. One telling indicator is that the faster-growing crops fetched lower returns under the commune system.[58] The rapid demise of the commune system is evidence of the improved incentives under the HRS. Another source of improvement came from the price adjustments. Research shows the substantial impact on the income of Chinese peasants resulting from the rising agricultural procurement prices, the reductions in rural taxation, and the increased flexibility to enter into higher-return nonagricultural activities (Sicular 1988).

My interest here is not to repeat this well-researched story of improved financial returns and the rising incomes of Chinese peasants during the early 1980s. Instead, I provide an account of a change in the way the Chinese political elites framed the incentive issue. Notice the wording by Deng Xiaoping quoted previously. He did not say giving money to peasants but to "give them the *power* to make money" (italics added by the author for emphasis). This is a critical distinction. Even during the Maoist period – and during the 1990s and under Hu Jintao in the 2000s, sometimes the government would raise the agricultural terms of trade to increase rural income. What is different about the 1980s is that there was liberalization – to give the peasants the power to make money.

To put it simply, the prevailing thinking during the Maoist era was a zero-sum mentality – gains achieved by the peasantry were viewed necessarily as losses incurred by the state. The reformist leaders very early on repudiated this idea and embraced a positive-sum thinking. That thinking had three essential elements, although they were never explicitly articulated. First, rural welfare, in and of itself, was important. Second, improving rural welfare was entirely consistent with improving the welfare of the country as a whole. Third, improving rural welfare was the mechanism by which to improve the welfare of the country.

The change in the policy idea was visible quite early on. In April 1979, *Red Flag*, the theoretical mouthpiece of the CCP, argued for an incentive approach. In order for the peasants to contribute more to the state, the article argued, the state should, first and foremost, guarantee the economic interests of the peasants (Zhou Reli 1979). In one of the first major policy pronouncements on agriculture adopted by the reformist leaders, "Decision of the Central Committee of the CCP concerning the acceleration of agricultural development" promulgated in September 1979, the issue of incentives was highlighted prominently. Consider the following statement (Central Committee 1979):

While strengthening socialist education among our peasantry, we must show genuine concern for their material welfare in economic work and must provide a complete guarantee for their democratic rights in political work. *Without material welfare and certain political rights, it is impossible for any class to have innate incentives* (italics added by author for emphasis).

Considering that this was three years after the Cultural Revolution, such an explicit recognition of fundamental market economy principles – stable future expectations, excludability, and individual welfare – is truly remarkable. Throughout this historic document, words such as reputation or credibility (*shixin yumin*), incentives (*jijixin*), material welfare or interests (*wuzhi liyi*), democratic rights (*minzhu quanli*), and political rights (*zhengzhi quanli*) frequently appear.

This positive-sum stance led to a host of concrete policies. For one thing, it justified the costly decision to raise procurement prices, a decision, as Naughton (2007, p. 89) points out, involved substantial trade-offs – planners had to reduce investments and scale back technology imports in order to pay for the grain imports.

The other implication is that the state came to trust the spontaneous forces of the market rather than imposing its own vision on the economy. This sentiment was best expressed by Wan Li, the vice premier in charge of the rural sector and a pioneering reformer. He had this to say: "Ordinarily, our work should accommodate the needs of agricultural development rather than forcing the peasants to accommodate to us" (Wan Li 1992 <1982>, p. 149). In the same speech, Wan put forward the view that officials should not prohibit activities even if they are at odds with the prevailing rules and regulations. In the form of a question, Wan asked whether the rules and regulations should be relaxed further (rather than, as implied, banning the activities themselves). He did not explicitly say yes, but he implored government officials at all levels to fully debate the merits and demerits of the issues. This kind of policy flexibility and market-consistent stance goes a long way toward explaining how China moved so far in the direction of a market economy in the 1980s, even as the overall political environment seemed to be prohibitively forbidding.

The accommodation to the reality on the ground is probably the single most significant hallmark of the 1980s. Naughton (1996) has a succinct formulation for this period, stressing the importance of the "crucial first move" by the central government – by reducing rural tax rates, raising agricultural prices, and increasing investments in the agricultural sector. But the fact that the Chinese leadership was willing to be so accommodating to the spontaneous market forces on the ground is not a trivial fact. Respecting market signals – by policy elites with unconstrained power – is a tall order. In the next chapter, I document the decisions of the leadership in the 1990s to dramatically curtail the highly productive credit allocations to rural entrepreneurs in order to carry out their own technocratic blueprint of economic development.

3.5 Microeconomic Flexibility

The policy of accommodation explains the expanding scope of microeconomic flexibility in the 1980s. The most impressive example can be found in the size of private-sector employment. In the early 1980s, the employment size of private businesses was considered ideologically sensitive. In 1981, the *People's Daily* carried a series of articles and readers' letters debating the issue of private-sector employment. The tone, as noted by Chinese researchers, was frank but measured and rational (Zhang Houyi and Ming Lizhi 1999). The root of the controversy was the Marxist theory of labor surplus. The 1983 No. 1 document issued a rule that rural household businesses – with two owners – could employ up to five "apprentices." This formulation established what was often viewed as the ceiling on private employment at seven workers per firm. (In *Das Kapital*, Karl Marx used a fictional example of a private firm employing eight workers to illustrate his labor surplus theory.)

The reality is that the reformist leadership never rigidly enforced the seven-employee rule. The World Bank TVE study could not find a single known case of private entrepreneurs being punished because they exceeded the seven-person employment rule (Lin 1990). Mr. Nian, as noted before, employed hundreds of workers and he was by no means alone. I have also provided survey evidence – based on PSS1993 – that rural businesses employed far more workers than the seven-employee ceiling. This is true both in terms of the average employment size as well as the employment size of the firms in the 90th percentile.

The reason is not at all surprising. A close reading of the government decrees reveals that the employment restriction was never intended to be prohibitive. In fact, the 1983 rule itself contained deliberately flexible provisions. Local officials were urged not to promote but also not to crack down on those who exceeded the seven-employee rule. The overall tone of the 1983 No. 1 document, which set forth the seven-employee rule, was pro private sector rather than restricting its development.[59] The operative phrase in the internal policy deliberations on the employment issue was "wait and see" (Zhang Houyi and Ming Lizhi 1999), a phrase that nicely captures the essence of the policy approach in the 1980s.

Ever pragmatic, the reformist leaders proposed measures that would ease the ideological tensions of the employment issue while permitting the practice itself. The 1984 No. 1 document asked the private-run businesses to create and contribute to a "collective reserve fund," which in effect was a form of profit-sharing with employees. The document also proposed a cap on dividend payouts. These measures, although not attenuating the private nature of these businesses, were designed to ease any tensions with labor.

Another form of microeconomic flexibility was private entry into the nonagricultural sectors. Very early on, private entry was not only allowed but also *encouraged.* Consider the following paragraph (Ministry of Agriculture 1985, p. 2):

The state, collectives, and individuals should *simultaneously* embark on businesses in *all* sectors of manufacturing, supply and procurement, science and technology, and services in the rural areas. The government should especially support voluntary forms of businesses. Supply cooperatives should be *completely* autonomous, responsible for their own profits and losses and managing operations on their own. They should be subject to democratic supervision by the masses (italics added by the author).

The 1985 No. 1 document gives explicit permission to individual businesses to bid for infrastructural construction projects and encouraged private mining (Editorial Committee of TVE Yearbook 1989b, p. 502). As pointed out in the last section, the private TVEs had a dominant market position in the transportation sector compared with the collective TVEs. The private TVEs also seemed to have engaged in building infrastructure. For example, in one city of Fujian, private TVEs built and financed three railways and they won the right to operate them as well (Editorial Committee of TVE Yearbook 1989b, p. 84). Private infrastructure financing and construction were even more substantial in Wenzhou. According to one estimate, 70 percent of the small township construction was financed by TVEs (most of which were private). Private financing and construction extended to primary and junior high schools, movie theaters, roads, tap-water facilities, bridges, electricity generation, and so on (Editorial Committee of TVE Yearbook 1989b, p. 118).

Private businesses were allowed to raise equity capital. In the same 1985 document that authorized the establishment of shareholding enterprises, individuals could purchase shares with capital or acquire shares through contributions of production materials and labor. Lifting the restrictions on TVEs occurred even earlier – in 1979 when a State Council circular removed the restrictions on the large-scale expansion of nonagricultural activities by TVEs. Around the same time, the restrictions on a number of nonagricultural activities by rural households were also lifted. The latter policy change stimulated a great spurt of private-sector development in rural China (Byrd and Lin 1990, p. 7).

I detail the financial liberalization during this period in the next chapter. Financial experiments were one of the unheralded areas of microeconomic flexibility in the 1980s. In a 1985 document, the State Council outlines 10 policy measures to revive the rural economy,[60] one of which is financial liberalization. The rural credit cooperatives were allowed to retain all profits after the reserve deposits at the central bank. They were encouraged to source deposits and lend across regions, in effect making it possible for the credit cooperatives to compete with one another. Interest rates were allowed to float within a band (as in the statement, "Some rates can approach market rates"). The rural credit cooperatives were authorized to lend to peasants in industrial and commercial businesses on the condition that the agricultural needs for credits were given priority. The document permitted informal financing.

4 Conclusion

It is no exaggeration to say that an understanding of Chinese economy and reforms requires a detailed, direct grasp of the economic policies and institutions in the 1980s. The story of the 1980s was written by the tens of millions of Chinese rural entrepreneurs. The vigor of rural entrepreneurship during that period is as remarkable as the lack of knowledge in the West about some of the basic facts. By far, the single most significant development in the 1980s was the TVE phenomenon. It is hard to identify another economic phenomenon so important and yet so systematically misconstrued.

Among top economics journals, one finds many illustrations – often backed up by sophisticated mathematical models – of how publicly owned

TVEs can nevertheless be efficient. The trouble is that the vast majority of TVEs were never publicly owned in the first place. In this chapter, I provide numerous factual details to show that TVEs, as referred to by the Chinese, designate the *locations* of firms, not the *ownership* of firms. TVEs, as used by the Chinese, include private-sector businesses and, in the 1980s, the absolute majority of TVEs were private and almost all the new entrants were private. Although individually smaller, private TVEs in the 1980s began to account for a large share of employment and output. In some regions, especially the poor regions, they produced a majority of the output.

Among 12 million or so TVEs in the mid-1980s, 1.5 million were collective TVEs. For now, let me leave aside the issue that the efficiency claims made by economists were meant to apply to all TVEs rather than to their collective subset. Let's consider the *raison d'être* of collective TVEs. One prominent theory is that collective TVEs deterred private stripping of public assets (Stiglitz 2006). Facts are, once again, inconvenient. Consider the example of Kelon. The founding entrepreneurs registered the firm as collective because there was really no feasible alternative. The collective registration provided a mechanism for Rongqi township to expropriate what ought to have been straightforward private assets in the first place.

The Kelon example illustrates the treacherous side of directional liberalism. For many years, Kelon was effectively run as a private-sector firm. The Rongqi township respected the control rights of its true founders in part because of its goodwill and its self-constraints. But, it is also because Kelon was small and there was little to expropriate. When Kelon was worth billions, the incentives began to change. The helping hand turned into a grabbing hand. This is the price of directional liberalism: Property rights security was not institutionalized. This is the difference between directional liberalism and institutionalized liberalism. (Another difference, as I show in the next chapter, is that directional liberalism can be reversed.)

A factually correct interpretation of collective TVEs is that they enabled public stripping of private assets. Kelon was not alone. A Chinese academic draws the following conclusion, "No matter whether it contributes any capital, as long as an enterprise is established, in order to be licensed it has to be classified as township-sponsored or village-sponsored in some regions" (Editorial Committee of TVE Yearbook 1990, p. 255). Zhang and Ming (1999, p. 180) state, "Due to government regulations, construction projects could not be awarded to private firms directly, which forced rural private construction teams to wear the red hats of collective enterprises." This is expropriation *par excellence.*

Let me end this chapter where I started it. In 10 years from 1978 to 1988, the number of the Chinese poor – by the Chinese definition – was reduced by 154 million, compared with 62 million during the next 10 years from 1989 to 1999. The vibrancy of rural entrepreneurship was an important contributory factor. Table 2.2 shows the deep and wide geographic and economic reach of the private TVEs. By 1987, 688 million rural Chinese – out of a total of 860 million – lived in provinces that had private TVEs producing a moderate (above 30 percent) to high (above 50 percent) portion of rural output. And this took place only eight years after the start of the reforms. It is probably history's single biggest private-sector success story.

The achievements of the 1980s are notable because the decade was bereft of many of the factors that are widely thought of as key components of Chinese success. There was very little FDI and trade, and "Chinese infrastructures" then implied the same connotations as the Indian infrastructures today. The single-minded policy focus was absent because the politics were very complicated. Many of the conservative elders were alive and well and they were always poised to intervene. The reformist leaders, such as Hu Yaobang, Zhao Ziyang, and Wan Li, had to constantly settle for compromises and intermediate solutions. Recall that only 3 out of 29 Party secretaries supported agricultural reforms at the outset. The most salient feature of the rural reforms is that the reforms started without a solid policy consensus.

And there was no ideological commitment to economic liberalization. Just fresh from the Cultural Revolution, none of the Chinese policy makers had been exposed to free-market ideology, unlike reformers in Latin America or Indonesia (the so-called "Chicago boys" or "Berkeley boys"). Chinese reforms did not happen by "a blueprint approach" whereby the policy makers devised economic policy solutions on the basis of abstract ideas. In this aspect, I agree with the view that the key ingredients of Chinese success in the 1980s were the context-specific innovations, a heavy reliance on local knowledge and a learning-by-doing experimentation (Naughton 1996; Rodrik 2007). My disagreement has to do with how the outcome of that Chinese experiment is characterized. As I showed in this chapter, the outcome of the Chinese experiment in the 1980s was actually private ownership and vibrant entrepreneurship and a degree of institutional convergence. It was not selective interventionism by the government and public ownership of firms.

A policy approach based on learning by doing may be technically simple and straightforward, but it requires a massive dose of self-constraint on the part of the policy makers. Policy makers have to learn to hone to the realities on the ground rather than imposing their own visions. In an unconstrained political system, that the policy makers were willing to let peasants experiment and to trust them to come up with right solutions is nothing short of extraordinary. This political economy dynamics is the single most important feature of the decade of the 1980s. This point will become clearer in the next chapter where I show that the Chinese authorities in the 1990s responded to the rising problems caused by financial centralization with more financial centralization. Maybe there is no such thing as an ideology-free policy approach. Being pragmatic is an ideology in and of itself.

In its very essence, the story of the economic transition is one of two Chinas – the rural and more market-driven China versus the urban and more state-controlled China. The pace of the transition depends on which of these two Chinas has the political upper hand. In the 1980s, rural China dominated, as evidenced by the vibrant rural entrepreneurship facilitated by policy liberalization. Many of the desirable economic and social consequences ensued. In the 1990s, urban China asserted itself and, as I show in the next chapter, Chinese economic performance took a turn for the worse. We can apply the same framework to different regions in China. Shanghai is the classic and the extreme version of the urban policy model. Like China of the 1990s, GDP growth was fast but the income of average households stagnated and income disparity widened substantially. (I come back to the Shanghai story in Chapter 4.) Zhejiang represents the continuation of the rural model of the 1980s. Its GDP grew very fast but, unlike Shanghai, the household income of average residents of Zhejiang also grew very fast. Both the rural and urban policy models can produce fast GDP growth but the implications for the welfare of the average Chinese differ substantially between them.

Finally, we pay attention to the rural entrepreneurs because the rural entrepreneurs, by definition, are indigenous entrepreneurs. Many of the rural entrepreneurs are located in poor and interior regions of the country and, unlike Mr. Liu of Lenovo, they cannot easily escape from the straightjacket of illiberal economic and financial policies and institutions by accessing Hong Kong's capital market and its legal institutions. The welfare consequences are severe. The rural entrepreneurs are the poorest and yet they are most burdened by the credit constraints on private sector and regulatory restrictions. The next chapter focuses on the decade of the 1990s and I show what happened to China's rural entrepreneurs and to rural income growth as the policy environment was reversed from its liberal direction of the 1980s.

APPENDIX

A.1 TVE Semantics and Data

There are two Chinese terms that are indiscriminately expressed in English as TVEs. One term is *xiangzhen qiye*, literally meaning rural and urban township enterprise. The second term is *xiangcun qiye*, or township and village enterprise (TVE). "TVE" is now a standard reference in English but it is important to note that TVEs are actually a subset of *xiangzhen qiye*. The official Chinese documents and policy pronouncements use *xiangzhen qiye* to refer to the entire TVE phenomenon. As explained in the text, the Chinese term for TVEs – *xiangzhen qiye* – is a broad classification of firms that includes both collective TVEs sponsored by townships and villages as well as straightforward rural private enterprises. *Xiangcun qiye*, on the other hand, refers to collective TVEs only. To keep the exposition straightforward, I have retained the English usage of the term to refer to *xiangzhen qiye* in the text. I use collective TVEs to refer to *xiangcun qiye*.

In the Chinese economic studies, the standard source of data is *Chinese Statistical Yearbook* (CYS). CYS, as well as the Ministry of Agriculture cited in the text, report data on TVE employment. A reader familiar with CYS may find some inconsistencies between CYS and the data reported by the Ministry of Agriculture. CYS reports rural employment data under three categories: TVEs, private-run enterprises, and individual businesses. For 2002, CYS reported TVE employment of 132.9 million, 14.1 million in the rural private-run enterprises, and 24.7 million in the rural individual businesses (NBS 2005, p. 121).

Notice the discrepancy with the figures provided in Table 2.1, which is based on the Ministry of Agriculture (2003). Table 2.1 reports a much larger private-run enterprise employment and individual business employment (35 million and 59.8 million, respectively). Notice also that the TVE employment reported by CYS, 132.9 million, matches exactly with the data from the Ministry of Agriculture. Thus, both publications are based on the same data source, but they report the employment data differently.

The Ministry of Agriculture breaks down TVE employment into collective, private-run, and individual components but CYS does not do so. From the reporting of CYS, 14.1 million in the rural private-run enterprises and 24.7 million in the rural individual businesses are not included in the 132.9 million total. One possibility, of course, is that this is a reporting error. Another possibility is that CYS data refer to those stand-alone rural private-run and individual businesses that do not simultaneously carry a

TVE label (and, therefore, they are outside the coverage of Ministry of Agriculture data). If this is the case, the size of the rural private sector is even larger than that reported by Ministry of Agriculture. Thus, the true rural private sector consists of rural private TVEs and stand-alone rural businesses. For 2002, this would yield a rural private employment of 136 million rather than 94 million only in the private TVEs.

A.2 Surveys of Private Business

In this chapter, we drew data from three surveys on private business. All three datasets were obtained from the Universities Service Centre at the Chinese University of Hong Kong. The first is the self-employment business survey conducted in 1991 (SEBS1991), which covered individual businesses in industry and commerce (*geti gongshang hu*). These are essentially self-employment proprietorships, although some also had outside employees. Under Chinese law, those businesses that employ less than seven workers are considered self-employment businesses. The survey was implemented in November and December 1991 and included 10 provinces or cities: Shanghai, Shandong, Hubei, Guizhou, Guangdong, Chengdu, Shenzhen, Xi'an, Shenyang, and Dalian.

The survey was designed by the State Economic Reform Commission and the All-China Industry and Commerce Federation. It covered a wide range of topics, from size of business, status of development, socioeconomic characteristics of the business owners, family finance, and views of the business environment. However, many variables contain a large number of missing values. The maximum number of observations is 13,245. I have used the portions of the survey that have the most complete information and the least number of missing values.

Our second and third surveys cover the more established private businesses. In Chinese, these firms are known as *siying qiye*, or privately run enterprises. They differ from the self-employment businesses in that they are much larger and they typically employ seven or more workers per firm. I drew data primarily from three such surveys. One was conducted in 1993 (private-sector survey in 1993, or PSS1993), another was conducted in 2004 (PSS2004), and the third one was conducted in 2006 (PSS2006). PSS1993 covered 1,440 firms, PSS2004 covered 3,012 firms, and PSS2006 covered 3,837 firms.

These surveys were a part of a regular series of nationwide surveys of the private sector, covering all the provinces in China. The surveys were organized by the Department of the United Front, the branch of the Communist

Party in charge of managing relations with the non-Communist components of Chinese society and the economy, and the All-China Federation of Industry and Commerce, the organization that represents the private sector. The surveys were designed with heavy input from researchers and academics at the Chinese Academy of Social Sciences, the Beijing Academy of Social Sciences, and China People's University.[61]

The sample selection is stratified by both economic and political criteria. The private-sector surveys focus on six types of regions selected on the basis of both political and economic criteria. The political criteria were (1) the provincial capital, (2) a prefecture-level city, and (3) a county-level city. With respect to the economic criteria, the survey sampled firms located in the advanced, medium, and least advanced areas. Within each region, the firms were randomly selected from the registration lists maintained by the local bureaus of industry and commerce. This means that these firms already operated in the formal sector at the time of the survey. The potential bias here is that those private firms most severely discriminated against – and that therefore chose to go underground – are not included in the survey. This is not a debilitating factor for our purposes because it is the formal sector that provides the meaningful benchmark on entrepreneurial development in a region. The second potential bias is that the survey is probably more heavily weighted toward the larger private-sector firms because the members of the All-China Federation of Industry and Commerce are more established firms. Therefore, the results presented in the chapter should be interpreted as reflecting characteristics of the larger private-sector firms.

The main questions in the two surveys cover (1) firm size, status of development, organization, and operation; (2) management system and decision-making style; (3) socioeconomic background of the enterprise owners; (4) social mobility and network of the owners; (5) source and composition of employees and employee–employer relations; (6) self-assessment by the entrepreneurs on a range of issues related to government–business relations, the business environment, and financing; and (7) income, expenditures, and assets of the entrepreneurs. Important for our purposes, both the 1993 and 2004 surveys contain information on employment and a number of critical entrepreneurial characteristics.

THREE

A Great Reversal

I used two phrases to describe rural reforms in the 1980s of the last century: "Advancing of non-governmental sector and retreat of the state." As for the 1990s of the last century, I also have two descriptions – "Advancing of the state and retreat of the non-governmental sector" and "retreat of rights of the people and advancing of the rights of the government." In the 1980s, the standard of living of the peasants improved day by day and the level of tensions was low in the rural area. In the 1990s, although rural economy continued to develop, the livelihood of the peasants was difficult and the level of tensions in the rural area accelerated considerably.
  – Li Changping (2005), a former Party secretary in Jianli county of Hubei province

We began the last chapter with the story of Mr. Nian, the impoverished and self-deprecating rural entrepreneur who created a marketing storm in the early 1980s with his Idiot's Seeds. The decade also ended with him. In September 1989, Mr. Nian was arrested. The local procuratorate of Wuhu city where Mr. Nian's business was headquartered charged him with crimes of corruption and "embezzlement of state property." In 1990, the city government shut down his firm. It was an inglorious end to a once sensational brand – and brand-name – of Chinese indigenous capitalism.

The charges against Mr. Nian were so trumped up that they did not even pass muster with the low evidentiary threshold of the Chinese courts. The municipal court of Wuhu city found Mr. Nian guilty on the corruption and embezzlement charges, but the intermediate court of Anhui province overturned the verdict. Mr. Nian, after all, was running a private firm so the charge of "embezzling state property" was rather strange in the first place. The intermediate court found him guilty on charges of something else – hooliganism – and sentenced him to three years in prison for having had immoral relationships with 10 women between 1984 and 1989. (Upon hearing the verdict, Mr. Nian reportedly retorted, "No, twelve.")

The fate of Mr. Nian signified a new economic and political era for China's rural entrepreneurs. Politically, the post-Tiananmen conservative leadership mounted a nationwide crackdown on China's private sector. This eased somewhat in 1993 and 1994 and substantially thereafter, but a more binding constraint began to impinge on rural entrepreneurship for the rest of the 1990s (and still persists to this day). The prevailing economic policy in the 1990s was to favor the urban areas over the rural areas and to favor foreign capitalists – FDI – over indigenous capitalists. There are other components of this policy model as well, including an emphasis on technocratic development and an industrial policy approach in favor of large firms. The cumulative effect of all these policies was a dramatic change in the balance of power between the two Chinas – the rural China that is more capitalistic and market-driven and the urban China that is more state-controlled. In the 1990s, the balance tilted decisively in favor of the urban China.

Fittingly, 1989 marked both the decadal and policy turning points. As is well known, 1989 was a year of political turmoil. Young university students protested and held hunger strikes on Beijing's Tiananmen Square for almost two months before the authorities decided to forcibly clear the square. In this book, my focus is on the economic implications of what famously is known as the "Tiananmen crackdown." Most Western analysts, although acknowledging the political importance of the Tiananmen crackdown, view the event as a brief pause in China's economic reforms. Barry Naughton, in his textbook on the Chinese economy, has a section devoted to this period entitled, "The Tiananmen Interlude." He notes (2007): "The conservative attempts to roll back reforms were completely without success, however, and are often forgotten."

Naughton is correct that the immediate ideological effect of the Tiananmen crackdown was short-lived. The political assault on the private sector fizzled out fairly quickly after Deng Xiaoping's famous "Southern Tour" in 1992. But, the quote by Li Changping – noted at the beginning of this chapter – that reforms in the 1990s stagnated or even reversed themselves reveals a different judgment, at least about rural China. Li Changping is intimately familiar with rural China. He began his career as a rural official in 1983 and, by the late 1990s, he was the Party secretary of a rural county in Hubei province. We should take his view seriously.

The issue is whether Li's judgment can be supported by aggregate data. It is not sufficient to cite the view of one official – even one as knowledgeable about rural affairs as Li Changping. It is possible that Li was simply noting one data point about what was happening in his own county, and we should not extrapolate the observations of a region to the entire country. As in the rest of this book, I have gone through pages and pages of government documents, including more than 20 volumes of detailed bank documents, directives, and regulations that as far as I know, have never been analyzed by Western academics. I have also assembled a dataset that consists of household income surveys and private-sector firm surveys. The totality of both the qualitative and quantitative evidence strongly supports Li's judgment that there was a substantial policy reversal in the 1990s, primarily in the rural areas.

My conjecture, although not yet an empirically settled view, is that the economic effects of Tiananmen were actually far more long-lasting than we previously believed. One observable effect of Tiananmen is that the backgrounds and outlooks of Chinese leaders before and after Tiananmen were very different. Many of the reformist leaders before Tiananmen – symbolized by Zhao Ziyang in particular – had first gained national prominence as a result of their economic stewardship of the poor rural provinces. More than any other politician, Zhao Ziyang and Wan Li had launched China's transformative rural reforms, in Sichuan and Anhui provinces, respectively. The leaders of the 1980s represented the rural and, by implication, the more market-driven part of China. Their demise was behind the increasingly urban biases in the orientation of China's economic policies in the 1990s.

The leaders of the 1990s came from entirely different backgrounds. The two top leaders, Jiang Zemin and Zhu Rongji, had built their political credentials in the most state-controlled and least-reformed urban bastion of China – Shanghai. They were consummate technocrats, trained as engineers, and they had spent many years primarily in the SOE system. Shanghai, as I detail in the next chapter, represents the apex of the urban bias in a political and economic system already laden with urban biases. Their ascendancy to national positions was a direct result of the political aftermath of Tiananmen.

The second policy development after Tiananmen was a significant reversal of the policy approaches prevailing in the 1980s. The sharpest reversal occurred in rural finance. Many of the very productive financial experiments were terminated and credit constraints on small-scale, low-tech, and labor-intensive rural entrepreneurship were tightened. There were other policy reversals as well, including backtracking on political reforms and centralizing the administrative and fiscal affairs of rural governance, and a fiscal recentralization in 1994 that substantially reduced the autonomy of the provinces. (The latter development is under-researched. A much-heralded Chinese innovation, "federalism, Chinese style," in fact ended in

1994, with potential long-term harmful effects.[1]) The cumulative effects of all these policies brought a change in the trajectory of capitalism in China. In the 1980s, a version of market-driven, small-scale, and welfare-improving rural capitalism was developing vibrantly. In the 1990s, China continued to march toward capitalism but toward a very different kind of capitalism. Whereas Chinese capitalism in the 1980s was a rags-to-riches capitalism, the capitalism in the 1990s led to sharp income inequalities, a reduction of social opportunities available to the rural population, slower income growth, and an investment-heavy growth pattern. In this chapter, I begin by describing the sharp reversal in the fortunes of the hundreds of millions of rural Chinese in the 1990s. In the 1990s, their income growth slowed down considerably compared with the 1980s. One notable development was that rural entrepreneurship experienced many difficulties. While farming became increasingly less lucrative, rural Chinese flocked to labor markets to contribute their labor rather than to start their own businesses. This was so despite the fact that the returns from entrepreneurship exceeded labor income and that labor income, adjusted for inflation and time allocation, in fact declined drastically in the 1990s. The TVEs began to languish after the mid-1990s, and they languished as essentially *private* firms rather than as collective firms.

Sections two and three of this chapter describe the policy and political dynamics behind this monumental change in China's countryside. I first contrast developments in the financial sector between the two decades. A little-known fact about the 1980s is that significant and imaginative innovations occurred in rural finance. The pro-private sector tilt in policies regarding access to bank credits was substantial. There was also an explicit effort to permit private entry into the financial sector and to benchmark the performance of the state-owned banks against that of the informal financial sector. All of this was to change in the 1990s. Decision making in loan policies became more centralized and many of the productive financial innovations were discontinued. The state reversed its stance on informal finance completely, no longer viewing private credits as a useful complement to formal finance but rather as lethal competition to be firmly stamped out.

Section three of this chapter describes other broad changes between the two decades. In particular, the promising political reforms that began in the 1980s were thoroughly repudiated. Those reforms had aimed at fostering some intra-Party democracy and moving in the direction of more accountability of the CCP. Between 1989 and 2002, these reforms stagnated completely. There was a massive effort to recentralize the fiscal and political management of China's vast countryside. Last, but not least, an important development in the 1990s was the rise of a technocratic state. A core feature of that state was that it viewed economic development in engineering terms and that it had the strength of conviction – and invested a huge amount of political capital – to force through its policy visions, at staggering immediate political and social costs and, in the long run, at huge economic costs as well. Above all, this was a state that went to extraordinary lengths to empower itself both politically and economically. All of these developments reinforced the effects of the increasing financing repression of the rural private sector and were directly responsible for the social and economic malaise in the form of what came to be known in China as the "three rural crises" – the crisis of agriculture, the crisis of rural governance, and the crisis of the peasantry.

1 A Tale of Two Decades

Recall the finding in the introductory chapter of this book that the fixed-asset investment (FAI) share by the private sector contracted beginning in 1993. Between 1981 and 1989, the private sector's share of fixed-asset investments was 21.4 percent; it declined to 19.8 percent during the 1990–1992 period and then to 13.3 percent between 1993 and 2001. The annual growth of rural private fixed-asset investments slowed to a crawling pace in the 1990s from its torrential pace in the 1980s.

This monumental reversal in the 1990s, affecting the fortunes of hundreds of millions of rural Chinese, has received scant attention. The prevailing view is that in the 1990s, China not only continued but actually deepened the reforms of the 1980s. This is the famous gradualist perspective on China. A central theme of this chapter is that in the 1990s, China reversed many of its productive policies of the 1980s, with real consequences. I show in this section that the income growth in rural China slowed down in the 1990s. In particular, business income growth – the income derived from owning and operating a business – slowed down drastically. I show that in the 1990s, rural Chinese, who otherwise could have entered into entrepreneurship under more propitious conditions, instead "chose" to crowd into the already highly competitive labor markets. They did so despite the fact that not only did the returns from their labor contributions pale in comparison with their business income, they were decreasing as well. The blocking of entrepreneurial opportunities must have been a factor behind this development.

Like the rest of this book, I rely heavily on government reports and documents as the empirical basis from which to draw my findings. The following excerpts are from a report prepared by a researcher at a think tank associated with the State Council. The researcher, Zhao Shukai (1999), published his findings in the *State Council Investigation and Research Report* in 1999:

- "For peasants in certain regions, their burdens began to increase in the 1990s."
- In Li village of Henan province, "starting in 1992, most rural households began to experience something new: Their hard-earned money was taken away by the village cadres."
- In Xuantanggang village, "in the 1980s peasants turned over 170 *jin* of grain per *mu* to the state; it is now 430 *jin* per *mu*."
- "As evidenced by government documents, [the taking of the peasants' belongings] by force began to occur on a large scale in the early 1990s."

The sentiments expressed by Mr. Zhao and Mr. Li quoted at the beginning of this chapter are the tale of the two decades to be told in the following pages. I show that the qualitative assessment reached by Mr. Zhao and Mr. Li are systematically supported by the findings based on large-scale survey data.

1.1 A Reversal of Fortunes

A central theme of this chapter is that the decades of the 1980s and 1990s are extremely different from each other and that economic performance in the 1990s was inferior to that in the 1980s. Any alleged performance differences between the 1980s and the 1990s bear directly on the validity of any explanations about China. The gradualist view of China is supported by data that show China's performance growing stronger over time. The view that China retreated from the reforms will find support in data that show China's performance to be weakening over time.

Let me first cite a finding that directly contradicts my views. It is important to address these data issues up front because we should be explicit about how the data are organized and presented. We again return to Naughton (2007) because it is the most comprehensive collection of the views and data schooled in the gradualist perspective of China. Using the urban and rural household survey data collected by the NBS, Naughton (2007, Table 9.1, p. 210) calculates real per capita household income for rural and urban residents. He shows that between 1985 and 1991, the average rural net household income grew at 2.8 percent per year, compared with 4.9 percent per year on average during the 1991–2004 period. (I mainly focus on the rural areas here, but Naughton also shows in his calculations the superior performance of urban disposable income in the 1990s, compared with the second half of the 1980s: 7.7 versus 4.8 percent.)

It turns out that the findings are highly sensitive to how the calculations are periodized. The average figure for the 1985–1991 period includes three years (1989, 1990, and 1991) in which rural households registered the slowest ever rates of income growth in the reform era. In fact, in 1989, rural households registered a negative income growth. The inclusion of these three years in his calculations will necessarily depress the growth rates for the 1980s.

Treating the three years of the Tiananmen interlude as part of the 1980s is problematic. Zhao Ziyang, who presided over economic stewardship of the country in the 1980s, was purged in May 1989 and Jiang Zemin formally assumed the position of Party general secretary in June 1989. It was Jiang, not Zhao, who presided over China between 1989 and 1991. A more analytically accurate approach would be to consider the Tiananmen interlude as a part of the 1990s. Those three years represented a massive retreat, or even an explicit repudiation, of the policies of the 1980s. Credit financing for the private sector was reduced drastically; new restrictions on private businesses – the vast majority located in the rural areas – were enacted; and, as we saw in Chapter 1, rural private fixed-asset investments declined. At a minimum, the three years of the Tiananmen interlude should be considered separately from the 1980s.

If we start with the basic premise that economic policies have a substantial bearing on economic performance, we should categorize Chinese economic performance on the basis of political leadership and economic policies. I do so here on the basis of the same source of data used by Naughton. Panel (1) of Figure 3.1 graphs the annual average growth rates of urban and rural household income against four distinct policy periods. The first policy period is that of rural entrepreneurship between 1979 and 1988 (and the subperiod between 1984 and 1988); the second period is the Tiananmen interlude between 1989 and 1991; the third period is the era of Jiang Zemin and Zhu Rongji; and the fourth period is that of Hu Jintao and Wen Jiabao. The income figures are deflated to their 1978 prices using the official urban and rural income deflators. (Naughton's data are deflated to their 2004 prices.)

A striking pattern in the graph is how low the rural household income growth was during the Tiananmen interlude. Average growth in 1989, 1990, and 1991 was only 0.7 percent compared with the double-digit growth during the first eight years of the 1980s. This underscores my earlier point – that classifying the Tiananmen interlude as a part of the 1980s substantially

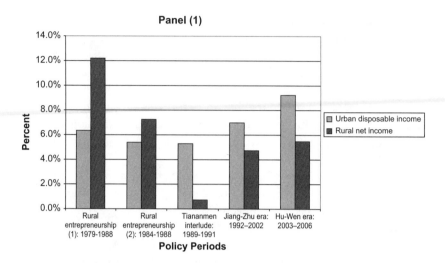

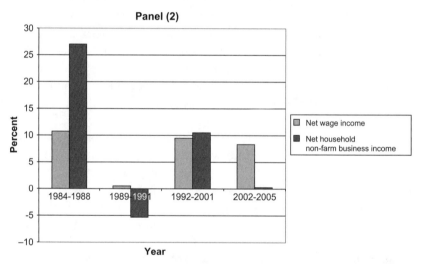

Figure 3.1. A great reversal. Panel (1): Average real growth rates of urban and rural per capita household income (based on household surveys, %). Panel (2): Real average annual growth rates of wage and non-farm business income (based on rural household surveys, %). *Note:* The data for the 1984–1988 period are reported separately here because some analysts believe that the price deflators for the first half of the 1980s are not reliable. *Source:* Based on rural and urban household surveys, various years.

understates the achievement of the 1980s. A second noteworthy feature of the graph is the discrepancy between urban and rural income growth. In the 1980s, rural income grew significantly faster than urban income; in the 1990s, it was the other way around. Again, as in so many areas of the Chinese economy, the Tiananmen interlude marked the change.

Rural household income in the 1980s grew at an extraordinarily robust rate. The average growth for the 1978–1988 period was 12.2 percent (after inflation is excluded). This was the decade of entrepreneurship referred to in the previous chapter. A legitimate issue is the reliability of the data. Naughton points out that the data for the earlier period are inaccurate because the rural consumer price index understates rural inflation (and thus overstates growth). This is an important insight. It explains an otherwise paradoxical contraction of income growth in the mid-1980s when rural policies became even more liberal. Whereas there may have been some reduction, the more important reason is the correction in the data series rather than a real policy change.

Let me assume the income growth for the entire decade of the 1980s to be at the rate prevailing in the second half of the 1980s – 7.2 percent rather than 12.2 percent. Even by this conservative estimate, the 1980s were still substantially stronger than the 1990s. During the Jiang Zemin–Zhu Rongji era, from 1992 to 2001, the average growth rate was 4.7 percent, a reduction by 35 percent compared with the rate during the second half of the 1980s. If we look at the entire Jiang Zemin period from 1989 to 2001, the average growth rate of rural income was only 3.8 percent, slightly under half of the growth rate in the second half of the 1980s. During the Hu–Wen period since 2002, growth recovered somewhat, to 5.5 percent. It is important to stress that these growth differences were not a result of the migrant labor income. The net rural household income includes labor income earned by household members working in locations outside the residence of the polled households.

The annual difference between the rural entrepreneurship growth rate of 7.2 percent and the state-led growth rate of 3.8 percent is not an abstract matter. It entails real and substantial income and welfare implications for hundreds of millions of Chinese peasants. This is not only because of the difference in the two growth rates but also because of the extraordinarily long tenure of the Jiang–Zhu leadership – 13 years. If, in the 1990s, the income of Chinese rural households had grown at the rate prevailing in the 1980s – that is, 7.2 percent as opposed to the actual 3.8 percent between 1989 and 2001 – compounded over 13 years, the two rates translated into a massive difference in the levels of rural income. Roughly, a Chinese peasant was 52 percent poorer than he would have been under the lower of Zhao's growth rates (i.e., assuming 7.2 percent for the entire decade of the 1980s).

That rural income growth began to recover under the Hu–Wen leadership is an important finding. For one thing, it illustrates the importance of policy. It is widely known that the Hu–Wen leadership began to address the rural problems in a proactive manner, even copying the format of the 1980s by issuing consecutive No. 1 policy documents dedicated to rural issues. We can debate whether their measures are adequate to the monumental task – many of these measures were designed to reduce the rural tax rates rather than to augment income growth, an issue I return to in the concluding chapter of this book – but there is no doubt that Hu and Wen take rural issues more seriously than did the Jiang–Zhu leadership.

The recovery of rural income growth under the Hu–Wen leadership is also analytically significant. Some may argue that rural income in the 1990s would naturally slow down after a period of rapid growth in the 1980s. After all, rural income would have had to grow from a higher base in the early 1990s than in the early 1980s. Simple logic says that it is harder to grow from a higher base than from a lower base.

It is extremely important to debunk this view because it attributes the slowdown to a natural economic process rather than to the policies of the 1990s. First, let me emphasize that in 1992, the per capita rural net income was only 449 yuan (in 1978 prices); this was about 81 dollars. It is absurd to believe that income at that low level would cap the growth. The reasoning is also squarely contradicted by the urban data: The level of urban income growth accelerated in the 1990s over the level in the 1980s despite it being from a higher base. The fact that rural income began to recover under the Hu–Wen leadership shows the importance of policy in affecting the growth rates of rural income.

1.2 From Entrepreneurs to Laborers

For rural residents, the most effective way to alleviate poverty is to transition out of low value-added agriculture and into higher value-added industrial or service activities. Theoretically, a Chinese peasant has two options to transition out of agriculture. He can start his own business, either providing services such as buying or selling of agricultural produce or production inputs, or going into the manufacturing of industrial products. Another option is paid employment: A rural resident can become a wage earner by working in a factory or a business owned by someone else. Chapter 2 describes the robust development of both sources of rural industrialization in the 1980s when rural households entered into entrepreneurship on a massive scale and TVEs grew rapidly to absorb the rural labor force.

We know from the previous section that the overall rural household income slowed down considerably in the 1990s. To understand the dynamics of this declining growth, we should decompose the components of the rural household income. By 1988, a typical rural household had 545 yuan in net per capita income. Of this, 118 yuan came from wage earnings and 58 yuan came from non-farm business earnings (i.e., profits from operating non-farm businesses). These two non-farm sources of income constituted 21.6 and 10.6 percent, respectively, of the overall household income. Because in the long run, agricultural income was not expected to grow substantially, the growth of rural household income critically depended on the growth of these two non-farm sources of income. Once again, the decades of the 1980s and 1990s differ substantially on this dimension.

Panel (2) of Figure 3.1 presents the annual real growth rates of wage income and non-farm business income averaged over the four policy periods. (Unless otherwise noted, business income refers to non-farm business income in the subsequent paragraphs.) The most visible pattern in the graph is the huge decline in business income growth after 1989. Between 1984 and 1988, growth averaged 27 percent, but during the Tiananmen interlude, growth tanked into negative territory (−0.58 percent). In the 1990s, business income grew in real terms but at a fraction of the rate prevailing in the 1980s (10.5 versus 27 percent). Then, during the Hu–Wen period, growth collapsed completely, to only 0.3 percent. This latest development is very worrisome and evidence that the ameliorative policy measures to solve the rural problems during this time fall far short of addressing the root cause of the problems in rural China – the difficulties faced by rural entrepreneurs to move out of agriculture.

During the 1990s, the business income share of rural income was higher than the level prevailing in the 1980s: 12.4 percent during the 1992–2001 period versus 8.5 percent during the 1984–1988 period. The point here is that the speed at which rural Chinese transitioned out of agriculture through the entrepreneurship channel slowed down in the 1990s, not that non-farm entrepreneurship in the 1990s was at a lower absolute level than that in the 1980s. That said, it is important to point out the following huge difference between the 1980s and the 1990s. In 1984, the non-farm business income share of rural income was only 5.6 percent. Within four years, this ratio almost doubled, to 10.6 percent in 1988. Therefore, the low ratio of the 1980s was primarily a function of the fact that the rural households had started out as completely agricultural producers in the early 1980s and thus they had much distance to go to make the transition to nonagricultural producers. That rural households in the 1990s had a higher business income share than in the 1980s owes largely to the fact that this ratio was already quite high in the late 1980s. Indeed, in the 1990s, this ratio fluctuated widely rather than increasing linearly. The ratio was 13.2 percent in 1993,

10.7 percent in 1995, 14.9 percent in 2000, and then it fell back to 11.5 percent in 2005.

In interpreting these data, let us keep in mind three sets of facts. First, overall rural income growth slowed down substantially in the 1990s compared with the 1980s. Therefore, the share of non-farm business income was rising in the 1990s in part because of the slowdown of overall household income. Second, recall that in 1988, this ratio was already 10.6 percent but in 2005 this ratio was only 11.5 percent, a very small increase. Third, the decade of the 1990s is associated with rapid industrialization and urbanization. Relative to the pace of structural transformation of the Chinese economy in the 1990s, the income composition of rural households experienced only a modest change.

In the 1990s, rural households largely maintained the same growth rate in wage income as they did in the 1980s. This is shown in Panel (2) of Figure 3.1. During the Tiananmen interlude, wage growth was very low. But, during the 1990s, real wage growth recovered to a level close to – but still lower than – wage growth during the 1980s: 9.5 percent during the 1992–2001 period versus 10.7 percent during the 1984–1988 period. During the 2002–2005 period, the growth slowed to 8.33 percent. Still, compared with the huge contrast in the growth rates of business income, these differences between the two decades appear to be small.

That the wage growth kept up while the business income did not provides a keen perspective about the 1990s. In the 1980s, rural residents had two options to transition out of agriculture – they could start non-farm businesses themselves by becoming entrepreneurs or they could contribute labor by becoming workers or paid employees in businesses owned by others. Consistent with our portrayal of the 1980s as an entrepreneurial decade, business income grew much faster than wage income. In the 1990s, the trends were reversed somewhat as the business income growth slowed down considerably, while the wage income stayed at a level close to that of the 1980s.

This was a major development in the 1990s: Rural entrepreneurship as a method to transition out of agriculture was curtailed, whereas transition through labor contributions remained a viable option. The next question is whether this change from rural entrepreneurship to labor participation was a predictable process of a market economy or whether it was the result of policy change. One can think of a perfectly logical explanation for the change – that the returns from labor contributions exceed those from entrepreneurial business income. Rational individuals would then choose to allocate more of their efforts toward paid employment rather than toward entrepreneurship.

The differentials between the per capita levels of wage and business income are not terribly revealing about what was occurring. The reason is that in both the 1980s and the 1990s, the per capita wage income always exceeded the per capita business income. In 1985, for example, the per capita wage income was 72.2 yuan, compared with the per capita business income of 32.2 yuan, a ratio of 2.24. In 1995, the per capita wage income was 353.7 yuan, compared with per capita business income of 169.3, a ratio of 2.1. So, clearly, the higher level of wage income relative to business income was a constant in both decades; thus, it cannot explain the change in growth rates between the two decades.

To understand the change in the 1990s, we need a measure that better captures the concept of returns – income earned per unit of labor or capital expended to generate those returns. We turn to a dataset compiled by the Central Committee Policy Research Office and the Ministry of Agriculture (2000). The volume reports on data aggregated from a large-scale survey effort conducted on some 20,000 rural households. The survey, known as the "300 Fixed Rural Observation Villages," commenced in 1984 and tracked the same 300 or so villages every year thereafter. The survey was not conducted in 1992 and 1994 and the published volume provides data only since 1986. We refer to this survey as the fixed household survey hereafter. (The Appendix to this chapter contains more detail about the survey.)

The survey asked the respondents to provide estimates of the number of labor days devoted to the following types of production activities: (1) operating household businesses (broken down by farm and non-farm activities), (2) paid employment activities in the region, and (3) paid migrant employment activities elsewhere. The survey also records streams of income per household attributed to these three production activities. This enables us to calculate the income earned per labor day devoted to a particular activity. To compare data across different years, we deflate all the earnings per labor day to their 1978 prices using the implicit rural income deflators.[2]

Table 3.1 presents earnings per labor day and the number of labor days devoted to two kinds of non-farm activities – household business and paid employment. Household business is essentially an entrepreneurial activity. An entrepreneur owns and operates the business and his income is the total of all the profits after the business expenses and taxes are deducted.

Table 3.1. *Earnings per day and labor-days devoted to household business and paid employment activities*

	1986–1988	1989–1991	1992–1999
	Panel (1): Household Business		
Non-farm business:			
–Income per day (yuan)	9.4 yuan	9.6 yuan	12.0 yuan
–Labor-days (% share of business and paid employment)	82.6 days (34.2%)	83.9 days (36.1%)	97.3 days (29.0%)
Of non-farm business: Industry			
–Income per day (yuan)	12.5 yuan	12.1 yuan	17.0 yuan
–Labor-days (% share of non-farm business)	22.8 days (27.6%)	22.5 days (26.8%)	19.6 days (20.1%)
	Panel (2): Paid Employment		
Local employment:			
–Income per day (yuan)	9.0 yuan	10.3 yuan	6.0 yuan
–Labor-days (% share of business and paid employment)	86.9 days (36.0%)	71.0 days (30.6%)	143.4 days (42.7%)
Migrant employment:			
–Income per day (yuan)	3.7 yuan	4.2 yuan	6.8 yuan
–Labor-days (% share of business and paid employment)	49.1 days (20.4%)	55.0 days (23.7%)	75.3 days (22.4%)

Note: The fixed household surveys were not carried out in 1992 and 1994. I calculated the values for these two years by taking the average of the two neighboring years. The rural income implicit deflators were used to convert all the values to 1978 prices.

Source: All the calculations are based on data compiled by the Central Committee Policy Research Office and Ministry of Agriculture (2000).

Examples of non-farm businesses include trading, transportation, and industrial production. Paid employment, as the term implies, is employment at a business owned by someone else. The income from paid employment is the wage. We have data on two kinds of paid employment – employment activities within the region of the household and migrant employment activities elsewhere.

Table 3.1 shows that the returns – defined as earnings per labor day – increased for non-farm businesses as a whole, especially for industrial businesses. During the 1986–1988 period, the per-day earnings from non-farm business were 9.4 yuan per rural household; this increased to 12 yuan during the 1990s. (Unless otherwise noted, all monetary figures refer to the household average amount per labor day.) This represents a 28 percent increase in real terms. For those households engaged in industrial business, the returns increased even more, from 12.5 yuan per day in the 1980s to 17 yuan per day in the 1990s, an increase of 36 percent. So, clearly, whatever the alleged constraints on rural entrepreneurship were in the 1990s, they did not reduce the returns from entrepreneurship as compared with the level in the 1980s. The returns from labor contributions to local employment establishments declined substantially in real terms. In the 1980s, per-day earnings were 9 yuan; in the 1990s, they averaged 6 yuan, a reduction of 33 percent. Migrant employment earnings experienced healthy growth, from 3.7 yuan to 6.8 yuan.

Putting these findings together suggests the following hypothesis about the 1990s. In the 1990s, there were policies in place that restricted the expansion of rural entrepreneurial businesses. I detail what these policies were in the next section, but credit constraints were among those that increased sharply in the 1990s. The existence of these constraints shows up in the pattern of labor days allocated to business and paid employment activities. Let us look at industrial business earnings. Earnings increased sharply in the 1990s but the time allocations by rural households went in the opposite direction. The number of days allocated to industrial businesses not only declined relatively but also absolutely. In the 1980s, the number of labor days dedicated to industrial business was 22.8 days but, in the 1990s, it was only 19.6 days. The share of labor days also declined, from 27.6 to 20.1 percent.

This is puzzling for several reasons. One is that although industrial business fetched the highest returns among the non-farm business activities, Chinese entrepreneurs in the 1990s allocated an increasing amount of time to other less lucrative activities, such as trading and transportation. The same puzzle exists regarding the time allocation between non-farm business and paid employment. Non-farm business fetched higher returns, and yet it was the paid employment that claimed the highest share of labor time. On a per-day basis, a Chinese rural household in the 1990s earned only half of what it was earning in the 1980s from local paid employment, and yet the same household allocated 143.4 days, an increase from 86.9 days in the 1980s, to this sharply less remunerative activity. The time allocation decisions are systematically mismatched with the relative returns from the various economic activities.

Both of these puzzles can be fairly easily explained by the existence of barriers to rural entrepreneurship. The barriers to entry or to expansion of rural entrepreneurship increased profits to incumbent businesses, thus explaining why non-farm business income increased in the 1990s. A plausible hypothesis explaining the paradoxical decline of labor days allocated to the higher-margin industrial business compared with the lower-margin service business is that industrial business is more capital-intensive; thus, it is more sensitive to credit constraints than is service business. This is consistent with our aggregate knowledge about China's private sector – that it is highly concentrated in the capital-extensive service sector.

If this reasoning is correct, contrary to the conventional view, rural China in the 1990s suffered from a lack of competition, not from excessive competition. Instead, all the competition converged on the labor markets. Because private businesses and TVEs were constrained from expanding, they created fewer job opportunities and, given that the agricultural income was declining, rural Chinese competed fiercely with one another in order to secure a job. This description is consistent with the wage compression documented previously as well as with the anecdotal accounts of rural Chinese bracing the cruel labor practices, huge wage arrears, and even labor indentures as they navigated the highly unfamiliar urban labor markets.

The other consequence was an increase in the flow of migrants. Because the local employment markets were overcrowded, rural residents sought jobs elsewhere. This latter explanation is consistent with what we know about the 1990s – that rural job migration increased substantially during the decade. This explanation is also consistent with a more recent story that shows that when the income prospects improved somewhat in the rural areas, places such as Guangdong suddenly began to experience a shortage of migrant labor. As Table 3.1 shows, the per-day earnings from migrant employment were not high in the first place, so a modest increase in earnings from other sources, such as agricultural earnings, would tilt the incentives away from migrant labor.

What does all of this mean? First, the rural industrialization that propelled the Chinese economy in the 1980s seems to have taken a very different turn in the 1990s. In the 1980s, the economy was entrepreneurially driven, with the labor deployment split almost evenly between entrepreneurial self-employment activities and paid employment activities. In the 1990s, the rural industrialization continued but it became more of an employment industrialization. The rural Chinese who were exiting from agriculture increasingly crowded into factories or establishments run by others rather than starting their own businesses. They made this "constrained choice" despite the demonstrably lower and decreasing returns from paid employment.

This finding entails enormous welfare implications. An activity that tied up the largest share of nonagricultural labor deployment by Chinese rural households actually yielded declining returns over time in the 1990s. This is puzzling, especially given the fact that the labor days devoted to household businesses not only experienced a relative decline compared with other lower-yielding activities, they also experienced an absolute decline over time. A natural question emerges, "Why did Chinese rural households not go into the higher-yielding business operations and instead crowded into the lower-yielding local paid employment?" The answer is that rural China was beginning to be afflicted with increasing financing constraints, and business creation, as an economic activity, was increasingly out of reach for many rural Chinese.

2 What Happened to the TVEs?

We disagree with the inappropriate exaggeration by Comrade Zhao Ziyang on the role of TVEs and with his policy of introducing some unhealthy TVE practices into the large and medium SOEs. But we do not deny the importance of the TVEs. The main challenge facing the TVEs is how to utilize raw materials and inputs in their local rural areas. The markets for the TVEs, except for a few TVEs aimed at the cities, should be primarily in the rural areas, providing for agricultural production and the daily commodities needed by the peasants.
                                        – Premier Li Peng, October 11, 1989 (Li Peng 1989)

It is now widely acknowledged that the TVEs faltered badly in the 1990s. The pace of job creation by TVEs dropped off sharply after 1996. In the 1980s, TVEs had been a primary source of employment and economic growth but, after 1996, the TVEs began to decline steadily. The value added of the TVEs in the share of GDP peaked in 1999 and then leveled off. The financial performance of the TVEs worsened, saddling the rural financial institutions with bad debt. According to survey data, township enterprises as a whole were incurring losses beginning in the mid-1990s (Park and Shen 2000) and today, the very term *TVE* has almost completely disappeared from the Chinese economic lexicon. The TVEs are history.

Understanding the downfall of the TVEs is critical. China is still a deeply rural society. In 2005, of 778.8 million people classified as active labor force in the official data, 484.9 million were rural employees (or 62 percent of the total). The TVEs were the most dynamic economic force in the 1980s and provided a ready channel for the rural Chinese to transition out of the low value-added agriculture. Their failings in the 1990s had a huge effect on the economic well-being of the rural population. The fate of the TVEs is also a barometer of the policy environment. As I showed in the last chapter, the vast majority of the TVEs were purely private; thus, policies toward TVEs were equivalent to policies toward the private sector. In this section,

I show that the policies toward TVEs became adverse in the 1990s and that it was this change in the policy environment more than those other factors emphasized by economists that explains the demise of TVEs.

2.1 The Downfall of the TVEs

The period from 1978 to 1996 was the "golden era" for TVEs. The period since then has been one of retrenchment. China scholars have provided many explanations for the changing dynamics of the TVEs. There are three prominent strands. One identifies the increasing competition in the market place as an important factor. In the 1980s, according to this explanation, the TVEs were protected from competition. The SOEs had not been reformed and competition from foreign firms was absent. Thus, the rise of the TVEs owed to the specific circumstances of China at the time. Another explanation identifies the public ownership of the TVEs as a problem. The TVEs might have been more efficient than the SOEs, but they still lagged behind the private firms. As private firms began to operate more freely, the position of the TVEs eroded. The third explanation focuses on the change in political incentives. For whatever reasons, in the 1980s, local governments are said to have favored collective firms but, in the 1990s, they began to withdraw their support for collective firms in favor of private firms.

The unstated takeaway of all three of these explanations is that the demise of the TVEs should be appropriately viewed as a sign of progress and deepening reforms. China's maturing marketplace, its more competitive landscape, and the success of its purely private firms are all positive developments. If the demise of the TVEs is the consequence, this is a sign that China is moving forward. Within official Chinese circles, there is another version of this type of reasoning. The TVEs were technologically backward and lacking in brand recognition and international expertise. They were ill-suited for a more modern and technologically advanced China.

In this section, I dispute all these claims about why the TVEs faltered in the 1990s. My own view – and I supply data to support this view – is that the TVEs failed because the national policy environment became inhospitable toward rural entrepreneurship. Before I make this argument, let me first illustrate why some of the commonly accepted explanations for the failure of the TVEs are problematic.

The view that TVEs failed because they were uncompetitive vis-à-vis private firms lacks even surface plausibility. As I detailed in the previous chapter, as early as 1985, an overwhelming number of TVEs were *private*. By the mid-1990s, it was even more the case that the TVE phenomenon was private. In the 1980s, although the private TVEs outnumbered the collective TVEs, their output and employment share was smaller. By 1996, the private TVEs were larger than the collective TVEs by employment, accounting for 56 percent of TVE employment. In terms of output value, in 1987, private TVEs accounted for 23.3 percent of gross industrial output value. By 1997, the share was 51.2 percent. Therefore, in the 1990s, the TVE sector was already substantially private, so it is a rather strange explanation that the TVEs failed because they were not private. The same rationale applies to the explanation that the local support for private firms was the reason for the demise of TVEs. In 1997, 18.8 million TVEs, out of a total of 20.1 million TVEs, were private. There was no better way to support private firms than to support TVEs.

The view that TVEs failed because they were out of step with the rest of the Chinese economy is at best incomplete and at worst misleading. This view somehow casts 18.8 million private TVEs as rigidly wedded to the old business models, incapable of adapting to a new market environment, and unwilling to upgrade their products. Unless one accepts the view that competitiveness is completely exogenous (Is it the water that the rural entrepreneurs drank?), it is reasonable to argue that many of the private TVEs could have gained competitiveness if the business environment had been more hospitable.

In fact, many of them did become competitive, but they tended to be concentrated in one geographic region – the province of Zhejiang (and within Zhejiang, the city of Wenzhou). The private firms based in that province are now designing brands, moving up on the technological chain, and actively investing in R&D. Almost all of these firms started out in the 1980s as private firms registered as TVEs.

The success of Zhejiang points to one explanation for why the TVEs failed in the 1990s that is insufficiently emphasized by Western economists – the increase in credit constraints on TVEs.[3] Zhejiang, especially the Wenzhou region, has China's most liberal financial policies toward private firms. In 1999, the short-term bank debt outstanding to the private sector from all financial institutions (including RCCs) was 57.9 billion yuan (People's Bank of China 2000). Zhejiang alone accounted for 11.4 billion yuan of this amount. The other two top provinces were Guangdong (8.4 billion yuan) and Fujian (3.4 billion yuan). Improving competitiveness and upgrading product quality require investments, and investments require capital. This is why Zhejiang firms came to dominate China's corporate landscape and this is why other regions, which repressed their private TVEs through financial and other constraint policies, lagged.

The TVEs succeeded in the 1980s and failed in the 1990s for exactly the same reason – that they were substantially private. It was the national policy environment that changed between the two decades. In the 1990s, mainly in the rural areas, it became increasingly difficult to obtain financing. This was in part because of a retreat from the financial liberalization of the 1980s and also in part because the TVE policies changed. The quote from Li Peng at the beginning of this section provides a useful way to reconstruct the TVE policies of the 1990s.

Li Peng's prescription for the TVEs is that they should primarily aim at the rural markets. (To the extent that the view of Chinese elites on TVEs – that they were low-tech – held any truth, it was a result of deliberate government policies tying the TVEs to low-tech rural China.) This perspective on TVEs constituted a dramatic shift from the 1980s. In the 1980s, the reformers viewed the TVEs as a source of competition to the urban-based SOEs and as a platform for rural residents to transition themselves out of low value-added agriculture. (Presumably, these are the unhealthy practices referred to by Li Peng.) Completely contrary to the view held by many Western economists, the reformers in the 1980s actively encouraged the TVEs to compete with the urban firms, rather than insulating them in an exclusively rural environment.

In fact, the reformers went even one step further. They actively encouraged the urban firms to establish direct production and sourcing links with the TVEs. In 1978, the government directed urban factories to shift their procurement to rural enterprises and to transfer technology to them. By the mid-1980s, according to Naughton (1996, p. 155), many regions in Jiangsu – still rural in the 1980s – had a significant amount of subcontracting work from Shanghai. One of the earliest beneficiaries of this policy was Wanxiang Auto, now China's largest private automobile-component producer. In 1980, Wanxiang was selected by the China Automotive General Corporation as one of three suppliers of gears. This was a turning point in the development of the firm (Wu Xiaobo 2006, p. 57).

Li Peng's criticism of the TVEs in the 1980s was not idle talk. Nor was it a temporary policy departure in the aftermath of the Tiananmen crackdown. In fact, the 1997 TVE Law, promulgated eight years after Li Peng made those remarks, closely reflects Li Peng's thinking. In his 1989 speech, Li Peng viewed the TVEs as *agricultural* businesses, mainly serving rural areas and markets. Article 2 of the 1997 TVE Law defines the TVEs as those enterprises "undertaking to support agriculture" (Editorial Committee of TVE Yearbook 1997). The second marker laid down by Li Peng was the emphasis on the collective ownership of TVEs. Again, the 1997 TVE Law reflects this thinking. Article 4 spells it out clearly: "TVE development must observe the principle of rural collective ownership as the main form, together with economic diverse ownership forms." The 1997 TVE Law also sanctioned county governments to establish "TVE development funds" to invest in the TVEs.

In the 1990s, the liquidity constraints on the TVEs were substantial. In 1993, the state banking system allocated 16.8 billion yuan for all TVEs. But the Ministry of Finance believed that the TVEs needed 200 billion yuan each year (Ministry of Agriculture 1995). There was also another source of liquidity constraints. China scholars have documented that the SOEs operated with increasing losses since the late 1990s. One effect was that the SOEs accumulated a large sum of accounts payable. It has been estimated that the accounts payable to the TVEs was 381.3 billion yuan in 1994 and 494.2 billion yuan in 1995. To put these numbers in perspective, the entire bank credit to the TVEs in 1994 was just 368.6 billion yuan (Ministry of Agriculture 1996, p. 14 and p. 2–2). The effects of the credit curbs were instantaneous. According to an internal report prepared by the Ministry of Agriculture, in 1994 the number of private TVEs fell by 21.5 percent and their employment fell by 10.8 percent. All of the increases in the TVEs occurred at the collective end. Township and village TVEs increased both in number of establishments and in employment (Ministry of Agriculture 1995).

2.2 TVE Privatization

Many Western economists believe that the private sector grew vigorously in the 1990s because the government increasingly came to support the privatization of TVEs. In the 1990s, the purely ideological opposition to private ownership eased considerably, but in rural China private-sector development was not as straightforward as many have assumed. For one thing, it is important to keep in mind the fact that the vast majority of the TVEs had started out as private businesses in the first place. In terms of establishments, as I showed in the last chapter, as early as 1985 more than 10 million out of 12 million TVEs were private. One significant development in the 1990s was that the coastal and richer provinces began to privatize their TVEs. Because these provinces have a large weight in the national data, the private share of TVEs grew in terms of output and employment.

It is important to address this view that much of the TVE privatization occurred in the 1990s because it fits with the gradualist interpretation that Chinese reforms got deeper over time. My argument is that this view overstates the importance of the decade of the 1990s in terms of TVE privatization. The overstatement comes in two forms. One is that this view uses the rising number of one type of TVE, known as a shareholding cooperative (*gufen hezuo qiye*), in the 1990s as evidence of increasingly liberal privatization stance. In reality, many of the shareholding cooperatives grew organically from smaller private rural businesses rather than as a product of privatization of collective TVEs. Second, many local governments did privatize in the 1990s, but it is not true that local governments did not privatize TVEs in the 1980s.

Shareholding cooperatives are essentially employee-owned firms and, by the late 1990s, many of the TVEs took this particular corporate form. Some of the shareholding cooperatives were no doubt converted from the collective TVEs, but many others were, in fact, an organic outgrowth of household businesses. In Wenzhou, by 1987, the shareholding cooperatives were already quite sizable, accounting for 47.9 percent of the total TVE output value. Of the 15,000 shareholding cooperatives, two thirds actually evolved from household businesses and one third were a result of TVE privatization (Editorial Committee of TVE Yearbook 1989b, p. 346). A 1987 Politburo document provides two rationales for the shareholding cooperative experimentation. One is that it led to a separation of government and enterprise management and the other is that it helped private enterprises raise capital (Editorial Committee of TVE Yearbook 1989b, p. 520). The second rationale has nothing to do with privatization; it is about helping household businesses that have attained scale to raise capital.

Another issue about the shareholding cooperatives is that the number of shareholding cooperative TVEs did not increase linearly. The peak was reached during the 1993–1994 period after Deng's Southern Tour and before many of the financing constraints on the rural private sector were institutionalized. This was the most liberal period in the 1990s. But, after the initial growth between 1993 and 1994, the number of shareholding cooperatives declined sharply in 1995 and 1996. According to the Ministry of Agriculture (1995), in 1994, there were 200,000 shareholding cooperatives, a rapid increase from 130,000 in 1993. But, in 1995, their number had decreased to 182,427 and then to 143,477 in 1996. The number of township/village–level TVEs also declined during this period but less rapidly. Therefore, the ratio of shareholding cooperatives to collective TVEs started at 7.7 percent in 1993, rose to 12.2 percent in 1994, and then fell to 9.3 percent in 1996.

Western academics believe that TVE privatization occurred largely in the 1990s (Whiting 2001, pp. 289–290). In their survey conducted in Jiangsu and Zhejiang, Brandt, Li, and Roberts (2005) report that cumulatively between

1993 and 1998, 34.2 percent of the TVEs were privatized and another 15.4 percent were shut down. The authors link the TVE privatization to "a fundamental shift in central government policy" in the early 1990s (Brandt, Li, and Roberts 2005, p. 525). Similarly, Oi (1999) reports on the privatization of TVEs in Shandong province in the 1990s.

In fact, what these academics have documented might very well be the tail end of the TVE privatization, not the beginning. Jiangsu is a well-known bastion of collective TVEs and it was among the last to privatize, not a pioneer. Zhejiang also privatized many of its collective TVEs in the 1990s. However, the first wave of the TVE privatization occurred in the 1980s and mainly in the poor, interior provinces, and it was poorly documented. As I showed in the last chapter, the share of private TVEs in the total TVE output was much higher in the poorer and more agricultural provinces than in the richer and more industrialized provinces. Coastal provinces might have finished the TVE privatization; they did not start it.

This empirical detail is important because it helps us assess policy developments in the 1980s and in the 1990s accurately. The explicit policy endorsement of TVE privatization happened much earlier than asserted by Brandt, Li, and Roberts. The first national policy endorsement that I found is a major Politburo document entitled, "Deepening rural reforms," issued on January 22, 1987. Article 4 of the document states, "small [rural collective] enterprises can be leased or sold to individuals to operate" (Editorial Committee of TVE Yearbook 1989b, p. 519). But, this 1987 document acknowledged and sanctioned the apparent large-scale privatization of collective TVEs already underway. Although the evidence is scattered, the poor performance of the collective TVEs at the very start of the rural reforms had already prompted a spontaneous wave of privatization of these loss-making firms.

As early as 1987, in Wuxi of Jiangsu province – the progenitor of the Sunan model – 100 collective TVEs had been acquired by other firms; 200 were leased out to managers, and 11 were converted into shareholding companies (Editorial Committee of TVE Yearbook 1989b, p. 328). If a stronghold of collective TVEs already began to privatize as early as 1987, it is only logical to assume that privatization might have occurred on a larger scale elsewhere. In fact, the rapid growth of private TVEs documented previously was, in part, a product of the privatization process. It was their initial source of financing.

According to the World Bank researchers, as many as 50 percent of the private entrepreneurs in the poor regions of the country got their startup capital from seizing control of collective fixed assets. According to Lin (1990, p. 177), village governments "sold some or all of their enterprises to

individuals at extremely low prices, leased them at a fixed rent, or contracted them out in return for a certain percentage of after-tax profits."
In Jieshou, "wholesale" privatization and "outright" sale of collective TVEs
occurred as early as 1979–1980. In one township, every single collective TVE
was privatized and in another township, half of the collective TVEs were
privatized. In Shangrao county, the share of private TVEs rose from 0 to
50 percent, in just three years from 1983 to 1986, through both the organic
growth of the private TVEs as well as privatization of the collective TVEs
(Byrd 1990).

Chinese sources also report on numerous instances of collective TVE privatization during the 1980s. Editorial Committee of TVE Yearbook (1989b,
p. 222) notes the transformation of "originally commune and brigade enterprises" into shareholding cooperatives through employee stock options and
new share issues in Sichuan, Shaanxi, Shanxi, and Henan. An investigation
into Qinhe county in Hebei province states, "In that region, there were
not many collective enterprises in the first place. Of the ones that were
collective, the majority were already divided among households" (Editorial
Committee of TVE Yearbook 1989b, p. 232). In Wenzhou city, by 1987, more
than 4,000 collective enterprises were converted into shareholding companies through either outright privatization or new share issues (Editorial
Committee of TVE Yearbook 1989b, p. 346). In Zhejiang province, in 1988,
605 collective TVEs were sold through auctions, 2,210 were leased out, and
364 were acquired (Editorial Committee of TVE Yearbook 1989a, p. 40).
An article on shareholding cooperatives details the various privatization
practices in Shandong, Shanxi, Shaanxi, Hebei, Wuhan, and Liaoning. The
practices ranged from dilution of government shares to outright sales. In
Hebei, these various ownership experiments involved some 14,000 firms
(Editorial Committee of TVE Yearbook 1989a, pp. 154–155).

The privatization of the collective TVEs financed the initial startup of
the private firms. This observation turns on its head the idea that the
development of TVEs owed their legacy to the Great Leap Forward. Lin
(1990, p. 177) gets the causal direction right when she remarks, "So, in
a sense, failure in the management of the original TVCEs [township and
village collective enterprises] was a factor in the successful development
of today's private enterprises." Here is an ironic twist to the conventional
wisdom of the TVEs: To the extent that the collective legacy of the Great
Leap Forward contributed to the TVE development in the 1980s, it was
through the failure, not the success, of the collective TVEs.

In the 1980s, private TVEs expanded from both rapid organic growth as
well as privatization of collective TVEs. This observation suggests that we

need to rethink about a common view in the writings of the Chinese economy – that TVEs owed their lineage to the collective TVEs from the Great Leap Forward period. This view errs on the facts because most of the TVEs were founded during the reform era. The view also errs on the reasoning. It is predicated on the belief that collective TVEs were successful.[4] When the TVEs are segmented correctly – into their true ownership categories such as township, village, or private categories – the evidence is very clear that the private TVEs were more efficient than the collective TVEs. For example, township TVEs reported heavy losses in the World Bank TVE study (Wang Xiaolu 1990). Nationwide statistics for 1985 show that the average output, profits, and wages of private TVEs were between 50 and 70 percent higher than those of comparable collective TVEs (Lin 1990, p. 181). The collective TVEs appear to have begun to incur losses as soon as the reforms began. Even in Wuxi, a region known for the best-performing collective TVEs, 11 percent of the township TVEs suffered losses. The much-touted Sunan model actually began to flounder at the very start of the reform era. Between 1980 and 1984, the collective TVEs in Jiangsu experienced a plunge in after-tax profits by 25 percent (Zhang Yi 1990, p. 192).[5]

2.3 The Resurgence of Collective TVEs

An additional source of complications in interpreting the TVE privatization in the 1990s is that in the 1990s, there was also a resurgence of collective TVEs. However, this resurgence of the collective TVEs occurred in the backward, small provinces; thus, this development did not show up in the national data. In the 1980s, there was a standard reference to government policy on TVEs – the "four-wheel drive" policy (*silun juedong*). The four wheels here refer to the four levels of TVEs: (1) townships, (2) villages, (3) alliance and multihousehold businesses, and (4) households. The first two represent the collective component of the TVEs and the last two represent the private component. Throughout the 1980s, the standard policy formulation was to support the development of all four "wheels" of the TVEs. For example, the 1987 policy document adopted by the Politburo, "Deepening the rural reforms," uses the phrase "simultaneous" development (*yiqi shang*) of four wheels (Editorial Committee of TVE Yearbook 1989b, p. 520). I know of no policy document in the 1980s that explicitly differentiated among the four different types of TVEs; quite the opposite. Numerous policy documents went out of their way to stress equal treatment of different types of TVEs.

This was to change in the 1990s. A speech by the Minister of Agriculture on January 5, 1990, portended a new policy formulation. In this speech, the

Minister revised the so-called four-wheel policy and added that the collective TVEs were the mainstay of the TVE sector (Editorial Committee of TVE Yearbook 1990, p. 8). One policy document even invoked a term customarily associated with the nationalization campaign of the mid-1950s to describe the policy visions for the TVEs.[6] The reformulation of the TVE policy to favor collective TVEs was reiterated throughout the 1990s, not just in the immediate ideological aftermath of the Tiananmen crackdown. Several articles in the 1997 TVE Law stress the primacy of the collective TVEs. Investment allocations closely follow the new policy formulation as well. Chapter 1 shows that fixed-asset investments in the rural collective sector grew rapidly in the 1990s. During the 1993–2001 period, rural collective fixed-asset investments grew at an annual rate of 9.1 percent compared with rural private-sector fixed-asset investments growing 7.5 percent.

Although the overall size of private TVEs increased in the 1990s, there are two important observations. One is the rate of this increase. In 1989, private TVEs already accounted for 50 percent of TVE employment. This ratio remained roughly constant, around 51 percent, until 1994. Only after 1994 did the private share of TVE employment begin to rise significantly above the level prevailing in the late 1980s.

The second observation is that this overall rise in private TVEs at the national level masks a huge variation at the regional level. This was not just a variation in the speed of the rising private TVEs but also a variation in the direction of private TVE development. In some regions, private TVEs actually *declined* in the 1990s relative to the size of the collective TVEs. In 1987, at the national level, private TVEs accounted for 32.1 percent of the gross output value; 10 years later in 1997, the share was 51 percent, a gain of 19 percent. Against this overall increase, however, seven provinces experienced a decline or stagnation of the share of private TVEs. The greatest decline occurred in Heilongjiang province: In 1987, private TVEs already accounted for 47 percent of TVE output; by 1997, this share had declined to 19.5 percent, a reduction of 27.5 percent. The six other provinces are (with the reduction magnitude in brackets) Guizhou (−17.3 percent), Qinghai (−16.6 percent), Hebei (−3.2 percent), Henan (−0.6 percent), Beijing (−1.4 percent), and Anhui (0 percent).

We do not know what happened in these seven provinces but it is important to understand the implications. One is that these seven provinces are relatively small in terms of their total weight in the national data on TVEs. In 1997 Anhui, with the largest weight, accounted for 5 percent of the national total. All the others accounted for less than 3 percent. Because private TVEs expanded in those provinces with a large TVE sector, national data show an increase in private TVEs. Zhejiang, which contributed 9.8 percent to national TVE output, increased the private share of TVEs by 35.8 percent. Jiangsu, another large TVE province, increased the private share of TVEs by 17.7 percent. The expansion of the private TVEs in these large TVE provinces masks the retrogressions in the smaller TVE provinces in the national data.

Private TVE development is not a mere statistical matter. It entails real welfare consequences. Provinces such as Jiangsu and Zhejiang, the two coastal, richer regions in China, had favorable endowment factors – such as access to FDI, trade, and an urban economy – to fall back on. It was the poor regions of China that most needed indigenous, bottom-up entrepreneurship because they lacked alternative means of economic development. We saw in the last chapter that rural residents in poor provinces such as Guizhou went into entrepreneurship to improve their standard of living. Except for Beijing, the agricultural population represented about 80 percent of the total in those provinces in which private TVEs contracted. They also had a high concentration of poverty. So, the welfare implications of their lagging private-sector development were substantial.

With more data available in the future, we ought to revisit this period and try to understand exactly why the rural private sector contracted in these poor provinces. Here, let me provide another corroboration of the lagging private-sector development in China's poor provinces. Recall the finding in the World Bank TVE study that in the mid-1980s, the private sector was already substantial in size in two of their poorer research sites, Jieshou county of Anhui province and Shangrao county of Jiangxi province. In the richer research sites – Nanhai of Guangdong and Wuxi of Jiangsu, the private sector was relatively small. The World Bank researchers reasoned that this was an organic result of the respective endowment factors. The richer regions started out with a more developed collective sector and they naturally gravitated toward collective mechanisms of economic and industrial development. The poorer regions never had the luxury of the choice. Private-sector development became a default mechanism for the economies of these regions to grow.

This highly convincing explanation, however, makes the policy making look easier than it was in reality. A vital condition is necessary to enable the process of natural selection to work – policy makers have to accommodate themselves to the economic reality on the ground rather than to forcibly impose their own visions. My contention is that the latter occurred on a large

Table 3.2. *Percentage shares of gross industrial output value by private TVEs in four regions: 1985 and 1998 (%)*

	Based on World Bank Survey: Firms of all Sizes		Based on NBS Industrial Firm Dataset: Large Firms Only (Sales >5 million yuan)	
	1985 (1a)	1986 (1b)	1998 (2a)	(2b)
Regions/TVE indicators	Private share of TVEs	Private share of TVEs	Private share of TVEs	Private share of all firms
Jieshou (Anhui)	51		12.4	3.95
Shangrao (Jiangxi)	35		24.6	9.5
Nanhai (Guangdong)	10	12	17.1	15.1
Wuxi (Jiangsu)	3		13.2	9.7

Note: The private firm classification is based on the Guangdong definition; i.e., registered private-sector firms plus those nonstate firms with individual share capital exceeding 50 percent.
Sources: The 1980s data draw from Table 9.1 in Byrd (1990, p. 195). The 1998 data are based on the NBS industrial firm dataset.

scale in the 1990s – that the local governments in the poor regions, instead of facilitating a natural, organic process of private-sector development, poured financial and other resources into the collective sector. Table 3.2 presents the estimates given by the World Bank TVE study of the share of private TVEs in the four counties in the mid-1980s. Consistent with the view put forward in this book that the poorer regions in the 1980s pioneered private-sector development, Jieshou and Shangrao counties – the two poorer research sites in the World Bank TVE study – had a higher share of private TVEs than the two richer research sites, Nanhai and Wuxi. In the 1990s, the situation reversed itself. Our data for the 1990s come from the NBS industry census and the year is 1998. The census data, which cover larger firms above 5 million yuan in sales, show that the private shares of TVEs declined in Jieshou and Shangrao but they increased in Nanhai and Wuxi.

Given that the collective TVEs began to incur losses as soon as the rural reforms began, it is implausible that the collective TVEs gained against the private TVEs in Jieshou and Shangrao as well as in the aforementioned seven provinces in the 1990s due to their efficiency and dynamism. Instead, they gained market shares in the 1990s due to policy support. These policy developments were hugely destructive. The collective TVEs wasted the resources allocated to them. They might have gained market shares against the private TVEs located in the same regions but because the resources went to the less competitive TVEs, compared with the country as a whole, the TVEs in those provinces lost market shares. Guizhou, Henan, Hebei, Heilongjiang, and Guangxi, the poor provinces that experienced a contraction of the share of private TVEs between 1987 and 1997, also experienced a contraction in their share of TVE output – inclusive of both collective and private TVEs – in the national total. The TVEs of Henan accounted for 6.62 percent of the national output of TVEs in 1987; in 1997, the share was 3.54 percent. Guizhou's share declined from 0.55 percent in 1987 to 0.38 percent in 1997. In the case of Hebei, it went down from 6.6 percent in 1987 to 4.55 in 1997.

We still have one piece of the puzzle to solve before we can close the loop on the subject of the TVEs. If the private TVEs lagged in some of the poorest provinces, why did they grow in the richer provinces? Jiangsu province, the progenitor of the collective TVE model, privatized many of its TVEs in the 1990s. By 2004, even among the largest TVEs, individual share capital was very important, accounting for 47.5 percent of the total share capital (Ministry of Agriculture 2005). A plausible hypothesis centers on the role of industrial policy. During the 1990s, the Chinese state adopted a policy platform officially known as "grasping the big and letting go of the small." "Grasping the big" means policy support for the large incumbent firms and "letting go of the small" means privatization of small firms.

Here is how this policy approach might have led to the divergent developments between the rich and poor provinces in terms of TVE development. The most valuable and the largest assets in the rich provinces resided in the traditional state sector, rather than in the TVEs. Thus, the logical approach in those regions was to restructure the SOEs, often by massive fresh investments and/or by forming alliances with FDI. The TVEs in these regions were small relative to the incumbent SOEs and were thus relegated to the privatization part of the policy program (i.e., "letting go of the small").

The poor regions had entirely different endowment conditions. They had a relatively under-developed state sector (and this is the reason why the private sector was allowed to develop there in the first place). They also had a paucity of FDI supply, which precluded this particular restructuring option. Their incumbent large firms comprised collective TVEs, which were then targeted for support under the policy of "grasping the big and letting go of the small." So, ironically, exactly the same dynamics behind the rise of private TVEs in the poor provinces in the 1980s then explains the endurance and even the resurgence of collective TVEs in the 1990s – the absence of viable developmental alternatives.

3 The Great Financing Squeeze

Under the banking regulations, individuals are not allowed to engage in financial operations. The emergence of private (siren) credit shows that our financial
work falls short of what is needed. This requires that our credit cooperatives and
agricultural banks improve their services. This is a huge task.

> – Chen Muhua, governor of the People's Bank of China, January 31, 1986
> (Chen Muhua 1987, p. 105)

Those funds, mutual assistance associations, savings associations, capital service
departments, share capital service departments, fund clearing centers, and investment companies established prior to this order and operating above the state law
should be restructured with a deadline according to the regulations of the State
Council. Those entities that operate after the deadline and continue to engage in
illegal financing should be stamped out according to this order. Those with serious
violations of a criminal nature should be held accountable for their legal responsibilities.

> – An order from the State Council to ban all illegal finance
> (State Council 1998)

The first quote comes from Madame Chen Muhua, who was the governor
of the People's Bank of China (PBoC), China's central bank, between 1985
and 1988. In this quote, Madame Chen, viewed by many Western journalists
as conservative in outlook and wooden in character, was using private – and
essentially illegal – financial transactions as a benchmark for the state-
owned financial system. In her judgment, China's formal financial system
was not up to the task and she urged it to reform. In other speeches given
between 1985 and 1987, she constantly implored the state-owned financial
institutions to do a better job – whether to draw deposits or to provide
loans – in order to compete with private financing. Several times, Madame
Chen held up Wenzhou – the bastion of capitalism in China – as a model
to be emulated by the rest of the country.

Chen Muhua used the term *siren* to describe some of the financial practices. Two Chinese terms connote the idea of private ownership. One is *siren*,
meaning private or individual; the other is *minjian*, literally meaning among
the people or nongovernment. *Siren* is more overtly private and thus more
ideologically sensitive than *minjian*, although the two terms do not differ
conceptually. So, there is a preference for using *minjian* rather than *siren*
in Chinese political discourse. But Madame Chen did not shy away from
using *siren*. In fact, Chinese financial officials went even beyond Madame
Chen. A statement by Han Lei, president of the Agricultural Bank of China
(ABC), used the term *siren* as early as 1984 in a discussion on the direction
of the financial reforms. Bank documents in the 1980s were peppered with

references to *siren* or *minjian* when discussing bank reforms. In the 1980s, rural China experimented with substantial financial liberalization, the main elements of which were (1) adoption of an accommodating and supportive credit policy toward the private sector by state banks, (2) the proliferation of informal financial instruments, and (3) tacit permission for informal financial instruments exclusively servicing the private sector.

With an ever-increasing intensity, much, if not all, of the financial experimentation in the 1980s was terminated or completely reversed beginning in the second half of the 1990s. The 1998 State Council order, whose stern warning is quoted in part at the beginning of this section, is extremely telling of the winds of change in the 1990s. Rather than viewing the informal finance as a useful complement to the official finance, the Chinese state began to systematically stamp out those providers of capital outside the state banking system. The government began to curb the operations of nationwide semi-official financial institutions, rural cooperative foundations (RCFs), in 1993 and completely banned their operations in 1998. In the 1990s, the two terms *siren* and *minjian* completely disappeared from bank documents (except when announcing bans on private financial transactions).

The crackdown on informal finance was both determined and ferocious. In 1991, an illiterate housewife in Wenzhou paid the ultimate price – Zheng Lefang was executed for "financial fraud." Zheng personified the turning point in China's financial policies. She had committed her alleged crimes in 1986 but she was not executed until 1991 (Wu Xiaobo 2006, p. 175). In the 1990s, numerous rural entrepreneurs who had been forced to tap into or organize underground financing because of the massive inadequacies of China's banking system were arrested. A famous case involves Mr. Sun Dawu, a rural entrepreneur who ran an animal feed company in the impoverished province of Hebei.[7] In May 2003, Mr. Sun was arrested for "illegally absorbing public funds." Mr. Sun had refused to bribe bank officials to obtain loans. Instead, he turned to the employees of his company and asked them to contribute funds. This practice, widespread in the 1980s and a legitimate source of start-up capital for many TVEs, now ran into the iron fist of the Chinese financial regulators determined to stamp out all forms of informal finance. Sun's company was destroyed. (In his prison cell, Mr. Sun coined a phrase thereafter invoked by many Chinese journalists, "Chinese peasants, your name is misery.")

Western scholars are keenly aware of the inadequacies of the Chinese banking system.[8] In 1998, Nicholas Lardy argued that the Chinese reforms were unfinished because the financial system was unreformed (Lardy 1998). Other researchers as well have reported on backpedaling of the financial reforms. For example, Park and Shen (2001) note that authority to issue new loans became highly centralized during the course of the 1990s and a study by the International Finance Corporation, based on a survey in the late 1990s, shows that newer private firms faced greater financing constraints than older firms (Gregory, Tenev, and Wagle 2000).[9] Other studies have reported on the deteriorating rural finance in the 1990s (Nyberg and Rozelle 1999; International Fund for Agricultural Development 2002).

I would agree with all of these assessments but I go one step further. My argument is that China reversed many of the productive and innovative financial practices it had adopted in the 1980s. In this section, I first present evidence that rural finance became very constraining in the 1990s. I then contrast the financial policies in the 1980s with those in the 1990s. The primary empirical basis to determine China's financial policies in these two decades is the thousands of pages of bank documents in 22 volumes.

3.1 The Poor State of Rural Finance

Recall the finding in Chapter 1 that rural private fixed investments grew rapidly in the 1980s. Fixed-asset investments are typically heavily financed by external sources of capital – bank loans or new share issues. It is not unusual that the construction of a new production facility is 50 to 70 percent financed by outside capital.

The rapid growth of rural fixed-asset investments in the 1980s illustrates a phenomenon virtually unknown in the West – the supply of bank capital to the private sector in the 1980s was plentiful. The ample supply was a function of two developments. One was a dramatic policy shift by Chinese banks toward a more business-friendly stance and more supportive of private-sector clients. The other was substantial financial liberalization, defined as those policy measures that made control of existing financial institutions more private and allowed private players a greater role in providing financial intermediation services. On both fronts, China moved backward, rather dramatically, in the 1990s.

Survey research undertaken in the 1980s shows a surprisingly high level of loans provided to private entrepreneurs when they first started their businesses. (Data on loan availability during the operating stage are scarce.) Two Chinese sociologists, Zhang Houyi and Ming Lizhi, summarize the findings from six large-scale surveys conducted in 1987 (Zhang Houyi and Ming Lizhi 1999, Table 9, p. 55). One survey, covering 97 firms in 11 provinces, shows that 40.6 percent of the start-up capital came from bank loans. (Unless otherwise noted, bank loans here refer to those funds made available to the firms when they first started.) For 281 firms in Hebei, the ratio was 54.8 percent, for 56 firms in Hunan the ratio was 28.5 percent, for 130 firms in Shaanxi it was 66.3 percent, for 10 firms in Guangdong it was 34 percent, and for 50 firms in Wenzhou it was 23.3 percent. The average ratio in these aforementioned six surveys is 41.3 percent.

The World Bank TVE study, referenced in the last chapter, also reports very high levels of credit availability to the private sector. Lin (1990, fn. 3, p. 188) reports on a survey of 56 private firms in Tianjin in 1985. Of those firms with a total investment of less than 50,000 yuan, bank loans accounted for 38.8 percent of their funds; of those with an investment between 50,000 and 100,000 yuan, bank loans accounted for 43.6 percent; and of those firms with investments of more than 100,000 yuan, bank loans accounted for 69.9 percent. One of the World Bank researchers, William Byrd (1990, p. 209), thus observes, "Banking institutions already see well-established private enterprises as solid borrowers." Byrd also reports that local banks that lent heavily to private-sector firms had lower non-performing loan (NPL) ratios.

It is definitely not true that private entrepreneurs in the 1980s were unable to access bank loans. But did access to loans become more or less difficult in the 1990s compared with the 1980s? To compare the two decades directly, we go to three sources of information that organize and report data on a consistent basis for both the 1980s and 1990s. A head-to-head comparison shows that private-sector access to finance, especially in rural China, was substantial in the 1980s, but it became extraordinarily constrained in the 1990s.

The first source of information is the fixed rural household survey we used to demonstrate the changing labor time allocation of Chinese peasants in the 1980s and 1990s. The fixed rural household survey provides data on loans obtained from banks and rural credit cooperatives (RCCs) from 1986 to 1999. To see the trends over time, I deflated the bank loans to their 1978 prices using the rural price index. In 1986, an average rural household obtained 84.2 yuan from banks and RCCs. This rose to 99.5 yuan in 1987 and to 92.3 yuan in 1988. Then, it contracted to 52.3 yuan in 1989. From that point on until 1999, the average rural household bank loans in real terms never exceeded their 1987 level. The peak year of the 1990s was 1996 when the average rural household bank loan was 92 yuan; in all other years, the figure was either below 80 yuan or only slightly above. Only in 1999 did the level exceed the peak reached in 1987. In that year, the amount of bank loans was 103 yuan.

In absolute terms, the average amount of formal loans per household did not increase in the 1990s compared with the 1980s. In relative terms, it declined. Because we are mainly interested in the role of bank loans to help

Chinese peasants transition out of agriculture, we compare the amount of bank loans with the amount of non-farm operating income. In 1986, 84.2 yuan of bank loans represented 28.3 percent of the operating income from non-farm sources. For the next three years, this ratio remained above 28 percent. In the 1990s, the ratio declined on a continuing basis. By 1999, the ratio was only 21.9 percent, a 20 percent reduction from the 1986 level. (Later in this chapter, I present data on the supply side to show that a main source of financing in rural China, the RCCs, shrank to a point of total irrelevance.)

Our second source of information is the private-sector surveys we used in Chapter 2 to ascertain the rural origins of Chinese capitalism. Question 8 in the PSS2002 asked the respondents to select their sources of start-up capital from the following sources: (1) savings from running small businesses, (2) savings from running small-scale productions, (3) donations from friends and relatives, (4) wages, (5) informal loans, (6) bank loans, and (7) inheritances. Let me compare the number of firms that checked off bank loans versus those that checked off informal finance in their responses. The PSS2002 contains information on the year in which the firm was founded so we can compare the responses to this question in the two decades. Because very few firms in the PSS2002 were established before 1984, I exclude those firms in the data analysis. Also, I report on the findings only on rural firms, although the findings on the entire sample do not differ.[10]

During the 1984–1989 period, 32.6 percent of rural firms reported receiving bank loans in the first year of their business. The highest ratio was in 1985 when 50 percent reported receiving loans. The year 1987 was also high, at 38.5 percent. During the 1990–2001 period, this ratio declined sharply, to 26 percent. Some years show very low numbers. For example, in 2001, the year often touted as an ideological breakthrough for China's private sector when Jiang Zemin unveiled his doctrine of the "three represents," only 13 percent of rural private firms received bank loans. The highest ratio was in 1999 when 34.6 percent of rural firms received bank loans, but this is nowhere near the 50 percent already reached in 1985.

As we already saw in the rural social–economic survey, informal finance skyrocketed to meet the unfulfilled credit demand. We find exactly the same dynamics in the PSS2002. During the 1990–2001 period, 29.7 percent of rural firms reported receiving informal loans, as compared with 26.3 percent during the 1984–1989 period. Thus, formal finance was more important to rural firms in the 1980s than it was in the 1990s; in the 1990s, the importance of these two sources of finance were reversed, with informal finance surpassing formal finance as a source of start-up capital.

One interpretation of the emerging role of informal finance is that the government became more tolerant of private providers of capital. Thus, it can be a sign of openness, not of closure, as Tsai (2002) explains the prominence of informal finance in some regions of China. This is the right perspective to explain the 1980s when the reformers endeavored to make the state financial institutions cater to private entrepreneurs and to allow a degree of opening and competition in the financial sector. The formal and informal sources of finance complemented one another.

In the 1990s, rather than being complementary, the formal and informal sources of finance became substitutes for one another. The authorities oriented the banking system away from the private sector; thus, the credit constraints on the private entrepreneurs drove them to rely more heavily on informal finance. The way to distinguish the substitution and complementary relationship between the two sources of finance is to look at how they relate to one another. In the 1980s, the reliance by the private sector on formal and informal sources of finance moved together: In those years when private rural firms drew in more bank loans, they also drew in more informal loans. The simple two-way correlation between the two series of data based on PSS2002 is 0.33. In the 1990s, the relationship became negative (-0.05); in those years when rural firms received fewer bank loans, they received more informal loans. This must have been a costly outcome for rural private firms. The drying up of bank loans drove up the costs of the informal loans.

Our third source of information concerns bank financing of fixed-asset investment activities. Fixed-asset investments – purchases of new equipment and property – are heavily financed by external capital. The high level of fixed-asset investments by rural households in the 1980s suggests the availability of external finance. Do we have direct evidence that this was the case? The answer is yes, although the information is not complete.[11] According to Lin Senmu (1993), a senior official in the State Planning Commission, between 10 and 20 percent of fixed-asset investments of the individual economy were financed by bank loans in the mid-1980s. The NBS (1988, p. 560) provides data on bank loans for private fixed-asset investments in 1987. In that year, the total amount of bank loans for the private sector was 5.1 billion yuan, all of which was in the rural area. This was about 7.3 percent of the rural private fixed-asset investments.

We already saw in Chapter 1 that rural private fixed-asset investment was to fall sharply in the 1990s. Bank financing fell even more sharply. Throughout the 1990s, bank financing as a ratio of rural private fixed-asset investment hovered between 3 and 4 percent, half of the level prevailing in 1987. In 2003, rural households invested 320 billion yuan. Of this amount, 12.5 billion yuan was financed by bank loans (NBS 2004b, p. 447), accounting for 3.9 percent of total investments. In 2004, bank financing fell further, to only 2.7 percent (NBS 2005c, p. 435). This is not even remotely close to the level prevailing in the 1980s.

3.2 Financial Liberalization in the 1980s

Some comrades asked about lending to individual business owners (*getihu*). For example, do you lend to him if he applies for $1,000 to import equipment? My opinion is that as long as his business is permitted by policy (*fuhe zhengce*) and contributes to economic development and as long as he has a permit from the Industry and Commerce Bureau and he can repay, of course, you can lend to him.

– Jin Deqin, President of the Bank of China, October 18, 1984.

Rural areas need state-owned banks and credit cooperatives for finance but at the same time, under bank supervision, we need to allow the existence of private (*siren*) free lending and borrowing.

– Han Lei, President of the ABC, July 20, 1984 (Han Lei 1984, p. 51)

The easing of the financing for rural private entrepreneurs did not occur by chance; it occurred because financial policy was tacitly or even explicitly supportive of the private sector. This is one of the least known aspects of the 1980s. Between 1980 and 1988, the Chinese financial system became increasingly flexible as the reformers directed banks and RCCs to lend to the emerging private sector. They also introduced proactive reforms of financial institutions by reducing state controls of RCCs and permitting entry by private players. The two quotes that begin this section are telling of this era. The first quote comes from the president of the Bank of China, Mr. Jin Deqin. In the 1980s, the Bank of China was tightly controlled by the central government as it was charged with the management of China's foreign exchange, considered a vital strategic and, at that time, scarce financial asset. Even in the area of foreign exchange, as early as 1984, officials were already expressing a willingness to lend to private entrepreneurs. This was only eight years after the end of the Cultural Revolution – a sort of financing re-engineering by comrades, if you will.

Second, the two men who made these statements were not some random financial officers; they were, respectively, president of the Bank of China and president of the Agricultural Bank of China. This underscores an important point about the 1980s: The financial reforms in the 1980s were not a stealthy act by renegade local officials behaving against the controlling strictures by the central policy makers. The financial reforms were enacted by the central policy makers themselves. Later in this section, I provide statements by the topmost financial officer of the country – the governor of China's central bank – to illustrate this very point. The financial reforms in the 1980s did not occur randomly and haphazardly.

To be sure, these measures did not amount to a full-scale financial liberalization. Financial controls remained tight in the form of lending quotas and interest-rate caps, and the urban areas were immune to these financial reforms. Also, it is true that not all of the proposed measures were fully implemented. Keep in mind that the reformist leaders in the 1980s had only a few years to implement reforms, in contrast to the long tenure of the leaders in the 1990s (from 1989 to 2002). There were also policy reversals. For example, in 1986, to curtail the rapid credit growth, the ABC sharply curtailed credit supply to individual business owners.

These caveats aside, it is important to document and provide a paper trail of the rural financial reforms in the 1980s. A running theme of this book is that analyzing Chinese reforms is about ascertaining the directions of institutional or policy change, not about the level of institutions and policies. How to characterize the rural financial reforms is an art, not a science. One could argue that these were modest changes in making Chinese financial institutions more "business friendly" (in the sense that Hausmann, Pritchett, and Rodrik [2004] analyzed the policy changes in India under Rajiv Gandhi). Or one could argue that reducing the blockage of competitive entry into the financial sector and making credits available to the private sector marked a monumental change from the central planning era. My emphasis throughout this book is on *directional liberalism* as the most relevant benchmark. Regardless of one's views of the rural reforms in the 1980s, the fact is that rural financial practices were trending in a liberal direction in the 1980s and in an illiberal direction in the 1990s. Getting the China story right requires a dynamic perspective.

The pioneer in the financial reforms of the 1980s was unquestionably the ABC. This is not surprising given the fact that the rural reforms were at the forefront of the economic transformation in the 1980s. (In the 1990s, due to massive mismanagement and conservative reversions, the ABC became the most problematic bank in China.) In December 1984, the ABC unveiled its "Provisional methods of lending to industrial and commercial rural households" (Agricultural Bank of China 1986 <1984>). In the same year, the ABC authorized floating interest rates for loans to individual business owners and waived loan-guarantee requirements for those borrowers with a good credit history and with a high self-funding ratio (Agricultural Bank of China 1986 <1984>, p. 364). In 1988, after passage of the Private Enterprise Law, the ABC revised its 1984 regulations and added private rural enterprises – as opposed to the less ideologically sensitive household businesses – on the list of firms eligible for its non-farm loans (Agricultural Bank of China 1988a).

A consistent theme running through the bank-policy documents of the ABC in the 1980s is that the ABC and the RCCs should provide loans to rural residents to engage in non-farm activities. An ABC document dated July 1984 reveals that loans provided to finance commercial production by rural households increased between 30 and 50 percent "above the targets set for the year." The document, transmitted to all RCC branches in the country, describes the success story of a client of a RCC in Hunan province – clearly intended as an exemplary model for other RCC branches to follow. In this case, 28 farmers jointly founded a business, specializing in sourcing and distributing agricultural produce. Its operations were massive, sourcing from 17 townships and selling to 13 cities located in 5 provinces (Agricultural Bank of China 1984).

The most important financial institution in rural China was the rural credit cooperative. In 1985, RCCs accounted for 76.8 percent of all agricultural loans and 47.8 percent of all loans extended to TVEs. These numbers understate, however, the true importance of the RCCs. Many of the loans originating from the ABC were actually handled by the RCCs (China Finance Association 1986, p. II-19). The RCCs were first established in 1951 as genuinely private financial institutions. RCC members elected the officers and determined the lending priorities and criteria of the RCCs in their respective regions. In the 1960s and 1970s, RCCs lost their operating autonomy and were placed under the administration of the ABC and local governments.

One of the first acts introduced by the reformist leaders was to move the RCCs back to the management system prevailing in the 1950s. This vision was mapped out in 1980, at the very start of rural reforms. In that year, the Politburo convened a finance leadership group specifically dedicated to the issue of rural financial reforms. The principle formulated by this group was called "restoring the original three features of the RCCs," meaning that they would be organizationally reliant on RCC members, managerially democratic, and operationally flexible. The 1980 policy document is remarkable in many ways. For one thing, it shows that in the 1980s, the financial reforms in rural China were being implemented at the same time as the general economic reforms. There was no lag in timing. Second, the document – issued only four years after the end of the Cultural Revolution – harshly criticized the "government-run" nature of the RCCs. (The Chinese term for government-run is *guanban.*) This criticism of RCCs as a "government-run" institution appeared in numerous bank documents in the 1980s.

Starting in 1983, the Chinese state began to take concrete steps to implement this vision. Under the reform plan, the RCCs would put aside 30 percent of their deposits at the ABC as reserve and the RCCs would determine how to use the rest of their deposit capital on their own. The RCCs were also allowed to compete directly with banks both in the deposit-taking business as well as in the loan business (Agricultural Bank of China 1985 <1983>-b). By the end of 1985, 80 percent of the RCCs in the country had adopted reforms along these lines (Agricultural Bank of China 1986 <1985>, p. 34). Governance reforms of the RCCs began in the late 1980s as the RCCs moved toward more operating autonomy. In 1988, the ABC drafted a regulation on RCC employment practices. Article 11 of the regulation specifies that the local heads of the RCCs should be selected through "democratic elections" (Agricultural Bank of China 1988c, p. 200). The same regulation also discourages a common administrative practice in the Chinese bureaucracy – the rotating of heads of departments across geographic jurisdictions. My point here is not that the RCCs became truly self-governing credit cooperatives in the 1980s. Rather, my point is that in the 1980s, the RCCs were moving explicitly in the direction of autonomy and self-governance, whereas in the 1990s, the RCCs moved in the opposite direction, both in letter and in spirit.

Another sign of policy flexibility was the treatment of informal finance. In both the 1980s and 1990s, informal finance played an active role in meeting the financial needs of rural entrepreneurs and households. The difference, however, is that informal finance was not only tolerated in the 1980s but also was actually used by the reformers to benchmark the reforms of the formal financial institutions. In the 1990s, there was a protracted, costly, and ultimately futile effort to stamp out informal finance on the one hand and to intervene and micromanage the operations of the formal financial institutions on the other. The combination of these two led to substantial credit constraints in rural China in the 1990s.

The official stance toward informal finance in the 1980s was extraordinarily liberal. There were periodic crackdowns on specific private money houses (usually after fraud was discovered and a large amount of money was lost). But there was no attempt to stamp out the entire sector of informal finance, a huge difference with the 1990s, as I detail later. Again, the policy stance was not just an *ad hoc,* grudging official recognition of the actual informal finance practices on the ground, but rather it represented a positive endorsement. The best way to illustrate this point is probably to point to statements made by none other than the governor of the PBoC. In a 1986 speech, Governor Chen gave a highly positive assessment of the financial experimentation in Wenzhou, the most liberal and the most capitalistic region in China. It is worth reproducing some of her statements at some length to illustrate the explicitly pro-private stance of the central bank at the time (Chen Muhua 1987):

- "[T]he gradual formation of Wenzhou's capital market is suited to the requirements of commercialized production in Wenzhou. In addition to the capital provided by the state banks and rural credit cooperatives, there are now various kinds of businesses with deposit-taking and lending operations. Non-governmental (*minjian*) capital mobilization and non-governmental rural cooperatives have emerged. The various methods of financial mobilization have made a positive contribution to local economic development."
- "Although the comrades working in banks, credit cooperatives, and insurance companies have made a lot of efforts to mobilize a substantial amount of capital and to support the legitimate financial requirements of economic construction, the needs of economic development are still not met. Now, there are so many non-governmental cooperatives in Wenzhou, with interest rates so high and with so much cash injection. There are so many rich people and so many speculative activities. All of these suggest that our banking work is not adequate, which calls for solving these problems by deepening the reforms of the financial system."

To be sure, Madame Chen did not give blanket endorsement to the various financial practices in Wenzhou. In particular, she singled out clandestine pyramid schemes known as escalating associations (*taihui*) for criticism. But the overall tone of her speech, as these excerpts show, was unmistakably positive. (She began her address to the Wenzhou government officials and bank managers by stating, "Today, I am not here to make a speech. I am here as a student.") She endorsed lending to private enterprises by the state-owned banking system, interest-rate flexibility, and the operation of private financial institutions subject to certain regulatory limitations. This high-level policy endorsement is particularly noteworthy considering the fact that, as Tsai (2002) reveals, there were some large-scale collapses of private financial houses in 1985 and 1986. (The money house run by Zheng Lefang, the Wenzhou housewife executed in 1991 for financial crimes, collapsed in 1986.)

Throughout the reform era, Wenzhou served as a barometer of the fundamental policy orientation toward the private sector. Madame Chen's highly positive assessment of Wenzhou exposes one of the biggest myths about the Chinese reforms – that the Chinese reforms were somehow pushed clandestinely by liberal local officials who connived against a conservative and controlling central leadership. Nothing can be further from the truth, at least for the 1980s. The private sector succeeded in Wenzhou because of the actively permissive, if not encouraging, stance of the central leadership in the 1980s. Madame Chen revealed in one of her speeches that the central government had sanctioned financial reforms in Wenzhou as early as 1982. The Chinese financial regulators had full knowledge of and endorsed many of the financial practices in Wenzhou. We know this because the president of the ABC, Dai Xianglong, who was to assume the governorship of the PBoC in 1995 and who cracked down on rural informal finance in the 1990s, detailed the practices of the Wenzhou RCCs in a 1987 speech.[12] Ma Yongwei, a senior manager at the ABC, hailed the "new breakthroughs" by the RCCs in Wenzhou in moving toward flexible interest rates and achieving fund mobility across different regions (Ma Yongwei 1987 <1986>, p. 85).

Another noteworthy aspect of her speech and several bank documents from this era is the implicit, and sometimes explicit, view that the state-owned financial system was not competitive enough to satisfy the funding requirements in rural China. Chen's point that "we are not doing an adequate banking job" is entirely consistent with the main thrust of the RCC reforms – to decentralize the control rights of the RCCs so that they would be more responsive to the needs of rural households. In the long run, as the formal financial institutions became more competitive, this thinking goes, the market positions of loan sharks and usurious financial practices would be undermined. It was a remarkably market-based approach rather than an administrative instinct that sought to criminalize informal finance.

Because of the high degree of policy tolerance, informal finance flourished in many regions of the country. Western scholars believe that informal finance emerged mainly in the free-wheeling and dynamic regions of southern China, such as Wenzhou of Zhejiang province (Tsai 2002). A factor that correlates more strongly with the informal finance is not geography but the extent of private-sector development. Keep in mind that informal finance itself is a form of private entrepreneurship and its operations are both a result of and a condition for the flourishing of private businesses. Thus, one finds informal finance wherever private entrepreneurship was present and, as I pointed out in the last chapter, private entrepreneurship thrived in the poor, rural, interior provinces. It is thus not surprising to find informal finance in those regions as well, not just in coastal provinces.

Take the example of Guizhou, a province that had a vibrant private sector in its rural areas. Guizhou, China's poorest, agricultural, and landlocked province, experienced surging informal finance activities in the 1980s. Streets were lined up with pawnshops and rotation associations (Editorial Committee of Guizhou Pan County Financial History, 1994), very similar to the description of the back-alley finance provided in Kellee Tsai's book about the more developed parts of the country. Informal finance was even present in a province known as the stronghold of the urban SOEs, Jilin province in China's northeast (home to one of the oldest and most established SOEs, First Automotive Works). A study conducted by the Jilin branch of the PBoC in 1987 reveals that 68.9 percent of the rural households in the survey borrowed from the informal credit market. The investigation details the uses of informal credit: 81 percent of underground loans were used for production purposes.

This study is revealing of both the extent of the informal finance in Jilin as well as the policy orientation of the PBoC in the 1980s. Jilin is not known as a pioneer in the economic reforms and has a well-deserved reputation of being cautious and economically conservative. Yet, PBoC's Jilin branch was highly positive in its assessment of the role of informal finance and concluded that informal finance "eliminated some of the inadequacies of the bank credit and contributed to the commercialization of the rural economy" (Jilin Branch of the People's Bank of China 1987, p. 151). That informal finance was present both in regions with an initially low endowment of state assets – such as Wenzhou – and in regions with a substantial presence of SOEs – such as Jilin – is evidence that the permissive stance toward informal finance was a central government policy rather than a discretionary policy of the local governments.

The best example of the market-based view of the Chinese reformers in the 1980s is the financial innovation called rural cooperative foundations. The background to the RCFs was the large-scale privatization of collective assets in the early 1980s. Although rural China privatized the control rights of collective land, some of the assets, such as plow animals or heavy-duty equipment, either were too expensive to be acquired by individual households or were indivisible assets – a donkey cannot be divided in two. So these assets still remained on the books of the villages, but they became illiquid as the collective entities shed their production role and the ability to generate revenue.

The RCFs rose in response to this problem. Villages securitized the collective assets by selling ownership shares to the members of the villages. The funds pooled from what amounted to private placements were then used to meet the short-term liquidity needs of the members of the villages. After the first round of initial privatization of the collective assets, the role of the RCFs migrated to something akin to the role of a savings and loan institution. The RCFs began to compete directly with official savings and loans institution such as the RCCs. In the 1980s, many RCFs were explicitly private, and in many ways they represented the model of what the financial reformers wanted the RCCs to become. (Some Western researchers believe that RCFs were tightly controlled by the local governments. They were, to some extent, but much of the research on RCFs was conducted in the 1990s, reflecting the state of affairs in that decade.)

The scale of the RCFs was enormous. By 1990, the RCFs covered more than 38 percent of Chinese rural townships (Rural Work Leadership Team of Fujian Communist Party Committee 1997). In 1990, the RCFs in Wenzhou pooled 20 million yuan from their members. This was a huge sum of money. In the same year, the total outstanding loans by the ABC amounted to 26.5 million yuan. At least in Wenzhou, by the end of the 1980s, the RCFs were beginning to approach the ABC in both size and reach (Editorial Committee of Wenzhou Financial History 1995, p. 152 and p. 225).

The RCFs are an excellent illustration of the fundamental differences between the 1980s and the 1990s. In the 1980s, policy makers wanted to make the RCCs more autonomous because they wanted the RCCs to become more competitive vis-à-vis other institutions such as the RCFs. Despite the fact that the RCFs competed with the RCCs, the Chinese government did not stamp out the RCFs. This was remarkable considering that the RCFs were never explicitly recognized by the PBoC as a legitimate financial institution. Unlike other financial institutions that were either regulated by the PBoC or were operating illegally, the RCFs enjoyed a semi-official status because they were loosely supervised by the Ministry of Agriculture, the most reformist central ministry in the 1980s.

3.3 The Financing Repression of the 1990s

The financing of the private sector contracted immediately after the Tiananmen crackdown. In 1989 and the 1990s, the credit financing of rural private fixed-asset investments amounted to half of the level in 1987 and 1988. Fixed-asset investments by the private sector slowed down substantially, as we saw in Chapter 1. During this period, the collective sector began to receive the bulk of bank loans. Data show that Henan, a province that had a large private TVE sector, expanded loans to collective TVEs enormously. In 1984, the household-to-collective ratio of loans by RCCs was 1.90; in 1993, the ratio was 1.02.

The motivation in part was political in nature as the conservative central planners mounted an ideological assault on the private sector. The other reason was the macroeconomic retrenchment effected through a tightening of the credit supply. During the reform era, in years that inflation was high, private-sector development tended to be robust. For example, during the heyday of private-sector development in 1984 and 1985, rural credit expanded rapidly. In 1985, the ABC took in deposits of 93.4 billion yuan and lent out 168.5 billion yuan, injecting liquidity into the rural economy (People's Bank of China 1987, p. 4).

One of the few ways to finance the private sector, which operated outside the credit rationing plan, was to create more credit. This is why reformers such as Zhao Ziyang always seemed to have favored an expansive credit policy whereas the private sector tended to suffer under the inflation hawks, such as Li Peng. Credit extensions to the private sector are the microeconomic link between reforms and inflation. By implication, during the macroeconomic retrenchment, the private sector becomes the first policy casualty.[13]

The political assault on the private sector ended in 1993 after Deng Xiaoping conducted his famous "Southern Tour." The substantial financial repression of the private sector that occurred after 1993 was not motivated by political ideology but rather by technocratic ideology. The private sector, much of it rural, small-scale, low-tech, and hailing from the poorer parts of China, was considered not worthy of the country's precious financial capital. Much of the capital, then, was directed to what were considered the high-tech, urban parts of the country.

The financing repression of the private sector took two forms. One was a change in the lending priorities of Chinese banks. Banks were now instructed to support agriculture rather than to support rural entrepreneurs transitioning out of agriculture. This is an industrial policy mentality *par excellence*. Because of the view that agriculture is strategic – ensuring cheap agricultural supplies to industry and to cities – and because of distrust of the price mechanism, the idea is that the state had to use policy levers to affect the relative returns between farm and non-farm activities. Restrictions placed on non-farm activities were used to raise the relative returns on farm activities so as to ensure a steady supply of agricultural produce. The same rationale justified loan subsidies to agricultural production.

The other form of financing repression was a retreat from the financial opening and the tacitly encouraging stance toward competition that had prevailed in the 1980s. Private, unsanctioned financial intermediation competed with the financing tools of the state's industrial policy and reduced the ability of the state to direct resources. Thus, at an ever-intensifying pace, the state began to crack down on informal finance.

The RCCs, the primary credit facility to the non-farm rural entrepreneurs, were ordered to focus on agriculture. The ABC issued numerous specific quotas for the RCCs. Usually, 40 percent of the new lending was to be allocated to agricultural projects; in the agricultural provinces, the ratio was at an even higher level. Agricultural producers had priority over other borrowers, and those providing agricultural services, such as processing, transportation, and trading of agricultural produce, enjoyed top priority (State Council 1996). In the 1990s, the RCCs were used as a mechanism to subsidize agriculture. This policy development explains the drastic slowdown in non-farm business income in the 1990s. Because strictly agricultural activities always have a lower value added, the sectoral restrictions also explain the reduction in the overall growth of rural income.

Non-farm lending by RCCs was not banned but it was scaled back. Basically, non-farm lending became a residual. RCCs were to lend to non-agricultural projects only after the agricultural lending was fulfilled. This is how Dai Xianglong, the governor of the PBoC, outlined the priorities of the RCCs: "After the priority lending to satisfy the capital needs of agricultural production, if there are still funds available, then the capital needs of the TVEs and other industrial and commercial businesses can be considered" (Dai Xianglong 1997). The loan qualification requirements were made more stringent. The self-funding portion had to be 60 percent, an increase from the 30 to 50 percent range specified in the bank documents of the 1980s (People's Bank of China 1999, p. 146). Article 37 of the 1995 Loan Guarantee Law explicitly excludes plots of land for private farming and private housing as collateral assets.[14]

The restriction of RCCs to agricultural lending amounted to effective credit constraints on rural private entrepreneurs, the vast majority of whom started their businesses *to get out of agriculture*. This represented a fundamental shift from the focus of the RCCs in the 1980s, which was to facilitate the transition of rural residents out of agriculture. In Wenzhou, for example, a high share of RCC loans had gone to non-farm projects in the 1980s, about 39 percent cumulatively between 1984 and 1990 (Editorial Committee of Wenzhou Financial History 1995, p. 149). Another form of discrimination, more implicit than the sectoral restrictions, was that bank policy favored production over construction of new facilities. In a 1996 State Council document, fixed-asset loans were capped at 30 percent of all RCC loans. This handicapped the private entrepreneurs, who had just started their businesses and needed capital to construct new facilities.

The discrimination against private entrepreneurs was not just *de facto* but was *de jure* as well. In the 1990s, there was a rising sentiment among Chinese financial regulators that private entrepreneurs posed higher credit risks (despite the mountains of evidence to the contrary). In 1992, the ABC (Agricultural Bank of China 1992a) instructed the RCCs to mandate individual business owners and private enterprises to deposit "a risk guarantee fund" before loan disbursements. Although private borrowers always faced higher costs, this policy was quite onerous. In the 1980s, the RCCs had charged higher interest rates to private borrowers as a way to mitigate the perceived risks of these borrowers. Good borrowers could generate profits to ease the higher interest costs. But the 1992 policy required an upfront payment and it made no distinction between a good and a bad borrower.

Chinese financial regulators felt that even this safeguard was insufficient. In 1994, the ABC issued another rule requiring the RCCs to impose an extra hurdle on loan approvals for individual business owners and private enterprises. Each loan to private entrepreneurs required two signatures, one from the loan officer and the other from the director of the regional RCC (Agricultural Bank of China 1994). This development is behind the observation by Park and Shen (2000) that loan approvals were centralized.

In the 1990s, the greatest change in rural finance was the increasing bureaucratization of the RCCs. Recall the 1988 draft regulation by the ABC to envision a system of selecting the RCC leadership on the basis of competitive elections by RCC members. This system was to replace the appointments of RCC managers by the ABC. This reform was now discontinued. Throughout the rest of the 1990s, among the large number of bank documents on RCCs issued by the ABC or the PBoC, not a single one refers to this 1988 draft regulation. Instead, management of RCCs was centralized. In a 1993 document entitled, "An opinion to speed up the rural financial reforms and opening," the ABC (Agricultural Bank of China 1992a) stated, "On the basis of the current leadership system, the emphasis should be on changing the operations and increasing the flexibility of the RCCs at the grass-roots level." The emphasis of this statement is on "current leadership system," signaling that the management system of the RCCs was not going to change.

Some of the key phrases used in connection with the RCC reforms in the 1980s disappeared in the 1990s. The three characteristics that the reformers wanted to restore to the RCCs – that they be organizationally reliant on RCC members, managerially democratic, and operationally flexible – did not appear in any of the copious bank documents issued on RCCs in the 1990s. Other terms that did not survive in the 1990s include *siren* or *siying*, meaning private-run, or *minjian*, meaning non-government. In its stead, the operative term used to describe the RCCs was cooperative (*hezuo*). In Chinese parlance, these terms have very different and specific connotations. The term "cooperative" falls into the same category of terms such as collective (*jiti*). Cooperative and collective institutions usually have some private revenue rights but their control rights are effectively governmental. (For example, in the mid-1950s, the production cooperatives formed by the peasants were viewed as a transitional stage between private and state-owned means of production.) *Minjian, siren,* and *siying* all imply full private ownership defined as both private revenue and *control* rights. In this connection, the 1988 ABC decision to experiment with the democratic election of the RCC management is fully consistent with the vision to make the RCC a *minjian* institution.

Almost every other year in the 1990s, the State Council or the PBoC would issue a major decision on "accelerating and deepening reforms" in the financial sector. This is a salient feature of the financial-sector policies in the 1990s. A close reading of these "reform" measures almost always reveals in essence a centralization of control rights, an increase in the extent of micromanagement by the government, and a restriction on the activities of private actors in the financial sector. This is especially true of those measures concerning the operations of the RCCs.

One example is the sanctioning of rotating RCC branch directors in an ABC directive issued in October 1992 (Agricultural Bank of China 1992b). A rotation means that an official of one region is assigned to a position at the same bureaucratic rank in a different region. The practice is a mockery of democracy as it nullifies any election results in the rotated regions. (Imagine rotating the governor of Massachusetts to Maine.) For this reason, in the 1980s, the reformers explicitly discouraged the rotations of top managers of the RCCs. The practice was resurrected in 1992.

Rural finance became increasingly centralized in the 1990s. In 1996, after the authorities completely severed the administrative relationship between the ABC and the RCCs, the RCCs were placed under the administrative supervision of the local governments. In a top-down political system, this was a logical consequence. Control rights are always vertical, running from a higher level of the bureaucracy to a lower level of the bureaucracy. The PBoC actively encouraged the RCCs to link up with the local governments.

The specific mechanism was the control by the Communist Party. The idea of Party control of the RCCs was completely absent in all the documents related to the RCCs in the 1980s. It appeared for the first time in a 1998 policy speech by Shi Jiliang, the vice governor of the PBoC. He urged the county RCCs to be linked up (*guaikao*) and to actively report to the local Party committees (Shi Jiliang 1999 <1998>, p. 25). In another speech, Shi defined RCCs as "local government financial institutions," by which he meant that the local governments should exercise active leadership over the RCCs (Shi Jiliang 1999). These directives were explicitly contrarian to the letter and the spirit of RCC reforms in the 1980s.

Prior to 1996, the directives and rules issued by the ABC paid lip service to respecting the autonomy of the RCCs. After all, the RCCs were defined as "cooperative" financial institutions by the State Council in 1993. Toward the late 1990s, however, the PBoC dropped all pretenses, as indicated by Shi's definition of RCCs as local government financial institutions. Even the word "cooperative" appeared infrequently in bank documents. In March 1998, the PBoC issued a detailed decree, containing 35 articles, entitled "Provisional methods on managing the appointment qualifications of the principals of RCCs and union associations of RCCs" (People's Bank of China 1999 <1998>). According to the decree, the PBoC was to assume control over all aspects of personnel appointments, including the screening of candidates, account examinations (mandated after each principal's departure), and the termination of appointment.

By the late 1990s, after a decade of mismanagement, bad policies, and poor governance, the RCCs experienced massive operating problems and they contracted dramatically in number. In 1985, there were more than 400,000 RCCs in the country. This number was to decline sharply in the 1990s. In 1990, there were 384,320 RCCs and 286,389 in 1992. By 2003, only 91,393 RCC branches remained.[15] This was the level of financial services in a massive country like China with more than 800 million rural residents. The performance of the RCCs also deteriorated. In the 1980s, the RCCs had non-performing loans (NPLs) on their balance sheets but most of them had been accumulated from the Cultural Revolution period. In 1994, 31.4 percent of the loan assets of the RCCs were non-performing and, in 1996, the NPLs increased to 38 percent, according to Dai Xianglong, the governor of the PBoC (Dai Xianglong 1997). The shareholder equity of the RCCs was reported to be 63.2 billion yuan in 1995, 54.8 billion yuan in 1996, 31 billion yuan in 1997, 15.1 billion yuan in 1998, and −8.5 billion yuan in 1999 (China Finance Association 1997, p. 452; 2000). In less than 10 years, an institution that had contributed substantially to the takeoff of the rural sector was completely insolvent.

Despite – and most likely because of – the layers of detailed controls instituted by the government, the RCCs' lending practices became progressively more egregious. The following is a telling list in a PBoC document of the degeneration in lending practices of the RCCs (People's Bank of China 2001a):

- making loans to peasants in the form of goods rather than money and forcing peasants to sell the goods to designated buyers
- expropriating the share capital contributions of the members of the RCCs when extending them loans
- collecting taxes and fees from peasants when making loans to them
- making loans to township and village governments to finance their fiscal obligations to higher-level governments
- forcing peasants to purchase shares of the RCCs and deducting their share contributions from their loans
- building office buildings and purchasing sedans while operating at a loss

It is clear from this description that by the end of the 1990s, a decade of mismanagement and poor governance had made the RCCs into the policy pawns and cashiers of local governments. Corruption and fraudulent practices were rampant. The RCCs had completely stopped serving the financial needs of their members, a goal the reformist leaders in the 1980s had set out to achieve. The policy response to the mounting RCC governance problems is as telling of the policy makers in the 1990s as their measures that had created these problems in the first place: If centralization created performance problems, the solution was more centralization.

Instead of trying to resolve the deep-seated incentive distortions and increase transparency and accountability, the authorities opted for command and control at a rapidly escalating pace. In October 1995, the ABC issued the directive, "Provisional regulation on the auditing of rural credit cooperatives and punishment measures" (Agricultural Bank of China 1995). Regional branches of the ABC were to conduct regular audits of the RCCs within their jurisdictions and mete out penalties according to the provisions in the regulation. This was an exceedingly detailed decree containing 4 sections and 18 articles. All the penalties had a monetary price, ranging from 100 to 2,000 yuan. For example, the penalty associated with lending to an incorrect borrower, for the wrong uses of loans, for loan contracts that do not meet specifications, or for borrowers violating loan contracts or government policy ranged from 20 to 1,000 yuan (Article 7). Provision 9 of Article 9 spells out the penalties for mishandling computer software, leading to data losses or the leaking of secrets. For some reason, mishandling computer software was considered more egregious than lending to the wrong clients, exacting a penalty starting at 100 yuan. Another rule issued by the PBoC concerned evaluations of the PBoC staff who monitored the RCCs (People's Bank of China 2001b). After all, those who monitor also need to be monitored. The style is classic command and control and the rule is numbingly detailed. (The set-up of a file system on the supervised RCCs is awarded two points in the evaluation, for example.)

In the 1990s, the authorities began to crack down on informal finance in a systematic fashion. The primary consideration was that informal finance was a source of competition with the state-owned financial institutions and that it drew resources away from the industrial policy programs of the state. The motivation was not the stability of the banking system. The available evidence indicates that financial institutions that were less tightly controlled by the state had better operating performance, but yet it was those state-owned institutions with poorer performance that were charged with the oversight of the better-performing institutions.[16] The 1997 Asia financial crisis had very little to do with the crackdown on informal finance, which took place before the financial crisis and, in all likelihood, weakened China's financial system.

In the 1980s, the government tacitly tolerated the operations of the RCFs, but this policy stance was to change in the 1990s. In 1993, the State Council (State Council 1994 <1993>, p. 7) pointedly singled out the RCFs, claiming they were not financial institutions and could not engage in deposit-taking operations. Instead, the role of the RCFs was to provide "mutual assistance" – small-scale, short-term revolving credit – to their members. The State Council decreed that the RCCs should take over those RCFs already engaged in deposit-taking businesses. In the next year, the government stepped up both the scale and the intensity of the campaign against the RCFs. The 1994 decision on restructuring RCFs prohibited lending and absorbing capital across different regions, and it established specific steps to absorb the RCFs into the RCC system. It also vastly limited the scope of the RCFs to agricultural lending because RCFs were not allowed to lend to urban residents or to develop branch networks beyond their home base (Rural Work Leadership Team of Fujian Communist Party Committee 1997).

The authorities stepped up the rhetoric against the RCFs in 1996. They were declared to be completely in violation of the financial regulations and engaged in "vicious competition" with the state-owned banks for deposits (State Council 1996). The 1996 decree announced that all RCFs would be absorbed into RCCs, a change from the 1993 decision that absorbed only the deposit-taking RCFs into RCCs. The final blow to the RCFs came on July 13, 1998, when the State Council, in a decree signed by Zhu Rongji, categorically banned all informal financial institutions and practices, including RCFs (State Council 1998). The tone of the decree was extremely harsh, criminalizing all forms of informal financial practices and mandating the involvement of the public security bureaus in the investigation and punishment of the informal financiers. Those PBoC officials who failed to refer the cases to the public security bureaus were deemed to have committed criminal offenses (Article 27).

We began this section with a lengthy quote from the stern 1998 State Council order to close down, ban, or even prosecute the informal finance operations in the country. We also began this section with a 1984 quote from Governor Chen of the PBoC that sanctioned informal finance as a useful supplement to the operations of the formal finance. The two contrasting policy statements came from the very top decision makers – the 1998 State Council was signed by Premier Zhu Rongji – and they capture the essence of the difference in the financial policies of the two decades.

4 The Power of the Chinese State

The policy reversals on rural finance, financial reforms, and TVEs took place in a larger political context. From 1989 to 2002, China was led by a group of individuals imbued with heavy urban biases in their views of economic development and with a strong industrial policy conviction. In the 1990s, the key economic policy makers were all engineers by training.[17] They followed a typical career path in a communist system – first serving as chief technicians and engineers at large SOEs and then ascending through the bureaucracy. Many of them came from overwhelmingly urban backgrounds. The top two national leaders in the 1990s, Jiang Zemin and Zhu Rongji, both had come from Shanghai prior to their elevation to their central posts. This represents a huge contrast with the 1980s when the top decision makers, such as Zhao Ziyang, Wan Li, and Tian Jiyun, gained prominence first as officials in the poor, agricultural provinces. (Interestingly, Hu Jintao comes from a background similar to the leaders of the 1980s, having first presided over Guizhou and Tibet in the 1980s.)

In the 1990s, FDI, technology, national champions, massive infrastructural developments, and urban renewal were elevated to the top of the economic policy agenda. In each one of these areas, the state is perceived as an indispensable instrument to make things happen. FDI was wooed through the construction of industrial parks and the bestowal of tax breaks. Technological acquisitions required state-sponsored and state-financed R&D programs. National champions were selected from incumbent large businesses, many of which were SOEs. Infrastructural developments and urban construction called for the intensive mobilization of a completely state-controlled resource in China – land assets. The direct economic role of the state in the 1990s remained substantial despite the fact that the Chinese state was shedding its ownership role.

In this section, I show that despite an economic transformation that is viewed by many as revolutionary, the size and the reach of the Chinese state have not diminished. In fact, by several measures, the Chinese state has grown massively since the early 1990s. Because Chinese capitalism is heavily rural in origin, the political environment in rural China has a direct bearing on private-sector development. Whereas governance deteriorated across the board in the 1990s, the extent of the deterioration probably was the most pronounced in rural China. One reason, apart from the economic policy reversals, was the strengthening of the political control by the state in China's vast countryside.

4.1 The Three Rural Crises

I have been a village cadre for nearly forty years. Even during the era of the commune system, control was never this tight. Today villages have no power whatsoever.
    –A Hebei village official quoted in a research report published by the Development Research Center of the State Council (Zhao Shukai 2005)

In 2000, as foreign firms and Western analysts were celebrating China's prospects to join the World Trade Organization (WTO), inside China an entirely different sentiment prevailed. That sentiment is best captured by the term *san nong weiji*. *San nong weiji* – coined by Li Changping, a rural official in Hubei province, in his now famous 2000 open letter to then-premier Zhu Rongji – refers to the three rural crises: the crisis of agriculture, the crisis of village governance, and the crisis of the peasantry. Li details the egregious abuses of the Chinese peasants in the hands of local officials, the helplessness of the rural residents, and the onerous burdens shouldered by them. As Party secretary of a township in Hubei province and part of the political establishment, Li was in a position to know. He intimately understood the situation in the Chinese countryside.

Li's assessment contrasts sharply with outside views of China. In writings about the Chinese economy, there is a remarkable discrepancy between insiders and Western analysts. This is not because of a lack of information. In fact, in many cases, the Chinese government has been surprisingly and brutally honest. A 1996 report by the Politburo and the State Council acknowledges "severe incidents of clashes between cadres and masses leading to deaths and injuries." The report lists a set of banned practices, evidence that local officials were actively engaging in these practices, including dispatching the police to confiscate the money and property of the peasants and forcibly removing property and herds from the homes of the peasants (Rural Work Leadership Team of Fujian Communist Party Committee 1997).

I have already documented the recentralization of credit controls. In the 1990s, there was also a significant attempt to recentralize the administrative and fiscal management of Chinese villages. In the immediate aftermath of the rural reforms in the 1980s, there was a quick and initial decline in the power of the CCP. Rural self-governance at the village level began to emerge. In the 1990s, however, there was an explicit and substantial effort to "rebuild" the CCP in rural China. Any progress that had been made in the direction of improving self-governance in rural China was eroded by the fiscal and administrative recentralization. This recentralization is captured in the statement – quoted at the beginning of this section – by a Hebei village official that "today's villages have no power whatsoever."

Very early on during the reform process, the CCP was already in a state of decline in rural China, a trend the Chinese state was determined to reverse in the 1990s. One immediate effect of the rural reforms was to render the title of Party secretary vacuous. The title did not connote any specific managerial or administrative responsibilities. In 1983, a village Party secretary issued what he called "a confession" – confessing to having nothing meaningful to do (Cui Anban 1983). An agenda of a township Party committee meeting contains rather mundane and marginal action items such as running an entertainment center for youth, conducting a campaign to extol courtesy, and cleaning the sidewalks ("A Report from the Shi Township" 1983). In his confession, the village Party secretary reveals that not a single person had applied to join the CCP for several years.

In the 1990s, the central government began to incorporate and then to increase the weight assigned to strengthening the local Party apparatus in its performance evaluations of subordinate officials. A major decision by the Politburo in 1994 laid out various measures to reclaim Party control of the countryside. The document sanctioned practices such as the stationing of higher-level cadres in villages and the appointment of outsiders to the post of village Party secretary. A 1995 policy document prohibits private marketing and trade of fertilizers and reestablishes the state monopoly over grain procurement (Rural Work Leadership Team of Fujian Communist Party Committee 1997).

Based on survey research, academics Oi and Rozelle (2000) show that democratically elected village committees met infrequently, with the number of their meetings decreasing from 5.4 times per village in 1988 to 5.2 times in 1995. The low frequency of these meetings implies that truly important decisions were made elsewhere. Oi and Rozelle also report that Party members accounted for a very high share of the village representatives.[18]

A second related development was an administrative and financial recentralization of power in the hands of the townships that sharply curtailed the operating autonomy of villages. In the 1990s, the Chinese state resurrected some of the administrative practices that originated from the commune era of the 1960s and 1970s. For example, under the commune system, there was a practice called "area management" (*guan pian zhidu*), whereby designated township officials were put in charge of specific areas comprising several villages. The person in charge was called area head (*pian zhang*). In the 1990s, this practice was reinstitutionalized and vastly expanded. Even provincial officials were stationed in villages.

In the 1980s, China made tentative but meaningful efforts toward village self-governance. The Organic Law of Village Committees mandated popular elections of those village officials in charge of fiscal management, allocation of land rights, and education. In the 1990s, the majority of those sitting on the village committees were elected. But there may be a less benign explanation for this seeming success: The village committees had no real power. In the 1990s, the modest level of village self-governance was completely supplanted by the administrative and financial centralizations. The village elections were becoming increasingly meaningless because the township governments used the Party system to counteract the outcomes of the village elections. In a 2005 report, one township Party official was brutally honest when he said, "As for those village officials who do not obey the township Party committee and government, we can dismiss the [village] Party secretary. If we cannot dismiss the village head, then we can push him aside and not invite him to the meetings or use other ways to get rid of him" (Zhao Shukai 2005, p. 5).

This 2005 report reveals the extent of the micromanagement by township governments, rivaling that during the commune system period. Compensation for village officials is financed by the villages but the compensation norms and standards are set by higher-level authorities. There are four components to the compensation: (1) a basic salary, (2) a seniority component,

(3) a position salary, and (4) a discretionary component. The report is based on data from 10 provinces, as varied and diverse as poor provinces such as Ningxia and Gansu on the one hand and Zhejiang and Shandong on the other, but the monetary guidelines seem to follow a uniform standard across all provinces, another indication of centralization. For example, the seniority wage is set at 10 yuan per job-year and the position wage is set at 500 yuan for village Party secretary, 300 yuan for village head, and 200 yuan for village accountant. The discretionary component, implemented since 1996, is set by a detailed performance evaluation by the township, ranging from population planning, budgeting, Party building, law and order, tree planting, FDI, the building of schools, the paving of roads, and so on, by the township.

In the 1990s, villages lost independent budgeting power. According to a 2005 State Council report, written based on extensive field research, a practice called the "village account managed by the township" (*cunzhang xiangguan*) was implemented in the 1990s. The level of budgetary centralization is remarkable. The township governments set three approval levels – 300 yuan, 500 yuan, and 1,000 yuan – above which the signatures of township officials, such as the deputy heads or heads of the townships, were required. The village cadre quoted at the beginning of this section was referring to this feature of township control. (He also said that he had enough authority to dig a small well.)

In a significant portion of the villages, the township governments not only approve budgetary applications but also directly take over management of the budget and cash-disbursement functions at the village level. This is called the "double centralized management" (*xuan daiguan*) – both budgetary approval and management at the township level. The 2005 report reveals that 16 villages had "single centralized management" and 14 villages had "double centralized management." Of the fifteen townships for which data are available, one started the budget centralization in 1991, five in 1997, two in 1998, five in 2002, and two in 2003. Thus, this was completely a 1990s phenomenon.

Let me underscore the huge operating implications of this move to transfer decision-making power from the villages to the townships. In 2005, there were 640,000 village committees and 18,900 townships. Moving decision making from the former to the latter entails a massive centralization of power. There is another issue here as well. In both the letter and the spirit of Chinese law, a village and a township are treated very differently in the Chinese political hierarchy. For example, the Organic Organization Law permits elections at the village level but not at the township level (Saich

2001). A village is not a formal part of the Chinese bureaucracy and village officials are not on the government payroll. Chinese political norms explicitly acknowledge the rights of villages to self-governance.

In contrast, a township is a formal part of the Chinese political hierarchy – it is the lowest level of the Chinese state. Township officials are officially on the government payroll and their expenditures are incorporated into the government budget. The township has an articulated government structure that is a near duplicate of the structure of the immediately superior government.[19] There are also real ethnographic differences between a township and a village. A village is far smaller and, therefore, more close-knit than a township. In the 1980s, a village averaged around 30 households with a total of 150 people. Many Chinese villages are populated by members of the same clan. This is why these villages are known as natural villages. They have a cohesive and tight culture and kinship networks in a way that distinguishes them from large, artificial, and far more permeable townships.[20] Centralizing the operating management of villages in the hands of townships nullified both the legal and the built-in autonomy of Chinese villages.

4.2 A Political Reversal

–"Individual laborers are the socialist laborer of our country. . . . As long as they meet the standards of the Party and [the Communist Youth] League, they should be recruited into the Party and the League according to the rules."
> –From a circular by the Party Central Committee and the State Council issued on October 17, 1981 (Central Committee and State Council 1982 <1981>, p. 987)

"There exists, between private entrepreneurs and workers, a relationship of exploitation and being exploited. Private entrepreneurs cannot be admitted into the Party."
> –From a circular by the Party Central Committee issued on August 28, 1989 (Central Committee 1991 <1989>, p. 598)

"Since reforms and opening, the social structure of our country has changed substantially. There are now non-governmental high-tech entrepreneurs and technicians, managers and technicians employed at FIEs, individual households, private entrepreneurs, employees at intermediation organizations, and free-lance workers so on and so forth. . . . They are also contributors to the socialism with Chinese characteristics."
> –From a speech given by Jiang Zemin on July 1, 2001 (Jiang Zemin 2006 <2001>, p. 286)

The last quote is from a famous speech Jiang Zemin gave on July 1, 2001. That speech is often described as path-breaking and credited as the one that finally conferred the belated political and ideological legitimacy on China's private sector. This view is simply incorrect.

The first quote is an excerpt from a circular issued by the Central Committee of the CCP and the State Council – in 1981. That circular already called for recruiting members of the private sector – called individual laborers at that time – into the Party. That circular addressed at great length and in great detail the need to equalize the economic and political treatment of the people working in the private sector with those in the state sector. The political environment for China's private sector started improving not in the 1990s but in the early 1980s.

Recall my account in the last chapter of Hu Yaobang's support for the emerging private sector in the 1980s. He coined the term "glory project" in 1983. This term was resurrected in 1994, by 10 private entrepreneurs, but there is a difference between how the term was used by Hu and how the term was interpreted in the 1990s. Hu Yaobang had argued that the economic contributions by the private sector were "glorious" but, in the 1990s, "glory projects" referred to the social contributions by the private sector – in the form of charity and donations to poverty alleviation and reforestation. An important feature of "glory projects" is noteworthy – it is specifically tailored to soliciting contributions from the private-sector entrepreneurs but not from the general corporate sector.

This is corporate social responsibility, Chinese style. Glory projects carry a rather subtle implication – that the charity contributions by the private sector are a form of indemnity against the political liabilities otherwise associated with private ownership. The unstated assumption is that the economic contributions by the private sector – output growth and employment generations – are insufficiently glorious. Private businesses need to make social contributions to make up their political deficit. This is very different from Hu Yaobang's original rationale for "glory projects."

This is a nice, if subtle, illustration of the substantial ideological hostility toward the private sector in the 1990s. Many assume that this ideological hostility was rooted in central planning and in the radicalism of the Cultural Revolution. This is true but part of the ideological hostility toward the private sector was revived by the leadership of the 1990s. The second quote is from a CCP document issued in August 1989 explicitly excluding private entrepreneurs from joining the Party.

I provide this documentary evidence here not to suggest that the ban was rigidly enforced in the 1990s but rather to argue that Jiang's 2001 speech eased the political and ideological restrictions that were created under *his own leadership*. It was the leadership of the 1980s that had taken on the ideological legacy of the central planning and Maoism; the leadership of the 1990s was revising its own views of capitalism. This is progress, to be sure, but let's give credit where credit is truly due. The easing of political constraints in the early 1980s preceded and enabled the entry of private businesses. Despite the praise Western observers lavished on them, the achievement by the leaders of the 1990s amounted to providing the lagging political recognition of a private sector already substantial on the ground. Let's also keep in mind that the private-sector policies, as measured by fixed asset investments, became illiberal in the 1990s.

We do not know nearly as much about the politics of the 1990s as about the economics of that decade, but we can be certain of one thing – the Chinese state was not retreating. In the 1990s, the Chinese state reversed the gradualist political reforms undertaken by the leadership in the 1980s. This assessment comes from a well-placed insider, Mr. Wu Min, a professor at the Party School under the Shanxi Provincial Party Committee.[21] In a 2007 article, Professor Wu reveals that the political reform program adopted at the Thirteenth Party Congress in 1987 made some substantial headway in terms of implementation during the one-year period after its adoption (a clear reference to the period leading up to the Tiananmen crisis in June 1989). According to Professor Wu, there were significant efforts to redefine and reduce the functions of the Communist Party. The Party committees were abolished in many government agencies and the functions of the Party and the state were explicitly delineated. Since 1989, however, despite the occasional rhetoric, there was no progress in the political reforms, especially in the area of reducing and streamlining the power of the Communist Party. Professor Wu argues that the stagnation of the political reforms is directly responsible for the multitude of the social ills plaguing China today.

The political reforms in the 1980s were designed to enhance the accountability of the government by creating some checks and balances over the power of the CCP and by fostering intraparty democracy. Professor Wu cites one specific measure in the 1990s to derail the reforms of the 1980s. According to Professor Wu, in the 1990s, China instituted explicit provisions prohibiting the National People's Congress (NPC) from conducting evaluations of officials in the executive branch, the courts, and the procuratorate. Professor Wu comments, "This is obviously a step backward and how can the system of people's congress be improved?"

Just how far did this step set back China? How about 1979? Three years after the end of the Cultural Revolution, the NPC began to exercise some real power. In 1979, in the aftermath of the capsizing of an oil rig during a storm in the Bohai Sea that resulted in 72 deaths, the NPC held hearings at which officials in the Ministry of Petroleum Industry were called to testify. The minister was determined to have been negligent and was sacked.[22] (Incidentally, since the late 1990s, there have been numerous explosions and industrial accidents in China's coal mines. Thousands of lives have been lost. Not a single official at the rank of minister or provincial governor has ever been held explicitly responsible.)

The stagnation or reversal of the political reforms was compounded by a substantial expansion of the scale of the Chinese state. Whereas the direct ownership role of the Chinese state declined, the magnitude of the state did not. In fact, since the early 1990s, the Chinese state has expanded in size substantially. There are several measures. One is a headcount of the number of civil servants. According to a researcher affiliated with the State Council, the number of officials on the government payroll was 46 million in 2004 (or 1 out of every 28 Chinese). In the early 1990s, the number was around 20 million. The researcher provides data on two poor provinces in China, Hebei and Anhui. In Hebei, between 1995 and 2003, the number of officials increased from 1.57 million to 2.19 million. In Anhui, between 1991 and 2003, the number increased from 1.2 million to 1.67 million (Zhao Shukai 2004b).

This expansion is especially noteworthy at the lowest level of the government apparatus. According to a 2004 government report, the number of township officials increased twofold during the course of the 1990s. In the mid-1980s, a small township had about 10 to 20 officials and a large township had between 20 and 30 officials. In 2004, an average township had more than 100 officials and sometimes even one department in a township had between 40 and 50 staff members (Zhao Shukai 2004a). The trend of these aggregate accounts is supported by micro survey data (although accounting differences mean that the match is not perfect). The fixed rural household surveys collected data on the number of village officials. In 1986, the number of officials per village was 6.2 persons; this number increased moderately to 6.29 in 1987 and 6.44 in 1988. In 1989, the number jumped to 9.08 persons. Between 1993 and 1998, the number of officials per village exceeded 7; it was 6.95 in 1999.

One relatively systematic measure of the size of the government is the fixed assets it has acquired for itself. Fixed assets here refer to the buildings, properties, and also possibly the vehicles operated by the government agencies.[23] Along with the headcount of government officials, this is a superior measure of the size of the government than government revenues and expenditures. The fiscal size of the government is a better measure of the role of the government in the economy, not necessarily its size. (For example, the United States can have a large government budget relative to its GDP, but the employment size of the government itself is relatively small compared with the size of the private sector.)

Another advantage of the fixed-asset investment data is that they are organized on a systematic basis and the series go back to the early 1980s, which allows for an analysis of the trends over time. There is also more disclosure. Many of the operations of the Chinese government are shrouded in secrecy, but we have more information on the fixed-asset investment activities.

In 2002, the fixed-asset investments by the apparatus of the state – defined as the agencies of the government and of the CCP – were 137 billion yuan, or about US$17 billion by the exchange-rate conversion.[24] This figure reflects the fixed-asset investments made by the entities of the state – government agencies and CCP departments. In the same year, the same state entities spent 56.6 billion yuan in fixed assets in the agricultural sector. In Chapter 5 of this book, I provide further evidence that the Chinese state today is self-serving. Here is a concrete illustration of this judgment: 800 million Chinese peasants claimed less than half of what 46 million Chinese bureaucrats claimed in fixed-asset investment resources. In the same year, the educational sector received 95.2 billion in fixed-asset investments, 68 percent of what the apparatus of the state invested in itself.

Let us also look at the trends over time. In 2002, the fixed-asset investments in the state apparatus amounted to about 7.1 percent of the total fixed-asset investments made by the state sector. In order to match this ratio, we have to go back to 1982 when the ratio was 7.0 percent. Here, once again, we have a tale of two decades. Throughout the 1980s, this ratio steadily declined, from 3.5 percent in 1985, 2.9 percent in 1988, to 2.3 percent in 1990. Beginning in 1991, the trend began to reverse. The ratio was 2.6 percent in 1991, 4.7 percent in 1995, and then 6.2 percent in 1998. By 2002, the ratio at 7.1 percent was more than twice the ratio in the last year of the 1980s.

4.3 An Industrial Policy State

The prevailing view in the West is that the Chinese state carried out a massive privatization program in the 1990s. An explicit turning point in the policy stance toward privatization is believed to be the 15th Party Congress convened in September 1997. Privatization did increase in scope and in intensity at that time when, by various estimates, between 30 million and 40 million workers were laid off from the SOEs (Garnaut, Song, Tenev, and Yao 2005; Yusuf, Nabeshima, and Perkins 2006).

Often missing in these accounts is another development that occurred during the same period: Massive investments in those large incumbent enterprises in which the state retained substantial and controlling equity shares. This is the industrial policy aspect of the Chinese state in the 1990s. The Chinese government is explicit and completely open about its own industrial-policy proclivities. The policy program officially sanctioned by the 15th Party Congress was "grasping the large and letting go of the small." "Letting go of the small" was the privatization component of the program with which Western academics are familiar; "grasping the large" was the industrial-policy component seldom emphasized in the works on this period.

The industrial policy agenda shaped China's privatization agenda. The purpose of "letting go of the small" was to limit the scale of privatization. According to a government estimate, small SOEs accounted for only some 18 percent of the assets in the state sector as of 1997. However, small SOEs accounted for the majority of the losses in the state sector (State Development and Planning Commission 1998). This is mainly because the small SOEs had to compete with the non-state firms, whereas the larger SOEs were protected from competition. Many of them were monopolies.

The standard economic rationale argues that the state should privatize the profitable SOEs first. The idea is that the profitable SOEs can be privatized with minimum social consequences. They have fewer employment redundancies and presumably they can fetch higher bids because of their sound financial conditions. The privatization proceeds can then be used to ease the pains to pay for the social costs of restructuring and privatization of the unprofitable SOEs in the future (Roland 2000, p. 248). This is an impeccable rationale. Presumably, private investors and entrepreneurs are better at managing and growing assets to create economic value, whereas the state has a comparative advantage in managing social responsibilities.

In the 1990s, the Chinese government did exactly the opposite, putting the country through an unnecessarily socially wrenching process. The privatization of small SOEs meant the loss-making SOEs were privatized. This policy stance maximized the social costs while it minimized the economic benefits. The privatization program financed a substantial build-up of the capital of those large SOEs that the state chose to retain. With an increasing intensity and level of specificity, several policy initiatives – in 1989, 1991, 1995, and 1997 – all aimed at supporting or creating ever larger SOEs. In 1991, the government selected 55 enterprise groups for experimentation and, in 1995, it expanded the list to 57. In 1997, the list was expanded again, to 120 (Institute of Industrial Economics 2000). Most of the beneficiaries of the government's industrial-policy program have been the SOEs. The target firms were given tax and debt relief, import licenses, greater access to domestic and overseas listing facilities, and substantially increased operating powers, such as powers to purchase and sell assets and to transfer assets across geographic and bureaucratic jurisdictions. The economic sectors covered by these firms also expanded to encompass virtually the entire economy. In 1990, the State Council issued a policy of "two guarantees" for 234 SOEs, guaranteeing them access to bank loans and raw materials. In 1994, the central government declared electronics, automobiles, petrochemicals, and construction to be the four "pillar industries" of the economy. The SOEs are dominant players in all of these four industries. Most of the 120 large enterprise groups slated for preferential policy treatments in the 1997 initiative were SOEs as well.[25]

The industrial-policy rationale for the SOE reforms forms another contrast with the 1980s. As is well known, Zhao Ziyang had begun to advocate SOE reforms in the late 1970s when he was Party secretary of Sichuan province, and Sichuan implemented one of the first programs to reform the SOEs.[26] What is noteworthy is that Zhao advocated reforms of the SOEs when the SOEs were *making huge accounting profits.* Zhao and his advisers clearly believed that the SOEs, as SOEs rather than as loss-making businesses, lacked competitiveness. A policy that limits privatization only to loss-making SOEs is based on a view that SOEs themselves were not plagued by distorted incentives and political control problems endemic of the state ownership. Rather, the diagnosis is that SOEs incur losses because they lack resources, technology, and investment opportunities.

The approach of Zhao toward SOE reform focused on solving a control-right problem. His contract approach, at least in terms of design if not in terms of the actual outcome, was trying to get at this control problem. Under this approach, SOE managers would sign contracts with the state that specified the obligations to the state and assigned the residual rights to the managers. There are differences of opinion as to whether the reform was successful, but the specific outcome of the reform need not detain us here. The important point is that the contract reform reveals an underlying, if implicit, intellectual framework that identified the core problem of the SOEs – their political control rights. Zhao's approach did not work because of the lack of complementary reforms and because of the short time frame of his leadership.

A view focusing on the control-right problems of the SOEs ought to have led to the next logical step of contract reforms – management buyouts of the SOEs. But, in the early 1990s, the Chinese leaders reversed the policy on the grounds that the contract reforms did not work. Instead, they embraced an industrial policy approach that actually augmented the control rights of those SOEs that the government had decided to retain. In the 1980s, collective TVEs, such as Kelon, had state revenue rights but private control rights. In the 1990s, in the case of the large SOEs, the situation was completely reversed. Most of the large SOEs, which were listed on China's two stock exchanges, had partial private revenue rights but complete state control rights.

Between 1990 and 2003, only 6.97 percent of the initial public offerings on the two Chinese stock exchanges were from private-sector companies. The rest were SOEs that issued minority shares but in which managerial control remained very clearly in state hands.[27] Put differently, because many shareholding firms in China have private revenue rights but their control rights still rest with the government, they should be considered as state-controlled. According to a detailed study of more than 600 firms on the Shanghai Stock Exchange (SHSE) and the Shenzhen Stock Exchange (SZSE) in 1995, the three main groups of shareholders – state, legal persons, and individual shareholders – each controlled about 30 percent of the outstanding shares (Xu and Wang 1997). This stock split has remained more or less constant since then, although the government has plans to reduce the state shares. The control rights of these firms were overwhelmingly state. According to the same study, although individual shareholding constituted 30 percent of the outstanding shares, on average individual shareholders occupied less than 0.3 percent of the seats on the boards of 154 companies, whereas on average the state was over-represented on the boards. On average, the state retained 50 percent of the seats even though its equity shares amounted to 30 percent. There were no proxy voting procedures, thereby putting the individual shareholders in a disadvantageous position vis-à-vis the institutional investors such as the government agencies. This usurpation of rightful shareholder power is direct evidence that the state harbors no intention of relinquishing its control rights even over those firms that have explicitly private revenue rights.

5 Conclusion

A widely accepted paradigm to explain Chinese reforms is the gradualist perspective – the idea that the Chinese reforms deepened over time in an incremental fashion. The economic and political logic of gradualism is powerful.[28] Gradual or incremental reforms build both political and economic complementarities. Reforms are fraught with uncertainties about eventual outcomes, and the best reform program minimizes these political and social costs and generates a bottom-up demand for deeper reforms because the public and government can take advantage of the successes of the initial easy reforms. The economic logic is just as strong. In the case of China, for example, the entry of non-state firms reduced the SOEs' profitability, which forced the SOEs to reform. Naughton explains the feasibility of this self-enforcing reform mechanism in terms of the "interconnectedness" of the institutional features of the centrally planned economies. Reforms are contagious because "unhooking a single key connection can cause the entire fabric to unravel" (Naughton 1996, p. 311).

In this chapter, I question the claim that China followed a gradualist strategy in the 1990s. My argument is that the gradualist perspective fits the China of the 1980s but not the China of the 1990s. Many of the productive reforms in the 1980s were partially or completely reversed in the 1990s. Fiscal decentralization, which is credited as an important positive incentive for growth, was largely reversed in 1994. The control rights of the small SOEs that had been delegated to managers in the 1980s were recentralized in the early 1990s, although many were fully privatized in the late 1990s. Private-sector financing became more difficult in the rural area. The political reforms stagnated completely. By far, the greatest reversal occurred in rural China. The financial innovations to lend to rural households to start non-farm businesses and to allow private financial intermediation were discontinued.

These reversals imply real consequences. In Chapter 5, I show that the ratio of investment to Chinese GDP rose steadily in the 1990s, unlike other East Asian economies in which the investment/GDP ratio declined as they became richer. By 2005, China was investing close to 50 percent of its GDP, a level that we do not see anywhere else in East Asia. One possible explanation behind this rise of investment is a shift of sources of growth. Because of the increasing policy and credit obstacles placed on the indigenous private sector, the ability of entrepreneurs to contribute to economic growth by product and process innovations was suppressed. The repression of the broad-based, small-scale private entrepreneurship would also depress income growth, thus limiting domestic consumption as a driver of growth. To maintain the same pace of GDP growth would require increasing the investment levels. This hypothesis dovetails with the fact that China launched huge infrastructural and urbanization projects since the mid-1990s. A large portion of those investments occurred within the state sector.

The massive investment boom, however, happened at a price. In the concluding chapter, I come back to this issue and ask the question, "If China invested so heavily in transportation and urban infrastructures and skyscrapers, what is it that the country is not investing in?" The answer, as it turned out, is education, especially education in the rural areas. In the 1990s, as China succeeded in creating world-class infrastructures, the government was charging fees for basic education and even for administering immunization shots to rural children. The result was a sharp rise of illiteracy and a slowdown in the pace of reducing infant mortality.

Another price of this investment boom is productivity growth. Beginning in the late 1990s, by some estimates, productivity growth slowed down and by other estimates it completely disappeared. (More data is presented in Chapter 5.) This is a very worrisome development. We know from economic research on East Asia that productivity slowdowns presaged the general economic contractions or even financial crises (Young 1995; Krugman 1994). China is facing a governance crisis of a significant magnitude. Corruption is rampant, the nature and scale of which began to take the form of grand theft in the 1990s, as opposed to the controllable, low-intensity corruption of the 1980s. The extreme policies, accelerating in intensity since the late 1990s – such as the laying off of tens of millions of workers without adequate social protection, the charging of ever higher fees for basic government services, the land grabs, and the growing crony capitalism – aggravated social tensions and contributed to income inequity. Social protests, some extraordinarily violent, are occurring at an increasing frequency.

I have already shown that the income growth of rural households slowed down dramatically in the 1990s. The TVEs, which were largely private, began to languish. I go into greater detail about the costs of the strategy in the 1990s in the final chapter of this book, but let me highlight a few of them here. One is that GDP growth in the 1990s increasingly was disconnected from the welfare of Chinese citizens. The ratio of household income per capita – gathered through surveys – relative to GDP per capita declined continuously during the decade. Yes, GDP was still growing rapidly, but each increment in the GDP growth entailed smaller improvements in the welfare of Chinese citizens. In the 1990s, education and health care were made more expensive and less accessible in rural China.

The true China miracle is a story of the 1980s when a vibrant rural entrepreneurial class emerged. This was the phase of what Baumol, Litan, and Shramm (2007) describe as entrepreneurial capitalism. The story of the 1990s is one of substantial urban biases, huge investments in state-allied businesses, courting of FDI by restricting indigenous capitalists, and subsidizing the cosmetically impressive urban boom by taxing the poorest segments of the population. This period is closer to what Baumol, Litan, and Shramm term as state-led capitalism. The epitome of this statist form of capitalism took place in Shanghai, a city that was left untouched by the reforms in the 1980s but became a political power base in the 1990s. The Shanghai model, with its skyscrapers and Maglev train, has impressed countless foreign observers of China and has inspired both the admiration and the fear of a rising China. But, a hard look into Shanghai leads to a very different perspective. At its core, Shanghai is substantially state-controlled and state-led. Its private sector is very under-developed. Personal income has not grown nearly as fast as the GDP of the city. This is the subject of the next chapter, "What is wrong with Shanghai?"

FOUR

What Is Wrong with Shanghai?

Why can't India plan bullet trains when China can smoothly roll hi-speed trains between Shanghai and Pudong covering a stretch of over 450 km in one hour?
– Jayant Patil, finance minister of the Indian state of Maharashtra

We must acknowledge that relative to the needs of economic growth and social development, Shanghai is not dynamic enough. The praise for Shanghai's dynamism mainly comes from the mouths of international friends based on impressionistic comparisons with metropolises of foreign countries.
– A report by the Shanghai Association of Industry and Commerce (2006, p. 29)

Nowhere else in the world has Shanghai inspired more imagination – and despair – than in the Indian city of Mumbai (particularly during its mon-soon season). Indian intellectuals and business people ask, often in great exasperation, "Why cannot Mumbai be more like Shanghai?" Prime Minis-ter Manmohan Singh, an Oxford-trained economist and a man steeped in humanistic values, nevertheless sees the heavy-handed Shanghai as a model. This is an excerpt from a speech he gave in March 2006[1]:

When I spoke of turning Mumbai into a Shanghai, many wondered what I had in mind. It is not my intention to draw a road map for Mumbai's future. But I do believe that Mumbai can learn from Shanghai's experience in reinventing itself; in rebuilding itself; in rediscovering itself.

This chapter begins with a quote by Jayant Patil, the finance minister of the Indian state of Maharashtra. His observation of Shanghai is fascinating. It shows the depth of admiration Indians have for Shanghai as an economic model. His comment, however, also shows that he knew next to nothing about the city he so admired. The high-speed train, known as Maglev, referred to by Patil, travels not from Shanghai to Pudong but rather between two locations within Pudong. It does not cover 450 km but rather only 30 km and it completes its journey 52 minutes ahead of Patil's schedule – in less

175

than 8 minutes. Patil is Exhibit A of the deeply flawed infatuations foreigners have about Shanghai, as pointed out by the report prepared by the Shanghai Association of Industry and Commerce (quoted at the beginning of this chapter).

The story of Shanghai is one of two extremes. At one extreme, Shanghai is viewed as a model of economic development and as a symbol of a rising and prosperous China, as the quotes from the Indian politicians show. At the other extreme, there is virtually no real knowledge about this city. It is unlikely that Prime Minister Singh has any detailed information about how Shanghai actually generates economic growth and creates wealth. He simply presumes the existence of these mechanisms firmly in place in Shanghai.

Much of the admiration for Shanghai is based on visual evidence. Just look at Shanghai's impressive and imposing skyline and the conclusion is obvious. Simon Long of *The Economist* opined that India has been "lapped" in its race with China. Why? For Long (2005), the proof is in the contrast between his experiences traveling in Shanghai and Mumbai. Returning to Shanghai was "a bewildering experience" as "[o]ccasionally, through the new skyscrapers, a familiar building appears, lost in the concrete jungle." Returning to Mumbai was infinitely more assuring. There was no new airport and the only innovation was an improved queuing system in the immigration hall. Long thus concludes, "Whereas its neighbor has been transformed out of all recognition, India has, in most visible essentials, stayed the same."

It might seem preposterous even to ask the question, "What is wrong with Shanghai?" Yet, this is precisely what this chapter is going to do and to argue that plenty is wrong with Shanghai. Much of the hype about Shanghai is heavily based on impressions (and on GDP data). The "Shanghai miracle" is assumed but not demonstrated. The "tyranny of numbers," in the words of Alwyn Young (1995), has led me to question the very foundation of this miracle. As in the rest of this book, I rely heavily on micro data for analysis. Three sources of data have been especially important in uncovering the economic dynamics of Shanghai: the well-designed rural and urban household surveys by the NBS; the series of private-sector surveys on larger and more established private enterprises; and a comprehensive, professionally managed patent database. Apart from the fact that these data get at the important microeconomic dimensions of Shanghai, they have another distinct advantage over GDP and FDI data: GDP and FDI data are explicit benchmarks used by the Chinese political system to promote or demote officials. The likelihood that the Micro data I report are politically tainted is much less and they thus reflect more accurately the economic dynamics on the ground.

Let me summarize the main findings based on detailed analyses of these data sources. First, although it is true that Shanghai has had excellent GDP performance, much of this performance seems to have only moderately improved the living standards of the average Shanghainese. A huge portion of Shanghai's GDP accrues not to Shanghai's households as personal income but rather to the government in the form of taxes and to corporations in the form of profits. Corporations in Shanghai are either heavily controlled by the government or their control rights are shared with foreign companies. The exalted GDP numbers translate into only modest levels of household income in Shanghai. Relative to the country as a whole, Shanghai's households are not nearly as rich as the city's GDP level suggests.

Second, in the 1990s, Shanghai's GDP growth was not pro-poor and since the late 1990s, its growth has been sharply anti-poor. The poorest segments of the Shanghai population have lost absolutely – relative to their income position in the past – since 2000. As recently as 2005, rural Shanghainese, who still accounted for a sizable share of the workforce,[2] had about the same income level as they did in 1989 relative to the rural income level of the country as a whole. The income position of urban Shanghainese, compared to the urban income of China as a whole, improved only marginally since the early 1990s. Whereas Shanghai households enjoy the highest wage level in the country, they earn very little money from their asset ownership, not just compared with households living in rich provinces but also compared with households living in some of China's poorest provinces. The huge construction and real estate booms that outside analysts associate with Shanghai appear to have done very little to benefit the average Shanghai households. Their rental income is among the lowest in the country. Third, despite its reputation of being a high-tech hub of China, there is no hard evidence that Shanghai is innovative. Measured in terms of patent grants per year, Shanghai consistently under-performed two of China's most entrepreneurial provinces, Zhejiang and Guangdong.

These little-known facts about Shanghai raise the question whether there is a Shanghai miracle at all. Our chapter begins with this question. Throughout the chapter, I benchmark Shanghai against Zhejiang and Guangdong (as well as some other provinces) for a very specific reason: Despite a rich history of business creation and risk-taking, entrepreneurship is almost completely missing in Shanghai today. This is the subject of the second section of this chapter. The "missing-entrepreneurship" phenomenon is extreme. In terms of small-scale household businesses, Shanghai ranks at the bottom of the country. In terms of larger, established private-sector businesses, Shanghai is under-developed relative to some of China's poorest agricultural provinces.

There is no good economic rationale why this is the case. Shanghai's lack of entrepreneurial development is entirely the result of its policy choices. The Shanghai model can be characterized as having three key elements. The first is heavy-handed intervention by the state in most micro affairs of the economy. The second is that the city has the most blatant anti-rural bias in its policy orientation in the country. (And, according to the line of reasoning developed in this book, an anti-rural policy orientation is strongly anti-market.) The third is a biased liberalization that privileges foreign capitalists – namely, FDI – and restricts and discriminates against indigenous capitalism. The chapter concludes with some broad conjectures about the true reasons behind the Shanghai miracle – that the city, taking advantage of its privileged political position, was heavily subsidized by the rest of the country.

1 Is There A Shanghai Miracle?

It is not an exaggeration to say that Shanghai is the most admired city in China in the eyes of foreign observers. Thomas Friedman, the influential *New York Times* columnist and an occasional Shanghai visitor, is a fan. The playing field has been leveled between "Shanghai and Silicon Valley," he stated. This is his description of Shanghai: "You can work where you want, live where you want, wear what you want, study abroad if you want, get from the Internet most of what you want and start a business if you want."[3] Academics are equally enthusiastic. Doug Guthrie (1999), a NYU professor who did all his field research in Shanghai for his book, *Dragon in a Three-Piece Suit*, described Shanghai as "the head of the dragon." Shanghai is the vanguard of the market reforms in China and, as Guthrie put it, it is one of "the most legalistic and institutionalized areas." No empirical evidence was actually produced to demonstrate that Shanghai was the vanguard of the economic reforms. The fact is so obvious that one has only to assert it.

Yusuf and Nabeshima (2006), two economists at the World Bank, provide more data about Shanghai in their book, *Postindustrial East Asian Cities*, but much of their data are really the statistical equivalent of tourist impressions. These include the fact that Shanghai constructed more than 3,000 buildings taller than 18 stories since the mid-1990s, it has a Maglev express train – the most advanced in the world – it has restored its historic buildings to their original grandeur on a massive scale, and it revitalized the cultural life of the city. The World Bank as an institution has long been enamored with Shanghai. In 2004, the Bank convened a large international conference on poverty in a posh Pudong hotel. The delegates to the conference had a chance to personally observe what China was supposed to have accomplished. One of the main themes emerging from the conference was that China succeeded in reducing poverty precisely because it did not protect its peasantry. Rapid urbanization was the only way out of poverty, the Bank pronounced at the end of the conference.

The World Bank has been intellectually consistent about Shanghai. China – and Shanghai in particular – has been the Bank's best student and its most admired teacher in FDI liberalization and globalization. Shanghai has indeed moved quite far on the path of globalization. The annual flow of FDI now amounts to 6.5 billion dollars, equivalent to the entire FDI inflow of India today. Not only does Shanghai attract a lot of FDI, it is able to attract the cream of the FDI – investments made by large and technologically sophisticated multinational corporations (MNCs). Just after China joined the WTO, some 300 global MNCs had already made investments in Shanghai, and 30 percent of them were contemplating making Shanghai their regional headquarters. The companies that have invested in Shanghai read like a who's-who list of the most prominent MNCs in the world, such as Delphi, GE, Mitsubishi, Itochu, Siemens, Hitachi, and Carrefour. Although Shanghai accounted for 5.5 percent of China's GDP in 2004, its share of exports was more than double its GDP share, around 12 percent. In 2004, FIEs accounted for 63.2 percent of Shanghai's gross industrial output and 67.3 percent of its total exports.

This would be the end of the conventional analysis of Shanghai. The excellent GDP performance and the massive FDI inflows must have improved the welfare of the average Shanghai residents enormously. The inference is so obvious that it obviates a need to actually examine whether this is true in reality. In this section, we take Shanghai's GDP performance as the start of our analysis and explore the answer to the question, "Has Shanghai's GDP performance improved the welfare of the average Shanghainese?"

1.1 Welfare and GDP

Shanghai has some exalted GDP numbers. For example, in 2004, Shanghai's GDP per capita was 55,037 yuan (about US$6,880). This was 5.2 times China's GDP per capita. By this measure, Shanghai unquestionably deserves the title as the head of the dragon. GDP data, however, are extraordinarily tricky.[4] GDP per capita is often loosely referred to as income per capita. That phrase leaves the impression that an average Shanghai resident earns an income close to its GDP per capita (i.e., 55,037 yuan). Many foreign firms, for example, use GDP per capita data to design sales strategies in their regional marketing plans, but this assumption is deeply flawed.

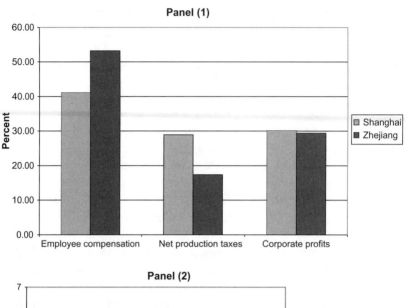

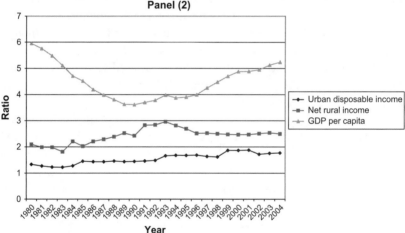

Figure 4.1. Benchmarking Shanghai: Various indicators. Panel (1): Components of net regional product in Shanghai and Zhejiang (based on income approach of GDP), 2002 (%). Panel (2): Ratios of Shanghai to national averages: Urban disposable per capita income, rural per capita net income and GDP per capita, 1980–2004. Panel (3): Ratios of Zhejiang to national averages: Urban disposable per capita income, rural per capita net income and GDP per capita, 1980–2004. *Sources:* The GDP data by income approach are from NBS (2004a, p. 64). Other data are drawn from *China Statistical Yearbook*, various years and rural and urban household surveys by NBS, various years.

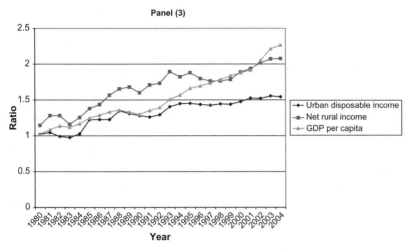

Figure 4.1. (*Cont.*)

There are two ways to disaggregate GDP data. One is the expenditure approach, under which GDP is disaggregated into consumption, investment, government spending, and net exports. The expenditure approach is the most common method by which GDP data are reported for China and for other countries. The alternative approach is the income approach, under which GDP is divided into the following components: (1) labor income (i.e., wages and benefits), (2) capital income (i.e., business profits, interest, and rent), (3) depreciation, and (4) taxes (i.e., income to the government). Depreciation is otherwise known as consumption of fixed capital and it refers to the amount that businesses set aside to replace worn-out structures and equipment. Calculations of the income components of GDP often require removing the depreciation amount from GDP. GDP minus depreciation becomes the net national product.

The other three components of GDP represent income accruals to the three main players in an economy: labor, capital owners, and government. This decomposition of GDP immediately illustrates the fallacy of the common assumption: That GDP per capita was 55,037 yuan in 2004 does not at all mean that an average Shanghainese earned 55,037 yuan. The 55,037 yuan was shared among labor, capital owners, and government. Importantly, it matters how the GDP is distributed among them.

Panel (1) of Figure 4.1 presents the percentage shares of the three components of what is known as the net regional product for Shanghai and Zhejiang in 2002. (The year 2002, the last year of Jiang Zemin's rule, marked the apex of the urban bias model.)

The Chinese data on employee compensation include both wages and benefits as well as proprietors' income. In 2002, employee compensation comprised 41 percent of Shanghai's net regional product. This is a remarkably low ratio. In the United States, the labor income and proprietors' income together typically exceed 70 percent of the net national product.[5] Shanghai's ratio is also low compared with Zhejiang. This comparison is both to minimize any differences in statistical reporting and other discrepancies as well as to illustrate a difference in the income accruals between Shanghai and the entrepreneurial economy of Zhejiang. An entrepreneurial economy has a high share of employee compensation (inclusive of proprietors' income), whereas a statist economy has a low share.

Employee compensation comprised 53 percent of the net regional product in Zhejiang, a full 12 percent higher than in Shanghai. The two provinces have almost identical shares of corporate profits, about 30 percent, which implies that the key difference between the two is the income accruing to the government. For Shanghai, the ratio is 28.9 percent; for Zhejiang, the ratio is 17.4 percent. The upshot of this analysis is that an average resident in Zhejiang captures 10 percent more of each increment in economic output than does her counterpart in Shanghai. She is 10 percent richer but her government is 10 percent poorer.

In fact, the difference is probably several multiples of a 10 percent differential in the employee compensation share. This is because Shanghai is significantly more state-owned than Zhejiang. Corporate profits in both regions account for about 30 percent of the net national product, but there is a difference in the ownership of corporations. Many capital owners in Zhejiang are private, whereas in Shanghai they are government agencies. We have fairly detailed ownership composition data on industry and we can assume that the ownership composition for the entire economy is similar to that for industry.

In 2002, SOE and government-controlled firms in Shanghai accounted for 39.4 percent of the industrial output value, compared with only 13.6 percent in Zhejiang (NBS 2003b, p. 461). Extrapolating from these output shares would lead to the conclusion that the private income share of GDP is 52.7 percent in Shanghai and 69.3 percent in Zhejiang. To be precise, in fact, we need to make another adjustment. Foreign firms accounted for a far higher share of industry in Shanghai than they did in Zhejiang. The difference may have been as high as 30 percent. To get at the income share accruing to indigenous residents, we would have to deduct the foreign share of economic output. However, this is a difficult exercise because of the overlapping ways in which the Chinese report the data.[6]

Shanghai is rich but an average Shanghainese is not. A huge share of the economic gains go to the government and the state-controlled businesses. Recall that Shanghai's GDP per capita is 5.2 times the national GDP per capita. But urban household surveys show Shanghai residents to be considerably poorer than this GDP ratio implies. In 2004, the urban disposable income per capita in Shanghai was 16,683 yuan (just above 2,000 dollars); for the country as a whole, the figure was 9,421.6 yuan. This implies a Shanghai/China ratio of 1.77, nowhere near the 5.2 ratio calculated on the basis of per capita GDP data. On the basis of per capita GDP for urban areas only, the ratio between Shanghai and Zhejiang was 1.92 in 2004, suggesting that Shanghai was almost twice as rich as Zhejiang. The Shanghai/Zhejiang ratio will be reduced to only 1.14 if we use the urban disposable income data. By this measure, Shanghai was only 14 percent richer than the urban regions of Zhejiang.

Let us examine this discrepancy between GDP data and income data from the household surveys. The household surveys were conducted on typical households living in Shanghai; thus, they reflect the economic well-being of the average Shanghainese. That the two data series have a huge gap between them suggests that there is a disconnect between the ostensibly impressive GDP performance of the city and the economic well-being of the population (numbering around 13 million). Specifically, we ask the following question, "Given that Shanghai has a very high level of per capita GDP, how have average Shanghainese fared relative to the rest of the country?" To get at this issue, I calculated the ratios of Shanghai's GDP, urban disposable income, and rural net income – all on the basis of per capita data – to their national averages. The results are presented in Panel (2) of Figure 4.1.

The line at the top, representing the ratios of per capita GDP, is shaped like a V. Shanghai began in 1980 at a very high per capita GDP relative to the rest of the country, but that ratio declined steadily until 1990 when it began to rise rapidly. In 1980, the per capita GDP ratio was around 5.9; in 2004, the ratio was 5.24. Thus, during the 24 years between 1980 and 2004, Shanghai seemingly went through a full cycle: In the 1980s, the city lost relative to the rest of the country, but in the 1990s, it regained its previous dominant position. This would be the conventional-wisdom interpretation of the economic history of Shanghai based on the GDP data.

Let us look at the other two lines in the graph representing the rural net income per capita and the urban disposable income per capita, respectively. The indicators based on the household-income surveys, a more accurate measure of the economic well-being of the average Shanghainese than the

GDP data, would cast doubt on this interpretation. The line in the middle, which represents rural net income, is shaped like an inverted V or a pyramid, almost a flipped image of the GDP per capita ratio. After an initial decline between 1980 and 1983, the ratio steadily rose, peaking in 1993, and then it declined or stayed flat for the rest of the period. At its peak, the ratio was 2.96 in 1993. In 2004, it was 2.5, exactly the same ratio as in 1989. An apt description of the line representing the urban disposable income ratio is a staircase with elongated but low stairs: The ratio rose by very small steps with many flat years in between. The ratio rose in 1985 to 1.46 (from 1.28 in 1984) and stayed flat until 1993, when it rose from 1.49 to 1.66. It then remained flat for another six years and rose only in 1999 to 1.87 and then resumed the flattening pattern until 2002, when the ratio declined to 1.72.

What do these numbers mean? The first striking pattern is a systematic inverse relationship between the GDP measure and the income measure. In the 1980s, when Shanghai's GDP per capita declined against the rest of the country, the income of its average residents was actually gaining, and this was especially true for its rural residents. In the 1990s, the relationship between per capita GDP and per capita rural income was still negative, but the movements of these two variables reversed their directions. Shanghai's per capita GDP grew substantially faster than the rest of the country beginning in 1990. (Again, the change came during the Tiananmen interlude.) In 1990, the ratio was 3.62. It was 3.98 in 1993, 4.25 in 1997, 4.88 in 2000, and 5.24 in 2004. At 5.24, Shanghai was roughly where it was in 1983 (5.11) in terms of its position vis-à-vis the rest of the country.

Many hail Shanghai's GDP development as evidence of its boom and miracle – many, that is to say, except those people living in Shanghai. After peaking in 1993, rural Shanghainese steadily lost ground relative to rural Chinese elsewhere in the country. Rural Shanghainese were still the richest in the country but, in 2004, their margins relative to the rest of the country had decreased. In 1993, the ratio was 2.96; in 2004, it was 2.49. This is exactly where Shanghai was in 1989. Urban Shanghainese fared only slightly better. They managed to increase their income margins relative to the rest of urban China but at an extraordinarily modest pace. Their margins rose every seven years or so, in 1985 (1.45), in 1993 (1.66), and then in 1999 (1.87). In 2004, the ratio was 1.77, a decline from the 1999 level.

Let me more formally demonstrate the negative relationship between Shanghai's GDP and its income levels – both relative to the rest of the country. A measure of simple two-way relationships between two variables is a Pearson correlation coefficient. When the coefficient is negative, the two variables are negatively correlated with each other; otherwise, they are positively correlated with each other. The Pearson correlation coefficient for Shanghai's GDP per capita and urban income per capita is −0.12; the Pearson coefficient for Shanghai's GDP per capita and rural income per capita is −0.62. In other words, there is a systematic *negative* relationship between Shanghai's GDP and the income levels of its population, although the strength of the relationship is much greater for the rural data than it is for the urban data.

The next question is why Shanghai exhibits such a pattern. One hypothesis is that a state-controlled economy can grow without improving the economic well-being of its average residents. For example, government-controlled corporations can invest heavily and reap huge gains through profit distributions. The government can finance heavy investments through taxes that reduce the income share of households. In contrast, an entrepreneurially driven economy can grow only by improving the personal incomes of the average households. We have already demonstrated that in entrepreneurial Zhejiang, the employee compensation share of GDP is much higher than it is in Shanghai. A logical inference is that GDP performance in Zhejiang is positively correlated with the household income of the average Zhejiang residents. This is confirmed in Panel (3) of Figure 4.1, which graphs the ratios of Zhejiang's per capita GDP, urban household income, and rural household income relative to the values of the national averages. In sharp contrast to the pattern visible on the Shanghai graph, the three lines move closely together. The Pearson correlation coefficient for the GDP per capita and urban household income is 0.91; it is 0.90 for the GDP per capita and rural household income data series. The welfare implications of the state-centered, interventionist Shanghai model and of the entrepreneurial Zhejiang model cannot be more clear.

1.2 Is Shanghai Poor?

In 2004, the World Bank convened a large-scale conference in Shanghai on global poverty. David Dollar, who wrote extensively about the supposed connections between globalization and poverty reduction in China, explained why the conference was held in Shanghai, "The World Bank looks around the world for successful stories, interprets it and then proselytises the interpretation – and that is often pretty good."[7]

Shanghai, according to the *Financial Times* article covering the event, is "a fitting location." It is one of the best students of globalization. In the 1990s and since China joined the WTO, the city has received a massive amount of FDI. In Chapter 1, I have already shown that much of China's poverty reduction occurred in the 1980s when the country was minimally globalized. In the 1990s, not only did the pace of poverty reduction slow

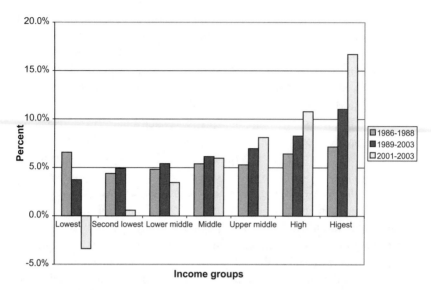

Figure 4.2. Real per capita urban income growth across three income groups in Shanghai: (1) 1986–1988, (2) 1989–2003, and (3) 2001–2003 (%). *Note:* The deflators used are Shanghai consumer price indices (1978 = 100). *Source:* The data are from the website of the Shanghai government. See http://www.stats-sh.gov.cn/2004shtj/tjnj/tjnj2006.htm#, accessed on July 13, 2007.

down dramatically, but also there were significant setbacks. (In the concluding chapter of this book, I return to this issue and note that China in the 1990s revised downward its poverty threshold several times so more people were lifted above poverty – in a statistical sense.) In this section, let's examine how poor people were faring in Shanghai, right under the noses of the World Bank delegates.

Figure 4.2 presents the real annual growth of urban household income averaged over three periods, 1986–1988, 1989–2003, and 2001–2003. The data were taken from the website of the Shanghai government and are based on the annual urban household surveys conducted by the NBS. The figure presents the real income growth rates. The nominal incomes were deflated to their 1978 prices (based on Shanghai consumer price indices). The Shanghai website breaks down income levels by seven groups: (1) lowest, (2) second lowest, (3) lower-middle, (4) middle, (5) upper-middle, (6) high, and (7) highest. These seven income groups are arrayed from left to right in the figure. I divided the data into three periods in order to detect any differences in the income-growth dynamics.

The pattern is very interesting. During the 1986–1988 period, the growth rates across the seven income groups are fairly even. The highest income group grew at the fastest rate (7.15 percent), but the second highest rate was registered by the lowest income group, at 6.57 percent. The other four income groups grew within a fairly narrow band. The dynamics during the 1989–2003 period is entirely different. This time there is an unmistakable pattern: The higher the income level, the higher its growth rate. And the differentials at which income grew between the income groups became very large. The lowest income group registered a growth rate of 3.73 percent, whereas the highest income group registered a growth rate at 11.05 percent. This is more than a threefold difference.

During the 2001–2003 period, the anti-poor bias of Shanghai became blatant. The lowest-income group lost 3.4 percent of their income and the second-lowest income group made no gains (0.6 percent). The growth rates of the next two income groups – lower middle and middle – slowed down considerably, both against the 1980s as well as against the rest of the 1990s. The upper-middle, high, and highest income groups gained enormously during this period. The highest income group grew at 16.7 percent annually, exceeding its already supersonic rate of 11 percent by almost 7 percent.

Two notes about the data. First, the household surveys do not include unregistered migrants and thus we could have an upward bias in the income data given that the unregistered migrants have historically been poorly treated by their employers and often go on for months without pay. Second, starting in 2004, the Shanghai government stopped reporting income figures for the lowest and second lowest income groups and the high and highest income groups separately. The seven income groups in the previous years are now consolidated into five income groups, which makes a detailed analysis difficult.

The difference in the growth rates between the highest income group and the lowest income group in Shanghai is 20 percent (16.7 percent minus −3.7 percent). All of these developments occurred right on the eve of the World Bank's conference on global poverty in Shanghai. Shanghai is a fitting location for a poverty conference but the rationale is diametrically opposite from the World Bank's "proselytisation." Shanghai's top-down model and state-led urbanization programs are inherently anti-poor.

1.3 Is Shanghai Rich?

Shanghai's Xintiandi – New Heaven and Earth – exhumes the wealth and affluence. It is located in a district, most ironically, where the first congress of the Chinese Communist Party was convened in 1921. Today, it houses avant-garde fashion boutiques, expensive bistros, and art galleries. Its architect, Benjamin Wood, who revitalized Boston's Faneuil Hall, applied the same formula to Xintiandi – in his words, he wanted to give Shanghai "a great European-style public space where people could go enjoy themselves."[8] With such a visible symbol of affluence, it is tempting to draw the conclusion that Shanghai is the consumption capital of China. Indeed, many MNCs use Shanghai to illustrate their strategy of targeting China's emerging consuming middle class. McKinsey, for example, foresees the rise of an urban middle class in China by 2025, with a spending power of some $2.4 trillion, equivalent to what Japanese households spend today. Shanghai features heavily in this type of analysis.

Elites in Shanghai are wealthy. This is not in doubt. The issue here is whether the level of wealth of the average Shanghai residents compares with the level of wealth elsewhere in China. To examine this question, we go to the NBS urban household surveys.[9] The NBS surveys collect information on incomes derived from owning property. The sources of property income are comprised of interest and dividend payouts or income from property rentals. All else being equal, there are some very good reasons why households in Shanghai should do very well on this score. For one thing, the rental income ought to be high because Shanghai experienced a real estate boom in the 1990s. But, it turns out that Shanghai is remarkably poor in asset terms.

In 2004, Shanghai's per capita property income was 215 yuan (about US$26) and in 2002 it was only 94.4 yuan (US$11). These are fractions of what urban residents in Zhejiang and Guangdong earned from property income. In fact, Shanghai urban households are not only asset poor compared with Zhejiang and Guangdong, they are also asset poor compared with the rest of urban China. Relative to all of urban China, the per capita property income of Shanghai households was between 0.6 (in 1996 and 1999) and 0.8 (in 2002) of the national average. In 2004, there was a sharp increase in the ratio of Shanghai to the rest of urban China, to about 1.3. The rise was mainly driven by the growth in rental income between 2002 and 2004. Even at 1.3, Shanghai is not particularly wealthy. Keep in mind that Shanghai's GDP per capita is 5.2 times the national average.

The low level of Shanghai's property income warrants further exploration. As low as the property income was in Shanghai in 2002 and 2004, this was already a substantial improvement over earlier years. Shanghai began to turn around in 2002, as indicated by the huge improvement from 94.4 yuan in 2002 to 215 yuan in 2004. In 2001, the per capita property income was only 39 yuan (US$5) and, in that year, Shanghai was ranked 25th out of 31 provinces in terms of the level of its property income. A Shanghai resident was worse off compared with residents in some of China's poorest provinces, such as Gansu (42 yuan), Shaanxi (53.8 yuan), and Ningxia (40.4 yuan).

An even more remarkable development is that between 1992 and 2001, an average Shanghai resident, in fact, experienced a *decline* in property income. This is not a decline in relative terms – relative to other sources of income. The property income declined in *absolute* terms; an average Shanghai resident was worse off in 2001 than she was in 1992 as measured by her property income. In 1992, the average property income was 44 yuan, compared with 39 yuan in 2001. All of this took place when GDP in Shanghai was growing at a double-digit annual rate. (These are all nominal values before inflation is taken into account.) In 1992, only four other provinces generated a higher level of property income than Shanghai (Zhejiang, Fujian, Guangdong, and Hainan). That Shanghai slipped from number five in the country in 1992 to number 6 from the bottom in 2001 is truly dramatic. Many observers believe that Shanghai experienced a Renaissance in the 1990s. The truth is that for Shanghai's average households, the massive growth brought about very little in wealth creation.

A comparison with entrepreneurial Zhejiang is revealing. In 1992, urban residents of Zhejiang, on average, earned property income that was 1.58 times that of a typical Shanghai resident. By 2001, this Zhejiang advantage had grown to 4.3 times. We can rule out a potential confounding factor – that Shanghai residents may consume a lot and, therefore, earn very little in the way of interest income. The huge difference between Shanghai and Zhejiang is due to the two components of property income – dividend income and rental income. The average dividend income in Zhejiang in 1996 was 27.65 yuan, 4.3 times that in Shanghai (6.43 yuan). The differential in the rental income was even larger. In Zhejiang, it was 22.54 yuan but in Shanghai, it was only 0.37 yuan – US$0.045 – a differential of 60.9 times. In fact, in 1996, the only reason why Shanghai avoided being dead last in the country was that rental income in Tibet was zero in that year.

The incomes from interest and dividend payouts represent the incomes derived from the savings set aside by households in previous years. That Shanghai's property income is so low indicates that there is a very low savings rate. Based on the income approach of GDP, we can know how much income was earned by households in a given year, and from the expenditure approach of GDP we can also know how much households spend in a given year. The difference between the two is the household savings. By this calculation, in 2002, the household savings rate in Shanghai was only 1.29 percent.[10] This compares with 13.7 percent in Zhejiang. There are many complications involved in calculating an accurate household savings rate, including the fact that the income approach of GDP does not include transfer payments, which can also be saved. The point of this exercise is not to argue that Shanghai's household savings rate is actually only 1.29 percent. The point is that the same estimation shows that Zhejiang has a significantly higher savings rate than Shanghai.

1.4 Jobless Growth

One of the most perplexing developments in the 1990s was that employment failed to grow. Employment growth in the 1990s in China as a whole did not remotely match employment growth in the 1980s, and several studies show that for the country as a whole, employment elasticity with respect to growth fell substantially in the 1990s.[11] This growth in joblessness took an extreme form in Shanghai. In the 1990s, not only did employment grow at a slower rate than GDP, the size of employment actually contracted.

Chinese statistical sources provide data on two employment measures.[12] One is the narrower measure covering staff and workers in formal establishments, mainly in the urban areas. This measure excludes employment in private-sector firms and self-employed businesses but does include employment in SOEs, collective firms, and FIEs. The second is a broader measure that includes both staff and workers in formal establishments as well as workers located in rural areas who receive remunerations. Workers in TVEs are included in the second measure but not in the first. We call the broad measure *aggregate employment* and we call the narrow measure *urban employment*.

Both measures show a sharp reduction in employment in Shanghai in the 1990s, especially in the second half of the 1990s. In 1995, aggregate employment stood at 7.9 million; by 2000, it was 6.7 million, a reduction of 15 percent. Since 2000, however, there has been a recovery in the creation of employment. Only in 2004 did aggregate employment in Shanghai recover to its 1995 level (8.1 million). That Shanghai had about the same level of employment in 2004 that it had 10 years earlier is quite remarkable. During those 10 years, Shanghai experienced an unprecedented boom in real estate; FDI; and industrial, commercial, and cultural activities. Its GDP expanded several-fold, and there were massive infrastructural investments. It is also remarkable in comparison with other regions that also experienced rapid economic growth but were also able to create jobs. The aggregate employment in Zhejiang expanded from 26.2 million in 1995 to 32 million in 2004. In Guangdong, it grew from 35.5 million to 47 million during the same period. Guangdong and Zhejiang were able to generate GDP growth and to create something in scarce supply in a populous country such as China – a job.

The narrower measure of employment – urban employment in the state, collective, and foreign sectors – shows an even sharper reduction.[13] And this reduction began to occur earlier than that in the aggregate measure of employment. In 1990, the number of staff and workers in Shanghai stood at 5.08 million; this number shrank by almost 50 percent in 2004, to 2.64 million. Although aggregate employment expanded modestly between 1990 and 1995, urban employment began to decrease even in the first half of the 1990s. In 1995, urban employment was 4.7 million. Again, the contrast with the more entrepreneurial provinces is substantial. Between 1990 and 2004, urban employment in Guangdong expanded from 7.86 million to 8.12 million. Zhejiang, however, experienced a decline in urban employment but not nearly as severe as that in Shanghai. Urban employment contracted by 8.7 percent between 1990 and 2004 (compared with 50 percent in Shanghai).

The rather poor job picture in Shanghai in the 1990s may help explain the shrinkage of property income of the average Shanghai resident as shown in the NBS urban household survey data. One possibility is that many Shanghai residents might have had to draw on their savings to support themselves. This would be due to a combination of the rising unemployment and the fact that single-proprietor income failed to rise. This hypothesis is consistent with something else I reported earlier – Shanghai's household savings rate is very low. The sharper reduction in urban employment as compared with aggregate employment raises another issue. Because Shanghai had a large state sector, a substantial component of the urban employment consisted of workers in SOEs. Thus, one could argue that the sharp contraction in urban employment was due to restructuring – the shedding of the excessive workforce in the SOEs. The sharp reduction in employment, although wrenching both politically and socially, can be viewed as a sign of a determined effort to reform the city.

Shanghai seems to have pursued one of the most aggressive restructuring programs in the country. In fact, the degree of the restructuring appears to have gone deeper and wider even compared with that in entrepreneurial Guangdong and Zhejiang. In 2004, urban employment in Shanghai's state sector was only 32 percent of what it was in 1990. In comparison, the SOE restructuring in Guangdong and Zhejiang was far less aggressive. In 2004, state-sector employment in Guangdong was 68.8 percent of its 1990 level; in Zhejiang, it was 60.6 percent.

This combination of a seemingly aggressive restructuring program aimed at SOEs and slower growth of the private sector casts doubt on a number of conventional explanations about the reforms in China. One popular explanation is that the Chinese government hesitated to privatize the SOEs because of the substantial negative social implications. Unemployment can lead to social unrest and thus even the inefficient SOEs had to be kept alive. But Shanghai does not seem to have been fazed by the social implications of the restructuring program. One would have expected Shanghai to have been extra cautious. After all, this is a city that has a high visibility abroad and any instances of social unrest would have a greater effect on foreign investors' confidence in China than social unrest elsewhere in the country. Relative to the high stakes involved, the aggressive extent of the SOE restructuring is quite surprising.

Shanghai also led the way in the labor reforms of the state sector. Shanghai began to shed its workforce in the state sector very early, before the large-scale restructuring was rolled out on a national scale. Between 1990 and 1995, Shanghai was one of only three regions in the country that experienced negative employment growth. The other two regions were Heilongjiang and Qinghai. Also between 1990 and 1995, Shanghai had already begun to reduce its workforce in the SOEs, from 3.97 million to 3.24 million. In contrast, in the entrepreneurial provinces, the size of SOE employment, in fact, expanded during this period. In Guangdong, employment in the SOEs increased from 5.3 million in 1990 to 5.5 million in 1995; in Zhejiang, it increased from 2.8 million to 2.95 million.

That the two entrepreneurial provinces actually added state-sector employment, whereas the normally statist Shanghai reduced it, is a fascinating observation. It suggests that Shanghai's restructuring program was not used to jump-start private-sector development in Shanghai. Shanghai reduced state-sector employment while imposing restrictions on the private sector. A plausible explanation is that Shanghai restructured its SOEs to maximize the tax and income gains from the SOEs. The purpose of laying off SOE workers was to reduce the cost base of supporting the struggling SOEs and the purpose of restricting competition from private-sector firms was to raise the revenue base of the remaining SOEs.

1.5 Is Shanghai Innovative?

Stephen Green, an economist working at Standard Chartered Bank based in Shanghai, wrote that Shanghai authorities liked to treat foreign visitors to a tour of the Fuxing Group, a Shanghai-based private-sector pharmaceutical firm. The purpose is to showcase "Shanghai's vibrant private, high-tech economy," Green (2003, p. 153) observed. But Shanghai's intentions erred in two areas – that Shanghai has a vibrant private economy and that its economy is high-tech. I have already shown that in terms of business income and income from holding assets, Shanghai is remarkably poor, not just in comparison with entrepreneurial Zhejiang and Guangdong but also in comparison with some of the poorest regions of China. In this section, I deal with the second of Green's observations – that Shanghai has a high-tech economy.

Shanghai Fuxing, the firm the Shanghai officials liked to showcase, is impressive but not at all for the reason that Shanghai claimed. The Shanghai firm has on its product portfolio a malaria-curing drug called Artesunate. In 2005, the World Health Organization (WHO) added this drug to its List of Pre-Qualified Medicines. This is the only indigenous Chinese firm on the WHO List of Pre-Qualified Medicines. (Another China-based firm on the list is the Chinese affiliate of Novartis.) To be certified by WHO is a major event for a firm because it signals the effectiveness of the drug and the reliability of the manufacturing process of the supplier. The standards used by WHO are identical to those used by the European Agency for the Evaluation of Medicinal Products and the US Food and Drug Administration.

But, to some extent, this was a hollow victory. For one thing, the fact that Artesunate is the only Chinese drug certified by WHO says something about the state of the pharmaceutical industry in China. On the WHO List of Pre-Qualified Medicines as of August 2006 – the list is updated regularly – there are eighty-three HIV/AIDs drugs supplied by five indigenous Indian firms and there are six tuberculosis drugs supplied by three Indian firms.[14] As impressive as Shanghai Fuxing is within China, it lags substantially behind its Indian peers.

For another matter, strictly speaking, Shanghai Fuxing had very little to do with developing Artesunate. Artesunate is registered by Guilin Pharmaceutical located in Guizhou province. Shanghai Fuxing acquired Guilin Pharmaceutical a few years ago, long after the drug discovery and development were well underway. In fact, Shanghai Fuxing is not really a pharmaceutical firm. It is a holding firm of many diverse assets. It operates in four unrelated areas – pharmaceuticals, real estate, steel, and retailing. Its founder has no background in the life sciences. He received a PhD degree in Chinese philosophy from Fudan University.[15]

The real reason that foreign visitors were repeatedly taken to tour the Fuxing Group is that there are so few prominent private-sector success stories in Shanghai. Shanghai has always fashioned itself as a leader of technology in China; as the pride in the Fuxing Group testifies, but its achievements seem to fall short of its ambitions or its capabilities. Beijing, not Shanghai, dominates the list of the technological startups that have gone public on the NASDAQ. As of 2006, there were 23 NASDAQ-listed firms based in China, of which 13 were based in Beijing and 6 were based in Shanghai.[16]

Let's examine Shanghai's technological development on the basis of a systematic and comprehensive measure – patent grants.[17] Patenting is widely used by economists as a measure of the innovations or competitiveness of firms or regions. The idea behind such a use is complex, but the main motivation stressed in the literature is that firms are motivated to build up their intellectual property rights in order to gain a competitive edge in the marketplace. Thus, patenting is a good measure both of innovativeness and of competitive business dynamics. Shanghai turns out to be terrible in terms of patenting activities and this is especially noteworthy considering the following two factors. One is that Shanghai started out as a leader in patents in the 1980s but ended as a laggard in the 1990s. The other is that Shanghai was showered with resources from the central government. With massive investments, a world-class infrastructure, and substantial FDI inflows, Shanghai does not seem to have much to show in an area that increasingly matters in China's competitive economic landscape – the ability to innovate and to upgrade technology and products.

In 1987, there were 575 patents awarded to individuals and institutions located in Shanghai. (All patents used in this chapter refer to patents granted by the Chinese patent authorities. Unless otherwise noted, all the patent data refer to annual patent grants rather than patent applications.[18]) This was second in the country, after Beijing (776 patents granted). In just four years, in 1991, Shanghai's position had slipped to No. 9 in the country in terms of the number of patents granted. Shanghai, with 1,025 patents, was not just behind Beijing (2,369 patents) but also behind two of China's largest agricultural provinces, Hunan with 1,174 patents and Sichuan with 1,232 patents.

The overall ranking is one indicator of what happened to Shanghai's innovative capacity in the 1990s, but it is not the most telling one. The more telling comparison is to benchmark Shanghai against provinces that have followed an entrepreneurial growth model. Let's compare Shanghai with Zhejiang and Guangdong. Figure 4.3 presents the ratios of Shanghai's annual patent grants to those of Zhejiang and Guangdong, respectively. Panel (1) of Figure 4.3, graphing the ratios of all the patent grants from 1987 to 2005, shows a steep decline in Shanghai's patent ratios relative to Zhejiang and Guangdong between 1987 and 1991. In 1987, Shanghai had about three times the number of patent grants as Guangdong and 1.8 times

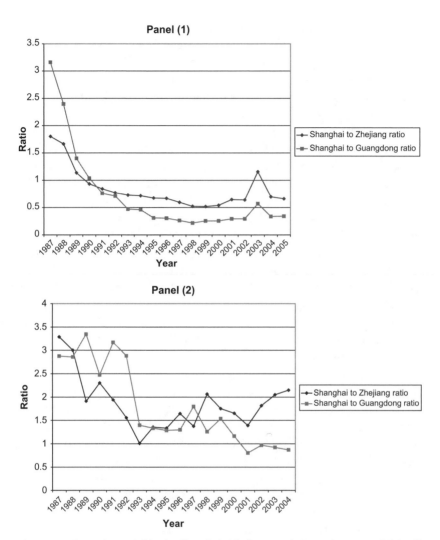

Figure 4.3. Patenting activities in Shanghai, Zhejiang, and Guangdong. Panel (1): All patent count ratios: Shanghai/Zhejiang ratio and Shanghai/Guangdong ratio. Panel (2): Invention patent ratios: Shanghai/Zhejiang ratio and Shanghai/Guangdong ratio. *Sources:* The ratios are based on data from the NBS and Ministry of Science and Technology (1999 and 2002).

that of Zhejiang. In 1991, the ratios were below one for both the Shanghai/ Zhejiang and Shanghai/Guangdong pairs.

Hu and Jefferson (2006) note "a patent explosion" in China since 2000. The fact is that Zhejiang and Guangdong experienced a patent explosion at least 10 years earlier. Like many economists, Hu and Jefferson (2006) attribute a large effect to FDI but this pickup in patenting activities in Zhejiang – almost without any FDI – is more difficult to explain. (So is the absence of a patenting explosion in Shanghai, a city with abundant FDI.) Another item in Hu and Jefferson's paper better explains our finding. They find that private-sector firms have a higher propensity to patent than either SOEs or FIEs.

This entrepreneurial explanation accords well with the fact that Shanghai struggled throughout the 1990s. Its ratios relative to Zhejiang and Guangdong declined throughout the decade, although at a more gradual pace compared with the late 1980s. Except for a blip in 2003, Shanghai consistently under-performed both Zhejiang and Guangdong. The ratio vis-à-vis Zhejiang was always smaller than one, except for 2003, and it was less than one vis-à-vis Guangdong in all the years between 1990 and 2005. Shanghai recovered somewhat vis-à-vis the other provinces in the late 1990s. Its patent ranking hovered between No. 9 and No. 10 in the first half of the 1990s and then between No. 6 and No. 8 in the second half of the 1990s. In 2004, Shanghai's ranking improved to No. 4 in the country, after Guangdong (No. 1), Zhejiang (No. 2), and Jiangsu (No. 3). Shanghai was able to stem the decline of its technological position, but it still did not recover its previous position of technological leadership in the mid-1980s.

Panel (2) includes only what are known as invention patents and excludes the two other categories of patents, utility models, and designs. Invention patents go through a more rigorous examination for utility, novelty, and non-obviousness. The utility model and design patent applications are held to a less rigorous scrutiny. Incremental improvement, rather than novelty, is sufficient for these two categories. The period of coverage is longer for invention patents. Under Chinese Patent Law, invention patents enjoy protection for 20 years, whereas the protection is only for 10 years for the utility and the design categories of patents.[19]

It is important to separate the invention patents from the other two categories of patents to see if Shanghai managed to maintain its edge in a more exacting innovative activity. It turns out that Shanghai lost much of its initial and substantial lead in invention patents as well. Its decline vis-à-vis Zhejiang and Guangdong was less steep and less linear, as the staggered lines in Panel (2) show. But, a clear downward trend is visible in the graph. The sharpest decline again was in the late 1980s, although, compared with the utility model and design patents, Shanghai largely stemmed its decline vis-à-vis Zhejiang but not vis-à-vis Guangdong in the second half of the 1990s.

Shanghai has many advantages, so this decline is quite puzzling. It started with a huge edge over Guangdong and Zhejiang in the mid-1980s when it commanded more resources that went into the production of patents. It had far more engineers, scientists, and universities than Zhejiang and Guangdong. In 1981, for example, there were 87,000 college students enrolled in Shanghai. Zhejiang and Guangdong had about half this number.[20] In 1981, in terms of engineers, the ratio of Shanghai to Zhejiang was 2.8 and to Guangdong 1.6. The gap was even greater in terms of the number of research scientists. The ratio of Shanghai to Zhejiang was 5.9; the ratio of Shanghai to Guangdong was 2.37. Shanghai also spent far more on R&D. The earliest figures we have are for 1992 and the data cover the R&D spending of only the large and medium industrial enterprises. Shanghai firms spent 2.4 times more on R&D than Zhejiang firms and 1.89 times more than Guangdong firms (see NBS 1993b, Table 18–59, p. 759).

Policy and legislative developments at the national level also should have been favorable to Shanghai. In 1993, the Chinese Patent Law was amended to extend protection to previously uncovered areas, such as pharmaceuticals, food, beverages, flavorings, and chemical compounds. In many of these areas, Shanghai firms possessed formidable preexisting capabilities. Yet, Figure 4.3 shows no pickup of patenting activities in Shanghai vis-à-vis Zhejiang and Guangdong since 1993.

Are there factors other than the entrepreneurial dynamics that may explain Shanghai's decline? One alternative explanation is that Shanghai's decline is simply a function of a natural process of technological diffusion whereby technologies originate in the advanced regions and then diffuse to other areas. The diffusion explanation would predict a relatively gradual and steady decline, but Shanghai's decline is very compressed. The sharpest decline occurred in the late 1980s and the early 1990s. Also inconsistent with the diffusion explanation, technological diffusions should first occur in the simpler category of patenting activities, such as utility and design patents, as the technological laggards climb up the learning curve. But, as we have seen in the data, Shanghai's decline was across the board, not just in the area of utility and design patents but also in terms of invention patents.

An alternative explanation is a measurement error. In our findings, we are comparing the absolute number of patent grants in Shanghai with those in Zhejiang and Guangdong. One may wish to point out that Guangdong and Zhejiang have a larger population and, therefore, they have a larger number of institutions and individuals involved in generating patents. But this explanation is not quite right either. Keep in mind that the phenomenon we are discussing is a reversal of Shanghai's fortune, not a permanent underperformance of Shanghai against the other two provinces. That Guangdong and Zhejiang have a larger population is a constant, not a variable. To identify the reason for Shanghai's reversal, we would have to locate a causal factor that has changed over time. In the end, it is not the total number of firms or individuals that matter for patenting activities; it is the number of inventive and innovative firms or individuals that matters. This is the crux of the matter – What explains the larger number of innovative and inventive firms and individuals in Zhejiang and Guangdong? One explanation is that these two provinces have a business environment that innovative firms and individuals find attractive.

2 Missing Entrepreneurship in Shanghai

Starting from last June, more than 7,000 private enterprises have moved out of Shanghai. Many of these Zhejiang entrepreneurs moved their headquarters to Hangzhou and Hong Kong. . . . It is time that we need to change policy.
    – Yu Zhensheng, appointed Party secretary of Shanghai in October 2007

In 1992, a book with the title *Shanghai: Her Character Is Her Destiny* became a best-seller in China. The Shanghai government sponsored the book project – its preface was written by Mayor Wang Daohan – to research the identity of the city. The theme is that Shanghai has a distinct culture characterized by "its great tolerance, diversity, individuality, and entrepreneurship." The book goes on to assert that the renaissance of Shanghai owed much to this distinct cultural heritage.[21]

The claim that Shanghai is historically entrepreneurial is accurate. In the first three decades of the 20th century, Shanghai was the major business and financial hub of Asia, similar to or even more significant than the role of Hong Kong today. It was the home of the country's largest textile firms and banks and the founding venue of a number of firms that are still major MNCs in the world today. These include Hong Kong Shanghai Banking Corporation (HSBC) and American International Group (AIG). A very powerful illustration of Shanghai's rich entrepreneurial heritage is the near absolute dominance of the Hong Kong economy by industrialists who left Shanghai in 1949.[22] During the take-off period of Hong Kong, the most important industry in Hong Kong was textiles. As recently as 1977, the industry produced 47 percent of the value of its exports and employed 45 percent of its workers. In the late 1970s, Shanghai industrialists owned 25 – out of a total of 30 – cotton-spinning mills in Hong Kong. Between 1947 and 1959, Shanghai industrialists created 20 out of the 21 cotton-spinning mills established in that decade. It is not an exaggeration to say that the Hong Kong miracle was a Shanghai miracle in disguise.

Today, Shanghai cannot claim any large-scale, well-known private-sector businesses. On the other hand, the city is at the bottom of the country in terms of our entrepreneurial measures. These two phenomena are closely linked with each other and they are a self-fulfilling prophecy created by its industrial policy approach toward economic development. Industrial policy always favors big, incumbent firms and in Shanghai, the large firms are not only subsidized, but also the small entrepreneurial businesses are restricted in terms of their access to market opportunities. Because Shanghai systematically discriminates against small firms, Shanghai's private sector never had the time, opportunities, or resources to grow from small to big, except in a few cases where private businessmen got big very quickly through corruption. (I return to the subject of crony capitalism in Shanghai in the concluding section of this chapter.)

The purpose of this section is to document and unpack this missing-entrepreneurship phenomenon in Shanghai. We rely on two datasets to do so. One is the urban and rural household surveys conducted by the NBS; the other is the private-sector surveys conducted by the All-China Federation of Industry and Commerce. The household surveys contain information on self-employed household businesses or single proprietorships. The private-sector surveys have information on larger and more established private-sector enterprises (*siying qiye*). Both types of businesses are entrepreneurial in the Chinese context.

The following is the main finding from the survey evidence: Shanghai appears to lack – almost completely – a microeconomic mechanism widely regarded as important for growth and innovation: private-sector entrepreneurship. Despite a rich history of creating some of the largest businesses in China and in Asia in the first part of the 20th century, the average size of Shanghai private-sector firms is among the smallest in the country by employment and is on the small side in terms of sales. Despite the image of the city as a high-tech hub, the private-sector firms in Shanghai, on average, are less likely to hold patents and/or hold fewer patents than private-sector firms based in the heavily agricultural, poor, and interior province of Yunnan. Fixed-asset investments by self-employed household businesses, after reaching a peak in 1985, collapsed in the second half of the 1990s.

The missing-entrepreneurship phenomenon is completely an artifact of policy, as Yu Zhensheng, the current Party secretary of Shanghai, pointed out. Yu, whose quote appears at the beginning of this section, recounted how the poor business environment of Shanghai drove out Alibaba – one of the most successful Internet entrepreneurial businesses in China – to Zhejiang province in the late 1990s. Alibaba first started in Shanghai. Shanghai should have thrived in entrepreneurship. It has history on its side, but it also has other huge advantages. It has a rich endowment of human capital. Its economic growth has been rapid and it has attracted a lot of FDI. It also has the agglomeration economics that economists believe to be important for economic and business development. The anecdotal "folk wisdom" in China is that people in Shanghai satisfy one particular definitional feature of entrepreneurs very well. According to Kirzner (1979), entrepreneurs are those who are particularly alert to business opportunities that often elude others. The reputation of Shanghainese is that they are well endowed with business acumen. Also, as I demonstrated before, Shanghai's unemployment was rising in the 1990s. To the extent that self-employment and paid employment are substitutes, we should expect to see increasing self-employment during this period. Other than policy factors, it is very difficult to think of a reasonable economic rationale why entrepreneurship should be missing in Shanghai.

The combination of high unemployment and restrictions on small-scale entrepreneurship during this period is especially intriguing. To the extent that this absence of entrepreneurship is a result of a deliberate policy, Shanghai did not at all follow what Western economists postulate as the essence of a gradualist strategy – delaying SOE privatization to avoid job losses while encouraging new entry (Roland 2000). Actually, Shanghai appears to have done precisely the opposite – aggressively downsizing the state sector while restricting entry.

Shanghai also fits with the analytical framework in this book to explain why capitalism developed in some regions but not in others. Shanghai is the consummate urban China. It is the progenitor of the industrial policy approach that China embraced in the 1990s at the national level. No other region in China better embodies complete domination by the urban, state-controlled China over the more market-oriented rural China than Shanghai. A group of Shanghai technocrats, who were direct political beneficiaries of the downfall of Zhao Ziyang and his associates, came to dominate Chinese politics and economic policy between 1989 and 2002. The divergence between GDP and welfare and the emaciation of rural entrepreneurship closely reflect the policy visions of this group of Shanghai technocrats.

2.1 Single Proprietorship in Shanghai

Single proprietorships are those businesses owned and operated by the owners themselves. They are also known as self-employment household businesses. Usually, these are on a very small scale. In China, a self-employed business is defined as one that has fewer than eight hired workers. In the 1980s, it was mainly this form of small-scale private businesses that propelled the growth of the rural economy. In the cities, they also began to mushroom quickly, setting up garment and noodle stalls in many areas. The ubiquitous presence of these small-scale entrepreneurs was a universe away from Russia, where entrepreneurial instincts were completely eliminated by the 70 years of communism.

But not in Shanghai. In this section, I show that this form of entrepreneurship is almost completely absent in Shanghai. I focus on the urban part of Shanghai. Our data come from the NBS urban household surveys conducted in 1991, 1994, and 2004. The NBS surveys are designed to track the living standards of households, not the performance of businesses. But this is precisely the appropriate venue to study entrepreneurship. In Asia, and in China particularly, capitalism runs in families. Many of the old commercial houses in Shanghai in the 1930s were all family affairs and the largest businesses in other ethnically Chinese economies, such as Taiwan and Hong Kong, are all family firms. To be included in the NBS survey, one has to be a long-term resident with a registration status in the surveyed city. This satisfies another requirement of our inquiry – that an entrepreneur has to be indigenous.

Two questions in the NBS urban household surveys bear on the question of entrepreneurship. One asks whether a respondent operates his own businesses; the other asks whether a respondent is employed by an individual business. The specific measure is the number of entrepreneurs or entrepreneurial employees per 100 households. For the first question, in 2004, Shanghai ranked third from the bottom among 31 provinces in China. For the second question, Shanghai fared better: It ranked 10th from the bottom. (That Shanghai has fewer entrepreneurs per household than entrepreneurial employees is in and of itself interesting.)

A comparison of the 2004 NBS survey with the NBS surveys in the previous years reveals that Shanghai's rankings vis-à-vis the rest of the country were always very low. It is easy to document the missing entrepreneurship in Shanghai in 1991. There was not a single self-employer in that year. Things improved a bit in subsequent years. In 1996, there were 2.3 self-employers per 100 urban households and in 2004 there were 5. But in terms of its relative rankings in the country, Shanghai was always in the bottom tier. It was No. 9 from the bottom in 1996 and No. 3 from the bottom in 2004.

Not only is entrepreneurial incidence low in Shanghai, those who choose to go into self-employment businesses in Shanghai also earn very little money compared with self-employers in other provinces. We already saw that Shanghai has a very low share of employee compensation in its GDP. In the Chinese data, employee compensation comprises two sources. One is the wage and benefits received by workers at paid establishments. The other source is what is known as proprietor income – income derived from owning and operating a business. (This is one major difference with the US data where income accruals, paid income, and proprietor income are reported separately. In the Chinese GDP data, they are combined.)

Fortunately, the NBS urban household surveys provide detailed break-downs of household incomes and we can thus compare Shanghai's proprietor income with that of other regions in China. In 2004, urban self-employers in Shanghai reported their per capita business income to be 500 yuan. In contrast, urban self-employers in rich – and entrepreneurially oriented – provinces earned far more. In Zhejiang, the per capita business income in 2004 was about 1,400 yuan; in Guangdong, it was about 800 yuan. Guangdong and Zhejiang, however, are among the richest regions in China. A more surprising finding is that Shanghai also compares poorly with what are often viewed as laggard provinces. At 500 yuan, Shanghai was squarely in the same earnings neighborhood as Hunan, Ningxia, Anhui, and Yunnan. The GDP per capita of these four provinces is a fraction of that of Shanghai. In terms of their GDP per capita ratios to that of Shanghai (based on 2003 data), Hunan is 0.162 of Shanghai; Ningxia is 0.143; Anhui is 0.138; and Yunnan is 0.121.

This finding is very significant. Some may argue that NBS household surveys, because they do not cover unregistered migrants, may under-count self-employers in Shanghai. But this omission clearly does not explain why the income of self-employers in Shanghai is low. The low level of self-employment income supports the hypothesis that entrepreneurship is suppressed in Shanghai.

There is no good economic explanation for why urban entrepreneurs in Shanghai and Yunnan earned about the same amount of per capita business income. Yunnan is located in China's southwest and is one of the poorest provinces in China. In the 1980s and 1990s, the central government teamed the coastal and prosperous provinces with China's poorer provinces in the interior and western regions of the country. Shanghai was teamed with Yunnan.[23] To illustrate how strange it is that urban entrepreneurs in the two provinces earned about the same amount of money, suppose a finding that self-employment incomes in the United States and Turkey were about the same. Turkey's per capita GDP in 2000 at US$3,000 was about 10 percent that of the United States, similar to the per capita GDP gap between Yunnan and Shanghai. The most plausible explanation is that Shanghai restricts its household businesses to the lowest value-added activities. It is not economics, it is policy.

2.2 Where Are Shanghai's Firms?

Let me turn to indigenous private-sector firms in Shanghai. These are larger, more established businesses compared with single proprietorships. But these are still entrepreneurial businesses in the context of China. They are the only category of firms in China without substantial ties to the government. (Even many foreign firms are joint ventures with SOEs.) They are very small. For example, in the private-sector survey of 2002 (PSS2002), the average number of employees was only 152 persons. This is far below the conventional World Bank 500-person cut-off threshold for large firms (Batra, Kaufmann, and Stone 2003). In an economy dominated by SOEs and, increasingly, by MNCs, indigenous private-sector firms are entrepreneurial in a Schumpetarian sense – these new private-sector firms challenge the market positions of the incumbent government-related firms.

They are also entrepreneurial because they are still start-ups. In PSS2002, of the 3,158 firms that provided data, only four had been established before 1980. The average age of the firms in the entire sample is only eight years. Shanghai has a younger cohort of firms. The average age in the Shanghai sample is only 7.1 years. One reason might be that Shanghai lagged behind the rest of the country in terms of development of entrepreneurial businesses, rather than a sampling bias targeting younger firms in Shanghai. As evidence, the 1993 survey also has this age difference between the Shanghai firms and the firms in the entire sample. In the 1993 survey (PSS1993), the average age of Shanghai firms is 5.3 years, compared with 6.9 years for all firms in the survey.

Many of the surveyed firms are still run by their original founders. In PSS2002, none of the firms is listed. The average number of shareholders is only 5.6 persons and the median number of shareholders is only 2. The largest number of shareholders is 54. So, unlike managers in SOEs and MNCs, the managers of these private-sector firms bear the residual risks and benefits of ownership. They also fit with a behavioral definition of entrepreneurship. The firms are very nimble, completely profit-driven and market-oriented. This is an attribute emphasized by writers such as Frank

Knight (1921) and Israel Kirzner (1979). Previous research on entrepreneurship in transition economies treat this type of firm as a form of entrepreneurship (McMillan and Woodruff 2002).

The private-sector surveys are biased toward the large private-sector firms in China since the members of the All-China Federation of Industry and Commerce are more established firms. This bias is not a problem here because our priors are that Shanghai firms should be larger. We borrow insight from the economics literature that firm size is a function of the legal and financial environment of firms, not of other influences such as market size and industry characteristics (e.g., Kumar, Rajan, and Zingales 1999). According to this reasoning, Shanghai ought to have some of the largest private-sector firms given its large GDP, superior human capital formation, connections to international markets, excellent infrastructure, and the city's long history of creating some of the largest businesses in China and the world.

From the NBS household surveys, we have already seen that self-employment businesses in Shanghai are scarce and perform less well compared with their counterparts elsewhere. One could argue that the reason for this is that Shanghai has an efficient *established* private sector. So, Shanghai may have a size bias but it does not necessarily have a bias against the private sector *per se*. The city may be more favorably disposed toward large private businesses than smaller private businesses.

We measure the development of entrepreneurship by the employment size of a private-sector *de novo* firm. Employment size is probably the most common measure of firm size in the general economics literature (Kumar, Rajan, and Zingales 1999; Cabral and Mata 2003). There is a special reason to pay attention to employment size in the context of a transition economy. The ability to generate employment by entrepreneurial businesses at a time when the SOEs are shedding jobs entails enormous welfare implications. For this reason, economists studying entrepreneurial dynamics in transition economies focus on employment (Johnson, McMillan, and Woodruff 2000). During the 1990s, as Shanghai's economy was growing rapidly, the city lost a large number of jobs, as shown previously.

Table 4.1 presents data on various indicators of firm development across a number of survey years. Panel (2) of Table 4.1 presents data bearing on the size of private-sector firms. We have two indicators. One is the average and the median values of sales per firm; the other is the average and the median number of employees per firm. Panel (1) presents data on the urban per capita income of these regions and their percentage shares of nonagricultural employment. We present data from PSS1993, PSS2002,

Table 4.1. *The state of the indigenous private sector in Shanghai, various years*

Regions/Year	Panel (1) Regional Indicators		Panel (2) Indicators of the Size of Private-Sector Firms				Panel (3) Indicators of the Development of Private-Sector Firms	
	Urban per capita income^a, yuan	Share of employment in urban area (%)^b	Average (median) sales, million yuan		Average (median) employment, person		% firms with patents (average # of patents per firm^c)	
	1996	1996	1992	2003	1992	2003	2001	2003
Shanghai	8,191	66.4	0.9 (0.34)	20.8 (2.8)	36.2 (23)	46.7 (16)	15.3 (3.7)	14.6 (2.97)
Zhejiang	6,960	23.4	2.4 (1.0)	91.6 (14.5)	49.5 (35)	299.8 (80)	17.4 (5.2)	22.1 (5.3)
Jiangsu	5,188	22.5	2.8 (0.35)	26.8 (5.4)	36.2 (12)	129.9 (53)	14.3 (2.3)	16.0 (3.1)
Guangdong	8,166	30.2	4.9 (1.3)	62.8 (8.4)	89.2 (38)	319.6 (60)	13.9 (5.7)	22.7 (7.9)
Yunnan	4,999	16.4	1.6 (0.4)	38.8 (4.45)	64.4 (30)	260.3 (47)	12.2 (1.8)	18.4 (2.67)
National average	4,844	28.9	3.8 (0.8)	34.0 (4.2)	61.3 (30)	166.7 (40)	16.6 (3.9)	15.7 (4.37)

Notes:

^a Based on the urban household survey data, not the national income accounting data.

^b Referring to employment located in urban areas.

^c Referring to those firms that hold patents.

Sources: The per capita household income data are from Urban Social and Economic Survey Team (1997). Employment data are from National Bureau of Statistics (2005a). Data on private-sector firms are from PSS1993, PSS2002, and PSS2004.

205

and PSS2004. All the findings reported in Table 4.1 are based on a descriptive analysis of the survey data. That is, these are the summary values of the indicator variables averaged over all the firms without considering firm-level characteristics. In the Appendix, I discuss findings based on a statistical analysis of the data; the results do not differ from those reported herein.

Shanghai under-performed in just about every dimension. Its firm size is not only smaller than that in rich and entrepreneurial provinces, such as Zhejiang and Guangdong, it is also smaller than the firm size in Yunnan. Recall the previous finding, based on the NBS household surveys, that the average business income and property income are higher in Yunnan than they are in Shanghai. Now, we know the reason why – Yunnan has a more developed private sector. Yunnan is much poorer than Shanghai. Urban income in Yunnan was about half of that in Shanghai in 1996, as shown in Panel (1), and the per capita GDP of Yunnan was a fraction of that of Shanghai because Yunnan has a sizable agricultural sector. Its nonagricultural employment is about one third of that of Shanghai. Yet, not only does Yunnan have larger private-sector firms, it has *substantially* larger firms compared with Shanghai. As shown in Panel (2), in 2003, Yunnan firms on average were 87 percent (38.8/20.8) larger by the sales measure and 457 percent larger (260.3/46.7) by the employment measure than Shanghai firms.

Shanghai firms look especially poor when firm size is measured by employment per firm. The average employment per firm in 2003 is 46.7. This compares with 260.3 persons in poorer and agricultural Yunnan and 299.8 persons in Zhejiang and 319.6 persons in Guangdong. The last row of Table 4.1 presents data on all the surveyed firms in China. Shanghai firms are smaller in sales and employment than the national average in all the years for which data are available, in 1992 and 2003.

In addition to the average size of sales and employment, I have included median values. Median values are a better reflection of the state of middle-sized firms than mean values. Several studies have shown that biased business environments often exhibit a "middle-sized firm" problem. The idea is that a difficult business environment is most detrimental to middle-sized firms because small firms are nimble enough to evade the regulatory imperfections and large firms have the political and financial power to overcome them. Middle-sized firms have neither.[24]

Shanghai exhibits a classic symptom of a "middle-sized firm" problem. The median values of sales and employment are much smaller than those indicated by the mean values. Take as an example the Zhejiang/Shanghai comparison. Measured in terms of sales, the Zhejiang/Shanghai ratio in 2003 was 4.4 for the average measure but 5.2 for the median measure. The differential between the mean and median measures is of a similar magnitude for the other paired comparisons as well (i.e., the differential in the median measure is always larger than the differential in the mean measure).

The employment measure reveals an even more remarkable development: The median employment declined for Shanghai firms between 1992 and 2003. This is telling on several accounts. One is that the average employment rose during the same period, suggesting that Shanghai's business environment eased for large firms but not for smaller firms. Second, Shanghai bucked the national trend. In the dataset as a whole, both the average and median employment rose between 1992 and 2003, but the median employment declined for Shanghai. This relative decline is striking because the period between 1993 and 2003 is usually regarded as the golden decade for Shanghai's economy. Nominal GDP expanded from 111.4 billion yuan in 1993 to 540.8 billion yuan in 2002. Between 1993 and 2002, real GDP grew in excess of 11 percent in every year. FDI increased from US$2.3 billion to US$5.03 billion.[25] It is curious that median firms located in this richest and fastest-growing market failed to take off.

We have already seen that Shanghai lagged behind Guangdong and Zhejiang in terms of aggregate patent grants. Here, we want to see if private-sector firms in Shanghai are more or less innovative than private-sector firms elsewhere. Both PSS2002 and PSS2004 asked respondent firms whether they held any patents. Shanghai firms in the 2002 survey show up very poorly in this respect. Fewer Shanghai firms held patents than in the national average. In the survey, 15.3 percent of Shanghai firms responded that they held patents, compared with 16.6 percent of all the firms in the survey. To the extent that they held patents, Shanghai firms in the 2002 survey held fewer patents than the national average. The average number of patents held by Shanghai firms was 3.7, compared with a national figure of 3.9. The number for Zhejiang was 5.2 and it was 5.7 for Guangdong. The 2002 survey also asked firms whether they developed products on their own. In response to this question, 28 percent of Shanghai firms said yes, compared with a national average of 34.2 percent. Interestingly, by this measure, Shanghai under-performed significantly against both rich provinces – Zhejiang and Guangdong – and poor provinces such as Yunnan. The findings based on the PSS2004 are very similar.

2.3 Does It Matter?

Economists and other scholars studying transition economies have conflicting views about the economic and political merits of mass privatization, financial reforms, and foreign-trade reforms. Few, however, would dispute the vital importance of fostering the development of new entrepreneurial businesses. Entrepreneurial businesses – defined as new entrants and as privately owned – create jobs and promote growth at a time when SOEs are downsized and retrenched. The *de novo* businesses also inject a much-welcomed dose of competition into economies that have poorly functioning product and factor markets and that are saddled with government distortions. It may be axiomatic for economists that entrepreneurship matters enormously for economic growth. China is not an exception. In the 1980s, rural incomes and economic growth improved rapidly because of rural entrepreneurship. The lack of this growth mechanism in Shanghai amidst surging GDP naturally leads to the question, "Does it matter not to have entrepreneurs?"

To get at this question, we revisit the issue of the divergence between GDP and personal incomes. We saw earlier that in Zhejiang, GDP growth and personal income growth tracked each other closely and that in Shanghai, the two diverged. The contrast between Shanghai and Zhejiang illustrates why entrepreneurship matters: Entrepreneurs promote economic growth because they are motivated to improve their own economic well-being. There is a built-in incentive mechanism for growth. State-led GDP growth can still be fast in Shanghai – and, it should be pointed out, in certain periods of the Soviet Union – without private incentives due to the huge government investments. This type of GDP growth is not sustainable and is less welfare-improving. In China, entrepreneurs tend to come from the least-privileged segment of the society. This is another cost of suppressing entrepreneurship – GDP growth can be anti-poor. As we saw already, the poorest people in Shanghai have lost absolutely since the late 1990s.

Is there a connection between the missing entrepreneurship and Shanghai's poor innovative capacity? Again, missing entrepreneurship means missing incentives. Shanghai is particularly poor in those innovative activities that convert inventions into useful commercial applications, as compared with entrepreneurial Zhejiang and Guangdong. There is an important distinction between being inventive and being innovative: Inventions are acquisitions of capabilities without reference to their underlying market value; innovations are acquisitions that are motivated by a realization of market values (Iacopetta 2004). A top-down bureaucratic system, such as that in the former Soviet Union, can be quite inventive because of massive investments in science and technology by the government. According to Iacopetta (2004), the former Soviet Union pioneered in cutting-edge research in a wide range of fields, as compared with the Western countries.[26]

The problem is that the economy was not innovative in new technologies and processes to convert the scientific breakthroughs into useful commercial applications. The massive R&D expenditures had very little effect on the economy as a whole.

Shanghai exhibits the classic Soviet syndrome – it is inventive but not innovative. In 2005, universities, research institutes, and government agencies in Shanghai were granted 1,895 patents. This is substantially more than in Zhejiang (841) and Guangdong (644), despite the fact that Zhejiang and Guangdong both had larger total patent counts. Because these are non-profit institutions, these are inventive activities without reference to their market value. Shanghai under-performed in the more market-oriented patenting categories. In 2005, there were 8,486 patents granted to firms in Shanghai but there were 11,518 granted to firms in Guangdong. (Zhejiang had far fewer than Shanghai: 3,892.) The greatest difference between Shanghai and these two other provinces lies in the number of individual patent grantees. In 2005, Shanghai had only 2,222 individual patent grantees; this does not even begin to compare with Zhejiang (14,333) or Guangdong (24,732).[27]

In one respect, Shanghai is fundamentally different from – and superior to – the former Soviet Union: Shanghai is open to FDI. So, the question is not whether it matters to have entrepreneurs but whether it matters not to have *indigenous* entrepreneurs. The answer is still yes, although the reasoning is a bit more complicated. The essence of the Shanghai model is to restrict the opportunities for Shanghai residents to become capitalists but to create an efficient and attractive platform for foreign capitalists to set up production facilities. This explains the paucity of asset returns to the average Shanghai households in the NBS household survey data. But, the low entrepreneurial income is partially compensated for by the fact that MNCs can offer a substantially higher level of wages than the majority of indigenous entrepreneurs. This again is consistent with the NBS household survey data that shows the average Shanghai residents to have the highest wage level in the country. The average Shanghainese are the richest proletariat in the country but among the poorest capitalists in the country. So, one can argue that it is a wash – that lower profit incomes are made up for by higher current wage incomes.

The Shanghai model will come back to haunt Shanghai if there is an external shock. One form of such external shock might be the rise of India as an attractive FDI location or the rise of other regions in China that can compete with Shanghai. Local firms have a home bias in that they have a preference to operate in their home base. The most detrimental aspect of the Shanghai model is that it has damaged the ability of local firms to attract top human talent. One of the few ways that local entrepreneurial businesses can successfully compete with the deep-pocketed MNCs in the talent market is that they can offer greater future payoffs – stock options or career paths to the top of the corporate hierarchy. (This is basically how Indian firms such as Infosys and Wipro were able to compete with IBM and GE to recruit and retain the best engineering talent in the country.) Suppressing the growth potentials of local entrepreneurs caps the value of the upside option these local entrepreneurs can offer to attract human talent. If the perception in the market is that these local businesses cannot grow big, then these local firms will have no choice but to compete on the basis of offering current payoffs. MNCs command a decisive advantage in competition on the basis of current payoffs. Greater talent flows to the MNCs will then reinforce their policy advantages and further solidify their market dominance.

3 Understanding the Shanghai Model

If I am not mistaken, in our country, private businesses contribute 40 percent of GDP. In our Shanghai, SOEs create nearly 80 percent of Shanghai's GDP. Who upholds socialism most rigorously? Who else if it is not Shanghai?
    – Quote attributed to Chen Liangyu, the Party secretary of Shanghai from
    2002 to 2006 (sentenced in 2008 to 18 years in jail for corruption)

Recall the finding that Shanghai relinquished its technological edge during the four-year period between 1987 and 1991. In 1987, Shanghai ranked No. 2 in the nation in terms of patent grants; in 1991, it ranked No. 9. This period thus warrants special attention. A central theme in this book is that China reversed many of its reforms in the early 1990s. There was a similar reversal in Shanghai, except that the reversal occurred five years ahead of the rest of the country. A little-known fact is that while Shanghai lagged behind the rest of the country in terms of reforms, Shanghai did implement meaningful reforms in the first half of the 1980s.

We again go to an indicator that reliably tracks private-sector policy developments – fixed asset investments by the individual economy. The individual economy refers to those business units run by single proprietors or self-employers.[28] The patterns are quite striking. Consistent with the portrayal of Shanghai as liberalizing in the first half of the 1980s, the share of the individual economy rose from 3.2 percent in 1978 to a peak of 10 percent in 1985. For the country as a whole, as we saw in Chapter 1, during the first half of the 1980s, the fixed-asset investments by household businesses already reached 20 percent. Thus, Shanghai was lagging behind the rest of the country but it was moving in a liberal direction in the first half of the 1980s. This is an important detail because much of the policy reversal documented in this book is associated with those leaders who came to Shanghai in the second half of the 1980s.

Descriptive accounts confirm this statistical portrayal. According to a 1986 State Council (1986) report on household businesses, by 1985, small daily consumer items traded in the private-market fairs in Shanghai already accounted for 77 percent of the total transaction value of these product groups. There were 1,558 so-called alliance businesses – a code name for the larger private firms at the time. The average number of employees was 12.6 persons, exceeding the seven-employee rule; 25 private businesses employed 50 to 100 each and some even employed more than 100 employees.[29]

Recall the case of Mr. Nian, who, as a private entrepreneur, was able to crack into Shanghai's food market in the early 1980s. In the late 1970s, Shanghai was already beginning to forge market ties with firms based in other provinces. Naughton (1996, p. 113) documents that the marketization of Shanghai's machinery firms – the most important in the country – began as early as the 1970s. In the 1980s, the central government substantially cut its investments in this sector and encouraged firms to create their own linkages with suppliers and customers. Shanghai led the way in this effort. In 1979, the State Council chose a number of SOEs in the country to experiment with profit-retention schemes. Because the program aimed at reforming the larger SOEs, the coverage of the program in Shanghai was quite large. According to Shirk (1993, p. 202), the Shanghai SOEs included in this reform program accounted for 80 percent of the total profits in the city.

The 1980s are commonly viewed as unfavorable to Shanghai. According to this view, the central government taxed Shanghai heavily. Although the view is mostly valid, it does not mean that Shanghai did not implement any reforms. (In the 1980s, Shanghai was taxed heavily but it was also a recipient of other forms of support. I present some data in the Appendix to illustrate this point.) In the early 1980s, Shanghai also experimented with shareholding reforms. Firms issued freely tradeable equities to investors. Shanghai led the country both in the launch of these financial instruments as well as in the size of their issuance. By 1984, 1,700 issues were recorded in Shanghai, totaling RMB 240 million (Walter and Howie, p. 23). This was a large amount of capital considering the overall size of fixed-asset investments at the time. In 1984, Shanghai's fixed-asset investments amounted to 9.2 billion yuan. In 1986, the Shanghai municipal government permitted the establishment of a new local bank that would directly compete with the incumbent state-owned banks (Harding 1987, p. 123).

The year 1985 marked the peak of private-sector development in Shanghai, at least as measured by the fixed-asset investments Shanghai's ratio of

10 percent in 1985 of fixed-asset investments by household businesses to the total fixed-asset investments would not be exceeded again. The ratio declined sharply to 7 percent in 1986, then to 5.8 percent in 1991, and to only 1.1 percent in 1993. (This period, as we saw earlier, also coincided with a sharp decline of Shanghai's patenting edge.) During the next 10 years, this ratio steadily declined further from an already negligible level in 1993. In 2004, the share was 0.2 percent. At 0.2 percent, this is less than one tenth of the level in 1978. The turning point thus seems to be around 1986.

The second half of the 1980s was a critical period for Shanghai and, as the circumstances would have it, for China of the 1990s. During this period, Shanghai set out some of the key elements of the top-down Shanghai model that we are familiar with today. The Pudong project, the essence of which rested on a massive taking of rural land, huge government investments, and subsidization of FDI, was formulated in the 1986–1987 period and won central approval in 1990 (Yatsko 2004). Urban control of the rural economy was tightened during this period under the doctrine of "rural–urban planning integration." (I go into detail about this later in this section.) The Shanghai leaders who ruled over Shanghai during this period were two of China's consummate urban technocrats, Jiang Zemin (1985–1989) and Zhu Rongji (1987–1991).[30] Under their leadership, Shanghai's private entrepreneurship declined sharply and Shanghai relinquished its patenting edge. With this kind of record behind them, they moved on to Beijing to govern China for the entire decade of the 1990s and beyond.

The Shanghai model has four integral components. The first is a highly interventionist state. The quote from former Party Secretary Chen Liangyu at the beginning of this section reveals this aspect of Shanghai. The second is a systematic and deep anti-rural bias in its economic policies. The third component is a biased liberalization in favor of foreign capitalists at the expense of indigenous capitalists. The fourth component is that Shanghai was favored by the central government and might have been showered with massive resources. The components of this model together produced rapid GDP growth but poor household income growth. In the following paragraphs, I mainly focus on the first three components of the Shanghai model we have fairly good data to illustrate them. I offer a conjecture about the fourth component in the concluding section of this chapter.

3.1 The Very Visible Hand of the State

Shanghai is a classic industrial-policy state. The industrial-policy approach comes in two related forms. One is that it is a highly interventionist government. The government sets ambitious policy visions and uses all of its administrative tools to accomplish them. In an otherwise positive assessment of Shanghai, two World Bank economists caution that Shanghai is too ambitious (Yusuf and Nabeshima 2006). The other is that this is a government with a lot of power. Foreign businesspeople often marvel at the ability of Shanghai to "get things done." World-class infrastructure can be built overnight and an entire neighborhood can be uprooted in a flash. There are no public hearings and eviction orders are carried out swiftly and, if necessary, forcibly. (The mayor of Beijing expressed an attitude that surely would be appreciated in Shanghai as well, "We never forcibly evict anybody, except those who refuse to move.")[31]

But, the hand of the state was not always so encompassing in Shanghai. As we saw earlier, in the first half of the 1980s, Shanghai was moving in a liberal direction. We also saw that rural household income in Shanghai relative to the rest of the country was rising between 1983 and 1993. This is entirely to be expected. Rural residents located in the proximity of the rich market of Shanghai should reap enormous income gains. The precondition for this pulling effect of the urban center to work is the existence of a market economy.

My conjecture is that the policy turning point occurred sometime around 1986. Some documentary evidence suggests that the blueprint for the top-down Shanghai model was established around this time. A 1987 government document might be the policy genesis of the Shanghai model: "A comprehensive development program for Shanghai" drafted by the municipal government. The program laid out many of the key elements of Shanghai's aspirations to transform itself into a world-class city in short order. The document did not include specific details about what would become the famous Shanghai landmarks in the 1990s, such as the Pudong district, the Maglev train, and so on. The 1987 document set forth a rationale that came to justify these highly costly projects – Shanghai was to join the ranks of the global, world-class cities by the early 21st century. Considering that Shanghai had a per capita GDP in 1987 of less than US$800, this was an extraordinarily ambitious goal.

The 1987 development program established two key mechanisms to leapfrog Shanghai. One was the internationalization of the Shanghai economy, not just any internationalization but one based on advanced technology and global brands.[32] The other mechanism was a systematic push to eliminate all vestiges of those extant features of the city considered to be backward by the policy elites. These included those small and informal market activities that were a ubiquitous sight in urban China in the 1980s – food and vegetable stalls operated by peasants at the intersections of cities and the countryside. In the first half of the 1980s, many spontaneous marketplaces had sprung up in various neighborhoods in central Shanghai, hawking goods ranging from vegetables and eggs to small-scale industrial goods, as detailed in a province-by-province study of self-employment businesses (State Council 1986). This is the sale or the demand side of the rural entrepreneurship miracle documented in Chapter 2. But, to the urban technocrats eager to project their city as an ultra-modern metropolis, these messy marketplaces represented not income-earning opportunities for rural merchants but rather unorganized, unlicensed, and unsightly activities to be stamped out.

The 1987 development program set up a bureaucratic mechanism to systematically cleanse Shanghai of these backward vestiges – a super municipal agency headed by the Shanghai mayor himself. This agency centralized all urban-planning decisions. The Pudong project, which was to convert an area of 350 square kilometers of farmland into a financial and commercial center in very short order, was first conceived of by this agency. The essence of the Pudong model is deceptively simple: The government, as the monopoly buyer facing no competition, was to requisition vast tracts of land from rural households at below-market prices and then auction off the land-use rights at prevailing market prices. The proceeds from the land sales were then used to finance the government's industrial policy programs, welfare and pension obligations, and last, but not the least, corruption.

The idea embodied by the Pudong project is what is known in the 1987 development program as "the rural–urban planning integration." As the name suggests, the idea was to closely coordinate planning of rural and urban economic affairs. It is worth elaborating on the implications of this seemingly simple planning conception. First, the reforms in the rest of the country and in Shanghai itself until the mid-1980s followed a so-called "two-track" approach – market reforms, private-sector development, and even financial liberalization in the rural areas but persistent central planning in the urban areas. The rural–urban planning integration implied an abandonment of this approach and the adoption of a single-track approach.

Second, the reformist leaders in the 1980s, Zhao Ziyang especially, advocated an extension of the mechanisms of the rural reforms to the urban areas when they began to contemplate how to reform China's industrial sector. Fixed, lump-sum taxation and enterprise contracting were both products of the rural reforms that the reformist leaders wanted to replicate in the cities. The policy intention – if not the actual result – was to converge the urban track with the rural track rather than the other way around.

(To be historically accurate, let's keep in mind that time was not on Zhao Ziyang's side to implement his policy visions. He lost much of his economic decision-making authority in late 1988 and was purged in June 1989.)

In Shanghai, the rural–urban planning integration amounted to the convergence of the rural track to the urban track. In the 1980s, urban Shanghai was substantially state-owned and controlled. As we saw previously, the 1991 NBS urban household survey did not uncover a single incidence of urban private household business in Shanghai. By contrast, in the urban areas of Guangdong, there were 6.47 self-employed businesses per 100 urban households. Relative to the urban areas, rural Shanghai had a higher level of a market economy. The non-farm rural business income was rising in Shanghai relative to the rest of the country throughout the 1980s. The rural–urban planning integration meant a complete domination by the state-owned urban economy of the (relatively) market-oriented rural economy.

A number of indicators suggest that rural entrepreneurship began to slow down as soon as the 1987 development program went into effect. We saw earlier that fixed-asset investments by household businesses, as measured in terms of their share of the total, reached a peak in 1985. Almost all of the fixed-asset investments were rural in origin. In 1985, the rural share was 98 percent of the total (and 95 percent of the total in 1995). We can also look at this issue by examining the real absolute amount of the household fixed-asset investments. (The deflator is the Shanghai consumer price index to the 1978 price levels.) In yuan amount, the peak was reached in 1988 when investments reached about 1 billion yuan (all in the 1978 prices). In 1989, it was below 800 million yuan and in 1993 it was 230 million. After a brief surge in 1996 and 1997, in real terms, the fixed-asset investments made by individual economy units simply disappeared. In each year after 2000, the investment level was below 200 million and, in 2004, it went down as low as 120 million yuan. This is exactly where Shanghai was in 1979 – at 110 million 1978 yuan, right back to the era of central planning. The emaciation of small-scale entrepreneurship was now complete.

The invisibility of entrepreneurship is the flipside of the visible hand of the state. There are telltale signs. Shanghai has very high tax rates. Several researchers have reported how Shanghai seemed to tax its firms beyond the tax quota specified by the central government. So, the high tax rates in Shanghai were not only designed to meet the central tax mandate but also to meet its own expenditure needs. There is evidence that the tax burdens have become more onerous over time. For example, Whiting (2001, p. 98) reported that Nantang Township of Jiading county in Shanghai did not aggressively tax private enterprises until 1989 when the tax-sharing rule was revised. Under the old rule, taxes collected from private enterprises had to be turned over to the county level, leaving few benefits for the township from heavily taxing private enterprises. Under the new rule, tax revenue above a set quota was shared between the township and the county.[33]

Another indicator is an extraordinarily puzzling pattern in the NBS urban household survey data: The average Shanghai households derived very little income from real estate rentals. In 2004, amidst China's hottest real estate market, Shanghai per capita urban rental income was only 157 yuan. This is 1.8 times the national average and only 0.81 and 0.62, respectively, of the urban averages in Zhejiang and Guangdong. That the average Shanghai households appeared to have derived modest gains from the country's most prosperous property boom is suggestive of the regulatory restrictions on the rental market. Shanghai pioneered the practice of massive urban renewal projects. Entire neighborhood blocs involving hundreds of thousands of residents were demolished to make way for new construction. The Pudong project, for example, involved relocating and resettling some 1.7 million people. According to one estimate, between 1992 and 1997, the government demolished 22.46 million square meters of building area and 541,400 households were displaced (Zhang 2002).[34] (Until the late 1990s, such urban construction programs were less frequent in Zhejiang and Guangdong, although in more recent years, this highly destructive practice began to be emulated elsewhere in the country.)

The staggering scale and rapidity with which urban renewal was carried out in Shanghai suggests a highly interventionist and often coercive role of government. One policy tool is strict business licensing. In 2004, China conducted an economic census of all businesses including those that were unregistered. Shanghai has the highest ratio of registered businesses in the country. This is not a reflection of a liberal business environment in Shanghai but rahter a strict enforcement of all the rules on the book pertaining to business registration. My interviews in Shanghai uncovered a range of highly restrictive policies toward household businesses in Shanghai.[35] These restrictions only began to ease in 2005. Following is a summary of some of these policy restrictions:

- The Shanghai government imposed onerous restrictions on who could start a second job as a private entrepreneur. University professors, civil servants, SOE general managers, and workers for the non-profit organizations were not allowed to start private businesses on the side. They had to quit their current jobs, the effect of which is that it took away the risk insurance that comes with a regular job, an insurance that was necessary at the beginning of the reforms. Since 2005, this restriction only applies to civil servants.

- The government imposed a registration capital requirement and required entrepreneurs to register the entire amount of the capital requirement on the day of registration. Thus, a potential entrepreneur would have to show the proof of the requisite capital rather than being able to pay in the registered capital by installments.
- Shanghai has very strict zoning regulations. Residential apartments cannot be used for commercial purposes and if a resident rents out residential space on commercial lease, it has to be approved by the government. The government enforces this law rigorously. One effect of this policy is that it raises the business and rental costs of household entrepreneurs.
- Shanghai government tightly controls land transactions. A concrete indicator is that in the demolition business – a huge business now in Shanghai as the city demolishes many old buildings to build new structures – all the firms are completely state-owned. This shows the intention of the Shanghai government to strongly control land allocation.
- In the critical infrastructure projects, the Shanghai government explicitly forbids private-sector firms from bidding for the projects. Because much of the GDP growth in Shanghai in the 1990s was generated by these investment projects, private-sector firms missed out on one of the key growth areas of the economy.
- Shanghai government favors FIEs – firms with at least 25 percent of foreign equity – both explicitly and implicitly. One implicit form of policy favoritism is that the Shanghai government allows FIEs to deduct the actual payroll costs from their tax liabilities. Domestic firms are allowed to deduct their payroll costs only to the extent of an average level specified by the government. The government purposely sets a lower level of salaries compared with the market rate, thus limiting the deductions by domestic firms.
- The World Bank does not classify China as having onerous business licensing procedures, as compared with other transition economies. The length of time to start a business is about 40 days and to register a business, 30 days. This is substantially better than Vietnam, where it could take six months to set up a business (McMillan and Woodruff 2002). The World Bank's reporting is based on China's business licensing regulations. A close reading of these regulations and other

accompanying documents at several business licensing offices in Shanghai reveal how misleading this classification is. The 40-day length refers to the amount of time required by the licensing office to notify an applicant whether his application for license is approved. However, before the business is eligible to apply for a license, an entrepreneur needs to assemble a large number of documents from numerous government agencies. For example, if an entrepreneur intends to set up a stall in a location, she has to obtain a permit from the agency in charge of that location. She also has to obtain certificates from health and labor bureaus. If she cannot provide a separate business address from her home address, she has to provide documentation that her home has been approved by the government for dual residential and business uses.

• The licensing office accepts an application for a business license *only after* all these documentation requirements are satisfied. A number of entrepreneurs commented that while these documentation requirements are uniform across China, they are being enforced with rigor in Shanghai.

The tight government control may explain both the paucity of the entrepreneurial supply in Shanghai as well as the modesty of the rental income accruing to the average Shanghai households. Consider the following characteristic of the urban private-sector activities: They are likely to cluster in the commercial sector, such as retail shops and restaurants, and so forth. There are two attributes of economic activities in the commercial sector. One is that they thrive in places with high population density; the other is that the location factor is an important determinant of business success. The nature of real estate regulations is likely to have a substantial impact here. Restricting the access of small private entrepreneurs to retail space has a double-whammy effect of constraining the development of urban private entrepreneurs as well as reducing the demand for rental property. We saw the effect of the former dynamic in the data on the paucity of single proprietorships in Shanghai and now we have a theory to explain why the average rental income of Shanghai households is so low.

3.2 The Consummate Urban China

Shanghai is the ultimate symbol of urban China. It has a very large urban population and the city boasts practically all of the amenities associated with a rapid pace of urbanization – infrastructures, skyscrapers, elevated highways, and Starbuck cafés. The Shanghainese are said to be urbane, sophisticated, and very wired. The city, according to *The Economist*, is now beginning to set international fashion trends.

Being urban in this book does not just refer to a geographic or demographic characteristic; it is also an ideology. At the political and economic levels, urban China represents the strong hand of the state, a heavy interventionist approach toward economic development, an industrial policy mentality, and an aversion to the messy and often unsightly processes of a free market and low-tech entrepreneurial activities. In this section, we focus on the fate of rural entrepreneurship in Shanghai. Rural entrepreneurship reflects the extent of urban controls. It thrives when urban controls are loose and it languishes when urban controls are tight. Shanghai is the consummate urban China in the sense that it has almost completely emaciated its rural entrepreneurship.

It should be noted that although Shanghai is widely viewed as a sophisticated, cosmopolitan metropolis, a surprisingly large number of people still work in the rural areas. By employment, in 2004, 2.48 million people out of a labor force of 8.36 million worked in the rural areas. Rural employment accounted for 29.7 percent of employment (NBS 2005a, p. 369), although many of these laborers had non-farm sources of income. Thus, rural entrepreneurship still entails significant economic implications in Shanghai even today.

We pay special attention to rural entrepreneurship in Shanghai because of our theoretical priors. We know from the early works of Schultz (1953) that urban/industrial centers exert a powerful boosting effect on the surrounding rural areas. Economic development emanates outward from the urban centers because farmers in the vicinity have greater access to industrial inputs, opportunities to improve their human capital, and non-farm business and employment opportunities. To the extent that this idea holds true in China, one would expect that, on average, rural entrepreneurs near Shanghai outperformed those in the rest of the country during the explosive growth period of the 1990s. A key unstated assumption in Professor Schultz's claim is that a market economy is in place. To the extent that his prediction is not borne out by the Shanghai data, it is a result of forces blocking the normal operations of a market economy.

We undertake two kinds of comparisons. One is to compare Shanghai with the rest of the country; the other is to compare Shanghai across different time periods. It should be stressed that all the comparisons presented in the following paragraphs are rural-to-rural comparisons; we are comparing the rural households in Shanghai with the rural households in other parts of

China. We are not comparing rural Shanghai with urban China. Our sources of information are the annual rural-household surveys conducted by the NBS.

We start on the side of the production inputs – machinery and equipment in the production process – and then we proceed to look at the earnings side of rural entrepreneurship in Shanghai. We use two measures of fixed assets. The first is fixed assets used for production in all economic sectors, including agriculture. We also look at industrial fixed assets and those fixed assets deployed for the service activities. (Service industries here refer to construction, transport, warehousing/postal services, and distribution/catering services.) We single-out industrial and service fixed assets because these industries should have thrived more rapidly given their proximity to Shanghai's huge urban economy and, therefore, rural entrepreneurship in Shanghai should have reaped substantial gains from this locational advantage.

But, the data point in the opposite direction. The size of production-related fixed assets per rural household is uniformly smaller in rural Shanghai than it is in the rest of rural China. This can be shown by calculating the ratios of Shanghai to the rest of China. In 2001, the ratios are 0.53 for the fixed assets in all sectors, including agriculture; 0.27 for the fixed assets in the industrial sector; and 0.82 for the fixed assets in the services sector. The small size of industrial fixed assets in rural Shanghai is particularly noticeable. Shanghai itself is a large industrial economy, but rural households located nearby do not seem to have developed a sizable industrial operation.

Another striking observation is that the fixed-asset size of rural households in Shanghai actually became smaller relative to the rest of the country between 2001 and 2005. All three ratios are smaller in 2005 than in 2001. This reduction occurred during a period when the Shanghai economy was expanding massively. In nominal terms, the GDP of the city expanded by 1.84 times between 2001 and 2005. The real GDP growth rates were 10.5 for 2001, 11.3 for 2002, 12.3 for 2003, 14.2 for 2004, and 11.1 for 2005.

We want to highlight one finding here – that the ratios of the fixed assets in the service industries in Shanghai declined from 0.82 to 0.56 between 2001 and 2005. The service industries are normally urban-intensive; whereas urban centers may decline as manufacturing hubs, normally they should expand in these service areas. In fact, the size of the two service components of GDP – transport/warehousing/postal services, and distribution and catering services – nearly doubled in Shanghai, from 89.5 billion yuan in 2001 to 159.2 billion yuan in 2005.[36] Shanghai was abundantly endowed with business opportunities in these service areas, but the benefits of these opportunities did not accrue to Shanghai's rural entrepreneurs. (Nor to the urban entrepreneurs, as we pointed out before; Shanghai's urban entrepreneurship lags behind the rest of the country.)

We now turn to the earnings side. Shanghai's rural income per capita declined relative to the rest of rural China in the 1990s. Here, we want to focus on one component of rural household income – what the NBS describes in its surveys as "household business income." According to the NBS, household business income is derived from "rural residents using households as the production or business units" and from "production coordination and management." The sources of the business income include agricultural production but also industry, construction, transport, distribution, and all other nonagricultural activities. Here, we want to focus on the non-farm portion of the business income, so we subtracted the agricultural income from the business income. One would expect the non-farm business income to be very high because Shanghai, as the hub of manufacturing and financial services, would normally possess abundant business opportunities.

The NBS rural household surveys provide detailed data on 1985, 1990, 1995, 2000, and 2005.[37] There is a clear linear development in the business income data. The level of business income in Shanghai declined during the five points in history for which we have data. The ratio began at 1.47 in 1985 and declined to 1.15 in 1990, 0.89 in 1995, 0.57 in 2000, and 0.37 in 2005. This is a dramatic development. In China's purportedly richest region, the level of rural business income in 2005 was only 0.37 of the entire rural China. The ratio of Shanghai's non-farm business income to that of the country as a whole also declined, although less linearly as the total business income ratio. The non-farm business income ratio began at 0.60 in 1985, declined to 0.56 in 1990, and rose to 0.71 in 1995. In 2000 and 2005, the ratios were, respectively, 0.52 and 0.54. While Shanghai's GDP per capita is five multiples of the country as a whole, its non-farm business income is only half of the country as a whole. We have already seen that the returns from urban self-employment businesses in Shanghai are about the same as those in some of the poorest provinces in China. Now, we have the rural data to complete the picture: Entrepreneurship across the board – whether rural or urban – does not pay in Shanghai.

In contrast, Shanghai rural households have a very high level of wage income. Wage income is, by definition, from non-farm sources and it represents returns from labor contributions to paid employment. According to the NBS data, in 2005, the ratio of Shanghai to the country as a whole was 4.29. The wage income also accounts for a large portion of the rural household income in Shanghai. It was 71 percent in 2005, a rise from 61 percent in 1990. It is largely because of the high level of wage income that rural households in Shanghai have the highest income level in the country.

But Shanghai has always had the highest level of rural wage income in the country. This is not news. The issue here is how to assess the contributions of policy. Policies have to be assessed on the basis of their contributions to economic outcomes given the stock conditions of history. That its wage income is high in and of itself cannot be the only evidence that Shanghai has the right economic policies. Shanghai falters when we look at the relative wage income levels of Shanghai over time. In 1980, the rural wage income ratio of Shanghai to the country as a whole was 4.31. The ratio then rose to 6.25 in 1985 and peaked at 7.69 in 1990. Throughout the 1990s, the ratio declined. In 1995, it was 6.53, 4.88 in 2000, and then 4.29 in 2005. So, in 2005, whereas the average rural Shanghainese still enjoyed the highest level of wage income in the country, they were actually comparatively poorer than they were 20 years earlier. The decline in their wage income relative to the rest of the country is consistent with a whole range of economic indicators such as business income and rural household income. Shanghai still enjoyed the highest wage income in the country but its relative level compared with the rest of the country had actually declined.

In the last chapter, we saw that the greatest reversal in the 1990s involved the growth rates of rural non-farm business income, not so much the wage income received by rural households. Shanghai is not only a microcosm of this development but also an extreme version of it. Judging by the gap between the non-farm business income and GDP per capita, we can safely infer that the policy repression of entrepreneurial opportunities in rural Shanghai must have been extreme. Rural households shed considerable production assets and lost their business income, all amidst a massive building boom, rising FDI inflows, and the emergence of a manufacturing hub that is now global in scale.

3.3 For Whom Does the Door Open?

In 1991, the Shanghai municipal government issued an order – known as policy document No. 287 – banning products of private businesses from being stocked in "large and famous department stores" located on Nanjing Road and Huaihai Road (Wu Xiaobo 2006, p. 109). (Nanjing Road and Huaihai Road are the main shopping avenues in Shanghai.) Was this an aberration in a market-oriented economy? Or was it an ideological gesture that the Shanghai government felt compelled to make against private businesses in the aftermath of the Tiananmen crackdown?

The following is from a dispatch by Xinhuanet dated March 1, 2007: "In Shanghai, the most prosperous commercial economy in China, some of the commercial districts simultaneously began to show the door to domestic brands and yielded their space to international brands."[38] The dispatch makes it clear that this was a decision by the government. One stall operator, who sold cosmetic products, was informed by the state-owned department store that the criterion was not the sales revenue but the nationality of the brand. His domestic brand, he was told, had "bad genes." Another stall operator, whose clothing line drew 40 percent of his customers, was denied an opportunity to renew his lease. He remarked, "Huaihai Road [a main shopping district in Shanghai] needs to introduce international brands and we do not even have a chance to put in a bid." A number of documents on urban planning in the Shanghai government outlined some specific goals in terms of increasing international brands. One document envisioned increasing international brands from the current 65 percent to 70 percent in three years. Another document revealed that a government agency had conducted an examination of a store claiming to sell an international brand. The conclusion of the investigation was that it was actually a domestic brand masquerading as an international brand.

In the 1990s, the Chinese government pursued a highly biased liberalization strategy to favor FDI at the expense of indigenous private entrepreneurs (Huang 2003). Governments at both the central and local levels showered expensive policy resources to attract foreign investors while systematically restraining the business opportunities of indigenous entrepreneurs. Government officials, when pressed for an explanation, often equate their policies with the investment-promotion programs in some of the market economies. The analogy is completely false. In the market economies, the objective is to create job opportunities. In China, indigenous rural entrepreneurs laboring under onerous regulations and credit constraints have created more than 100 million jobs, whereas the highly subsidized foreign investors have created between 15 million and 20 million jobs. Also, the governments in the market economies have not differentiated businesses on the basis of nationality in the way the Chinese government has done.

Shanghai represents the ultimate embodiment of the highly biased liberalization strategy, and it may have been the pioneer of this strategy. The 1991 and 2007 rules about stock-keeping units in department stores are indicative of both the extent of the micromanagement of the Shanghai government and the overtly discriminatory nature of its regulations. The rationale provided to explain the 2007 rule is explicitly anti-market. The issue, however, is whether there is any more systematic evidence illustrating the FDI policy biases in Shanghai.

Our evidence comes from a World Bank survey conducted in 120 cities in China in 2005. The research from this survey appears in *China Governance, Investment Climate, and Harmonious Society: Competitiveness Enhancements for 120 Cities in China* (World Bank 2006a). As noted earlier, the World Bank, as an institution, has always been enamored of Shanghai and this report is no different. The report awards Shanghai as a silver medalist in its overall assessment of its investment climate (World Bank 2006a, pp. 46–47). The World Bank survey has three main components: (1) city characteristics, (2) government effectiveness, and (3) social measures of environmental quality, health, and education. Shanghai ranks very high in a composite ranking of these three components. Shanghai is No. 6 in investment climate for domestic firms and No. 17 in investment climate for foreign firms.

Upon closer inspection of the data, it is clear that Shanghai scores high in the stock conditions. Of the three components in the World Bank survey, two of them – city characteristics and social measures – are strongly influenced by history and by the policy treatments of the central government. On these two measures, it is not surprising that Shanghai would score very high. It has an excellent geographic position augmented by massive investments by the central government in its port facilities. It has a high level of human capital and China's best hospitals and educational institutions.

Only the measure on government effectiveness truly reflects the portion of the investment climate that is subject to the discretionary influences of local governments. This measure is based on a range of indicators, such as taxes, bureaucratic red tape, and an indicator that is widely found to be closely correlated with corruption – time spent with government officials. The findings on government effectiveness are much more meaningful in terms of both analytical and policy implications. There is very little a Chinese city located in an interior region can do about its geographical isolation, but it can improve its competitive position by strengthening its policy effectiveness.

On this measure, Shanghai has a remarkably low score. Its government effectiveness is ranked No. 77 in the country as perceived by domestic firms (in comparison with No. 6 in the overall investment ranking). Its ranking improved substantially in the perception by foreign firms, where it ranked No. 26 in the country. In other words, Shanghai is ranked in the bottom third of the Chinese cities by domestic firms whereas it is ranked in the top third of the Chinese cities by foreign firms. This is a specific illustration of the biased liberalization.

Favoring foreign capitalists is often justified by the rationale that foreign capitalists bring financial resources and technology. This reasoning lacks both conceptual and empirical support. Economic research shows that technology transfer occurs in a competitive business environment. Restricting indigenous entrepreneurs curtails competition. China, for example, attracts a huge level of FDI in sectors that have very little technological content and in sectors where indigenous entrepreneurs are expected to possess superior know-how (e.g., herbal medicine). The distortions introduced by this strategy often result in fake or round-trip FDI, as the Shanghai bureaucrats discovered when they sought to ban domestic brands. Indigenous entrepreneurs simply dressed up their products as international products to evade the regulatory restrictions. These practices have led to dishonesty in business practices on the one hand and to further bureaucratic interventions on the other.

What about the argument that FDI brings in precious foreign exchange to Shanghai? The simple fact is that the FIEs in Shanghai incur chronic deficits in their trade balances. In 2005, the FIEs based in Shanghai exported 61.6 billion dollars of goods, but they imported 63.9 billion dollars of goods, incurring a deficit of 2.3 billion dollars (NBS 2006a, p. 175). This trade imbalance persisted throughout the 1990s. Although one should not rush to the judgment that the trade imbalances of the FIEs are bad for China, or for Shanghai, it is worth noting that provinces with a more dynamic domestic private sector have positive trade balances with their FIEs, and their surpluses are huge. In Zhejiang, the FIEs had a trade surplus of 12.1 billion dollars in 2005. In Guangdong, the surplus was 30.7 billion dollars and in Fujian, it was 7.7 billion dollars. By the way, the trade surplus of the FIEs in each one of these three provinces is larger, some by several multiples, than the annual FDI inflows into Shanghai.

In 1990, Shanghai – mainly the Pudong area – was designated a special economic zone (SEZ). In the late 1970s and early 1980s, four regions of China – Shenzhen, Zhuhai, Xiamen, and Shekou – were given SEZ status. It is tempting to put Shanghai in the same category as these four SEZs in the 1980s. In fact, Shanghai is categorically different from the first-generation SEZs. One difference is that FDI liberalization in Shanghai is biased to disadvantage the domestic private sector. The success of the four SEZs in the 1980s was a product of opening both to FDI *and* to the domestic private sector.

We can compare the most successful SEZ in the 1980s – Shenzhen – with Shanghai. Shenzhen attracted a huge amount of FDI but it was equally successful in attracting indigenous entrepreneurial talent. In Chapter 2, using the SEBS1991 to assess entrepreneurial mobility between rural and urban areas in the 1980s, we found that a large number of self-employers with operations in urban areas were, in fact, rural residents. (SEBS1991 covered 10,000 self-employed businesses in 1991.) SEBS1991 shows that Shenzhen was far more open to rural entrepreneurs than Shanghai. In the survey, 45 percent of those self-employers in Shanghai were rural residents compared with 93 percent in Shenzhen. (In Guangdong as a whole, the ratio was 71 percent.) In the 1980s, Shenzhen implemented an internal passport system that sharply restricted migration. Despite this restriction, however, Shenzhen had a higher level of economic mobility than Shanghai.

PSS1995 – the private-sector survey of 1995 – provides another comparison between Shanghai and Shenzhen, this time of more established, larger private businesses.[39] PSS1995 surveyed 83 private-sector firms in these two cities so the sample size is identical. PSS1995 shows that the employment size of private enterprises in Shenzhen was much larger than that of Shanghai (91 employees per firm in Shenzhen compared with 55 employees in Shanghai). Another indicator of the developmental level of private enterprises is the geographic scope of their operations. In the Shanghai sample, the majority of firms – 64.8 percent – sold their products locally, as compared with 35.7 percent in the Shenzhen sample. Because Shanghai's firms were immature, they were more beholden to the SOEs. In the Shanghai sample, 48.8 percent of the firms sourced products from the SOEs, compared with 28.9 percent in the Shenzhen sample.

Private entrepreneurs in Shenzhen were far better educated than those in Shanghai, suggesting that the business environment in the mid-1990s in Shenzhen was sufficiently enticing to attract quality human capital, but not in Shanghai. Among the Shenzhen entrepreneurs, 68 percent had at least an associate or college degree, compared with 24.1 percent in the Shanghai sample. Private enterprises in Shenzhen were present across all industries, whereas private enterprises in Shanghai were concentrated in a few industries. This suggests that the entry barriers for indigenous capitalists were lower in Shenzhen than they were in Shanghai.

4 Conclusion

We focus entirely on Shanghai in this chapter because of the oversized political and economic position of the city. Shanghai dominated Chinese politics throughout the 1990s (and beyond). In the late 1980s, Jiang Zemin and Zhu Rongji, both of Shanghai, assumed the two top positions of the

Chinese state. Jiang was the general secretary of the Communist Party from 1989 to 2002, and Zhu was the premier from 1998 to 2003 (and executive vice premier between 1991 and 1998). Other vital national positions were held, or are still held, by men and women rooted in Shanghai. Huang Ju, the vice premier in charge of finance and a former member of the Standing Committee of the Politburo until his death in 2007; Li Rongrong, the current chairman of the State Asset Holding Commission; and Chen Zhili, who ran China's Ministry of Education, all came from technocratic backgrounds based in Shanghai.

Shanghai is a window unto China of the 1990s. The Shanghai model, formulated in the last five years of the 1980s, was a precursor to China's anti-rural bias and repression of small-scale and labor-intensive entrepreneurship in the 1990s. The economic consequences for the rest of the country were grave. As I show in the next chapter, GDP performance and personal household income began to diverge at the national level in the 1990s. The Pudong project, which in its essence is built on a massive taking of land from rural incumbents, has had a powerful demonstration effect and was widely emulated in the rest of China beginning in the late 1990s. The Pudong model contributed to rising land grabs in China as many local governments sought to create their own versions of urban miracles. The tactics include forcible evictions of long-term residents, large-scale demolitions of existing housing stock, collusions with corrupt real estate developers, and below-the-market-price land requisitions.

The political power of Shanghai underscores an essential difference between the first-generation SEZs such as Shenzhen and Shanghai. In the 1980s, Shenzhen was always on the margins of Chinese politics and was often mired in political controversy. It never enjoyed the kind of carte-blanche political power that was freely wielded by Shanghai in the 1990s. And herein is an explanation for Shanghai's outward prosperity – its rapid GDP growth, rising skyscrapers, and construction boom: It might have been heavily subsidized by the rest of the country.[40] The Shanghai model is extraordinarily expensive. The Maglev train, expensive to build but very inconvenient to use, will take at least 160 years to get the investment back, according to an estimate by two economists at Hong Kong Banking Corporation (Qu Hongbin and Sophia Ma Xiaoping 2006).

That the Shanghai model is not dynamic suggests that the city might have been subsidized. More research should be done to understand how the resource transfer occurred. The potential mechanisms include fiscal transfers, financial flows through the banking system, reinvestments by SOEs controlled by the central government, and subsidized energy prices. I detail some of these developments in the next chapter, but suffice it to note here that there is a logical connection between the rural educational and health crises on the one hand and the huge urban biases in favor of cities such as Shanghai and Beijing on the other.

Herein lies the intimate connection between politics and economics. Because of its privileged position in Chinese politics in the 1990s, Shanghai was able to amass a huge amount of financial resources supplied from the rest of the country. These resources were then invested in modern infrastructures and luxury-amenity facilities and, importantly, they were used to finance very generous tax and other benefits conferred on foreign firms. It is in this sense that the Shanghai model can be described as being built on a Potemkin foundation.

Like any subsidy, someone has to finance it. The next question is, Who shouldered the financing costs of the rise of Shanghai? Deng Xiaoping is said to have famously ruminated why he had not opened up Shanghai earlier. It is not entirely clear that his remorse was justified. The SEZ designation of Shanghai was fiscally costly to the central government in a way that Shenzhen's was not. This is a second difference between Shanghai and the first-generation SEZs – the central government may have poured massive resources into Shanghai and taxed other regions of China to finance this resource transfer. In fact, one could reframe Deng's remorse as follows: The opening of Shanghai would naturally have to follow the opening of the other SEZs because the first-generation SEZs generated the resources to finance Shanghai.

I go into more details in the concluding chapter of this book, but let me mention here a few critical details. In the 1990s, as the Chinese central state was investing heavily in a few urban metropolises such as Shanghai and Beijing, the same central government under-funded rural health and education. The long-run implications of this resource allocation – investing in and supplanting the economic roles of entrepreneurs in the urban areas while taxing the rural and the poor populations heavily – are detrimental both economically and socially. From a social perspective, this policy choice planted the seeds of the jarring income inequalities and political instability. From an economic perspective, this policy choice undermined the micro-economic foundation for China's economic takeoff. I explain these views in the next chapter.

Let me end this chapter by returning to the main subject of this book – entrepreneurial development in China. The Shanghai model is not antithetical to capitalism *per se*; it is just antithetical to the virtuous kind of capitalism.

Recall our finding that small-scale rural and urban entrepreneurship does not pay in Shanghai. Small-scale household businesses operated by people with humble backgrounds languished in the 1990s. In their stead, there emerged a small coterie of politically connected crony capitalists who thrived in Shanghai's distorted business environment. Shanghai is the quintessential state-led capitalism as described by Baumo, Litan, and Shramm (2007).

In 2003, the All-China Federation of Industry and Commerce (CFIC) published a list of the 1,582 largest indigenous private-sector firms in China. Of the top 100 firms ranked by sales on the CFIC list, six were based in Shanghai. This compares with 35 based in Zhejiang and 17 based in Jiangsu, the two provinces bordering with Shanghai. To put Shanghai's ranking in perspective, on this list there were the same number of firms from Liaoning, a province in China's northeast that was saddled with inefficient SOEs and with a struggling economy in the 1990s. The six Shanghai firms were not ranked particularly high on the list. The top Shanghai firm is Shanghai Fuxing (No. 6 on the list); the five other Shanghai firms were ranked Nos. 15, 39, 60, 81, and 91, respectively. Another statistic is also telling. Of the six Shanghai firms, three were connected to real estate and construction, the most political sector in the Chinese economy.

A few private-sector firms in Shanghai did attain some fame. One is the Fuxi Investment Group founded by Zhang Rongkun, a private entrepreneur from Suzhou in nearby Jiangsu. Zhang was known in Shanghai as the "road king" because his firm successfully gained management rights over a number of critical highways around Shanghai. For a firm that was founded only in 2002, the rise was meteoric. In 2002, the same year of its founding, his firm spent 3.2 billion yuan ($400 million) to acquire the management rights for a Shanghai highway. This was followed by another massive acquisition in 2003, to the tune of 5 billion yuan ($600 million), and a 2004 acquisition of 588 million yuan ($70 million). By 2005, Zhang's firm had obtained the control rights of 200 kilometers of highways in Shanghai. *Forbes* magazine ranked him as the 16th wealthiest individual in China in 2005.

The Chinese media described Mr. Zhang as highly secretive and shy of publicity. So, little was known about him until July 2006 when publicity was forced on him – he was arrested.[41] It turns out that Mr. Zhang rose in the same way that the Russian oligarchs rose in the 1990s – through audacious corruption deals. It was revealed in the media that 30 percent of the investment capital that Mr. Zhang amassed came from Shanghai's pension fund, and the remainder came from bank loans and under-the-table privatization deals involving one of the largest SOEs in the city, Shanghai Electric. In other words, Mr. Zhang never built or developed a true business. He became big because of his political connections.

The cast of characters involved in this scandal reveals the depth of the crony capitalism in Shanghai. The head of the pension fund, which incurred a massive deficit of 4 billion yuan in 2002, was arrested, as was a secretary to the Party secretary of Shanghai. And, finally in September 2006, Chen Liangyu, the Party secretary of Shanghai, whose quote appeared before in this chapter, was detained on corruption charges. At the time of this writing (August 2007), the Chen Liangyu affair is still producing ramifications. The secretary to a prominent member of the Shanghai faction and former member of the Politburo's Standing Committee, Huang Ju was arrested in July 2007.

Incidentally, many foreign investors and observers would describe Shanghai as quite clean. They seem to know the trees of petit corruption but miss the forest of grand theft. Since late 2006, eight senior officials in charge of land management have been arrested.[42] One official, with a nickname "King of Land" because every deal had to go through him, was found to have received 4 million yuan in bribes. Another official, a deputy director of land management bureau, amassed 10 million yuan, about $1.25 million in his bank accounts, and 26 apartments valued between 70 million and 80 million yuan (between $8.7 million and $10 million), all on the strength of his 10,000-yuan civil-servant pay scale. Liu Jinbao, the head of the Shanghai branch of the Bank of China in the 1990s, reportedly took bribes amounting to 30 million dollars ("Bank Executive Arrested over $30 Million Fraud Scandal" 2004).

Probably the most notorious corruption case in Shanghai concerns that of Mr. Zhou Zhengyi, a real estate tycoon. Prompted by a lawsuit filed by a group of Shanghai residents whom Zhou had evicted with the help of the Shanghai government, Zhou was arrested but was given what was widely considered an extraordinarily light sentence – three years in jail – on stock-market fraud. This is not all. The Shanghai authorities arrested and sentenced the lawyer – Mr. Zheng Enchong, who led the lawsuit against Zhou – to the same jail sentence (three years) as the one given to Mr. Zhou. This is crony capitalism at its very worst.

The ascendancy of crony capitalism is a fitting testimonial to the Shanghai model and to the industrial policy approach of the 1990s. Shanghai represents the political triumph of the Latin American path, anchored on the prominence of statist interventions, huge urban biases, and distorted liberalization in favor of FDI at the expense of indigenous entrepreneurship.

Shanghai, as the world's most successful Potemkin metropolis, is both the sign of and the culprit for what is structurally ailing in the Chinese economy today. If the Chinese economy stumbles, future historians will look back at the dizzying rise of skyscrapers from the rice paddies of Pudong as a glaring warning sign that *almost* everyone missed.

APPENDIX

A.1 Statistical Findings on Entrepreneurial Underdevelopment in Shanghai

The findings presented in the text that private-sector firms are very small in Shanghai are based on a descriptive reading of the survey data. One might object that these findings do not sufficiently control for factors that might account for some of the differences between Shanghai and other regions. Yi Qian and I have conducted a detailed statistical analysis of both survey and industrial-firm census data (Huang and Qian 2008), and the results are consistent with the descriptive analysis presented in the text. After controlling for many firm-level attributes and detailed industry characteristics, Shanghai private-sector firms are fewer in number and are far smaller in employment, sales, and assets as compared with almost all the provinces and cities in China.

A.2 Did Shanghai Get a Rotten Deal?

There is a long-standing view that Shanghai got a historically "rotten deal" from the central government – that Shanghai paid heavily into the treasury of the central government. In 1985, Shanghai's tax collection as a ratio of its fiscal expenditure was about 4:1; in Guangdong, it was about 1:1. The difference was remitted to the central government.[43] But, the fiscal channel is only one of many ways in which the central government can transfer resources. Although the central government taxed Shanghai heavily, it also invested heavily in Shanghai in the 1980s and the 1990s. In 1986, Shanghai's GDP was about two thirds that of Guangdong (41 billion yuan compared with 62 billion yuan), but from 1986 to 1990, the central government invested 63 percent more in Shanghai than it did in Guangdong.[44] In the first half of the 1990s, the central government continued to invest more in Shanghai compared with Guangdong, despite the fact that the economy of Shanghai was smaller.

Another reason why the "rotten-deal" view is misleading is its implicit suggestion that Shanghai was somewhat unusual. In fact, it is Guangdong that was unusual, not Shanghai. Many other provinces bore a heavy tax obligation toward the central government, and some of these provinces still managed to create a dynamic entrepreneurial sector. Take Zhejiang as an example. In 1985, Zhejiang collected 5.83 billion yuan in tax revenue but only expended 3.74 billion yuan. The difference was remitted to the central government. To be sure, the difference between tax collection and expenditure is much greater in the case of Shanghai than in the case of Zhejiang. The ratio of tax to expenditure in 1985 was about 4 in Shanghai but 1.56 in Zhejiang. This is a large gap, but it shrank rapidly between 1985 and 1990 – 2.25 in Shanghai and 1.26 in Zhejiang – and, in fact, since 1995, Shanghai has been a net recipient of tax revenue from the rest of the country in the sense that it spent more than it collected. There is no evidence that entrepreneurship in Shanghai failed to take off because of the high taxes by the central government.

The central government favored Shanghai in another way as well – it restricted the access of other regions to some of the FDI opportunities. In 1992, the central government issued the first insurance license to the American International Group to sell life-insurance products only in Shanghai. No other cities were allowed a similar right despite the fact that in the 1980s, foreign insurance firms had already established representatives in a number of cities other than Shanghai. In 1997, the Chinese central bank granted licenses to eight foreign banks to conduct *renminbi* business in the Pudong district. The number of foreign banks subsequently increased to 24 by March 2000 (Lardy 2002).

FIVE

Capitalism with Chinese Characteristics

One day in August 2006, Mr. Cui Yingjie, a small-time street peddler, suddenly lunged toward a market regulator in the Beijing municipal government and knifed him to death. Mr. Cui had lacked a business license to operate his stall and the market regulator had confiscated his three-wheeled dolly – worth about US$50. This was the trigger to this tragic event.[1]

Media reports of clashes between stall operators and market regulators are increasing in frequency. In one report, market regulators in Qingdao city were fitted with bullet-proof vests and helmets as protection against rebelling private merchants. On March 20, 2006, according to a Hong Kong newspaper, thousands of traders in Dongguan, a city in Guangdong province, clashed violently with the police. The protest was triggered when the market regulators beat and inflicted severe injuries on an unlicensed trader. The riot lasted for 12 hours and hundreds of police officers eventually prevailed by using tear gas to disperse the crowd. According to the Hong Kong newspaper, this was the third large-scale riot in the city of Dongguan in 2006 (and the article was published in March).

We have seen this type of violent clashes between government regulators and small traders before but not usually in an economy widely viewed as dynamic, rapidly growing, and liberalizing. The Stanford economist, John McMillan, in his book *Reinventing the Bazaar: A Natural History of Markets* (2002), describes how in 1979 the military government of Ghana resorted to violence and brutality to shut down the Makola marketplace in the city of Accra.[2] The soldiers, armed with machine guns, beat up the traders and looted their stalls. In one case, a soldier "ripped [a trader's] baby off her back and shot her." They also dynamited and bulldozed the entire marketplace. The military government accused these small traders of price gouging and placed the blame for its own poor economic performance – high inflation – on them.

In China, the repression of the small entrepreneurial traders was not motivated to eliminate them but rather to extract rent from them. This hypothesis is consistent with the fact that licensing fees were rising in the 1990s and local government regulators were acting with increasing ferocity to root out unlicensed traders. In the 1980s, unlicensed traders were merely fined, and thus they were allowed to continue to operate. But by the 1990s, market regulators were seeking to incapacitate the unlicensed traders. Their tactics included confiscating their equipment, destroying the commodities, and even inflicting physical injury. The pecuniary interests to the bureaucrats must have been massive as judged by the determination of their efforts – such as equipping with bullet-proof vests – and by the willingness to incur the huge political and social costs of their actions.

Probably the best illustration of the rent extraction occurred in Xiushui Market in Beijing.[3] Xiushui Market was a thriving outdoor market fair, located not far from the US Embassy. It started spontaneously in 1985 when a few traders began to sell fruits and vegetables. (The folk wisdom in Beijing holds that Xiushui Market created the first generation of millionaires in Beijing.) By 2004, it was one of the most successful retail operations in the city. Xiushui Market, specializing in fake brand-name goods, was extremely popular with foreign tourists. With a huge volume of business, it was nicknamed "Little Hong Kong" or "Little Paris." According to one estimate, it was doing US$12 million in sales annually; on weekdays, the market would attract 10,000 visitors a day and up to 20,000 visitors a day on weekends.

Xiushui Market became a valuable brand name, with the full value accruing to the traders operating there, almost all of whom had set up their shops in the 1980s and who single-handedly had contributed to the value of the Xiushui brand. Then, the bureaucrats moved in to capture the handsome rent embodied in the brand. The specific details are lacking but we know the broad contours of the story. In 2004, Chaoyang district government, where Xiushui Market is located, decided to close the entire outdoor market to build a nearby indoor market. They gave two rationales. One was that Xiushui Market posed a fire hazard; the other was that Xiushui Market was illegally selling fake products. Although Xiushui Market never had a documented case of fire, this rationale at least was theoretically plausible. The marketplace was narrow and crowded, but it is not clear that closing down the entire market was the only way to minimize the fire hazard. The second rationale was patently false. One week into the opening of the new Xiushui Market, journalists spotted numerous pirated goods on display.

The true reason was probably rent extraction. In China's real estate market, the buy-and-sell sides of a transaction are governed by diametrically opposite rules. On the buy side, the government, acting as the monopsonist, does not permit competition. No bids are held and all transactions are carried out in top secrecy. On the sell side, the government, now the monopolist, maximizes competition by organizing bids and auctioneering. This deal is similar. Without any bidding, Chaoyang district government awarded the right to build and operate the new Xiushui Market to a private entrepreneur who did not have a stall in the old market. Not a single detail of this deal was disclosed. Even a promised public hearing on the demolition of the old Xiushui Market – not on the right to operate the new market – was apparently never held.

Without any input from those merchants who actually created the value of the Xiushui brand and without any explanation on the choice of the entrepreneur to build the new market, Chaoyang district government arbitrarily assigned control of this very valuable asset to an outsider. There is another irregularity here. Under Chinese law, all land belongs to the state. So, Chaoyang district was the landlord of the original Xiushui Market. One can think of a public policy rationale to strengthen public finance by charging high rents to the Xiushui merchants and to benefit from the government's nominal ownership of the Xiushui brand. But this is not what happened. The government transferred the windfall gains to a private entrepreneur. A postulation that the deal at least was tainted with shadiness is not farfetched.

In January 2005, the government demolished the old Xiushui Market. The police were there to suppress a last-ditch, desperate protest by the stallholders. The private entrepreneur awarded with the right to operate the new market then auctioned off the new stalls competitively. The highest bid fetched 4 million yuan (US$480,000). Because of the high bids, only one third of the original Xiushui merchants were able to set up operations in the new marketplace. In essence, the original Xiushui merchants were paying the market price for the right to the brand they themselves had created. For the other merchants who failed to win a bid, the brand was completely expropriated from them.

Xiushui Market is not alone. Another is the closing of Xiaoyang Lu Market in Shanghai in 2006. The official rationale is again grand – rooting out pirated goods from Shanghai. Xiaoyang Lu Market, like Xiushui, specialized in fake products. (In fact, Xiaoyang Lu Market was known as Shanghai's Xiushui.) But, as the reporter for *Economist Intelligence Unit* discovered, the real reason was property sales. Shanghai government, as soon as it closed down the Xiaoyang Lu Market, leased the plot to Sun Hung Kai group from Hong Kong for a substantial amount of money. According to this report, the authorities told the merchants to sell their pirated ware elsewhere (Washburn 2006). We do not know if this land deal was tainted with corruption; all we know is that eight senior officials who presided over Shanghai's real estate have been arrested for corruption since late 2006.

The fate of Xiushui Market is a microcosm of the evolution of Chinese capitalism during the last 30 years. The most laissez-faire phase was in the 1980s when the market, founded with little bureaucratic interference, developed and expanded spontaneously. The new Xiushui Market carries all the elements of the Chinese economy today. For sure, it is not socialism; Chaoyang district government awarded management rights to a private entrepreneur rather than retaining management itself. So China is capitalistic, as I point out in the first chapter of this book, but it is capitalistic in a particular way. It is crony capitalism built on systemic corruption and raw political power. Property rights are not secure. A politically connected entrepreneur, with the full backing of the coercive power of the state, could simply expropriate the value of the Xiushui brand from hundreds of entrepreneurs who had created the brand. This business environment is especially detrimental to small-scale entrepreneurs. Two thirds of the poorer original Xiushui merchants lost absolutely. They could not even enjoy the future gains from the Xiushui brand.

We saw in Chapter 2 that many of the first-generation rural entrepreneurs came from humble backgrounds. Mr. Nian, the poor farmer in Anhui province, was able to enter the retail market of Shanghai, Beijing, and Dalian. Mr. Cui, the unlicensed peddler who committed a capital crime, came from a similarly humble background. He was a retired soldier unable to find a job in his native province so he eked out a meager living by baking sausages. Although Mr. Nian thrived in the 1980s, under the grabbing hand of the state today, millions of poor people like Mr. Cui are now denied a similar opportunity. There has been a sharp decline in self-employment businesses since the late 1990s. In 1999, the number of self-employment businesses in the urban areas stood at 31.6 million, but in 2004, it had declined dramatically to 23.5 million, all during a period of a seemingly urban boom. The reason was the rising and exorbitant fees levied on such self-employment businesses. The situation improved slightly in 2006. As of June 2006, the number of urban self-employment businesses was 25.1 million.[4]

The fate of Mr. Cui and millions like him is pregnant with significant implications. In this final chapter, I delve into some of them. Although not all of these implications have been rigorously tested and empirically examined, they are natural inferences based on the findings in this book. As such, they should be viewed as conjectures that call for future debate and exchange of ideas. I take stock of the finding that the evolution of capitalism during the last 30 years has been highly heterogeneous. In their book, *Good Capitalism, Bad Capitalism*, Baumol, Litan, and Schramm (2007) offer a taxonomy of different capitalist systems in the world. There is state-guided capitalism, in which government sets industrial policies and directs investments. Then, there is oligarchic capitalism that empowers and enriches the few at the expense of the many. The third variety is big-firm capitalism that accentuates the dominance of big firms and suppresses innovation. The last category, which the three economists argue is the only sustained path to economic prosperity, is entrepreneurial capitalism in which small and innovative businesses drive growth.

This taxonomy of capitalism offers a productive way to examine the evolution of capitalism in China during the last 30 years. In the 1980s, China moved fast and far toward entrepreneurial capitalism in its vast countryside. In the 1990s, this development was reversed and China today resembles the state-led capitalism prevailing in Latin America. The most important question is, "Did it matter for China that the government reversed the directional liberalism of the 1980s?" The consensus view among China economists is that reforms continued and deepened in the 1990s. The most tangible support for this consensus view is that GDP continued to expand. It is legitimate to ask about both the evidence for the policy reversals as well as the evidence of the effects of the policy reversals. In the previous chapters, I presented the evidence on policy reversals; here, let me offer evidence on the effects of the policy reversals.

The ultimate criterion to assess the quality of an economic system is whether it is conducive to the improvement of human welfare. The most powerful intellectual justification for China's partial reforms is that they have produced a Pareto-optimal outcome. This is the idea behind a 2000 paper that claims that the Chinese reforms have produced all winners and no losers (Lau, Qian, and Roland 2000). Published in one of the most prestigious economics journals, *Journal of Political Economy*, the paper assumes that Chinese reforms *always* improved rural welfare and that the reforms were a homogeneous process. In 2000, our systematic knowledge of the state of rural China during the 1990s was partial and incomplete. (There was no shortage of anecdotal reports of dire situations in rural China, however.) With more data, we can now revisit the claim that the Chinese reforms produced no losers.

The first section of this chapter assesses the welfare impact of the policy reversals in the 1990s. Probably the most tangible evidence of the adverse effects of the policies of the 1990s is the sharp rise in illiteracy in China, all of which most likely took place in rural China. Between 2000 and 2005, the number of illiterate adult Chinese rose from 85.07 million to 113.9 million. I provide more details on this grave development later in the chapter, but it is important to note here that the way adult illiteracy is measured in China implies that all the newly illiterate Chinese between 2000 and 2005 were the products of the country's basic education system in the 1990s. There is a near-perfect match in terms of timing between the policy turns toward urban biases, financing constraints in rural China, and constrictions of rural entrepreneurship on the one hand and the deterioration of educational performance on the other. Although we have less direct evidence on the state of health in rural China, available evidence suggests that the state of health care deteriorated in rural China as well.

I look into the issue that GDP grew as rapidly in the 1990s as it did in the 1980s. Measured in terms of the growth of GDP per capita, the difference between the entrepreneurial decade of the 1980s and the state-led decade of the 1990s is minuscule. However, Shanghai provides an important clue – the fast GDP growth did not necessarily translate into fast growth of personal income. I show that in the 1990s, relative to the fast pace of GDP performance, the growth of personal incomes lagged significantly. This lag was in sharp contrast to the pattern in the 1980s when the growth of personal incomes *exceeded* the growth of GDP. The divergence is descriptively consistent with a host of other indicators that raise questions about the economic and social performance in the 1990s, including the rising illiteracy and the rapid escalation of income inequalities.

One of the strengths of China is its geographic heterogeneity. Although the country as a whole moved toward a statist version of capitalism in the 1990s, some regions continued with the economic model of the 1980s. One of the most famous and most successful regions is Zhejiang province. In the second section of this chapter, I argue that this is "the other path" for China and that the Zhejiang model is closer to the entrepreneurial capitalism based on rural entrepreneurship and small-business dynamism. To sharpen the contrast, I provide the example of another development model – this one adopted in the neighboring province of Jiangsu. Jiangsu, although similar to Zhejiang on many dimensions, was more state-led but has been outperformed by Zhejiang across the board.

Within China, even some of the most ardent supporters of the Chinese approach – such as economist Wu Jinglian – have come around to the view that without deep political reforms, reforms of economic institutions cannot succeed (Pei 2006). This is a full circle back to a position embraced by

Zhao Ziyang as early as 1987, when he made political reforms a central component of his policy agenda. However, a widespread view among Western analysts is that a sharp tradeoff exists between democracy and economic growth. Normatively, some believe that democracy is a luxury good, which a poor country like China cannot afford. Positively, democracy is viewed as a constraint on economic growth. It slows down decision making when decisiveness is most needed to jump-start economic development.[5]

Increasingly, this view that poor countries are faced with a Faustian political and economic choice is being contradicted by the very country that supposedly supplied the clearest evidence in favor of this hypothesis – India. India has begun its own economic takeoff as its GDP has grown above 8 percent for a number of years. Skeptics may point out that India also registered episodic high growth rates in the 1970s and 1980s but its growth faltered in subsequent years. In this book, I advocate an "Indian model" on the basis of the belief that the current round of high growth will be sustained. In the 1970s and 1980s, the Indian economy was primarily agriculture-based, which means that its growth at that time was very sensitive to the vicissitudes of weather. (India has the added disadvantage of being located in a tropical zone with unpredictable weather conditions.) This time around, India's growth is broad-based – in services, in manufacturing, and even in agriculture. The lesson from this emerging economic miracle is that "soft infrastructures," such as financial and legal institutions, are more important than hard infrastructures for economic growth. In the second section of the chapter, I present a stylized comparison of China and India.

The third section of the chapter returns to the big question that started this book – the nature of Chinese capitalism today. Chapter 1 presents data showing that the size of China's indigenous private sector is very small even after 30 years of economic reforms. I put this finding against a broader, international perspective. My argument is that the best way to characterize the Chinese economic system today is that it is a commanding-heights economy. This system has many failed antecedents among the statist developing economies of the 1970s. Many view the Chinese economy as another East Asian economy. I dispute this perspective and show that the East Asian economies, notwithstanding the high levels of industrial policy interventions, were far more privately owned than China is today. Commanding-heights economies are typically corrupt because they place enormous power in the hands of the government. Capitalism with Chinese characteristics is also deeply corrupt. I discuss some of the manifestations of the corruption problem in China and the phenomenon of land grabs that poses a systemic threat to China's political and social stability as well as to its economic prospects.

Lastly, I try to assess the prospects for the Chinese economy going forward in the next five to ten years. Here, the most alarming sign is a virtual collapse or stagnation of productivity growth in the Chinese economy since the late 1990s. The country today is still saddled with considerable problems in its financial system, a weak social foundation, and a corporate sector divided between the highly profitable state monopolies and private-sector businesses operating on the margins of technology and innovations. On a more hopeful note, the current Chinese leaders, Hu Jintao and Wen Jiabao, have pursued a different policy agenda from the leadership of the 1990s. They have put the rural issues again on the forefront of the policy agenda and have revived some of the rural financial reforms of the 1980s. Rural income has registered its fastest rate of growth since the late 1980s, as we saw in Panel (2) of Figure 4.1 in Chapter 4. In many ways, the Hu–Wen leadership is seeking a return to the directional liberalism of the 1980s.

There are, however, significant risks ahead. One risk is expectational – that people expect governance to improve when objective conditions for an improvement do not exist. This may happen when a more liberal political rhetoric raises expectations of the public but fails to change the behavior of the Chinese bureaucrats. There are also economic risks, including the challenge of managing asset bubbles inflations, and rising cost pressures. In the final section of this chapter, I speculate about some of these risk factors and assess the likely trajectory of the Chinese economy during the next critical period.

1 Does It Matter?

In the introductory chapter, I quote a number of highly positive views of China's economic performance by Nobel laureates. Such sentiments are widespread. Many regularly tout those indicators of a rising China: its massive foreign exchange reserves, its huge economic size as measured in purchasing power parity (PPP) terms, and its voracious appetite for raw materials and energy that power economic growth from Latin America to Africa. Books with titles such as *The Chinese Century, One Billion Customers,* and *The Rise of China* convey the impression of a rising economic super-power. The World Bank, an ardent fan of China, recently elevated China from a "lower income" to a "lower middle income" country.

On the surface, it does not seem to matter whether Chinese capitalism is entrepreneurial or state-led. In both the 1980s and 1990s, China's GDP grew rapidly. As of August 2007, the Shanghai stock market index, hovering around only 1,000 points as recently as 2005, reached above 6,000 points. The real estate market was booming. The 2008 Olympics fed a feverish investment boom across the country. Amidst these signs of prosperity, it is fair to ask, "Does it really matter whether Chinese capitalism is entrepreneurial or state-led ?"

I show that it matters along three dimensions. First, I present new evidence that social opportunities – arrangements for health care and education – contracted during the fast GDP growth period of the 1990s. Recently available data show that illiteracy in China has risen sharply, and this increase is due to the poor performance of basic education in rural China in the 1990s. Rising illiteracy is probably the most monumental legacy of the policy model of the 1990s.

I single-out developments in health care and education for emphasis because they are considered fundamental components of human welfare. Many countries, including China, have enacted explicit guarantees for equal and universal access to health care and education. Health care and education are enshrined as human rights in the Chinese Constitution and they hold both intrinsic as well as instrumental values. The welfare gains from rising life expectancy and improved health are just as important as the welfare gains from income growth. They are also critical inputs to economic growth. China's own achievements in the social arena in the 1960s and 1970s are widely credited as important reasons behind its economic takeoff during the reform era.

Recall the finding in Chapter 4 that GDP per capita and personal income per capita in Shanghai have negative correlations with one another, whereas the two are positively correlated in Zhejiang. This finding shows one substantial implication of state-led capitalism vis-à-vis entrepreneurial capitalism – there is a difference in the welfare of the Chinese people under the two systems. This is the second topic of this section. GDP, along with personal income, grows rapidly under entrepreneurial capitalism. Under state-led capitalism, GDP may still grow very fast but personal income lags. Although a firm conclusion awaits more research, preliminary analysis shows that as a ratio of GDP per capita, personal income declined sharply in the 1990s as compared with the 1980s. Related to the welfare implications of entrepreneurial vis-à-vis state-led capitalism is an issue of who gained the most from the rapid GDP growth. Shanghai again offers a clue – it has a very unequal income distribution. In the 1990s, China's social performance deteriorated substantially. This is the third topic of this section.

1.1 Social Opportunities

In their book, *India: Economic Development and Social Opportunity*, Jean Drèze and Amartya Sen (1999) highlight a critical reason why India lagged behind China in the initial phase of economic development – India's highly inadequate and inequitable provisions of health care and educational facilities. The "social backwardness" of India prevented broad and effective participation in economic and political activities even when the opportunities for such participation presented themselves (as when the country moved toward a market economy and was a democracy). Later in this chapter, I come back to this theme in the China–India comparison and argue that the different levels of social opportunities, not FDI or infrastructure, are the central reasons behind the performance differences between the two countries.

For now, let me focus on the state of social opportunities in China. Social opportunities – defined as the arrangements a society makes for education and health care – interact with economic growth both as a precondition and as an outcome. It is well established that the initial endowment of human capital matters substantially for economic growth. The experience of China amply confirms this relationship. As I show in Chapter 2, micro data show that the first generation of Chinese entrepreneurs was quite well educated, confirming the idea of Drèze and Sen that health and education "prepare" a population for economic participation.

Initial conditions aside, economic growth can, in turn, exert an effect on social opportunities. Sen (1999, p. 45) presents a sharp contrast between two types of high-growth economies. In one, as exemplified by South Korea and Taiwan, high economic growth was accompanied by an expansion of social opportunities. In the other – for example, Brazil – GDP per capita experienced fast growth but without the comparable success in raising the levels of education and basic health care. Clearly, economic growth itself does not automatically expand social opportunities. The income growth of the poor, rather than the average income growth, and specific policy interventions such as public expenditures earmarked for education and health are more important than the simple GDP growth itself.[6]

We know that average GDP growth in China has been very rapid. The next question to consider is whether China falls into the category of South Korea and Taiwan or into the category of Brazil. Did social opportunities expand during the reform era? In terms of our demarcation of the two decades, which phase of Chinese capitalism expanded social opportunities more? These are deeply complex questions that require a more systematic treatment than I can provide here. My purpose is to suggest some clues for further discussion and research.

I focus the discussion on the rural population. It is reasonable to assume that the welfare of the rural people is more sensitive to the social arrangements regarding the financing and provision of health and education. In the rural areas, people are poorer and are more vulnerable, and the points of service provisions are more geographically dispersed than in the urban areas. So, the rural population already faces some extra difficulties in accessing health and education facilities regardless of the specific designs of the social arrangements. A theme running through this book is that rural China is particularly entrepreneurial. Thus, expansions or constrictions of social opportunities in the rural areas may have a disproportionate effect on the overall level of entrepreneurship in the society.

China is widely recognized – and admired – for having successfully educated a broad segment of the population, especially in the rural areas, during the 1960s and 1970s (Sen 1999, p. 42). Although studies on China's educational performance since 1978 identify concerns and challenges, the consensus view is that China has made steady strides in basic education during the reform era as well. A 1999 World Bank report is confident that China has successfully achieved the goal of universal nine-year compulsory basic education. The World Bank team recommends that China move to a system of 12 years of compulsory education, comparable to OECD standards (World Bank 1999).[7]

Much of this positive appraisal of China's educational performance is based on official data on enrollment and attainment, which clearly demonstrate substantial progress. The net enrollment ratio is nearly 100 percent at the basic education level and educational attainments at the upper levels of basic education – junior and senior secondary education – and at the tertiary levels were all increasing steadily.

Details matter. Local governments in China often automatically register school-age children as enrolled in schools. But we know very little about the actual attendance of these enrolled students, especially in the rural areas. It is almost certain that local officials falsified their educational data. Exaggerating GDP growth may lead to greater demands from higher levels to ratchet up tax collection, to which local officials are averse. There is no similar self-constraint in reporting false educational data. Chinese educational researchers and journalists have documented blatant cases of statistical falsifications. The most extreme case I have come across occurred in Wei county of Hebei province.[8] In 2000, the county government certified that schools in the region had successfully met all of the targets of "nine-year compulsory education." One of the targets was to achieve a dropout ratio below 3 percent. But, in 2003, a journalist discovered that only 3,000 students took the graduation examination in the junior secondary schools of Wei county. The class of 2003 had started in 2000 with 10,000 students. Thus, the cumulative three-year dropout ratio was 70 percent. In 2005, things "improved" a bit: 4,000 out of 10,000 students remained to take the graduation examination.

The attainment data overstate China's educational achievements. The data include partial attainment – attendance of a level of schooling, not graduation – as sufficient to be included in the category of educational attainment.[9] The Chinese definition of a given level of schooling specifically and explicitly includes dropouts from that level of schooling. The following is the definition of high school attainment given by the NBS in its household income surveys (NBS 2006b, p. 327): "Referring to the highest educational attainment at the high school level, including those who graduated from, attended in the past (*yiye* in Chinese), or are currently attending high schools." The definition also includes high school equivalents. The same methodology applies to all levels of schooling. Primary school attainment also includes those who never attended primary school but who are considered literate under the Chinese definition (discussed later).

Chinese data on literacy between 1990 and 2000 show a steep decline in adult illiteracy, from 180 million in 1990 (15.9 percent of the adult population) to 85.07 million (6.72 percent) in 2000. An adult is defined as someone at or above 15 years of age. The Chinese definition of literacy is the ability to identify 1,500 Chinese characters. Normally, a Chinese student attains this ability between the third and fourth grades – by the age of 7 to 9.

Given the way that adult literacy is measured, there is a six- to eight-year lag between the performance of China's basic education and its adult literacy data. A person reaching the age of 15 between 1990 and 2000 would have attained the Chinese standard of literacy before the early 1990s. The declining illiteracy between 1990 and 2000 primarily reflects the quality and performance of China's basic education up to the early 1990s. To know how Chinese basic education has functioned since then, we need the literacy data after 2005.

On April 2, 2007, *China Daily*, the official English-language newspaper, reported that the number of illiterate adult Chinese increased by 30 million between 2000 and 2005 (Wang Zhuoqiong 2007).[10] This implies that in 2005 there were 115.7 million illiterate adult Chinese. (In 2000, there were 85.07 million.) The *China Statistical Yearbook 2006* reports a slightly lower figure – in 2005, the number of adult illiterate Chinese was

113.9 million (NBS 2006c, p. 114).[11] Illiteracy not only increased in absolute terms but also in relative terms. The illiteracy rate of the adult population increased from 6.72 percent in 2000 to 11.04 percent in 2005, an increase of 64.3 percent. (To ensure that the definition of literacy has not changed, I checked the current definition of illiteracy and found that there is no change in the definition.)[12]

Prior to 2000, we have illiteracy data for 1964, 1982, and 1990 (NBS 2006c, p. 102). The number of illiterate adult Chinese totaled 233.3 million (33.6 percent of the adult population) in 1964, 230 million in 1982 (22.8 percent), 180 million in 1990 (15.9 percent), and 85.07 million in 2000 (6.72 percent). We do not have data for the intervening years, but it is safe to assume that Chinese illiteracy – measured both in absolute and relative terms – continuously declined up to 2000. The abruptness and the scale of the reversal are probably unprecedented in history anywhere else in the world.

Assuming the same rate of depreciation of human capital in China since 2000 as before 2000, then it must be true that all of this increase in illiteracy was due to new adults becoming illiterate, rather than due to relapses (i.e., previously literate adults losing literacy). Those reaching the age of 15 between 2000 and 2005 were born between 1985 and 1990, and all of their primary school education occurred in the 1990s. The rise in illiteracy was thus completely a product of Chinese education in that decade.

The timing coincides precisely with the period of urban biases and rural deprivations as depicted in this book. Because of the sheer size of the rural population and because of the greater sensitivity on the part of the rural population to the costs of education, rural basic education drives the Chinese data on illiteracy. Assuming all of the newly illiterate adults to be rural Chinese would imply that China's basic education failed 33 percent of the rural cohort between 10 and 14 years of age as of 2000. (In 2000, according to the population census, the number of rural Chinese in the 10 to 14 age cohort was 89.5 million.)

As I maintain throughout this book, the best way to understand China in the 1990s is to explicitly benchmark it against the decade of the 1980s. Consider the following fact: In the early 1980s, the enrollment rate initially dropped and by a substantial margin. Pepper (1990, p. 79) documents that the number of students enrolled in primary schools declined from 150 million in 1975–1976 to 140 million in 1982. Hannum, Behrman, and Wang (2008) report that the drop in the enrollment rate among secondary-school age men in rural areas was especially dramatic during the early 1980s. Yet, illiteracy data between 1990 and 2000 show a sharp drop, from 180 million to 85.07 million. (Most of those reaching the age of 15 between 1990 and 2000 received their primary education in the 1980s.)

It is important to understand what triggered this initial drop in the enrollment ratio in the 1980s as a contrast with the development in the 1990s. In the early 1980s, the rural reforms improved the income-earning prospects of farmers, thus leading to a shift in labor allocation away from education in favor of more remunerative activities. This dynamic explains in particular the sharp drop in male enrollments in secondary school. In other words, the decline in the enrollment rate in the early 1980s was due to the rising *opportunity* costs of education. But the rising opportunity costs were not a binding constraint on education. The main effect was a delay in education rather than forgoing education altogether, especially forgoing basic education. This is consistent with the fact that the gross enrollment ratio – the number of students enrolled at a given level of schooling divided by the number of people in that age group – bounced back very strongly in the mid-1980s.

This is the critical difference with the 1990s. In the 1990s, the *actual* costs of education rose substantially. High actual costs of education are prohibitive (absent of financing intermediation, which rural China does not have) and they force those who cannot afford it to forgo education altogether. The following is my hypothesis of what happened. In the 1990s, there were two developments on the financing side of Chinese education. First, there was a withdrawal of public funding for education, including basic education. Second, the costs of education were rising rapidly. The combination of these two developments led to high nonattendance in primary schools and, in all likelihood, contributed to the educational failures in rural China, the evidence of which is becoming available only now.

Public expenditure on education in China was never high to start with and it became even lower over the course of the 1990s. In 1998, public expenditure on education was 2.2 percent of GDP; in 1988, the ratio was 2.6 percent. At 2.2 percent of GDP, China spent less on education compared with India (3.2 percent), Brazil (4.9 percent), and Bangladesh (2.4 percent). In the group of countries selected by Hannum, Behrman, and Wang (2008) for comparison, China only spent more on education than Indonesia (1.5 percent of GDP) and Pakistan (1.8 percent of GDP). Moreover, in the 1990s, China spent almost all of its central-government education budget – 94 percent – on tertiary education, leaving the bulk of the financing responsibilities for basic education to the local governments (Pei 2006, p. 171). And, as is well known, local governments in the 1990s ran on a growing

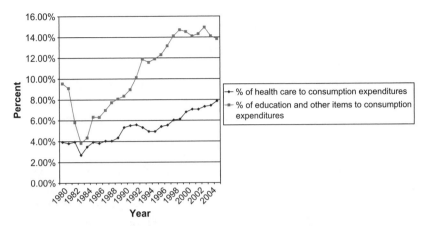

Figure 5.1. Health care and education expenditures as percentage shares of consumption expenditures of rural households, 1980–2005 (%). *Note:* Education expenditures also include cultural and entertainment expenditures. All the expenditure figures here exclude expenditures in kind and refer to cash expenditures only. *Source:* Rural household surveys by NBS, various years.

fiscal shortfall becuase the 1994 tax reforms recentralized revenue collection in the hands of the central government.

The declining public investments in education meant rising private financial burdens. A Chinese scholarly estimate suggests that the private share of the financing costs for primary school education as of the turn of the century accounted for 76 percent (quoted by Pei 2006, p. 172). We go to the NBS rural household survey data to look into the question of the rising costs of education. The rural household income surveys provide a category of "expenditures on culture and education." This category includes expenditures on tuition and textbooks, as well as newspaper subscriptions, tickets to cultural events, and so forth. The bulk of this category of rural expenditures is probably on education.

Figure 5.1 shows per capita cultural and educational expenditures by rural households as ratios to per capita consumption expenditures between 1980 and 2005. The expenditures are valued on a cash basis so the data exclude in-kind expenditures.[13] In the early 1980s, there was a sharp decline in the ratio, from 9.6 percent in 1980 to 3.8 percent in 1983, and then the ratio began to rise in 1984. It reached a peak in 2003 with a ratio of 14.9 percent. Recall the earlier discussion that school enrollments dropped in the early 1980s because of the rising opportunity costs of education. The decline in the ratio captures this effect when rural households reduced their educational expenditures as fewer rural children attended school. Consistent with the story that school enrollments began to rise in the mid-1980s, educational expenditure ratios began to rise as well.

Both cost increases and rising enrollments can lead to a rising ratio. Because we do not have data on education costs, we can only make some educated estimates. I adopt the following estimation procedure. First, I estimate an expenditure ratio at which a full enrollment is attained. Then, I attribute the spending in excess of this ratio to rising costs rather than to rising enrollments.

It is reasonable to estimate the full-enrollment expenditure ratio at 10 percent. From Figure 5.1, rural households spent 9.6 percent of their expenditures on culture and education in 1980 and about 10 percent in 1992. In those two years, China had more or less full enrollment at the level of basic education. In 2003, this ratio reached 15 percent, a 50 percent increase from 1992. Although a part of this increase was due to the expansion of more costly senior secondary and tertiary education, this is a smaller part of the picture. The ratio of rural residents attending school beyond junior secondary education was fairly low. Because the official data for basic education show consistent full enrollments throughout the 1990s, a reasonable hypothesis is that the rising costs of basic education reduced school *attendance*, about which there is no systematic data. To make sense of the illiteracy data from 2000 to 2005, one has to assume that enrollment and attendance diverged sharply in the 1990s (or the enrollment data were falsified).

A 2005 academic study, commissioned by the Ministry of Education and authored by 17 prominent educational researchers in China, uncovered widespread nonattendance at schools.[14] Based on field research covering 17 rural junior secondary schools located in 14 provinces during the 2001–2003 period, the average dropout rate among the 17 rural junior secondary schools was 43 percent. The highest documented dropout rate was 74.34 percent. The transition rate in the urban areas – that is, the percentage of students transitioning from junior to senior secondary schools – increased from 40 percent in 1985 to 55.4 percent in 1999. However, this transition rate in the rural areas *declined* from 22.3 to 18.6 percent during the same period.

In Chapter 3, we saw that the decadal shift in economic policies brought about an instantaneous slowdown in rural income growth. We are now beginning to see the staggering costs in human capital terms. Furthermore, the future prospects are grim. The urban biases began in the early 1990s, rapidly accelerated in strength in the mid-1990s, and probably peaked in 2002–2003. As of 2005, Chinese researchers were still reporting high dropout and nonattendance rates in the rural areas. The Hu–Wen leadership began to address this problem in 2004 with a policy initiative to waive tuition and other charges for rural Chinese by 2007. Even if their policy initiatives are successful, they only address the flow problem – reducing the rate at which China is producing illiteracy. Unless drastic action is taken, the stock problem – the legacy from the 1990s – will continue to plague the country for years to come.

In the area of health care, we do not have one clean data point – such as rising illiteracy – that sharply differentiates between the two decades, but we have multiple suggestive indicators that point to a deterioration in the 1990s. It is well established that during the reform era (i.e., in *both* the 1980s and 1990s), public financing of health care collapsed. In the 1970s, the community medical scheme (CMS) covered 90 percent of the rural population; by 2003, it covered only 20 percent of the rural population (World Bank 2005b).[15] The 2003 outbreak of Severe Acute Respiratory Syndrome (SARS) was a wakeup call and exposed the fragility of China's health system. SARS was confined to the urban areas, which have good health facilities. Had SARS spread to rural China, the consequences would have been much more severe. The new leadership of Hu Jintao and Wen Jiabao has taken public health more seriously and has rolled out a pilot insurance program in 300 counties (there are more than 2,500 counties in total). The commitment is to cover the entire rural population by 2010.[16]

An emerging body of evidence shows that the policy neglect of health care, stretching over the entire reform era, has begun to affect the health status of the Chinese population. Systematic research shows that Chinese health care performance has deteriorated both against its own past achievements and against expectations (conditional on past achievements and the values of those variables predictive of health care performance). The World Bank researchers show that in the 1960s and 1970s, China was able to reduce its under-5 mortality by 6 percent annually, but the rate of reduction began to decline in the 1980s and the speed of the fall accelerated in the 1990s. In the 1980s, the rate of reduction was 3 percent and in the 1990s it was 2 percent. In the 1960s and 1970s, China was out-performing Indonesia and Malaysia by a substantial margin in reducing child mortality under the age of 5. In the 1980s, China began under-performing against Malaysia; then, in the 1990s, it was under-performing both Malaysia and Indonesia. Because the under-5 mortality reduction is a function of both the past level of mortality and per capita income, the World Bank researchers have also calculated the predicted rates of reduction for China. It is the same picture. In the 1960s and 1970s, China out-performed relative to its predicted rates of reduction. In the 1980s and 1990s, China under-performed relative to its predicted rates of reduction (and in the 1990s by a substantial margin).

Rather remarkably, given the supposed economic miracle in the 1990s, China is one of very few countries in the world that has a higher infant mortality rate for girls than for boys. In the 1990s, the mortality rate for boys under the age of 5 declined by 2.3 percent a year on average, but the mortality rate for girls under the age of 5 *rose by 0.5 percent a year.* The World Bank report does not go into detail to explain these differential effects, but one fact identified by the report is that China was charging for immunizations in the 1990s. An explanation could be that the rising immunization costs have forced rural households to choose between boys and girls in allocating the shots. The same report concludes that "China is off-track for the majority of the health MDGs [Millennium Development Goals], and this is largely due to shortcomings in its health system" (World Bank 2005a).

Is there also a tale of two decades here – that the development in the health care sector was more adverse in the 1990s than in the 1980s? Although the policy neglect of health care, especially in the rural areas, was present during *both* the 1980s and 1990s, there are some substantial differences. One difference is that at least by the indicators presented herein, Chinese performance relative to international norms worsened at a faster rate in the 1990s than in the 1980s. The second difference is that the absence of any health insurance program in the 1990s was a purer case of policy neglect. One can plausibly argue that the initial collapse of the rural CMS was to a large extent inevitable. The CMS was intrinsically part and parcel of the massively inefficient commune system. The hugely welfare-improving collapse of the commune system was inevitably accompanied by a collapse of its embedded components, even though some of these embedded components served useful functions.

One can come up with a number of explanations that put the policy inaction in the 1980s in some perspective – such as the brevity of the time to deal with this issue, the recognition of which began around 1984; lack of knowledge; and the stringency of public finance.[17] But none of these explanations can be applied to the 1990s. The leaders of the 1990s had 13 years at their disposal, had presided over a steady rise in the tax/GDP ratio, and had ample access to information and knowledge about both the dire situation in rural China and the experiences of other countries in creating and managing social protection institutions during their period of rapid economic growth. There is no excuse for this level and duration of willful neglect of such a massive problem.

There is yet another difference between the 1980s and the 1990s. In the 1980s, although the burden of financing was shifted from the community to individuals or households, the Chinese state was not profiting from the provision of health care. In the 1990s, the government-run hospitals and their doctors began to increase charges for hospitalization and outpatient visits and for prescription drugs. According to a group of Chinese experts on public health, between 1992 and 2002, GDP per capita grew by 50 percent in real terms but per capita spending on hospital/clinic visits and on hospitalizations increased 2.15 and 3.76 times, respectively (Du Lexun, Zhang Wenming, and Zhang Dawei 2004). In the 1990s, China experienced an extraordinarily fast rate of inflation in the health care sector.

Figure 5.1 presents per capita expenditures on health care as percentage ratios of per capita consumption expenditures between 1980 and 2005 in rural China (on a cash basis). In the 1980s, the health care expenditure ratios were fairly flat, remaining very close to 4 percent. The turning point, yet again, was 1989. In 1988, the ratio was 4 percent; in 1989, it shot up to 4.3 percent and then sharply to 5.3 percent in 1990. Between 1992 and 1997, the ratio fluctuated around 5.5 percent and then in 1998 it began a linear climb, reaching 6 percent in 1998, 7.1 percent in 2001, and 7.9 percent in 2005. This is the social version of the economic tale of the two decades. In the 1980s, the social insurance system collapsed due to the rural reforms, but health care costs were more or less contained. During the next 10 years, between 1988 and 1998, however, the ratio increased by 50 percent and then another 30 percent between 1998 and 2005. The 2005 ratio is almost twice as high as that in 1988.

Although Chinese rural residents spent twice as much in 2005 on health care as they did in 1988, there is no evidence that the quality and quantity of health care have improved. According to the 1998 National Health Service survey conducted by the Ministry of Health, 37 percent of rural residents who were sick did not seek medical care due to the unaffordability of health care. In the same survey, 65 percent of those who should have been hospitalized were not because they could not afford it. Both of these figures were significantly higher than those in 1993, suggesting that health care became less available over time. China is ranked by the World Health Organization as one of the most inequitable countries in the world in terms of the distribution of and access to health care. By the measure of "fairness in financial contributions," China was ranked No. 188 in 2000, ahead only of Brazil (189), Myanmar (190), and Sierra Leone (191).[18]

Objective data bear out this picture. Although on the supply side China looks impressive in terms of the number of doctors or hospitals per population,[19] the prohibitive costs of medical facilities may have deterred their usage. Medical and health facilities, however abundantly available physically, do not improve health if they are not used. Chinese data show a sharp difference in the utilization rate of hospital beds between the 1980s and the 1990s.[20] In the 1980s, the utilization rate was increasing. In 1985, the rate was 82.7 percent, in 1987 84.3 percent, and in 1988 84.5 percent. The latter – 84.5 percent in 1988 – turned out to be the peak. Beginning in 1989, the utilization rate of hospital beds began to decline. In 1989, it was 81.7 percent, in 1992 78.6 percent, in 1996 64.7 percent, and in 2002 57.4 percent. Interestingly, 57.4 percent in 2002 – the last year of Jiang Zemin's rule – marks the trough of this measure. Starting in 2003, the rate began to rise. In 2003, it was 58.7 percent, in 2004 61.3 percent, and in 2005 62.9 percent. Again, as in so many other areas, the improvement coincided with the commencement of the leadership of Hu Jintao and Wen Jiabao.

1.2 Welfare and GDP Growth

Economics, John Stuart Mill famously stated, is the study of "the sources and conditions of wealth and material prosperity for aggregate bodies of human beings." "Aggregate" is the key operating word here because it gets to the heart of why economic growth matters. Economic growth matters because growth improves the welfare of the majority of the population. It is not sufficient that growth benefits only a few elitist members of the society. Throughout this book, I have stressed the point that economic growth under the entrepreneurial capitalism in the 1980s was broad-based, whereas the growth under the state-led capitalism in the 1990s was not.

Economists and other analysts rely almost exclusively on Chinese GDP data to formulate their views of the Chinese economy. GDP data are readily available and are assembled on the basis of standardized and systematic procedures. The assumption is that the Chinese GDP correlates closely with the "wealth and material prosperity for aggregate bodies of human beings." In this book, I raise the issue of whether this assumption is warranted. I propose a conjecture – not a settled claim – that Chinese GDP diverged from Chinese welfare in the 1990s.

I focus on two issues concerning Chinese GDP data.[21] One has to do with the construction of the deflators used by statisticians to calculate real GDP growth. This is related to the aforementioned cost inflation in health care and education in the 1990s. The second issue has to do with the observation first made by Khan and Riskin (1998) that personal income per capita – obtained through household surveys – grew much more slowly than GDP per capita. Khan and Riskin drew their findings from the two waves of the China Household Income Project (CHIP) surveys of 1988 and 1995. According to them, the weighted rural and urban income per capita grew at 5.05 percent a year in real terms between 1988 and 1995, compared with an annual average rate of 8.07 percent of per capita GNP growth. Because the CHIP surveys do not go back far enough, Khan and Riskin cannot examine whether GDP and income survey data diverged in the 1980s as well. We go to the NBS household survey data that go back to the early 1980s to find the following pattern in the data: In the 1980s, personal income grew faster than GDP, but in the 1990s, it was the other way around. The direction of the divergence differs systematically between the two decades.

One way that the Chinese deflators can be under-estimated is that the weight assigned to rural spending on health care and education may be too low in the construction of the Chinese consumer price index (CPI).[22] This is a hypothesis that requires more research, but we have some suggestive clues. As postulated before, the huge rise in adult illiteracy between 2000 and 2005 must imply large-scale nonattendance of – or dropout from – schools in the 1990s, to the tune of roughly 30 percent of rural school-age children. We also know from the 1998 National Health Service survey that 37 percent of rural residents were not treated when sick because of the high health care costs. By definition, the expenditure ratios shown in Figure 5.1 do not reflect the forgone expenditures by those who failed to attend schools or by those who did not seek medical care. The reported educational and health expenditures thus understate the welfare impact of cost inflation in health and education.

One can correct the Chinese CPI by assigning a weight to education and health care based on full schooling and full access to medical care. After all, this is what is guaranteed in the Chinese Constitution, so education and health care should be treated as entitlements rather than as normal goods and services. The adjusted CPI will thus exceed the official statistics. Health care and education experienced the fastest price increases in the 1990s. I have already pointed out the high inflation in health care. In education, according to Holz (2005), in the early 1990s, the growth in the cost of tuition and child care exceeded the CPI by about 10 percent. This divergence grew extremely large toward the late 1990s. In the late 1990s, China experienced a general deflation, but the costs of tuition and child care continued to rise. By 2000, the growth of tuition and child care costs exceeded the CPI by some 30 percent. Assigning a greater weight to the highest-inflation items would lead to a higher estimate of the CPI.

The under-statement of the Chinese deflators is not a narrow – and narrowly technical – issue. It has massive implications for gauging the true growth rates of Chinese GDP. The under-estimations of the CPI would

Table 5.1. *Per capita GDP and weighted rural/urban income: Real annual average growth (%)*

	1979–1988	1989–2002	2003–2005
Panel (1): Two alternative estimates of growth of GDP per capita			
(1a) Based on implicit GDP deflators	8.5	8.1	9.4
(1b) Based on household income deflators	9.5	6.9	10.8
Panel (2): Growth of per capita household income			
(2a) Weighted rural/urban income	11.1	6.3	8.7
(2b) Rural income	12.2	3.9	5.8
(2c) Urban income	6.3	7.1	8.8
Panel (3): Ratios of weighted rural–urban income per capita to GDP per capita			
(3a) Ratios	56.2	48.7	46.2

Notes: The NBS publishes the nominal values of GDP and household income as well as their real growth rates. The implicit deflators are then derived accordingly. The weighted rural–urban incomes are derived by using the rural–urban population shares.

Source: Statistical Yearbooks, various years, and rural and urban household surveys, various years.

naturally overstate Chinese GDP growth. This is another way of stating that the official data on GDP growth do not fully reflect the welfare gains and losses of the Chinese population. This analysis also shows that Chinese GDP growth rates are highly sensitive to the choice of deflators. As an illustration, in the following paragraphs, I present several estimates of growth rates based on different deflators. The idea here is not to argue that one set of deflators is superior to another set of deflators. Rather, the point is to illustrate a systematic difference in the pattern of growth rates between the 1980s and the 1990s.

Table 5.1 presents two groups of indicators: the real growth rates of per capita GDP and the real growth of per capita household income. There are three time periods – 1979–1988, 1989–2002, and 2003–2005 – coinciding with the tenure of the three generations of leaders during the reform era. The growth rates of GDP per capita are derived in two ways. One is that we use the official implicit GDP deflators to deflate the published nominal GDP numbers. These are the official GDP growth rates. The second method is to deflate the nominal GDP with the deflators that Chinese statisticians use when they report the real growth rates of household income. The household income deflators capture the price developments of those goods and services most pertinent to the well-being of the Chinese population.

For now, I concentrate on the 1980s and 1990s. I come back to the period since 2002 later in this chapter when I assess the leadership of

Hu Jintao and Wen Jiabao. Panel (1) of the table presents the growth rates of the GDP per capita as the annual averages during the three policy periods. Row (1a) uses the implicit GDP deflators and Row (1b) uses the implicit household income deflators. (The NBS publishes both the nominal values and their real growth rates. The implicit deflators are derived accordingly.) The growth rates based on the official implicit GDP deflators, which are the widely cited figures, show only a slight difference between the two policy periods under the first two generations of Chinese leaders. Between 1979 and 1988, GDP per capita grew at 8.5 percent per year, compared with 8.1 percent during the 1989–2002 period.

The performance difference becomes more apparent once we use an alternative set of deflators based on the household income surveys, as shown in Row (1b). By this measure, GDP per capita grew at 9.5 percent a year between 1979 and 1988, compared with only 6.9 percent during the 1989–2002 period. The difference becomes substantially larger in terms of the per capita household income measure, as shown in Panel (2). During the 1979–1988 period, the population-weighted household income per capita grew at 11.1 percent; over the subsequent 13 years, growth fell sharply, to only 6.3 percent during the 1989–2002 period. (The weights used in the calculation refer to the rural and urban population shares.) The rural income growth, as I point out in Chapter 3, contracted sharply between 1989 and 2002. Urban China did much better during the 1989–2002 period. Per capita urban household income grew substantially faster in the 1990s compared with the 1980s as well as compared with rural China.[23]

Our third indicator is the ratio of the weighted rural-urban household income per capita to GDP per capita. In Chapter 4 of this book, we saw that there is a large gap between household income and GDP in Shanghai, whereas in Zhejiang, the gap is smaller. Shanghai's GDP per capita is roughly 5 times the national average, whereas its per capita household income is only 1.7 times the national average. There is a similar difference in the national data between the decades of the 1980s and the 1990s, as shown in Panel (3). During the 1979–1988 period, the ratio of the weighted rural–urban household income to GDP per capita was 56.2 percent; this ratio fell substantially to 48.7 percent during the 1989–2002 period.[24]

More – and more systematic – research is needed to further explore the following conjecture: The divergence between welfare and GDP grew in the 1990s. The GDP data do not sufficiently differentiate the vast differences between the 1980s and the 1990s, but those measures bearing more closely on the welfare of the Chinese people do show rather substantial differences. Economic policies affect not only GDP growth but also how GDP growth does or does not improve welfare or to what degree it improves welfare. One piece of evidence apparent in Table 5.1 is that since 2002, GDP growth and personal income growth again began to converge. I discuss the details later but again, this development took place under the leadership of Hu Jintao and Wen Jiabao, who, as is widely known, began to put more emphasis on improving the living standards of the Chinese people rather than on GDP growth *per se.*

That there can be a divergence between GDP growth and welfare gains is a cautionary tale to those economic observers who formulate their grandiose views of the Chinese economy on the basis of GDP data alone. It is for this reason that this book treats GDP performance as the beginning of the analysis rather than as the end of the analysis. In Chapter 1, I cite research that contrives analytical devices to comport manifestly inefficient institutions and policies on the one hand with the excellent GDP performance on the other. Maybe a simpler and a more analytically productive approach ought to have been to probe more deeply into the complications and implications of GDP performance.

1.3 Equity

It is well established that China today is among the most unequal societies in the world. According to Khan and Riskin (2005), China had a Gini coefficient (which measures inequality of income distribution) of 45 in 2002, compared with 31.6 in Korea (1998), 32.5 in India (late 1990s), and 34.3 in Indonesia (2002). By 2006, China's Gini coefficient reached 49.6, according to a report by the Chinese Academy of Social Sciences based on a survey of 7,140 households (Dyer 2006). China has now surpassed or is in the process of surpassing the level in Latin America, the region widely known as having the worst income inequality in the world (and troubling economic performance). According to the data provided by Khan and Riskin (2005), the Gini coefficient was 46.5 in Costa Rica, 52.2 in Argentina, 57.1 in Chile, and 58.5 in Brazil.

A part of this increase in the dispersion of income distribution is not surprising. To be sure, the income distribution during the socialist period was compressed, but the price for this was an extraordinarily high level of poverty. One mechanism to achieve absolute egalitarianism under central planning was the complete suppression of incentives in resource allocation. Moving away from the absolute egalitarianism of the central planning era and toward a greater reliance on economic incentives is likely to lead to an expansion of income gaps among individuals endowed with different dispositions and capabilities. From an efficiency perspective, income disparities rise for "good" reasons.

There can also be an entirely different reason for rising income disparities. In this case, certain groups or individuals are privileged – by the political process, financial system, and regulations – over others to grab a larger share of the economic gains. For example, the privileged groups or individuals can enter into businesses that are off-limits to others; under this scenario, the income disparities rise because the economic processes are anti-competitive. A more subtle form of anti-competitive economic processes is the restrictions not on the economic opportunities *per se* but on the social opportunities – the acquisition of psychological inclinations and educational and physical capabilities to participate in economic opportunities. In this case, economic opportunities may be distributed equally, but the social opportunities to participate in them are not. Income disparities can rise as a result and for "bad" reasons.

But here is the analytical challenge: The "good" and "bad" mechanisms for income disparities lead to an observationally identical result – a rising Gini. We do not know which set of factors is behind the rising income disparities or which set of factors is more important. Both for analysis and for drawing the right policy implications, it is critical to identify the true mechanisms – economic incentives or blockage of economic opportunities – behind China's rising income disparities during the reform era. Let me suggest a way to think about this issue.

A simple, although crude, way to distinguish between the economic incentive story and the anti-competitive story is to assume that 100 percent of the income disparity in the United States is the result of market incentives. Under this assumption, the Gini coefficient of the United States can serve as an upper threshold between the "good" and the "bad" mechanisms for income disparity. It is an upper threshold because in the United States, racial discrimination and the political power of big business can also be construed as obstructions to economic opportunities. For our purposes, it is better to err on the side of caution against drawing a false positive and, therefore, it makes sense to set a high threshold on the basis of the US level rather than on the basis of the more egalitarian East Asian level.

Estimates of Gini coefficients often vary by sources and by analysts. For the sake of simplicity, I adopt the estimates provided in Khan and Riskin (2005) who directly compared the Gini coefficient for China with that of other countries, including the United States. According to them, the recent Gini coefficient for the United States is 40.8. If this is the threshold, China crossed it sometime in the early 1990s. China's Gini was 38.2 in 1988 and

45.2 in 1995 (Khan and Riskin 1998). In 1980, China's Gini was 28 (Khan and Riskin 2001). Based on these numbers, we can argue that in the 1980s, the rise in the Gini was due to the workings of the economic incentives, whereas in the 1990s, it was due to the blockage of economic opportunities.

One supporting piece of evidence for this hypothesis comes from Khan and Riskin (2005). According to their analysis, both urban and rural entrepreneurship – defined as self-employment businesses – improved income distribution, although each in different ways. Rural entrepreneurship was found to increase within-rural income inequality but it decreased rural-urban income inequality. Their analysis shows that within-rural inequality contributed very little to China's overall income inequality, whereas rural–urban income differences had a huge effect. Thus, the net effect of rural entrepreneurship was an equalization of income. Urban entrepreneurship, on the other hand, improved within-urban income distribution because small-scale self-employers in the urban areas tend to be poor. An extension of this finding to the theme of this book leads to the conclusion that in the 1990s, blockage of business opportunities for small-scale entrepreneurs exacerbated income inequalities. This dynamic also explains the income distribution pattern in Shanghai. Shanghai is the extreme version of the policy model that restricted small entrepreneurs, with grave implications for income distribution.

There are other telltale signs that in the 1990s the rising Gini was a result of factors other than economic incentives. The economic incentive story is most compatible with rising income disparities at the *individual* level – such as educated individuals earning more than uneducated individuals – rather than at the *group* level, especially groups of individuals with incidental characteristics (e.g., place of birth or race). The following is one of the most unusual findings by scholars who have looked at income distribution in China in some detail: In the 1990s, there was a sharp *decline* in individual income inequality and there was a sharp rise in group income inequality, primarily in the rural vis-à-vis the urban groups. This is from Khan and Riskin (2005), who report that both the rural Gini and the urban Gini declined between 1995 and 2002, whereas rural–urban income disparities rose sharply. This is true whether or not migration is taken into account.

Another intriguing finding is that factors such as place of residence, in fact, *increased* in importance in explaining income distribution. This is reported by Sicular et al. (2007). They show that the variables at the individual or household levels, such as the size of household, education, and age, explain about 54 percent of urban–rural income differences in 1995 but only about 20 percent in 2002. That is, in 2002, 80 percent of the income differences are a result of incidental factors such as the geographic residence of the households, compared with only 46 percent in 1995. This finding is rather remarkable considering the following. One is that their paper implicitly already incorporates the story of economic incentives by including education and other variables. So, another reading of their finding is that the importance of economic incentives declined between 1995 and 2002. The other factor is that between 1995 and 2002, China was supposed to have experienced an increase in the regional mobility of labor as rural migrants moved more freely between rural and urban areas. The rising importance of geographic factors in their econometric exercise is quite unexpected given this increase in labor mobility.[25] Although the scholars who have generated these findings do not explicitly make this argument, I would argue that these findings are largely consistent with the story of blocked opportunities rather than with the story of rising economic incentives.

Our third clue comes from the rising social tensions in Chinese society. Although few China economists take the sharp increase in social unrest in China as a data point in their perspectives on China (in sharp contrast to other China social scientists), these incidences of social unrest help to put the rising Gini in perspective. In general, economists are less concerned about the relative deprivation – rising incomes of all groups in the society but at different rates – than about the absolute deprivation (some groups losing income relative to the levels of their past incomes). If the rising Gini is a result of relative deprivation, the implications are relatively benign. If, however, the rising Gini is a result of absolute deprivation, it is altogether a different story.

The rising levels and the degree of severity associated with social unrest in China suggest the looming possibility of absolute deprivation. In the post-Tiananmen political environment in China, social unrest – demonstrations, protests, riots, strikes, and so forth – are highly risky undertakings. The individuals involved face realistic and swift prospects of arrest and severe punishment. It is unlikely that millions of Chinese participated in these highly risky activities simply because of relative income differences. A hypothesis centered on absolute deprivation seems to be more appropriate to the phenomenon in question.

Protests in China increased at a stunning rate. Between 1993 and 1997, the total number of demonstrations rose from 8,700 to 32,000.[26] According to official figures released by the Ministry of Public Security, there were 58,000 large-scale incidents of unrest in 2003, 74,000 in 2004, and 87,000 in 2005. In an ominous development, in September 2007, more than 2,000 demobilized soldiers rioted simultaneously in two cities 770 miles apart from each other, indicating a high level of coordination. The ex-soldiers were protesting their poor living conditions ("Thousands of Ex-Soldiers Riot in China" 2007). Another group of statistics is even more startling. According to Professor Li Shuguang, a vice dean at the graduate school at Chinese University of Politics and Law, in 2005 the central government received 30 million petitions from Chinese citizens address-ing various grievances. Professor Li also reveals that between 1979 and 1982, the Chinese government received only 20,000 similar petitions annu-ally (Chen 2006). Professor Li is in a position to know. His university is closely associated with the Ministry of Public Security, which handles petitions.

We already have some preliminary evidence of the absolute deprivation in China. In Chapter 4, we saw that the poorest 10 percent of Shanghai's population lost income every year since 2001. It turns out that this was a development at the national level as well. During the period when GDP growth averaged more than 10 percent, a World Bank study reports that the income of China's poorest 10 percent of the population declined by 2.4 percent every year between 2001 and 2003 (McGregor 2006b). This is the first documented evidence that a large number of Chinese people – 130 million people – have actually experienced an absolute reduction in their living standards. That this absolute deprivation occurred at a time of double-digit GDP growth is a worrisome sign that Chinese growth has taken on an inherently anti-poor bias.

2 The Other Path

The title of this section is taken from the seminal book by Hernando de Soto. Hernando de Soto (1989), a Peruvian economist, documents the barriers to indigenous, small-scale entrepreneurs in his native country of Peru. In a real social science experiment, de Soto assembled a research team to follow all the required bureaucratic procedures to set up a one-employee garment factory. The process took the team members 289 days and cost them a total of $1,231, equivalent to three years of an average Peruvian income. Hernando de Soto shows the massive, self-inflicted harm to a poor struggling economy because of policies repressing indigenous entrepreneurship.

The ideas of de Soto gained wide acceptance and acclaim among policy makers and academics around the world – until China came along. In his book, *The End of Poverty*, Jeffrey Sachs (2006), an influential development economist, questions the basic premise in de Soto's work. China's growth experience figures heavily in Sachs's critique. He argues that economic growth is not a single-factor process and many factors other than the security of private property rights and the policy treatment of private-sector firms contribute to growth. China's growth, Sachs argues, did not depend first on "solving the deeds and titles."

Sachs does not recognize the distinction I make in Chapter 1 between the personal security of a proprietor and the security of her property. Sachs is right that China did not first solve "the deeds and titles" and then grow its economy. But China did solve the personal security of millions of those holding deeds and titles as a first order of policy business. China was moving directionally toward liberalism and, by the "nasty, brutal, and short" standard of the Cultural Revolution, did so by leaps and bounds. The incentive effect was massive.

An empirically accurate framing of the China story is entirely consistent with the essence of de Soto's claim – the most important contributory factor to broad-based economic growth is indigenous entrepreneurship. Among Chinese policy makers as well as among Western observers in the 1990s, there was an obsession with the supposed growth-boosting effects of foreign direct investment (FDI). (Incidentally, just at the time when de Soto's experiment encountered numerous difficulties in registering an indigenous firm in Peru, the country, under President Fernando Belaunde from 1980 to 1985, enthusiastically wooed FDI by tax and policy concessions.[27]) The leaders of Shanghai routinely highlighted the number of *Fortune* 500 MNCs making investments in the city, not the growth of household income, as their achievement. For many years, Western analysts habitually wrote off the economic prospects of India simply because that country was unable to attract FDI.

My argument that the decade of the 1980s was the true China miracle implicitly assigns zero weight to FDI in explaining China's economic take-off. In the 1980s, very little FDI flowed into China. Let me make this view explicit here. I do it in two ways. First, I compare Zhejiang with Jiangsu. I have referenced Zhejiang several times in this book as the most successful entrepreneurial economy in China. There is another aspect to the Zhejiang story – it has attracted very little FDI. Jiangsu, a neighboring province, has exactly the opposite combination. Like Shanghai, Jiangsu has systematically repressed indigenous entrepreneurship with its left hand while lavishly courting foreign investors with its right hand. (The direction of the hand analogy is intentional.) Here is a contrast between the two provinces: Zhejiang has outperformed Jiangsu in every meaningful dimension of economic performance. I present more details on this in the following section.

I then present a stylized comparison between China and India. There are both positive and normative aspects to this comparison. On the positive side, the stellar performance of the Indian economy should debunk many myths about growth – the outsized role of FDI being one of them. On the normative side, the rise of India undermines, hopefully fatally, the intellectual underpinnings of an idea that, in fact, never had any empirical support in the first place – that democracy is anti-growth. As China ponders the question of whether to begin to reform its politics, a closer look at India's experience is highly relevant.

2.1 The Zhejiang Model

All our indicators are better than those of Ningbo [in Zhejiang province], except per capita income.
> – Wang Mang, the mayor of Suzhou of Jiangsu province, 2004

In this quote, Mayor Wang of Suzhou city of Jiangsu province gets right to the essence of our tale of two provinces. Compared with Zhejiang, Jiangsu has everything on its side – FDI, high-tech industrial parks (with heavy support from another FDI-heavy economy, Singapore), bank loans, and massive investments – except for one thing that actually matters, economic performance. Mayor Wang cites the GDP per capita data. In doing so, he is understating the true differentials between the two provinces. The relative difference between Zhejiang and Jiangsu – the ratio of Zhejiang to Jiangsu – in terms of GDP per capita was 1.11 in 2006 (NBS 2007a, p. 71). But the gap was much larger in terms of per capita household income, a better measure of the material well-being of the average person. In terms of urban household income per capita, the relative difference is 1.30 and in terms of rural household income per capita, the relative difference is 1.26. The gap is even larger when measured by specific components of household income. Consistent with the idea that an entrepreneurial economy is better at wealth creation, an average urban resident in Zhejiang earned an asset income 3.4 times that of her counterpart in Jiangsu province.

These differences are not mere statistical abstractions. They have real welfare implications. In 1990, an average resident in these two provinces had a roughly identical life expectancy at birth: 71.37 years in Jiangsu and 71.78 years in Zhejiang. In 2000, the gap increased: 73.91 years in Jiangsu and 74.70 years in Zhejiang. There are other objective differences. An average rural resident in Zhejiang consumes and owns more telephones, computers, color TV sets, and cameras than her counterpart in Jiangsu. She also lives in a bigger house.[28]

That Zhejiang's life expectancy surpassed that of Jiangsu is an extremely important data point: Zhejiang is a catch-up story. Today, Zhejiang is the richest province in terms of per capita GDP and per capita household income. (In this and the following comparisons, I exclude Beijing, Shanghai, and Tianjin because these three metropolitan areas do not have an agricultural sector.) To put it simply, Zhejiang is rich because it has grown faster. Jiangsu is also among the richest provinces in China today, but it is rich because it has always been rich. In 1980, Zhejiang was ranked No. 7 in the country in terms of per capita GDP, compared with Jiangsu's No. 3 position. Today, Zhejiang has the highest per capita GDP (minus Beijing, Shanghai, and Tianjin), whereas Jiangsu retains its No. 3 ranking. In 1980, Zhejiang and Jiangsu had the same level of rural household per capita income. By 1990, the Zhejiang/Jiangsu ratio was 1.15 and by 2006, it rose to 1.26 (NBS 2007a, p. 368). There are other performance differences as well. Jiangsu was more indebted, had much higher investment/GDP ratios, and a higher non-performing loan ratio. Thus, Jiangsu carries some of the same traits of China as a whole – it has grown very fast but it requires massive resources to power its growth.

A comparison of these two provinces is a near-perfect natural experiment. Their geographic conditions are almost identical. Located next to each other, both are coastal. Jiangsu is to the north and Zhejiang is to the south of Shanghai. The two provinces are also similar in terms of their history of entrepreneurial development. In 1952, private firms accounted for 57 percent of the sales value in the retail sector in Jiangsu and 60 percent in Zhejiang.[29] At the beginning of the reforms, the size of the industrial non-state sector was quite similar as well. Historically speaking, these two provinces were among the most entrepreneurial and culturally developed in China. In the first half of the 20th century, both supplied industrialists and entrepreneurs to Shanghai, and throughout Chinese history, the two provinces produced some of the most prominent literary and political figures.[30]

The two provinces differed in two critical aspects. First, Zhejiang relied substantially less on FDI for its economic performance as compared with Jiangsu. In the second half of the 1980s, both provinces drew very little FDI, as measured by the proportion of FDI to total fixed-asset investments. In Jiangsu, the ratio was only 0.63 percent, about the same as the ratio in Zhejiang (0.65 percent). In the first half of the 1990s, as China became more open to FDI, this ratio rose in both provinces but much more rapidly in

Jiangsu. On average, FDI accounted for 13.6 percent of fixed-asset investments in Jiangsu, which was more than twice the level in Zhejiang during the same period (5.7 percent). Other measures, such as output and export shares by FIEs, indicate the same contrast.

The second difference is that Zhejiang was a vibrant entrepreneurial economy, whereas Jiangsu was a more statist economy.[31] Jiangsu and Zhejiang represent two contrasting development models in China, a phenomenon first noted in 1986 by Professor Fei Xiaotong, China's most prominent sociologist. The Wenzhou model is characterized by a heavy reliance on private initiatives, a noninterventionist government style in the management of firms, and a supportive credit policy stance toward private firms. (Wenzhou is a city in southern Zhejiang province, hence the name of the model.) The foundation of the Wenzhou model was established in the 1980s, as a 1990 World Bank TVE study notes. Byrd and Lin (1990, p. 34) characterize the Wenzhou model as follows:

The famous "Wenzhou" model is characterized by free development of private enterprises (mostly household undertakings), a thriving financial market based to a large extent on private financial institutions, and extensive commercial relationships with distant parts of China.

In sharp contrast, the "Sunan model," which prevailed in Jiangsu, was highly interventionist and discriminatory against indigenous private entrepreneurship. In Jiangsu, private enterprises "are tolerated, but their development has been constrained by limits on loans, restricted access to inputs, and environmental and other regulations" (Svejnar and Woo 1990, p. 80). The Sunan model also carried a strong industrial policy approach with a heavy emphasis on the role of the government, rather than the private sector, in economic development. The model emerged in the 1980s and persisted until the late 1990s. (Since the late 1990s, the province has partially moved away from this model of economic development by privatization of the collective TVEs and more financial support for the private sector.)

The level of micromanagement in the Sunan model was extensive. Wuxi, a city in Jiangsu, is widely regarded as a progenitor of the Sunan model. In 1985, the Wuxi government adopted the following measures: (1) penalties for skilled workers who left collective TVEs for other jobs, including barring their family members from jobs in TVEs; (2) thorough status checks on enterprise registration documents and procedures; and (3) limits on managers' pay to three times the average payroll (Luo 1990, p. 150).

All of these measures were designed to constrain indigenous private firms by denying them access to quality human capital, raw materials, and finance.

And they all succeeded. In 1985, collective TVEs constituted 36 percent of the total number of industrial non-state firms in Wuxi but contributed 96 percent of the gross value of industrial output. The private sector in the industrial arena was inconsequential (Svejnar and Woo 1990, pp. 67–69). In terms of the share of private TVEs in total TVE output, in 1987, Zhejiang had a higher share, at 16 percent, compared with 11 percent in Jiangsu. But the differences grew greater in the 1990s. By 1997, in terms of the share of the private TVEs, it was 52 percent in Zhejiang and 28 percent in Jiangsu (Ministry of Agriculture 2003). Although the two models were formulated in the 1980s, it was the policies of the 1990s that accentuated their economic differences.

After Professor Fei proposed these two models, Chinese economists rigorously debated their respective merits. Now, the debate has been settled overwhelmingly in favor of the Wenzhou model. As I show earlier, the economy of Zhejiang grew faster and its residents are much richer than those in Jiangsu. We can speculate about why a stronger indigenous entrepreneurial economy is more efficient than a combination of statism and FDI. One reason could be that stronger indigenous entrepreneurship is associated with a larger local supply network, which expands local incomes more directly. In contrast, an FDI model relies heavily on export-processing that has low domestic value-added. The profits of this business model accrue to the foreign investors rather than to the local entrepreneurs. Another piece of evidence is that although both provinces have a similar export/GDP ratio, Zhejiang has a far lower import/GDP ratio, as compared with Jiangsu. A stronger local production base also enables foreign firms to source locally. In 2006, the foreign trade balance of FIEs in Zhejiang was US$18.6 billion, compared with US$16.2 billion in the case of Jiangsu (NBS 2007a, p. 741). However, FIEs in Jiangsu exported 3.3 times as much as FIEs in Zhejiang, suggesting a far greater domestic content of export production for FIEs in Zhejiang.

In a statist economy, the primary contributions of FDI may be ameliorative in nature rather than additive to economic growth. That is, efficiency-enhancing FDI contributes to growth by offsetting the inefficiencies of the state sector. So, its contributions to growth are stunted. A counterfactual scenario is that the Sunan model would have done even worse without the FDI. This reasoning may explain why Jiangsu seemed to court FDI more eagerly than Zhejiang: Because Jiangsu systematically suppressed indigenous entrepreneurship, it needed to expend precious resources on importing foreign entrepreneurship. In this scenario, FDI still contributed to growth, but not nearly as much if Jiangsu had had a more vibrant private sector.

2.2 The Indian Model

[T]he Indian manufacturing model, in my view, continues to suffer from three major deficiencies – a lack of infrastructure, a low national saving rate (a little over 20%) and anemic inflows of foreign direct investment (barely $4 billion in 2003).
– Stephen Roach (2004), chief economist of Morgan Stanley,
after an arduous six-hour trip from Mumbai to Pune

For a long time, academics and business analysts have compared India unfavorably with China. China grew faster, drew more FDI, exported more, and reduced poverty at a more impressive rate. According to a widely accepted view, the two countries started the decade of the 1990s at the same level of per capita GDP, but China ended the decade twice as rich as India. This latter view, based on GDP data adjusted for purchasing power parity supplied by the World Bank, has powerfully influenced the ways academics and analysts explained their respective growth experiences. The view that China left India behind in the 1990s tilts analytical attention to those developments that occurred in China in the 1990s. The hallmarks of China in the 1990s were massive FDI inflows and huge investments in infrastructure. An extension of this view to India is that the poor quality and the meager quantity of infrastructure explain India's lagging performance.

It is important to adjudicate the timing of China's economic takeoff vis-à-vis India. If it indeed is the case that China became richer than India only in the 1990s, then FDI inflows and heavy investments in infrastructure loom large in the explanation of why China surged ahead. If, however, China was already richer than India by the early 1990s, then it was the policy choices prior to the 1990s that mattered. I show that multiple indicators other than the PPP estimates by the World Bank cast substantial doubt on the notion that China overtook India only in the 1990s.

Although many believe that China left India behind economically, a closer look at the comparative economic performance of China and India reveals a more subtle picture. By the standards of wealth and value creation, the Indian economy, in fact, has some substantial strengths. Indians use less energy and fewer investment resources to generate growth. These attributes of Indian growth should be recognized because they offer a useful lesson to other poor countries. The most important implication from an Indian miracle in the making is the importance of what I call "soft infrastructures" to understand economic growth. Soft infrastructures, such as rule of law, financial institutions, and China's directional liberalism in the 1980s, matter more for growth than the massive investments in hard infrastructures.

Alternative GDP data to the PPP estimates show China to be a far richer country than India long before the 1990s. Dwight Perkins (1986), the world's foremost authority on Chinese economic history, estimated China's GDP per capita in 1985 to be US$500. In the same year, India's GDP per capita was US$270. According to a careful study, China's nutritional levels and consumption of durable goods as of the early 1990s broadly resembled the patterns in Taiwan in the 1970s. Because there is a close correlation between income and consumption patterns, Garnaut and Ma (1993), the authors of this influential study, concluded that GDP per capita for China in 1990 ought to be valued at around US$1,000. India's GDP per capita was US$350 in 1990.[32] Maddison presents other comparative data that put China significantly ahead of India as early as 1975. In 1975, China's gross value-added per agricultural worker was 2.3 percent of the US level, compared with India's 1.9 percent (Maddison 1998, p. 113).

The point here is not to suggest that China's GDP per capita was actually US$500 in 1985 or US$1,000 in the early 1990s. Rather, the suggestion is that we should be very skeptical about the prevailing view that China surpassed India due only to its policies in the 1990s. In fact, the PPP estimates of GDP per capita by the World Bank are the only indicator that I know of that shows the two countries to be at the same level of development as of 1990. Every other indicator suggests that China was substantially more developed than India, not just in 1990 but as far back as 1965. Let us take a look at the human development index (HDI) devised by the United Nations Development Programme. In 1975, China had a HDI of 0.527 compared with India's 0.413. (The higher value indicates more advanced development.[33]) In the 1960s, the Chinese had a longer life expectancy, lower infant mortality rate, and better educational attainments. In 1965, the life expectancy at birth for an average Chinese male was 54 years; for an average Chinese female, 55 years. In contrast, for Indian males, life expectancy was 46 years and for Indian females, 44 years. (India is one of the few countries in the world where men outlived women.) By 1985, the gap in life expectancy between China and India had grown larger. Chinese men averaged 68 years in terms of life expectancy, compared with 57 years for Indian men. For women, Chinese women averaged 70 years, as compared with 56 years for Indian women. In the mid-1980s, China's infant mortality rate was 54 per 1,000, compared with 122 per 1,000 in India. Furthermore, China's primary education enrollment ratio was far higher than that of India as early as the mid-1970s.[34] In 1973, the Chinese averaged 4.09 years in primary education, compared with the Indian's 2.6 years (Maddison 1998, p. 63). If the two countries truly had the same level of GDP per capita, one must be prepared to explain this huge gap in their broader socioeconomic achievements.

The idea that China's success owes to its infrastructural investments and FDI is heavily rooted in observation of China of the 1990s. Once we consider the experience of the 1980s, an entirely different picture emerges. In the 1980s, China's economy grew rigorously and the population-weighted household income per capita grew substantially faster than it did in the 1990s. In the 1980s, China attracted very little FDI. The highest level of FDI was US$3 billion, accounting for a trivial portion of China's total investments. Although their growth rates have become closer in recent years, it is beyond any doubt that China outperformed India by a large margin in the 1980s.

There is another little-known fact: In the 1980s, China, in fact, started with an infrastructural *disadvantage* vis-à-vis India. In 1989, India had a longer network of paved roads (1.4 million kilometers) compared with China (862,000 kilometers) and it had a more developed railway system. In 1975, India, the smaller country of the two, had a railway system 60,438 kilometers in length, as compared with 46,000 kilometers in China. As late as 1995, China still had shorter railway lines (Maddison 1998, p. 51). One measure of the "quality" of the railway system is the length of electrified railways. Here again, India held an advantage over China. In 1989, its electrified railways were 5,345 kilometers long, as compared with only 1,700 kilometers in the case of China.[35]

To attribute China's economic success to FDI and infrastructural investments is putting the carriage before the horse. FDI and infrastructural investments played a minor role in China's initial economic takeoff. The more factually accurate description of China's growth experience is that growth occurred first, and FDI and infrastructural investments followed, rather than the other way around.

Now India is repeating this story. Despite being a persistent FDI laggard and despite universal complaints about – and scorn for – the fact that India lacks the Chinese level of infrastructure, India's economy is gaining increasing strength. Its GDP growth has inched from the 4 to 5 percent range to above 8 percent in recent years, defying many pessimistic predictions that it could not grow without the Chinese levels of FDI and infrastructure. India will repeat the true China miracle in another way as well – FDI does not put a country on a high-growth trajectory, but once a country grows fast, FDI will come to the country regardless of its infrastructures. With a growth trajectory of 8 to 9 percent, India can easily triple or even quadruple its FDI inflows from the US$6 billion in 2006. This is a smarter way to attract FDI and to build infrastructures. Rising FDI and economic growth will generate resources to self-fund the construction of infrastructures.

India's growth experience is more relevant to that of other developing countries wishing to jump-start their economies. A universal problem among developing countries is the low savings rate. It will be valuable to learn from India how to use limited resources efficiently. India is investing half of what China is investing and yet it is achieving a growth rate around 80 percent of the Chinese growth rate. It will also be valuable to learn from India in terms of how it is able to overcome another massive disadvantage vis-à-vis China – its tropical geography. (China is a temperate country similar to the United States and Europe.) Growing an economy in a tropical environment entails special challenges (Sachs 2001).

India has other well-known disadvantages – its hugely unproductive and counterproductive caste system and its high level of illiteracy. One can focus on these liabilities and bemoan India's growth prospects. Another more productive approach is to focus on those conditions that have enabled India to grow at an impressive rate despite these liabilities. My own candidate variable is India's rigorous soft infrastructures. One can go a step further and argue that India's soft infrastructures must be so good to be able to offset its massive disabilities in other areas.

India's growth has accelerated in recent years, but it still pales in comparison with China. According to the *World Development Indicators*,[36] between 1978 and 2004, annual GDP growth averaged around 9.73 percent a year in China but only 5.37 percent in India. On that basis, many analysts would conclude that China has outperformed India substantially in the past two decades.

Details are important in making comparisons between China and India. The first important detail is that the growth gap between China and India has narrowed. On average, between 1978 and 1997, China grew nearly twice as fast as India, but between 1998 and 2004, China was growing about 50 percent faster. The second detail is that Chinese per capita GDP growth exceeded that of India by a larger margin than its aggregate GDP growth. Between 1978 and 2004, Chinese per capita GDP growth was roughly 2.5 times that of India, but its aggregate GDP growth was 1.8 times that of India. It is this difference in the growth rates of per capita GDP, more than the differential GDP growth rates, that explains the sharp visual difference between China and India. After visiting the two countries, countless visitors have reported that China feels far richer than India.

That China was able to grow substantially faster in per capita terms than in aggregate GDP terms is partially a political story. Although the economically induced declining fertility played a role, there is no doubt that China's draconian one-child policy led to lower population growth in China than in India. India tried a similar program in the late 1970s but voters thoroughly rejected the proposal by Indira Gandhi to enforce a forcible sterilization program. Because both countries have a chronic surplus of labor, it is plausible to argue that the higher GDP growth per capita in China – above that of its GDP growth – is due in part to the greater political capacity of the Chinese government to contain population growth. Leaving aside the issue of whether population control is economically desirable, very few countries can emulate this aspect of China's development strategy.

A hallmark of a market economy is wealth creation. A little-known fact is that the Indian economy is able to create more value and wealth for a given unit of GDP than is the Chinese economy. Despite the widespread belief that China is far more successful than India in the manufacturing industries, it is intriguing to note that, in fact, India has a higher manufacturing value-added per worker than China.

According to data in the *World Development Indicators 2001*, the value-added per worker in manufacturing was 2,885 dollars per year during the 1995–1999 period for China, but 3,118 dollars per year for India during the same period. More tellingly, however, is the fact that China's value-added in manufacturing declined over time. Most countries upgrade their products and increase their production sophistication as their economies grow, but not China. In the mid-1980s, the manufacturing value-added per worker per year in China was 3,061 dollars, but this figure declined to 2,885 dollars in the late 1990s. India displays a more normal pattern. It increased its manufacturing value-added from 2,108 dollars in the mid-1980s to 3,118 dollars in the late 1990s.[37]

Maybe India has a different industrial structure as compared with China. This is a point put forward in a paper by IMF economists (Kochhar, Kumar, Rajan, Subramanian, and Tokatlidis 2006). The paper does show some initial differences between China and India. In 1980, India "overly" specialized in those industries that are characterized by high skill intensity, at the expense of those industries characterized by labor intensity.[38] But the differences in their starting points still do not explain why manufacturing value-added should decline over time in China. The IMF paper shows that conditional on the initial industry mix between 1981 and 1996, China's share of output in skill-intensive industries was not only lower than that of India, but also China's share experienced a modest decline over time.

GDP is a flow measure, but a person's economic well-being is not just a function of his income but also of his assets – physical or financial – that are being accumulated. A path-breaking study by the World Bank (World Bank 2006b), *Where Is the Wealth of Nations?*, comes up with monetary estimates of a range of assets in a country. Of particular value, the study divides the assets into several classes – produced, natural, and intangible. This division allows an analyst to separate the endowment factors from those factors endogenous of the economic and political institutions. The data used in the study refer to 2000.

In 2000, the per capita GDP for China was $840 on the basis of the foreign exchange conversion and $3,940 on the basis of the PPP conversion. The two figures for India were $460 and $2,390, respectively. The ratio of the Chinese per capita GDP to the Indian per capita GDP ranges from 1.8 (the exchange rate conversion) to 1.6 (the PPP conversion). By the wealth measures as provided by the World Bank, the two countries are closer to each other. China's total wealth per capita is 9,387 dollars, whereas India's is 6,820 dollars. This gives rise to a China/India ratio of only 1.38. A better measure than aggregate wealth reflecting institutional effects is intangible capital. The vast majority of the wealth in rich countries takes the form of intangible capital because of the higher educational achievements and rule of law. And here is an intriguing finding: China and India are very close to each other in terms of intangible capital despite a near two-fold gap in terms of per capita GDP. China has intangible capital of 4,208 dollars per person, as compared to India's 3,738 dollars. Thus, the ratio of China to India is only 1.13. This is substantially lower than their income differentials. Here, we see a similar difference between the output measure and asset measure of China as we saw in a comparison between Shanghai and Zhejiang. A state-led economic model can build up output capacity very quickly but it does not lead to wealth creation.

It is high time to take a close and careful look at India's growth experience. Its growth, like China's growth in the 1980s, is a result of financial liberalization, private-sector development, and an evolving policy environment that nurtures and fosters indigenous entrepreneurship. Collectively, these constitute what can be termed as "soft infrastructures" for growth. One reason why India was consistently under-estimated by Western analysts is that the analysts focused only on those tangible and physical growth drivers, such as airports and roads. These hard infrastructures support growth, but so do soft infrastructures.

It is easier to see the results of building up hard infrastructures than it is to see the results of building up soft infrastructures. An airport, once built, is visible. It is much more difficult to tell whether or not a country's financial system has improved. Institutions are intangible and their importance shows up in their effects on investment and the work incentives of individuals rather than in a physical manifestation. Even a casual observer can tell the difference in the physical landscape of Beijing between 2000 and 2007 but, without due diligence and some expertise, it is difficult to tell the difference in Beijing's financial system between 2000 and 2007. (This is one reason why academics and business analysts after a superficial exposure to China – especially an obligatory exposure to Beijing and Shanghai – typically have a very positive view of the country.)

For the same reason, it is easy to under-appreciate some of the strengths of India because the progress it has made is mainly in the intangible area of institutions such as financial reforms and privatization, whereas its main deficiencies are in the visible area of hard infrastructures. At the beginning of this section, I quote from Stephen Roach, the chief economist at Morgan Stanley, expressing a widespread sentiment of "Indian pessimism." That pessimism is rooted in making an inference only on the basis of what is easily observable (to be more precise, what is observable during a short, skin-deep trip, which, by his own admission, left him "exhausted, head-spinning, and with a sore back"). It is a classic observational error that all students in an entry-level methodology class are taught to avoid. As a footnote, after Roach expressed his pessimism of Indian manufacturing in 2004, India registered a growth in manufacturing production and exports in excess of double-digit rates every year. It will not be the first time that India defies the pessimists and proves them wrong.

In the area of finance, the contrast between China and India is especially sharp and the precariousness of Chinese indigenous capitalism is most apparent. We have some fairly systematic evidence from a unique dataset – the World Business Environment Survey (WBES) – to assess the financing environment facing indigenous private businesses in China and India.[39] The WBES is the only dataset that this author is aware of that uses the same survey instruments for both countries and that was conducted during the same timeframe (2000–2001). It is this feature of the WBES dataset that allows us to compare the financing constraints in China and India in a somewhat systematic way. Another attractive feature of the dataset is that the majority of the surveyed firms are indigenous private businesses.

Question 38 in the WBES asks the respondents about how problematic the financing constraint is for the operation and growth of their firms. The responses to this question range from no obstacle, to a minor obstacle, a modest obstacle, and a major obstacle. Indigenous private firms in China reported a substantially higher level of financing constraints as compared with their counterparts in India: 80.2 percent of the Chinese firms described the situation as a moderate obstacle or a major obstacle, compared with 52.1 percent of Indian firms. The differential in their responses is even greater if we look only at those firms that gave "a major obstacle" in their responses:

66.3 percent of the Chinese firms compared with only 25.5 percent of the Indian firms.[40] I have undertaken a statistical analysis of the WBES data, which allows me to control for a variety of other factors that may also affect financing constraints. The statistical results are identical to the descriptive results reported here (Huang 2006).

The Chinese score for financing difficulties, at 80.2 percent, is very close to those for Russia (79.5 percent), Romania (80.5 percent), Belarus (82.3 percent), Bulgaria (73.3 percent), and so forth. China, although similar to the *European* transition economies, is dissimilar to its *Asian* capitalist neighbors, such as Indonesia (50 percent), Malaysia (41 percent), and Singapore (30.3 percent). By contrast, the level of India's financing constraints puts that country squarely in the same league as these Southeast Asian economies. The only plausible explanation for why China's financial system is similar to the European socialist countries is the legacy or the continuation of central planning. India's financial system may be inefficient and cumbersome, but it is at least capitalistic in its fundamental orientation.

The different levels of financing constraints are not an accident but rather a cumulative function of the pace of the financial reforms in the two countries. Both countries implemented some financial reforms at the start of the general economic reforms. China had an earlier start in the 1980s and in the rural areas, but it lagged behind India because it reversed these reforms in the 1990s. By Chinese standards, India's financial reforms were implemented at lightening speed.[41] In the first half of the 1990s, the focus was to reduce the ownership stakes of government in banks. (India had nationalized many of the major banks in 1969.) Between 1995 and 1998, several large state-controlled banks, such as Bank of India, Bank of Baroda, and Industrial Development Bank of India, launched initial public offerings. The government stake was reduced to around 50 to 60 percent. This kind of reform began in China's banking sector only after 2005, and the scale of the ownership diversification in Chinese banks has been considerably more modest. Very early on, in 1992, India permitted the entry of new private players into the banking sector. By 2003 or so, these new private banks accounted for 12 percent of the total credit (Banerjee, Cole, and Duflo 2005). In contrast, as Sáez (2004) points out, "the presence of private banks in China is negligible."

India is often criticized for being protective of its domestic industry, but in the financial sector, India opened itself to foreign competition far ahead of China. In 1998, the government permitted foreign investors to own 40 percent of stakes in Indian banks, doubling the foreign share prior to that time. In China today, foreign ownership is still capped at 20 percent. As of 2003, foreign banks accounted for 8 percent of India's banking assets; in China, at the end of 2002, foreign banks accounted for just 1.7 percent of total banking assets. The example of Citibank in the two countries is illustrative of their dramatic contrast. According to Sáez (2004), as of 2000, the total assets of Citibank in India amounted to $35.8 billion; in contrast, Citibank had $2.5 billion in assets in China, and the assets of all foreign banks in China in 2000 came to only $34 billion. This is about the same as the assets held by one single foreign bank in India: Citibank.

Another clear difference is the role of the stock market. India's stock market is substantially more supportive of indigenous private-sector development. Some of the most competitive technology firms in India today owe their rise to listings on the Bombay Stock Exchange. For example, Infosys issued shares in 1993. This share issuance was critical to the strategic growth of the company. Infosys used the proceeds to build its now famous "Infosys Campus," which differentiated itself from the dilapidated rest of the country. The firm explicitly used this strategy to win the trust of its multinational customers.[42] In contrast, as is well known, very few indigenous private-sector firms could gain access to China's stock exchanges. Unlike their Indian counterparts, some of the most famous Chinese technology firms, such as Lenovo and Huawei, are not listed on China's stock exchange.

Beyond the financial sector, the gap in soft infrastructures between the two countries appears to have grown over time. One example is revealed in the World Economic Forum's growth competitiveness index (GCI).[43] In the latest ranking (2007–2008), China is ranked at No. 34, far ahead of India's No. 48. China typically outranks India on the macroeconomic and overall benchmarks, but it is outranked by India on the microeconomic benchmarks. In the 2007–2008 GCI, China is ranked at No. 57 on the business competitiveness index (BCI) compared with India's No. 31. The detailed components of the BCI, such as company operations and strategy, all show China to have a lower ranking than India.

It is interesting to note two features of the GCI ranking. One is that there is an inconsistency between the macro and micro rankings vis-à-vis India. In the long run, an economy grows and performs on the basis of its strong micro foundation. China scores high on the macroeconomic ranking in large part because the macroeconomic rankings are heavily weighted by GDP growth. To the extent that China's GDP growth is faster and to the extent that its GDP growth is heavily powered by the government-sponsored investments, it can score high on the macroeconomic ranking but low on the microeconomic ranking. Either India's macro performance will improve, as it has in recent years, or China's macro performance will deteriorate. This macro-micro inconsistency is unlikely to last forever.

Second, this inconsistency is present only in the more recent GCI rankings. In the earlier versions of the GCI, China outranked India on both the macroeconomic and microeconomic rankings. In 1998, in terms of BCI, China was ranked at 42nd place compared with 44th for India. (This fact answers the skeptical view that the ranking differentials are due to the ways that the indicators are compiled.) Since 1998, India has steadily and quietly improved its microeconomic fundamentals. The effect of these improvements does not show up instantaneously but these improvements will position India well down the road. That India overtook China in microeconomic rankings also debunks the widespread idea that India is now ahead of China in certain areas because India has a longer history of capitalism. This view completely ignores the fact that for 30 years, until the reforms in the early 1990s, India had a highly organized central planning system modeled after that in the former Soviet Union. The fact is that China led India substantially in economic reforms in the 1980s and most likely in the first half of the 1990s as well. India has now overtaken China in microeconomic rankings because China failed to make meaningful reforms in the 1990s.

3 Capitalism with Chinese Characteristics

The economy is still the base; if we didn't have that economic base, the farmers would have risen in rebellion after only ten days of student protests – never mind a whole month. But as it is, the villages are stable all over the country, and the workers are basically stable too.

– Deng Xiaoping on May 19, 1989[44]

This quote is putatively from Deng Xiaoping, who made the comment at the height of Tiananmen turmoil – May 19, 1989, the day the Chinese government declared martial law. As usual, Deng had the most incisive observation of the country. After the collapse of the Soviet Union, many came to the view that China was spared the same fate in 1989 because it did not liberalize its political system. The real reason why China did not collapse in 1989 was that its rural population was reasonably content in the 1980s.

One of the most damaging effects of the policy model of the 1990s is that it undermined the rural stability. Much of the increase in the political and social instability in the 1990s – documented before in the form of rising protests – occurred in rural China. Rising illiteracy will lead to rising crimes. (In a Yunnan prison, 65 percent of the prison inmates were illiterate and 70 percent of them were rural residents.[45] The two populations likely overlapped substantially with each other.) The root of Chinese stability is its rural stability. The anti-rural bias of the policy model also entails significant economic implications: It slows down the pace and it alters the nature of China's transition to capitalism.

In this section, let me return to a broad theme of this book – assessing the nature of capitalism with Chinese characteristics. The consensus view among leading Western China economists is that China today is largely a market economy. Yingyi Qian (2003) remarks, "In the last 22 years of the 20th century, China transformed itself from a poor, centrally planned economy to a lower-middle-income, emerging market economy." Barry Naughton echoes this view. Writing in 2007, he states, "Today, many of the initial challenges of market transition have been overcome. The market is now the predominant economic institution in China" (Naughton 2007, p. 5).

Some of the prominent economists based in China, as compared with Western academics, have a far less sanguine view on the state of reforms.[46] Wu Jinglian, probably China's best-known economist, has forcefully argued that without genuine political reforms, China faces a real risk of falling into the trap of crony capitalism. Fan Gang, another well-known economist who sits on the monetary advisory committee of the Chinese central bank, has expressed similar concerns. The data and facts presented in this book are consistent with the views of these academics based in China. In this section, I place the state and evolution of capitalism in China against a broader, comparative perspective. First, I try to answer the question, "What is the best way to characterize the Chinese economy today?" My own characterization is that this is a commanding-heights economy, similar to that of many of the developing economies of 1970s vintage. Is this progress? Yes, in the sense that China has moved from a Leninist to a Nehruian system, but it is a far cry from claiming that the Chinese economy today is based on private-sector dynamism and a market orientation.

I then show that capitalism with Chinese characteristics is fundamentally different from capitalism with East Asian characteristics. The main difference has to do with the role and the size of the private sector. Another difference is the degree to which the state is a grabbing or a helping hand. The East Asian state, even the authoritarian state in Korea or that in Taiwan during the period of their respective economic takeoffs, was by and large benevolent. Corruption existed but the size of the corruption was not endemic. Social performance was excellent and it improved over time. I contrast these aspects of China with those of East Asia.

3.1 Commanding Heights

It was China, after 1978 under the influence of Deng, that accelerated leaving India far behind.... China did this paradoxically by adopting a much more "capitalist road." While India went on restricting its large native capitalist class after independence, China had to practically reinvent its own bourgeoisie after 1978.

  – Meghnad Desai, a former professor at London School of Economics and a
    member of the British House of Lords (Desai 2003).

It is a remarkable view that China is more capitalistic than India, the world's largest democracy and a country with a continuous history of capitalism. Professor Desai is by no means among the minority of scholars to make this claim.[47] Similar comparisons are frequently made in the business media, claiming that China is a more vibrant, more capitalistic economy than India. Let us confront these views with some data.

According to the OECD study cited in Chapter 1, the Chinese private sector – covering both agriculture and industry – accounted for 70 percent of GDP as of 2003. I explained why this figure is a substantial overstatement of the Chinese private sector: The estimate includes the output by those legal-person shareholding firms that are still substantially owned by the state. Let me add another reason here. The assumption that agriculture in China is completely private is increasingly questionable in light of a development since the late 1990s – the massive land grabs that have rendered land leaseholds insecure.

For the sake of argument, let me ignore these computational complications and take the OECD's claim of 70 percent at its face value. Clearly, by the OECD estimate, China has moved substantially away from the centrally planned economy of the 1970s. But, we need to have an appropriate perspective here. For sure, 70 percent is high by the standard of centrally planned economies, but it is not at all high by the standard of capitalist economies, even some of the most statist capitalist economies. To illustrate this point, let us go back to the 1970s. This was a decade at the apex of the commanding-heights ideology. Among developing capitalist and statist economies, many far exceeded 70 percent of GDP in the private sector. Take Tanzania as an example. Under the radical leadership of President Julius Nyerere, Tanzania adopted a socialist economic model and yet, in 1978, the private share of its GDP was nearly 90 percent. In Brazil, the private share of GDP was 94 percent; in Venezuela, 73.9 percent (World Bank 1995, pp. 300–302).

What about Professor Desai's assertion that China is more capitalistic than India? For the sake of the argument, I again take at face value the OECD claim that the Chinese private sector, inclusive of foreign firms, was producing 52.3 percent of industrial production in 2003 and 71.2 percent in 2005. I set a low bar for China – comparing China of the 2000s with India of the 1970s at the height of its economic statism. India at that time was at the apex of its commanding heights after Indira Gandhi nationalized all major banks, significantly expanded the scope of "License Raj," and created numerous barriers for the private sector. But, even at the height of the "License Raj," the importance of the Indian private sector was comparable to the level of the Chinese private sector in 2005. One estimate puts the share of private-sector firms in total manufacturing GDP in India at 93 percent in the early 1960s and at 69 percent in 1983–1984. The share of fixed-asset investments of the private sector was around 58 percent,[48] a ratio that is substantially higher than the broadest definition of the Chinese private sector as reported in Chapter 1: 33.5 percent in 2005 (and only 17.2 percent as recently as 1998). Thus, even a generous accounting of the current size of the Chinese private sector puts China roughly in the same league as one of the world's most statist economies of the 1970s. (It should be stressed that the OECD's estimate of China's private sector is inclusive of foreign firms, so this comparison is not affected by differences in FDI policies.)

One specific component of Professor Desai's comparison between China and India is especially off the mark. He argues that India restricted its "native capitalist class," whereas Deng's China encouraged it. China in the 1980s did encourage its "native capitalist class" (mainly in the rural areas), but in the 1990s, it went in a different direction. If we compare China of the 1990s with India, Professor Desai got the facts backward. The government of Indira Gandhi severely restricted the activities of multinational corporations (MNCs) in order to protect domestic businesses. Many firms, such as IBM and Coca Cola, left the country altogether.[49] Recall the finding in Chapter 1 that the size of the Chinese indigenous private sector relative to the foreign private sector is very small and the findings in Chapter 4 and earlier in this chapter that Shanghai and Jiangsu systematically restricted indigenous private entrepreneurship while eagerly courting FDI. My point here is not to suggest that India of the Indira Gandhi era pursued the right economic policies; there is plenty to suggest that her policies were hugely counterproductive. Rather, the point is that there is no evidence whatsoever that China since the early 1990s has been a more nurturing environment for indigenous capitalism than India.

3.2 How East Asian Is China?

Baumol, Litan, and Schramm (2007) classify China as an example of state-guided capitalism, similar to that in Japan and Korea. We can debate about the accuracy of this empirical classification. In the 1980s, as the present book shows, China moved quite far toward entrepreneurial capitalism in its countryside. Urban China remained state-controlled but, because the vast majority of the population was rural then (and now), the entrepreneurial capitalism in the rural areas had a disproportional effect on the economy and brought about broad-based economic success.

The issue is whether Chinese capitalism today is closer to that in East Asia or that in Latin America. (Here, East Asia refers to Japan, South Korea, and Taiwan.) Regardless of one's views on the wisdom of the industrial policy approach of the South Korean government during that country's economic takeoff, the microeconomic foundation of that country was completely private. Most of the corporate entities in the Korean economy, such as Hyundai, Samsung, Kia, and LG, were privately owned. The entire banking sector was privatized in 1982. According to one estimate, in 1990, bank claims on official entities – including local governments, government investment institutions, and SOEs – were only 4.5 percent the size of the claims on the private sector (Haggard and Huang 2008).

Taiwan is another private-sector success story. According to Kuo, Ranis, and Fei (1981, pp. 80–81), 24 percent of loans were going to private enterprises in 1953 and this figure increased to 77 percent in 1979.

Let us take a look at China. We have fairly detailed loan data by ownership for short-term loans. (Long-term loans to the private sector are most likely even smaller.) In 2002, the percentage of short-term loans to the private sector – defined here as all TVEs and agricultural and private-sector businesses – was 19 percent (People's Bank of China 2003). This is nowhere near the level in Taiwan in 1979, but it is close to that during the statist era of Taiwan in 1953. Other analysts identify China with East Asia in terms of performance. They point to the fast GDP growth, rising export competitiveness, and rapid industrialization as common features in both China and East Asia.[50] Since the late 1990s, China has been investing a rising portion of its GDP – almost half in 2005. China economists have rationalized that this is similar to investments of other East Asian countries.[51]

The claim that China's investment/GDP ratio is comparable to that in East Asia in the 1970s is not accurate.[52] The investment/GDP ratio in China increased substantially in the 1990s, from the 35 percent range in the 1980s to the 40 to 45 percent range in the 2000s. China seems to have acquired a permanent addiction to investments. In 2005, the country invested 48 percent of its GDP in new fixed assets; in 2006, it invested 52 percent (NBS 2007a, pp. 26–27).[53] At 35 percent, China in the 1980s was quite close to that in Japan – around 33 percent in the 1970s – and within striking distance of Taiwan (around 26 percent). In the 45 to 52 percent range, China is in an entirely different league. Korea had the highest investment/GDP ratio in East Asia. The height was 40 percent in 1990, but this was a one-off event. In the 1970s and 1980s, the ratio was within the normal East Asian range of around 30 percent.

The second difference with East Asia is the ownership composition of the investments. In East Asia, an overwhelming portion of investments took place in the private sector. In China, the opposite is the case. Take Korea as an example. It is true that the investment/GDP ratio rose from an annual average of 19.3 percent in the 1970s to about 32.3 percent in the second half of the 1980s, but the private sector led the way in this investment surge. On average, private-sector investments accounted for more than 70 percent of total investments in the 1970s and this ratio rose to more than 80 percent in the 1980s. So Korea started out in the 1970s with a higher level of private-sector investments and, over time, the private-sector investments grew even larger. China, on the other hand, started out with a weaker private sector in the early 1980s, when its share was only around 20 percent as shown in Chapter 1, and ended up even weaker in the 1990s. This is not an East Asian story at all.

The strength of the indigenous private sector is really the essence of the East Asian model. According to Campos and Root (1996), East Asia did not invest at an inordinately high level as compared with Latin America. What distinguished the higher-performing East Asian economies was the high proportion of private investments. The high state share of investments puts China closer to Latin America than to East Asia. There is another East Asian difference with China. Except for Singapore, FDI played an insignificant role in the extremely successful export production of the East Asian economies. In the mid-1970s, FIEs in Taiwan accounted for only 20 percent of Taiwan's manufactured exports.[54] In China today, the ratio is more than 60 percent.

Students of East Asia all agree that the state was interventionist during the growth period (Wade 1990), but the state interventions were ultimately market conforming.[55] Consider the famous example of Formosa Plastics. The government on Taiwan established the firm but it did not intend to run it. Instead, the government recruited Wang Yongching, a businessman who was not even living in Taiwan at the time, to run the firm. Wang subsequently built Formosa Plastics into the world's largest PVC producer. Li Kuoting, the father of Taiwan's economic miracle, constantly exhorted his government colleagues to look at "things from the entrepreneur's point of view."[56]

Contrast this with China's top-down approach. In the 1990s, China strongly promoted a number of industrial policies but the Chinese industrial policy initiatives drew almost no input from the business community, not even from the SOEs. According to a 1998 survey, only 4.5 percent of respondents believed that enterprises and enterprise associations played a key role in industrial policy making; 65 percent of the respondents said that only the central government was responsible. When asked if the government's market forecast was correct, more than half of the respondents answered in the negative (Zhao 1998).

There are sharp differences in the area of social performance between China and East Asia. Here, it is important to have a precise idea of what the "East Asian miracle" means. The East Asian miracle does not only refer to the fact that East Asia grew rapidly; during its period of growth, East Asia also had excellent social performance. In East Asia, the Gini coefficient was low at the start of the economic takeoff and remained low during the takeoff. In Korea, the Gini increased modestly from 34 in the mid-1960s to 36 in the early 1980s. In the case of Taiwan, the Gini actually declined from 36 to 31 during the same period.[57] China, as documented previously, has experienced a sharp rise in the Gini. This is not a story of "rapid growth with equity."

3.3 The Grabbing Hand of the State

Historically, some of the capitalist countries used all sorts of means to squeeze out the peasants, forcing them to enter into bankruptcies and to become a source of cheap labor. . . .
– Wan Li (1992 <1982>, p. 145), vice premier of China, 1984–1988

The poorest man may in his cottage bid defiance to all the force of the Crown. It may be frail; its roof may shake; the wind may blow through it; the storms may enter, the rain may enter – but the King of England cannot enter; all his forces dare not cross the threshold of the ruined tenement!
– William Pitt, Prime Minister of Britain, 1766–1768

The authoritarian states of East Asia, by and large, were benevolent. Park Chung-Hee, the leader who created Korea's economic miracle, exemplifies this combination of supreme power and deliberate self-constraint. Although ruling with the iron fist of a military general, Park was methodical and conscientious in his economic management. ("There was a method to his madness," as political scientist Meredith Woo grudgingly admired.) Never a man of political patronage, he ruthlessly held his subordinates accountable to his high and strict meritocratic ways. On the eve of each New Year, he would visit his cabinet ministers to discuss goals and strategies for the upcoming year and followed up with a performance check one year later. Those who failed more than 80 percent of the targets were fired on the spot

(Campos and Root 1996, p. 140). He scrupulously avoided creating perceptions of bias and cultivated policy credibility. He made a practice of meeting with businesspeople only in large groups in which the businesspeople acted as representatives of their industries rather than as representatives of their firms (Johnson 1987).

The East Asian states invested heavily in education and public health and expanded the social opportunities for their citizens. Corruption existed in East Asia but was unlikely to approach the pervasiveness of China today. Land grabs, currently an endemic problem in China, were unheard of in East Asia. It is widely acknowledged that land reforms, which solidified the private ownership of farmers, laid the foundation of the East Asian economic miracle. For whatever reasons, the East Asian states governed in ways that maximized the public interest.

By contrast, the Chinese political system became increasingly self-serving in the 1990s. A blatant illustration is how it enriched itself at the expense of the society at large. Between 1989 and 2001, the Chinese government increased the salaries of its civil servants five times – and four times between 1998 and 2001 – and each time by a double-digit rate.[58] As a result, civil servants today are among the best paid and the most desired professions in China. In a 2007 survey, college students in Beijing ranked a government job as the second most desirable, after a job in a MNC. (In the same survey, 13 percent wanted to work for SOEs and only 1 percent wanted to work for the domestic private sector.)

An official rationale for increasing the salaries of civil servants was to counteract the recessionary effect of the Asian financial crisis by boosting internal consumption. (Another rationale – i.e., to reduce bureaucratic incentives to accept bribes – was patently false given that the amount of bribes in the 1990s amounted to millions of yuan.) But the same bureaucracy repeatedly reduced the incomes of those with the highest propensity to consume – China's rural poor. Between 1997 and 2002, the Chinese state *lowered* the official rural poverty line – which entitled the poorest people to very basic assistance – three times, matching perfectly in timing with the four salary raises for civil servants. In 1997, the rural poverty line was stipulated at 640 yuan per person. This was reduced to 635 yuan in 1998 and 625 yuan in 1999. In 2001, it was raised to 630 yuan, only to be reduced again to 627 yuan in 2002. As in other areas, the poverty line was adjusted upward under the leadership of Hu Jintao. In 2003, it was 637 yuan and in 2006, it reached 693 yuan.[59] The aforementioned figures are nominal; after adjusting for inflation, the official poverty line has never exceeded the level established in 1987.

The Chinese state today – especially at the local level – is dangerously proximate to "a grabbing hand," a term coined by Frye and Shleifer (1997) to describe the Russian state of the 1990s. Exercise of power for pecuniary interest and corruption were hallmarks of Russia's distorted transition to oligarchic capitalism. In the Chinese context, the state *literally* grabs – for land. At the beginning of this section, I quote from Wan Li, the vice premier in charge of agriculture in the 1980s and a liberal reformer who launched the rural reforms in poor Anhui province. He was warning against what he believed to be a widespread practice in capitalist countries – the massive taking of land from the peasants that drove them to become a source of cheap labor. He might have worried too much about the capitalist countries. The quote from William Pitt, the prime minister of Britain during the primitive stage of that country's capitalist development, shows that property rights were more secure than credited by Wan Li.

With remarkable prescience, Vice Premier Wan was right on target in his 1982 comment, not about the capitalist countries but rather about China since the late 1990s. In Chapter 3, we saw that the per-day earnings in local non-farm activities dropped sharply in the 1990s (although the migrant per-day earnings increased). Many urban businesses refused to honor their wage contracts and they accumulated massive wage arrears to migrant workers. The situation became so egregious that the Chinese premier personally intervened to resolve several cases of late wage payments. A Chinese reporter, quoting from the All-China Federation of Trade Unions, reveals that the cumulative wage arrears at the end of 2003 stood at 100 billion yuan.[60] China has even resurrected slave labor. One infamous case, exposed in 2007, involved 570 slave laborers forced to work eighteen hours a day and seven days a week in a kiln in Shanxi province.

Macro data also show that the labor share of GDP declined throughout the 1990s. According to Li Daokui, an economist at Tsinghua University, the labor share of GDP declined from 53 percent in 1990 to 48 percent in 2005. Li points out that China has one of the lowest labor shares of GDP in the world. Most countries vary between the 60 and 80 percent range.[61] Land grabs may have contributed to this adverse development for the Chinese working class. The first effect of land grabs was the uprooting of a large number of farmers. These farmers then flooded the labor market and further reduced the bargaining power of labor in a populous country struggling to create employment opportunities. Taxing rural China heavily – by charging school fees – was another factor. One effect of failings in rural basic education has been the early release of young people onto China's labor market. We can view the 30 million newly illiterate Chinese as 30 million additional members of the workforce. The labor supply increased due to these dynamics.

The most systematic evidence for the scale of the land grabs comes from a joint research project between researchers at the Chinese People's University and Michigan State University.[62] They report that nationwide land grabs have increased 15-fold over the past decade. According to their survey, covering nearly 2,000 rural households scattered in 17 provinces, 83 percent of which comprised the rural population, 27 percent of the rural households either experienced or witnessed one or more incidents of government land-taking since the late 1990s. If their survey remotely captures the reality of rural China, the number of people and the degree of livelihood affected by the land grabs are on a truly phenomenal scale.

The land grabs may explain several phenomena documented in this book. In Chapter 3, we saw that although the aggregate rural income rose since 2002, the non-farm business income stagnated. In Chapter 1, we saw that private rural fixed-asset investments failed to grow despite a more pro-rural and liberal policy environment under Hu Jintao and Wen Jiabao. It is quite possible that the land grabs have undermined the security of property rights so much so that rural private entrepreneurs have stopped investing.

The land grabs are not only a rural affair. Forced evictions of long-term residents to make way for new development projects have occurred in numerous cities, including Beijing, Shanghai, and Guangzhou.[63] These evictions – as well as the land grabs in the rural areas – have often taken place with the full connivance of local governments and despite the repeated prohibitions issued by the central leadership of Hu Jintao and Wen Jiabao. The most likely reason for the land grabs in the rural areas and forced evictions in the urban areas is corruption. Politically connected developers bribe government officials to acquire sweetheart deals on the one hand and to lean upon the coercive power of the state on the other – as the entrepreneur who gained the management rights to the new Xiushui Market did – to enforce the eviction orders.

Corruption is not new in China, but the general consensus is that corruption intensified massively in the 1990s. The extent of the scale of corruption is illustrated by the amount of the bribes involving the highest levels in the Chinese political system. According to a study of all the reported bribery cases involving government officials at or above the rank of minister or provincial governor from 1986 to 2003, in the 1980s, the highest amount of a bribe was 16,000 yuan paid to a vice governor of Xinjiang province (Sun 2004, pp. 46–49). This compares with the highest bribe between 1990 and 2003 of 40 million yuan. The second highest was 25 million yuan and the third highest was 18 million yuan. The lowest amount of a bribe in the 1990s was 64,000 yuan, an offense committed in 1994. In nominal terms, the lowest amount of a bribe in the 1990s is four times the highest amount of a bribe uncovered in the 1980s and 2.3 times in real terms. Corruption in the 1980s can be described as individual cases of malfeasance; in the 1990s, it has intensified to a systemic proportion.

There is an entirely different style of corruption in China now. Pei (2006, p. 21) notes that corrupt officials in China have become younger. Of those officials caught for corruption in the province of Henan, 43 percent were between the ages of 40 and 50. One would normally think that officials in the prime of their careers would be more circumspect. Corruption today takes the form of grand theft and insider looting, not just under-the-table deals. Liu Jinbao, an executive at the Bank of China's branch in Hong Kong, stole 41 million yuan from the bank. In another case, managers at the Bank of China branch in Kaiping in Guangdong province stole US$483 million from 1997 to 2002 (Pei 2006, p. 118). Furthermore, corruption is no longer the exclusive domain of politicians and SOE managers. In a semi-official 2006 blue book on education, the authors devote two chapters to "unhealthy practices" and "corruption" in the field of education (Yang Dongping 2006).

4 China's Prospects

We had been in the largest boom in Mexican history. And for the first time in our history, in those years 1978 through 1982, we were being courted by the most important people in the world. We thought we were rich.
      – Silva Herzog, finance minister of Mexico, reflecting on the period leading to the debt crisis of 1982[64]

This quote from the Mexican finance minister in the 1970s reminds us of the era when countries such as Mexico and Brazil were viewed as economic miracles. They were the darlings of foreign investors and their GDP growth was extraordinarily rapid. But, over time, their growth began to stagnate. The entire decade of the 1980s was lost for Latin America and in the 1990s, after a brief period of surging growth and rising FDI, the Latin American region slowed down again. Many of the countries in the region are plagued by poor social and microeconomic fundamentals. If there is one lesson from the experience of Latin America for China, it is that FDI is neither the necessary nor the sufficient guarantee for economic prosperity.

China today is a darling of foreign investors, but it should heed another lesson from Latin America as well: The sentiments of foreign investors are poor predictors of long-run economic prosperity. In the final section of this book, I attempt to assess China's economic prospects for the next decade or so. The overall view of this book is that China faces substantial challenges in its transition to a genuinely efficient form of capitalism. I emphasize two microeconomic challenges in particular. The first microeconomic challenge is the deterioration of China's productivity performance. This is a very worrisome development, but few economists have noted or thought about its deep implications. The low productivity trend can be indicative of significant macroeconomic volatility and slowdown in the future.

The second microeconomic challenge has to do with what I call "a matching problem." This is a situation in which the most innately competitive and capable firms are not matched with resources – broadly defined to include capital and legal support. Private-sector firms, although efficient and innovative at the firm level, lack resources to compete effectively. They have devised various coping mechanisms – including, for example, focusing on less resource-intensive products or production technologies and adhering to low-cost and low-margin business models. This strategy has become increasingly untenable as China faces revaluation pressures on its currency and a sharply adverse external operating environment.

The next five years – the term of Hu Jintao – will be a critical period for China. The leadership of Hu Jintao is a monumental improvement over that of Jiang and we already have some preliminary data to illustrate this judgment. In this section, I provide an assessment of Hu's leadership so far. Although the assessment is largely positive, I also highlight some potential risk factors. One risk is expectational. A clear change associated with Hu Jintao is the rhetorical emphasis on equity, responsiveness of government, and accountability. This policy rhetoric may raise expectations in a political system fundamentally resistant to change. Another group of risks is economic in nature. These include the emerging challenge of managing transparently apparent asset bubbles and their deflation, rising cost pressures, and inflation. The Chinese state has "muddled through" many difficult problems before; the issue is whether the political system as currently constituted is capable of managing a perfect-storm scenario in which political and economic risks converge.

4.1 Is China's Growth Sustainable?

In the concluding section of Chapter 3, I posit that the repression of entrepreneurship in the 1990s led to a switch in growth strategy. In the 1990s, the Chinese government at all levels began to embrace a growth strategy centered on large-scale infrastructural and urban investment projects. The visual transformation of some of China's metropolises has been dramatic. Shanghai, Beijing, and Chongqing demolished massive tracts of old neighborhoods to make way for some of the world's most avant-garde skyscrapers. Many of these buildings carried astronomically high price tags. The Bank of China building and the National Theater in Beijing reportedly each cost more than US$200 million and the building for China Central Television, also in Beijing, is reportedly to have cost more than US$800 million. Across the country, local governments spent lavishly building office towers – for themselves. Fixed asset investments in government buildings and properties, as I showed in Chapter 3, rose sharply in the 1990s. With the 2008 summer Olympic Games scheduled to take place in Beijing, the investment boom has reached a frenzied level.

Many equate skyscrapers in Beijing and Shanghai with economic dynamism. I would argue that the rapid transformation of China's urban landscape – much of it forcibly induced by government rather than by market forces – is an exact symptom of what is deeply wrong with the country. Many of these urban building projects do not raise the long-run productivity and economic potentials of the economy, even though they boost growth in the short run. Since the late 1990s, China's GDP has grown at a double-digit rate every year, the highest growth during the reform era. But this rapid growth is deceptive. It is due in part to the fact that the state can mobilize a huge amount of resources very quickly and thus can invest a large quantity of capital within a very short period of time, whereas had there been investment spending by the private sector, this would have stretched over many years. The growth is thus more compressed as compared with investments by the private sector, but the quality is likely to be poorer.

The financial costs of these skyscrapers, as stratospheric as these skyscrapers themselves, do not even begin to describe the full adverse effects of these urban investment projects. The opportunity costs are massive. Because the country has chosen to invest so much in its urban areas, it must be true that it has not invested elsewhere. At the beginning of this chapter, I provided evidence for the emerging manifestation of this investment strategy: China's poor people in the rural areas were heavily taxed – in the form of high fees for public services – to finance the transfer from rural to urban areas. One result is rising illiteracy – to the tune of 30 million people – between 2000 and 2005. From both an economic and a social perspective, China made a costly tradeoff.

China made other economically unproductive tradeoffs as well. Consider the following postulation: Rural China is more market-oriented and more efficient. Taxing rural China to subsidize less efficient urban China entails a very specific consequence – trading off efficiency in favor of investment scale. We now have convincing evidence that productivity growth has slowed down substantially since the late 1990s. This slowdown of productivity means the current rapid GDP growth rates are not sustainable.

Much of the productivity research focuses on the reform era as a whole[65] rather than examining the different subperiods within the reform era. With the passage of 30 years since the reforms began, it is legitimate to ask, as I have throughout this book, if there is any difference in China's productivity performance during different periods of the reform era. Decomposing China's reform era shows that the total factor productivity (TFP) – a comprehensive measure of the productivity performance of an economy – has slowed down considerably since the mid-1990s compared with the 1980s and the early 1990s. I review several published and unpublished studies of TFP in China and summarize their main findings in Table 5.2.

Because of different assumptions, the estimates of TFP growth differ across these studies but they converge on trend findings. They all show that TFP growth in the last period (i.e., in the late 1990s or early 2000s) was considerably more modest than TFP growth in the 1980s and the early 1990s. For example, Zheng and Hu (2004) report that TFP grew annually by 3.26 percent between 1978 and 1995, but during the 1995–2001 period, TFP growth virtually disappeared (0.32 percent). Focusing only on Chinese industry, Ren and Sun (2006) report a reduction in TFP growth of a similar magnitude. During the 1988 to 1994 period, TFP grew annually by 3.83 percent, but it slowed down dramatically to 0.52 percent in the latter half of the 1990s.[66] Despite differences in the level of the data aggregation, every study shows declining TFP performance in the late 1990s.

The sources of TFP growth also bear upon this point. Heytens and Zebregs (2003) show that the role of labor re-allocation, rather than structural reforms, grew considerably in the late 1990s in accounting for Chinese TFP growth. In their estimation, the single largest source of TFP growth is the re-allocation of labor out of agriculture into the higher value-added manufacturing and service industries. During the 1979–1994 period, structural reforms – an index of the share of the non-state sector, the share of trade in total output, urbanization, and the rate of capital formation – accounted for about 33.8 percent of TFP growth. The importance of labor re-allocation increased dramatically during the 1995–1998 period and the importance of the structural reforms was reduced by half. The structural reforms accounted for only 17 percent of TFP growth during the 1995–1998 period. These findings contradict the view that the reforms were deepening

Table 5.2 *Estimates of annual TFP growth in the Chinese economy (%)*

		Reference Periods					
		1980s		1990s		2000s
Sources of Estimates	Level of Data	First Half	Second Half	First Half	Second Half	First Half
Heytens and Zebregs (2003)	National-level GDP data	2.78 (1979–1984)	2.11 (1985–1989)	2.81 (1990–1994)	2.30 (1995–1998)	
Zheng and Hu (2004)	National-level GDP data	3.26 (1978–1995)			0.32 (1995–2001)	
Kuijs and Wang (2005)	National-level GDP data	3.74 (1978–1993)			2.7 (1993–2004)	
Miyamoto and Liu (2005)	Provincial-level GDP data	5.45 (1981–1985)	1.73 (1986–1990)	6.28 (1991–1995)	2.91 (1996–2000)	
Wu (2004)	Provincial-level GDP data	n/a	n/a	1.88 (1993–1997)	1.19 (1993–2002)	
Wu (2003)	Provincial-level GDP data	2.35 (1982–1985)	0.43 (1986–1991)	1.75 (1992–1997)		
Ren and Sun (2006)	Industry-level data	6.45 (1981–1984)	3.14 (1984–1988)	3.83 (1988–1994)	0.52 (1994–2000)	

Notes: Kuijs and Wang (2005) estimate TFP growth to be 3 percent in the 1978–2004 period and 2.7 percent in the 1993–2004 period. On the basis of their estimates, I have calculated TFP growth to be 3.74 percent in the 1978–1993 period.

Sources: See the table for citation information.

in the 1990s and they are consistent with the theme of this book that the reforms stagnated in the 1990s.

The recent productivity performance is very ominous. Productivity performance is not only the most reliable indicator of China's long-run prospects for growth but also of the short- to medium-run stability of its macroeconomy. The Asian financial crisis in 1997 was preceded by the well-documented productivity slowdown (Young 1992; Krugman 1994). The structural conditions for a financial crisis are abundantly present in China today. There is a weak financial system, an overvalued stock market, a deteriorating social foundation, and an underdeveloped indigenous corporate sector. Compared with Southeast Asia, China is poorer, and the effects of a financial crisis in China will be very grave.

4.2 The Matching Problems

China is known as the factory of the world but, in 2007, this formidable image came under increasing strains. Massive quality problems in a wide range of imports from China, such as toothpaste, toys, food, and tires, were uncovered. Mattel, the maker of popular toy items such as Barbie dolls, had to recall millions of its products manufactured in China. In one case, Mattel discovered its supplier was using lead paint that was expressly forbidden in the order contract. Unlike South Korea and Taiwan 20 to 30 years ago, which also started with low-quality products but rapidly upgraded, China seems to have persisted with a low-cost and poor-quality business model over a prolonged period of time. Also unlike South Korea and Taiwan where the quality issues were a "teething" problem naturally characteristic of early industrializing economies, in China many of the quality problems were not due to lack of knowledge. Chinese firms knowingly and deliberately committed fraudulent business practices in order to skimp on costs.

There will be another challenge as well to China's low-cost and low-margin business model. China is facing enormous economic and political pressures to revalue its currency. On the political front, the United States and the European Union have threatened punitive actions if China does not revalue its currency further. On the economic front, the inflows of capital into the stock market and real estate sector have exerted upward pressures on the yuan. Currency developments hold grave implications for the export-oriented private-sector firms, on top of a probable slowdown in the export demand from the United States.

Between 2005 and 2007, Chinese currency has gradually appreciated by almost 10 percent (from Y8.3 to US\$1 in March 2005 to about Y7.5

in November 2007). The experience of the East Asian economies in the 1980s and 1990s can provide some guidance. Japan, Korea, and Taiwan faced similar appreciation pressures but at a time when they were far richer than China is today. When Japan revalued its currency between 1985 and 1995, the Japanese corporate sector boasted Sony, Toyota, and Honda. These extremely capable and agile Japanese firms rolled out new products, upgraded their technology, and moved production offshore to digest the costs of the revaluation.

The Chinese corporate sector today is in a far weaker position and we now have evidence that in the last two years, Chinese private-sector firms have done very little to prepare themselves for a new currency environment. The latest private-sector survey in 2006 (PSS2006) contains the most up-to-date information about the capabilities of private-sector firms. Because Chinese currency had already begun to appreciate prior to the survey, PSS2006 should reflect any strategic adjustments private-sector firms have made to prepare themselves for a new currency environment.

The experience of Japanese firms suggests that investing abroad was a critical component of the strategy to respond to the currency appreciation. In contrast, very few Chinese private-sector firms have set up operations overseas. In the PSS2006, only 1.9 percent of the firms reported having overseas operations. This is nearly identical to the 2 percent reported in PSS2004. Another test is whether Chinese private-sector firms have increased their R&D activities. The PSS2006 shows no change in R&D activities from those reported in PSS2004. In both surveys, about 41 percent of the firms reported having some R&D expenditures. Exactly the same number of firms reported owning intellectual property rights in the two surveys (about 16.7 percent). By one measure, in fact, the Chinese private-sector firms were less focused on R&D in 2006 than they were in 2004. The median value of R&D expenditures in the PSS2006 was 200,000 yuan, compared with 300,000 yuan in PSS2004. All of these indicators are not very encouraging that China will be able to withstand a substantial currency appreciation.

After 30 years of rapid economic growth, China's private sector today is still very immature. According to a comprehensive study of China's private sector conducted by the International Finance Corporation (IFC), a distinctive characteristic of Chinese private firms is their informality. Their business practices are opaque, on purpose. It is said that China's private-sector firms keep three sets of accounting books – one for the government, one for the bank, and one for themselves. They frequently shift their business focus and pursue short-term goals rather than building up long-term competitive capabilities. Very few private firms have graduated from the initial founding stage in the life cycle of the firm. They are tightly controlled by the immediate family members of the founders and are lacking in professional management (Gregory, Tenev, and Wagle 2000). More recent data, such as PSS2006, reveal exactly the same picture.

The persistence of a business model centered on low costs rather than technology and upgrading and the lack of maturity in the corporate development of Chinese private firms are results of two matching problems in the Chinese economy. One is that political legitimacy, legal support, and financial resources are not matched with the most efficient firms in the economy – private-sector firms and entrepreneurial businesses that have an arm's length relationship with the government. The adverse business environment then hampers the expansion and corporate development of Chinese private-sector firms. Private entrepreneurs, instead of focusing on business and product development, spend their time cultivating particularistic ties with the government and currying political favors. Rather than investing in technology and product quality, this is the focus of their competitive strategy. Valuable time, talents, and efforts are lost to rent-seeking activities. For example, an analysis of data from PSS2002, PSS2004, and PSS2006 shows that Chinese private businesses are far more interested in donating to "glory projects" – heavily prodded by the government – than financing social protection and health insurance programs of their employees.

The second matching problem is a function of the way in which capitalism has evolved in China. Throughout this book, I have shown that the most rigorous entrepreneurship is rural in origin. Rural China is more liberal but it is also less capable – in a technical sense. It lacks deep engineering talent and industrial know-how. Take the example of Zhejiang. The province is the most laissez-faire economy in China but it is heavily rooted in agriculture. The province received very few industrial investments from the central government in the 1960s and 1970s and is relatively poorly endowed with industrial and technical capabilities. This, in turn, means that firms in Zhejiang had to start at a lower level and with a steeper learning curve as compared with firms in Beijing and Shanghai. It took them a longer period of time to master the technology and acquire the sophisticated human capital.

There is a geographic mismatch: Economic efficiency is rural but technical efficiency is urban. This mismatch has a cost. Think of a counterfactual scenario in which Shanghai and Beijing firms were privately owned and were allowed to operate in a liberal environment. Those firms would have had ample access to the deepest talent pool in the country and could have upgraded their products and technology at a faster speed. Had the Chinese reforms unfolded in both the rural and urban areas, the Chinese corporate sector would have been more capable and competitive and would have been in a stronger position to withstand the shocks of a currency appreciation. The corporate and technical immaturity of the Chinese corporate sector is a long-lasting cost of the way in which Chinese capitalism has evolved.

4.3 Emerging Risks

China has made genuine progress in economic development and in market reforms. This is not to be denied. But the overall tone of this book is one of caution. Consider the following fact. If we redraw the poverty line at $2 a day rather than at the conventional $1 dollar a day, 45 percent of the Chinese population still lives below the poverty line (World Bank 2003). With 30 years of double-digit growth, China has successfully tackled extreme poverty but it is still a fundamentally poor country.

Can China succeed in becoming a prosperous country like its East Asian neighbors? I would argue that the policies of the 1990s detracted China from its growth trajectory and put the country on the wrong path. The good news is that the current generation of leaders – Hu Jintao and Wen Jiabao – is attempting to steer China in a different direction. Recall the finding in Table 5.1 that rural income growth began to recover since 2002. The average growth of rural household per capita income between 2003 and 2005 was 5.8 percent, compared with 3.9 percent during the Jiang Zemin era. This is a substantial improvement. Social performance began to turn around under Hu Jintao as well, such as a modest decline in household educational expenditures.

Hu Jintao's policy formulations, such as the harmonious society, scientific development concept, and energy efficiency, are significant adjustments to the model of heavy investments and rapid GDP growth at all costs in the 1990s. Some of the policy adjustments are subtle but deeply meaningful. For example, we have seen in the case of Shanghai very low levels of asset incomes. In his political report to the 17th Party Congress convened in October 2007, Hu Jintao explicitly stressed the importance of increasing average household asset incomes.[67] Although this is less explicit, he also seemed to recognize the divergence between GDP growth and household income growth, a development I identify in this book as a product of the policy model of the 1990s. In the political report, Hu stresses the growth of household income ahead of GDP growth.

Rural issues are once again the priority of the policy agenda. In a sign that signals a return to the policy model of the 1980s, since 2004, the leadership of Hu Jintao and Wen Jiabao has issued consecutive No. 1 documents focusing on rural issues. (I describe this approach of the 1980s in Chapter 2.) The Chinese government has also begun to acknowledge the dire situation of rural finance. Some efforts have been made to revive the deeply troubled rural credit cooperatives (RCCs) and to permit more competition in financial services. During his five years of leadership, Hu has also begun to address many of the social imbalances. The government has completely abolished agricultural taxes, started to reduce or waive educational charges in the rural areas, and experimented with a basic health insurance program that will cover the entire rural population by 2010.

In an unmistakable political gesture, Hu Jintao arrested one of the most prominent members of the Shanghai faction, former Shanghai Party secretary Chen Liangyu, on corruption charges. He has begun to tackle the ever-deepening corruption problems in a determined fashion, and he has signaled his intention to undertake some gradual and modest political reforms designed to permit a degree of intra-party democracy. According to one account, in his political report to the 17th Party Congress, he mentioned the word "democracy" no less than 61 times (Kahn 2007).

In a political system staffed with more than 40 million officials who have a deep-vested interest in the status quo and who are blatantly self-serving, a top-down political and policy adjustment will entail some substantial risks. One risk is expectational. The policy rhetoric of the central leaders is increasingly liberal and even progressive, but the everyday practice of the Chinese bureaucracy is not. The millions of entrenched political elites are unlikely to change their behavior overnight. Rising expectations against the actual delivery of results on the ground may exacerbate social and political tensions. The case of the coordinated riots by demobilized soldiers, referred to previously, may be a harbinger of things to come.

The year 2008 may be a year of significance for China. As China celebrates its 13th anniversary of reforms, the country may enter into a period of some economic uncertainties. At the time of this writing, there are visible signs of economic risks, including a potential recession in the United States, an induced slowdown in the export demand by the United States, rising energy prices, and even the subprime crisis in the United States. The issue is not whether these developments would translate into an economic downturn for China (as for other countries); the issue is whether they would trigger financial instability in the form of a crisis. In this aspect, there are worrying signs.

Between 2005 and 2007, the index on the Shanghai Stock Market rose from 1,000 points to more than 6,000 points, but within six months, the market lost almost 50 percent of its value. This meteoric rise in stock market valuations between 2005 and 2007 was not matched by any signs of improving microeconomic fundamentals, which may be one reason for its subsequent decline. Although natural resource and other state monopolies are reporting record profits, the profitability picture of those firms that actually drive the growth and create employment is not sanguine. According to an analysis by the investment bank Macquarie, whereas the returns on the equity of the big-cap listed firms were rising, they were declining for the small-cap listed firms (Carvey 2006). Data from the PSS2006 show no substantial improvement in the profitability ratios of Chinese private-sector firms compared with the PSS2004. Signs of a massive bubble in the making are everywhere. Chinese media report on numerous instances in which the stock prices of a number of companies go up sharply – after they are punished for business fraud. This is not an "irrational exuberance," as Alan Greenspan once described the US stock market and as he recently described the Chinese stock market in 2007.[68] This is exuberant irrationality.

The lack of supporting economic fundamentals suggests that China is highly vulnerable to shocks. One trigger of asset market meltdowns could be the full dissipation of the psychological effects of the 2008 Summer Olympic Games. The 2008 Olympic Games may have two effects on market valuations. The widespread belief that the Chinese government will act to bolster the stock market in order to ensure the success of the Olympics may have contributed to its latest runs. The other effect is a perception that the market will peak around the time of the Olympics. If this belief is sufficiently widespread, the probability of a market crash around the time of the Olympics will by no means be trivial.

Until 2005, the ups and downs of the Chinese stock market were almost completely divorced from the real economy. Given the poor corporate governance practices of the listed firms, the low regulatory standards, and the corruption, this was a blessing in disguise because the separation reduced spillovers from the financial dysfunctions to the real economy. This time, however, things are different. For one thing, the first generation of Chinese stock market investors in the early 1990s was a select species. They were few in number and they had a high risk forbearance. The current generation of Chinese stock market investors is very heterogeneous. They range from sophisticated institutional investors to novel and uninformed individual investors such as school teachers, migrant workers, and even nannies. This latter group of investors lives on meager incomes and some have apparently invested their lifelong savings. As of 2007, Chinese stock market investors numbered in the neighborhood of 100 million. Some research has shown that the Chinese savings assets are extremely concentrated in the possession of a small number of depositors. The vast majority of Chinese depositors only have a low level of savings assets. The economic – and political – consequences of sharp and precipitous investment losses for such a large group of people can be devastating.

The bursting of the stock-market bubble poses a systemic risk in a way that the Chinese government has never faced. The Chinese state has defused many of the crisis situations in the past in large part because of its formidable ability to control information and prevent *correlations* of risks. In the 1990s, there were several episodes of bank runs. But, because the government imposed strict blockades of information, these bank runs were isolated and contained to the distressed regions. Such information control was vital because it allowed the authorities to mobilize savings assets from one region to recapitalize the financial institutions in the troubled region. The information controls thus reduced the likelihood of panic runs. By contrast, the movements of stock market prices are transparent and the very institution of the stock market operates on the principle of the correlated expectations, sentiments, and behavior of tens of millions of investors. In other words, the stock market, by its very design, automatically coordinates the beliefs and actions of a large group of individuals. The traditional technique of relying on isolation and segmentation is no longer operative. This is a completely new environment for the Chinese government.

There are other looming risks. At the time of this writing, China's inflation is reaching a new level. This may be due to some transitory factors such as the rising international oil prices, but a structural cause could be the massive urban boom. The urban boom – the frenzied building of skyscrapers and luxury government offices – does not boost the long-run potentials of the economy but it does exert huge short-term demand pressures for raw materials and intermediate products. It is arguable that this decade-long urban boom pulled China from its deflationary spiral of the late 1990s and put the country on an inflationary course. The prices of commodities and raw materials are rising at an accelerated pace. Chinese media report long lines outside gas stations as the country is now experiencing a shortage of fuel.

Another related effect of the policy-induced urban boom is the rising energy intensity of the Chinese economy. The urban boom exerted particularly strong effects on those sectors and products that are most energy-intensive, such as cement, steel, and aluminum. (Skyscrapers, highway construction, and passenger cars are all heavily urban products and they are most energy-intensive.) Now, with oil prices more than US$150 per barrel and with China importing half of its energy needs abroad, China will pay dearly for its policy mistakes of the 1990s.

Another source of cost increases is induced by policy. The currency appreciation has already threatened the margins of the small and medium enterprises in the export sector. In 2008, it is very likely that political pressures from the United States – in an election year possibly going into a recession – for China to revalue its currency to another level will increase substantially. There will be another policy shock in 2008 as well. On January 1, 2008, China put into effect a new labor law that requires businesses to offer permanent employment to workers with more than 10 years of employment. This new labor law will be very damaging to the economy. Labor market rigidity will reduce the incentives of entrepreneurs to create businesses and will drive away existing businesses to countries such as Vietnam and India. Aggregate employment may drop and thus further exacerbate the weaknesses of domestic demand, even though the intention of the law is to provide relief to China's long suffering labor.

This new labor law is symptomatic of the leadership of Hu Jintao. The leadership has made many adjustments to the policy *goals* but not to the policy methods. The era of Jiang Zemin was associated with an industrial policy and big-push government initiatives. The government of Hu Jintao reassigned policy priorities, now giving greater weight to social objectives. But, it is implementing these objectives via the heavy interventionism of the government. There is little recognition that many of the social problems in China today are a result of a malfunctioning economic process, such as the blockage of small-scale entrepreneurship, and that the right recipe to correct these distortions is further liberalization. The 2008 labor law is one of many examples. Another example is the "construction of a new socialist countryside" program to improve farmers' income through heavy government investments. This is a direct reversal of the urban-bias policy model of the 1990s but the method is still entirely administrative, similar to the antecedent urban-bias policy model.

The worst-case scenario for China is a perfect storm in which several economic and political risks converge at the most inopportune moment. The tenure of the current leaders will run through 2012. The next five years will be a litmus test for whether the country will emerge as another East Asian miracle or as a Latin American version of a vicious cycle of dashed expectations and perpetual turbulence. The Chinese leadership under Hu Jintao and Wen Jiabao has begun to turn around the rural situation. By any reasonable benchmarks, this is an improvement from the 1990s. The bad news is that almost all of their accomplishments so far have been the result of adjusting and revising the policy goals rather than the policy methods of the 1990s.

Many of the endemic problems in the Chinese economy today – massive pollution, corruption, inefficient capital deployment, land grabs, and so forth – cannot be tackled without meaningful institutional reforms, in particular, reforms of Chinese political governance. So far, the policy rhetoric is encouraging. The issue is whether the current leaders will truly follow their policy rhetoric to its logical conclusion – empowering people through political reforms. Only history will tell whether Hu Jintao and his colleagues are the right leaders for the right moment, but one thing we know for sure is that whatever they do will have monumental consequences for China and for the world.

Notes

Chapter 1: Just How Capitalist Is China?

1. Lu provides a detailed account (Lu 2000).
2. Many of the details on the early history of Lenovo are chronicled in Lu (2000).
3. I explore this phenomenon in great detail elsewhere. See Huang (2003).
4. See Eckstein (1977).
5. See Qian (2003) and Naughton (2007). I provide more details on their views later in this chapter.
6. The lawsuit was covered extensively in the Chinese press. See http://arch. pconline.com.cn/news/suiji/10308/210452.html, accessed on December 11, 2004.
7. Table 4.5 in Bai, Li, and Wang (2003).
8. This has been done by Lin, Cai, and Li (1996).
9. It is interesting that some scholars, although recognizing the problems from equating the non-state sector with the private sector, nevertheless use the development of the non-state sector as a measure of the reforms. An example is Bai, Li, and Wang (2003, p. 99), who explicitly acknowledge this problem when they state: "In reality, collective enterprises are under close control of a government. Major investment and employment decisions could not be made without government direction or approval."
10. Their paper is a background paper for the OECD report on China. See Dougherty and Herd (2005).
11. Their methodology involves two steps. First, they divide the firms into state and non-state firms. State firms in turn comprise two types of firms: SOEs and collective firms in which the collective share capital exceeds 50 percent. The second step is to classify all those firms in the non-state category as those with more than 50 percent of share capital held by legal persons, individual investors, and foreign firms.
12. The NBS dataset does not contain industrial value-added for 2001, so in my calculations, I used a close substitute, industrial profits. The 28.9 percent in 1998 in my calculations is very close to the 27.9 percent of the industrial value-added reported in the OECD study.

13. Another problem is that the study treats domestic private-sector firms and FIEs as a single homogeneous category. This treatment does not recognize that China has favored foreign firms at the expense of domestic private-sector firms. Thus, the estimate implicitly incorporates a substitution effect between FIEs and domestic private-sector firms.

14. The history of this firm is easily accessible by checking its website. The website, in both English and Chinese, provides details about the organizational evolution of the firm. An analogy would be those firms owned and controlled by Temasek, the holding and investment arm of the Singaporean government. Whether Temasek behaves as if it is a private firm is a separate question, but from an accounting point of view, because Temasek itself is state-owned, the firms controlled by Temasek ought to be classified as state-owned as well.

15. I have dealt with this issue extensively elsewhere. See Huang (2003).

16. This is available online. See http://law.baidu.com, accessed on December 19, 2006.

17. Quoted in Yergin and Stanislaw (1998).

18. The calculations are based on data on the value of gross industrial output broken down by ownership. Private sector here refers only to individual businesses. The data are provided in NBS (1997b).

19. This theory was first proposed by Che and Qian (1998a). Roland (2000) then reiterates the theory. Stiglitz (2006) defends the China model by invoking the TVE reasoning.

20. Some scholars have also argued that given China's institutional environment, the organization of TVEs is, in fact, superior to that of purely private firms. The TVEs have the advantage of political protection provided by local governments and in the biased financial system they have access to capital because their borrowings are guaranteed by the state. See Chang and Wang (1994) and Li (1996).

21. Acemoglu and Johnson (2005) have shown that those institutional arrangements that protect property rights and constrain public officials from arbitrary behavior have the greatest effect on economic growth. Not just any institutions matter, but a particular set of institutions matters the most. See a comprehensive review and assessment of this literature (Acemoglu, Johnson, and Robinson 2005). Finance economists have demonstrated the critical role of financial institutions. Access to finance has been shown to be a very important determinant of long-run economic growth (King and Levine 1993; Levine 1997; Rajan and Zingales 1998). La Porta, Lopez-de-Silanes, Shleifer, and Vishny (1997) connect the design of legal institutions with finance. The literature on this topic is vast and the summary here is cursory. Some of the papers cited previously are survey papers that contain more comprehensive coverage.

22. In Chapter 2, I explain why this is the case and provide some evidence for it. The main reason is that central planning and the Cultural Revolution decimated capitalism in the cities but not in the countryside. In addition, agriculture, even at the height of central planning, was less planned than industry and rural residents never had job or social security protection as compared with urban residents.

23. For a good discussion on private plots during the commune era, see Perkins and Yusuf (1984).

24. For an explanation of the political holdup problem, see Acemoglu, Johnson, and Robinson (2005).
25. The polity data are compiled by Jaggers Keith at University of Colorado and Ted Robert Gurr at University of Maryland (source: http://www.bsos.umd.edu/cidcm/polity/). The polity scores in the exhibit are based on two variables in their database – DEMOC and AUTOC. Both variables are based on an additive 11-point scale (0–10). For DEMOC, 0 means least democratic and 10 means most democratic. For AUTOC, 0 means least autocratic and 10 means most autocratic. DEMOC and AUTOC are derived from codings of the competitiveness of political participation, openness and competitiveness of executive recruitment, and constraints on the chief executive. The polity scores here are derived from the following formula: Polity score = DEMOC − AUTOC. Thus, −10 means the most autocratic and 10 means the most democratic.
26. For a very good account of the role of Deng in the politics of reforms, see Harding (1987).
27. Whether Deng was actually politically distant from Mao is less relevant. In the end, Deng turned out to be far more politically conservative than suggested by his speech in 1980. But what mattered is how he was perceived in the early 1980s.
28. See Chua (2007).
29. Although there are complications, it is safe to say that FIEs are private firms, although in the foreign sector. Because we are primarily concerned with the domestic private sector, we do not discuss FIEs in great detail, except to make two points. One is that in the early 1990s, FIEs absolutely dominated the "other" ownership category of firms, with 71.2 percent of all the fixed-asset investments of these firms in 1993. Second, this juxtaposition of the seemingly liberal policy toward foreign firms, although imposing severe restrictions on the explicitly domestic private firms, is a fascinating topic, to which we return later.
30. It should be noted that the NBS no longer uses the "individual economy" in its data series on industrial output, although it still uses the "individual economy" category for its fixed-asset investment reporting. The 11.7 percent quoted in the text refers only to *siying qiye* and presumably does not include industrial *getihu*. See NBS (2003b), p. 459.
31. There is a related concern, which is that the rural collective sector actually incorporates some private-sector activities. Beginning in about 1993, the fixed-asset investment sources report separately on the collective economy and shareholding cooperative firms. Thus, although it is possible that the collective economy still incorporates some shareholding cooperatives, it is incorrect to assume that the rising rural private/collective ratio was primarily driven by the ownership changes of the collective TVEs.

Chapter 2: The Entrepreneurial Decade

1. This account of Nian Guangjiu is based on several sources. See Wu (Wu Xiaobo 2006) and Zhang and Ming (1999).
2. Detailed provincial data are available from the National Bureau of Statistics (1996).
3. The data come from the 1985 industry census (State Council 1988).

4. See http://209.85.165.104/search?q=cache:b2JPcTT l9MJ:www1.worldbank.org/ economicpolicy/globalization/dollarqa.htm+David+Dollar+China+World+ Bank&hl=en&ct=clnk&cd=2&gl=us, accessed on February 15, 2007.

5. The official source is the NBS rural household survey. See NBS (2007b, p. 43).

6. The World Bank advocates globalization as the reason for China's poverty reduction despite the contrarian evidence marshaled by its own economists. Ravallion and Chen (2007) devised their own poverty line that shows a higher number of poor people than that given in the official statistics. According to them, in 1980, 602 million Chinese rural residents lived in poverty, as compared to only 99.5 million in 2001, an enormous reduction indeed. But what is lost by merely looking at these two points in history is that an overwhelming portion of the poverty reduction took place in the 1980s. According to the same measure by Ravallion and Chen, by 1988, the number of rural people living in poverty was already reduced to 190.7 million. (In fact, in 1985, the poverty level was down to 183.1 million.)

7. This approach by the World Bank was first noted by Qian (2003). For more details on the World Bank's approach, see World Bank (1996), especially pp. 14–17.

8. The data in this section are reported in the Bureau of Industry and Commerce Administration (1990).

9. See World Bank development indicators for details.

10. A Western academic, John Burns (1981), documents that peasants in Guangdong engaged in fairly substantial speculative activities.

11. These are documented by Zhang and Ming (1999).

12. Dachai commune, located in Shanxi province, was flaunted by the Gang of Four for having thoroughly eliminated private ownership and the market economy.

13. This account is provided by Wu (2006, pp. 17–18). Zhou (1996) has some similar but less detailed accounts of private-economy activities during the Cultural Revolution.

14. Oi (1999, p. 73), for example, states that until 1987, "the hiring of more than seven employees was banned."

15. See Jiangsu Statistical Bureau (1987) and (1988) for details.

16. Information about these cases comes from Zhang and Ming (1999).

17. This is a study by the Rural Policy Research Office of the Central Committee and the Rural Development Research Office of the State Council (1987). The field research was conducted between the fall of 1984 and the spring of 1985 and provides a valuable and rare snapshot of the state of rural China five years after the rural reforms began to unfold. The data and cases came from 28 provinces and were based on surveys of and interviews with 37,422 rural households. Only Tibet was excluded from the study.

18. That many rural entrepreneurs operated in the services sector, which we cannot examine due to a lack of data, further implies that the usual measure – industry share of the private sector – would understate the significance of the private sector in the 1980s when service data were not collected by the government.

19. I am not aware of studies explicitly linking private rural entrepreneurship with developments in income distribution, but some have suggested that the rural industrialization was behind the rise in the income inequalities in the second

half of the 1980s (Rozelle 1996). However, it is important to be specific about the channels with which rural industrialization might have contributed to the rising inequalities. There are two ways that this could have happened, but these two mechanisms would entail opposite policy implications. One is that the rural entrepreneurs came from a privileged socioeconomic group and their gains were achieved at the expense of the gains of those from a less privileged group. The other scenario is that the rural entrepreneurs possessed a greater aptitude for success and this capability allowed them to be well-positioned when the regulatory environment became flexible. It is more likely that rural entrepreneurship contributed to the rise in inequalities through the second channel.

20. During the 1980–1985 period, rural inequality rose even as inequality at the national level declined. For the rest of the 1980s, rural inequality rose faster than inequality at the national level. Thus, the most significant development in the 1980s was a mild reduction in the gap in income inequality between the rural and urban areas (Ravallion and Chen 2007).

21. Data in this section are from Editorial Committee of Ten Years of Reforms in Guizhou (1989) and Editorial Committee of Contemporary China Series (1989).

22. See Rural Policy Research Office and Rural Development Research Office (1987).

23. All the data on banks cited in this section about Zunyi are from Editorial Board of Financial History of Zunyi (1992).

24. The quote is from the Guizhou branch of the People's Bank; other details are provided by Editorial Committee of Ten Years of Reforms in Guizhou (1989).

25. As recently as 2006, Stiglitz remained a proponent of TVEs despite the fact that many of the collective TVEs had failed in the late 1990s (Stiglitz 2006). His thinking on TVEs is heavily influenced by the modeling effort that shows that TVEs served as an effective bulwark against predation by the central state (Che and Qian 1998b). It should be noted that this model relies on two potentially incompatible assumptions to reach its conclusion. One is that the national government is predatory and self-serving. The other is that the same predatory national government trusts the local governments precisely because the latter are viewed as effective in public goods provision.

26. Details about this firm are contained in Huang and Lane (2002).

27. Aside from the confusion about the debt for equity capital, there was a practical reason as well: In the 1980s, the single-most binding constraint on private-sector development was the ideological sensitivity about employment size. From its first day, Kelon was a relatively large firm, recruiting some 4,000 workers.

28. As an article in *The Economist* recounts ("Infatuation's End" 1999):

When Whirlpool set up factories to make refrigerators, air conditioners, washing machines, and microwave ovens in China in 1994, it assumed that it was racing against other foreigners. Instead, its chief competitors turned out to be Chinese appliance makers such as Haier and Guangdong Kelon. Their technology was nearly as good as Whirlpool's, their prices were lower, and their styling and distribution were better suited to China. By 1997, having lost more than $100 million, Whirlpool had shut its refrigerator and air conditioner plants. The microwave factory survived mainly by devoting itself to exports, and Whirlpool's washing machine factory now makes appliances under contract for Kelon, which sells them under its own brand, a reversal of the usual hierarchy between Western and Chinese firms.

29. This finding is reported in Groves, Hong, McMillan, and Naughton (1995).
30. The story of Huabao is worth detailed examination. In 1993, the state-owned holding firm of Huabao decided to sell a majority of shares to a Hong Kong company at 10 million yuan. This was a highly questionable deal. Huabao itself was worth 1.8 billion yuan and the Hong Kong firm in question only had assets valued at 700 million yuan. The decision plunged the firm into turmoil among management, the Hong Kong firm, and the state-owned holding firm. Huabao, which was ranked No. 1 in the country in air-conditioner sales in 1993, deteriorated rapidly. By 1998, it was a deeply troubled firm. See Wu (2007, p. 39).
31. Putterman (1995) presents data showing that the industrial output share increased from 9 percent in 1978 to 18 percent in 1988. The private sector, by contrast, accounted for only 4.3 percent in 1988. Roland (2000, p. 281) cites data to show that the TVEs accounted for more than twice China's industrial output value as compared with that of private firms.
32. For example, Rodrik (2007, p. 87) has this to say about TVEs, "China did not simply liberalize and open up; it did so by grafting a market track on top of a plan track, by relying on TVEs rather than private enterprise...."
33. This theory was first proposed by Che and Qian (1998a). Roland (2000) then reiterated the theory.
34. TVEs have the advantage of political protection provided by the local governments, and in a biased financial system, they have access to capital because their borrowings are guaranteed by the state. See Chang and Wang (1994) and Li (1996).
35. For a historical account of the TVEs, see Whiting (2001).
36. A Chinese academic also notes this definitional change provided in document No. 4. See Zhang (1990, p. 31).
37. The excerpt of his speech appears in Editorial Committee of TVE Yearbook (1991, p. 128).
38. The 1990 regulations are found in Editorial Committee (1991, pp. 500–502). The 1997 law is found in Editorial Committee of TVE Yearbook (1997, pp. 85–87).
39. Naughton (2007, p. 271) also states that during the 1978–1996 period, "most TVEs were publicly owned," but Naughton fully acknowledges the heterogeneous nature of the TVE phenomenon. Figure 12.2 on p. 286 of his book clearly shows that very early on, private TVEs accounted for a significant share of TVE employment. In 1985, collective TVEs were only slightly larger than private TVEs in terms of employment (40 million versus 30 million) and by 1988, their employment size was quite comparable. So the data in his book actually do not lend to the notion that "most" TVEs were collectively owned.
40. The data in this section are based on the Ministry of Agriculture (2003).
41. At that time, the ministry was formally known as the Ministry of Agriculture, Husbandry, and Fishing. I have shortened it to the Ministry of Agriculture for expositional ease.

42. The TVE data used in this section are from Editorial Committee of TVE Yearbook (1989b, pp. 578–582). The TVE output data are broken down by economic sectors as well as by TVE ownership.

43. The World Bank and Chinese researchers conducted field trips and surveys of four counties in 1986, the results of which form the basis for this book. It offers a rich, nuanced, and accurate depiction of the complex ownership structures of TVEs. For example, the World Bank researchers reported that some of the private TVEs each employed more than 100 workers (Lin 1990, pp. 178–179). They also reported that although the collective TVEs had the size, the private TVEs had the momentum – they grew much faster than the collective TVEs. Between 1980 and 1986, the private TVEs grew at an annual average real rate 2.64 times that of the collective TVEs and, by 1986, the private TVEs accounted for 21.3 percent of the entire TVE output value, up from only 5.4 percent during the 1980–1983 period (Byrd and Lin 1990).

44. Micro data on the rural economy of Shandong are summarized in Shandong Rural Social and Economic Survey Team (1989).

45. This quote is from a fascinating book on China's economic history by Wu (Wu Xiaobo 2006).

46. Deng's quote appears in a report by a State Council research team on the rural economy. See Rural Economy Research Team (1998).

47. This size is massive, considering that rural China had poor infrastructures. The selection of the management committee of the commune was top-down, by Party officials at the county level (Barnett and with Vogel 1967, pp. 344–370). The management committee itself, ranging from nine to fifteen members, did not run the daily operations but had the ultimate power to veto decisions at the lower levels (brigades or production teams). The commune controlled all other levers of power by "absorbing or amalgamating with the various basic level organizations operating in the countryside...." These organizations included, for example, agencies for supply and marketing, credit unions, and the local branches of the People's Bank (Donnithorne 1981, p. 44). The state extracted exorbitant surpluses from the peasants through the commune system. A report by the Chinese government describes Chinese peasants under the commune system as "payers of tribute." Per capita grain consumption and other welfare indicators show no improvement between 1957 and 1977.

48. Data are from Lin (1983) and "Individual purchase of tractors has exceeded one million."

49. There are many references to this episode, in both Chinese and English. See Wang, Wei, and Chen (1981). For an English reference, see Zhou (1996).

50. For a concise reading of this period, see Meisner (1999).

51. This is how Daniel Kelliher, in *Peasant Power in China* (1992, p. 247), describes the reformist thinking during this period:

Deng's coalition feared that peasant dissatisfaction, expressed in traditional modes like passivity and noncooperation, could doom the whole enterprise. Consequently, Deng's government displayed unprecedented restraint toward peasant defiance, an urge to accommodate peasant desires, and, above all, an openness to peasant initiatives.

52. This meeting is disclosed in a study of individual entrepreneurs by a research team assembled by the State Council. See State Council (1986, p. 25). The study does not disclose the timing of the meeting, but judging by the publication year of the study and a biography of Hu Yaobang, published in 1997, we can put the date at August 1983. See Chai, Shi, and Gao (1997, p. 126).

53. This is disclosed by Zhang and Ming (1999, p. 24). In 1999, Zhao was a political persona non grata. So, the two authors do not mention Zhao by name and simply note that the "Party secretary" visited the business in early 1988.

54. See Deng (2005, pp. 185–186).

55. This episode is recounted in Wu (2006, pp. 85–86).

56. Zhang and Li (2001, p. 7).

57. The data are from Zhejiang Bureau of Statistics (1985, p. IV-123).

58. For example, the level of grain production in 1978 was 36.2 percent more than the 1965 level, but cotton production increased by only 2.8 percent. According to one Chinese economist's calculations, the net returns per area for grain production were only 39.6 percent of the net returns for cotton (Li Binqian 1982).

59. The document uses euphemisms such as "large rural employment households" to refer to private businesses.

60. These are outlined in the Ministry of Agriculture (1985, p. 2).

61. More information can be found in Zhang and Ming (1999), who discuss the survey method and summarize the findings of the 1993 survey. A detailed description of the 2002 survey is contained in the dataset available from the Universities Service Centre of the Chinese University of Hong Kong.

Chapter 3: A Great Reversal

1. In my earlier work, I argued that fiscal centralization, under the condition of political centralization, could lead to some unproductive economic decisions. When politics is centralized, fiscal decentralization serves as a way to check and balance the discretion of the central government. It is also a risk-sharing device in that if one province makes a wrong decision, the harmful effect is confined to that one province. See Huang (1996).

2. The NBS discloses nominal values and the real growth rates. The implicit deflators are derived on the basis of these data.

3. As far as I know, only one economist, Wing Thye Woo, has identified credit constraints as the reason why the TVEs failed (Woo 2005). His view on this subject is rarely cited in works on TVEs. I owe my own inspiration to Woo's writings on this issue.

4. Economists have produced some evidence that TVEs outperformed private firms in rural China (Chang and Wang 1994), but this finding hinges on an erroneous classification of assigning all TVEs to the collective sector. As I have noted, the majority of TVEs were actually completely private.

5. To be fair, this is the after-tax profit figure. One reason for this huge decline in the after-tax profit seems to be an increase in taxes. Taxes rose from 560 million yuan in 1980 to 1.5 billion yuan in 1984 (Zhang Yi 1990). But this huge increase suggests that the collective TVEs were vulnerable to government predation.

6. This document states in part, "In order that billions of assets accumulated by individual businesses and alliance enterprises be used for production rather

than for consumption and in order to guide individual businesses and alliance enterprises toward a path of collective development, from now on the regulation of these enterprises should put an emphasis on guiding them to adopt a shareholding cooperative system. This is to emulate the system of shareholding cooperatives in the transformation of the handicraft industry" (Editorial Committee of TVE Yearbook 1990, p. 4).

7. The Sun Dawu affair is described in great detail by Lei and Hong (2004).

8. I should mention that some scholars, although acknowledging credit constraints in general, believe that the credit constraints varied considerably across different regions in China, either in the formal financial sector (Brandt and Li 2002) or in the informal financial sector (Tsai 2002). It is worth putting this view against the broad context. In 1999, the short-term bank debt outstanding to the *de jure* private sector from all financial institutions (including rural credit unions) was 57.9 billion yuan (People's Bank of China 2000). The top three provinces with the largest credit outstanding to the *de jure* private sector in 1999 were Zhejiang (11.4 billion yuan), Guangdong (8.4 billion yuan), and Fujian (3.4 billion yuan). *These three provinces accounted for 40.3 percent of the entire short-term bank debt outstanding to the private sector; Zhejiang alone accounted for nearly half of that.* The view that there is considerable regional heterogeneity is thus true only for a limited number of provinces.

9. The IFC study on the private sector also shows that loans from banks and credit unions for sampled firms declined between 1995 and 1998. In 1995, loans from banks and credit unions accounted for 22.6 percent of finance but, by 1998, they had declined to 18 percent. Corporate bonds declined from 1 to 0.3 percent. The drying up of outside financing forced owners to put up more capital. In 1995, the principal owners' capital accounted for 21.9 percent; in 1998, it accounted for 35.8 percent.

10. I add some additional restrictions. For example, I exclude those firms that were subsequently privatized. We do not have information about when these firms were privatized and, therefore, we cannot know their ownership status when they received formal or informal finance. Moreover, in asking for information about the firm during its "start-up stage," the question contains an important ambiguity: We do not know whether the respondents interpreted the question to mean the start-up of the original firm or the start-up as a privatized firm.

11. Until 1988, the loan data on TVEs did not explicitly separate out the collective and private TVEs. By policy, loans to established private TVEs were reported together with the loans to collective TVEs. A 1983 decree by the ABC accorded the same loan policies to the new alliance enterprises – a contemporaneous euphemism for large private enterprises – as collective enterprises (Agricultural Bank of China 1985 <1983>-a). After 1988, private TVEs became a separate reporting category in the bank data with the promulgation of the ABC "Provisional regulations on loans to TVEs by rural credit cooperatives." Article 6 specifically includes private businesses as a part of the TVEs (Agricultural Bank of China 1988b).

12. The practices included that 57 percent of the Wenzhou RCC branches had moved to a system of flexible loan rates and that the reformed branches reported healthy profit growth (People's Bank of China 1987, p. 126).

13. During the years of a tight monetary policy, the credit squeeze was obtained essentially by freezing the loans extended to the non-state sector. Loans to the state sector continued, albeit at a lower rate of growth. In 1989, during the period of an austerity policy, loans to small-scale private firms contracted by 20 percent as compared with the previous year. Working capital loans and fixed-asset loans to the state sector rose by 21 and 14 percent, respectively. In 1994, loans to collective firms and TVEs contracted by 10 percent and in 1995 loans to private firms contracted by 36 percent. However, in both these years, loans to the state sector grew at double-digit rates. See Sehrt (1998, p. 83).

14. The 1995 Loan Guarantee Law is available in Rural Work Leadership Team (1997).

15. These numbers are reported in China Finance Association (1986).

16. In 1995, the central government compelled the genuinely private urban credit cooperatives (UCCs) to form shareholding ties with municipal governments. The official rationale was to impose better financial supervision. In a single sweep, the municipal governments became the largest shareholders of the UCCs (renamed Urban Cooperative Banks). But, the official rationale ran hollow as the financial performance of the UCCs was far superior to that of the state commercial banks, not to mention the fact that improving financial supervision is a regulatory matter, not an ownership issue. See Girardin (1997).

17. For comprehensive treatment of the Chinese leaders, see Li (2001).

18. One very interesting finding in their research is that village elections are more contested in those villages with more private entrepreneurs. This is clear evidence that private entrepreneurs are attempting to counter the power of the Party via the villager committees (Oi and Rozelle 2000).

19. For example, a township government has a Party committee, a court system, and a legislature similar to that at the county level. An interesting example illustrates how the Chinese government devised the different legal treatments of the township and village enterprises. A ruling by the State Land Administration in 1992 differentiates the assignment of land rental incomes between township firms and village firms. In the case of township firms, the rental income is accrued to the township governments. In the case of village firms, the rental income is accrued to the villages. Very tellingly, the State Land Administration applied the same assignment principle to village firms and private firms.

20. Field research indicates that these differences do matter in terms of perceptions. Kung (Kung 1999) reports that a village cadre deliberately crossed out the word *zhengfu* (government) on a questionnaire and remarked that the village was not a part of the government. Budget constraints differ as well. Again, according to Kung, the township managers, although often reassigned to other regions, could count on government bailouts, whereas there was "the unceasing pressure that the village Party secretary will inevitably face in the event a village enterprise goes under, in which case the burden falls disproportionately upon him."

21. The article is reprinted in http://www.singtaonet.com/china/200707/t20070717_577084.html, accessed on July 24, 2007.

22. For more details about this episode, see Lieberthal and Oksenberg (1988).

23. According to one estimate, in 2006, the Chinese government spent 70 billion yuan on official vehicles. See Pei (2007).

24. The Chinese data on fixed-asset investments are disaggregated by 15 broad sectoral categories, such as agriculture, manufacturing, construction, health, and education. Within each of these 15 broad categories, there are several subcategories. Manufacturing, for example, is further broken down into food processing, beverage making, and so on. One of the 15 broad categories is labeled "government, Party, and social organizations." The data allow us to separate out the investment activities of the social organizations, which are nongovernment organizations. It should be stressed here that the figures preclude investments in the provision of the public goods, such as public utilities and infrastructure. These investment activities are listed separately.

25. Apparently, a few non-state firms were incorporated into the target list but the precise number is unknown.

26. Naughton (1996) provides some detailed accounts of these early reform efforts.

27. See http://www.baidu.com/s?cl=3&wd=http://news.xinhuanet.com/stock/2004–09/07/content_1952118.htm, accessed June 5, 2006.

28. For an exposition, see Roland (2000).

Chapter 4: What Is Wrong with Shanghai?

1. The speech is printed on the website of the Indian embassy to the United States. See http://www.indianembassy.org/newsite/press_release/2006/Mar/35.asp, accessed on August 23, 2006.

2. In 2004, according to NBS (2005a, p. 369), the number of employed people in Shanghai was 8.37 million people and of this number, 2.48 million were classified as "rural." This suggests 29.6 percent of the workforce to be rural. There is a sharp discrepancy between the residency data and employment data. According to the same source, in 2004, only 80,000 people resided in the rural areas. However, Shanghai's residency data are highly unstable. In 1992, there were 4.1 million rural residents, but in 1994, this number declined to only 1.8 million. In 1995, this number was reduced to 390,000. This pattern suggests the likelihood that the number on rural residents is highly sensitive to administrative reclassifications rather than to the long-run economic and social dynamics, which tend to bring about changes more gradually.

3. The comment that Shanghai is leveled with Silicon Valley appeared in Pink (2005). See his *New York Times* column for his view on freedom in Shanghai (Friedman 1999).

4. For one thing, because GDP data are the explicit benchmarks used by the Chinese political system to promote or demote officials, they can be easily manipulated. During the 1990s, Shanghai was a showcase of Chinese economic progress and it is not altogether implausible to assume that Shanghai's GDP data might have been assembled in such a way as to match its outwardly impressive skyline. Chinese data are often suspected of statistical falsification, but this is not a problem for which a ready solution exists. In the following analysis, I proceed on the basis that the Chinese data are accurate, but I analyze the components of Shanghai's GDP to illustrate some of the particular dynamics of its economy.

5. In 1997, for example, the net national product of the United States was 7,231 billion dollars. Of this amount, 4,687 billion dollars was employee compensation and 551 billion dollars was proprietors' income. In the Chinese data, employee compensation and proprietors' income are reported together. So, in order to compare the two countries, I added the two items in the US data, which comes to 72.4 percent.

6. The main problem is that we do not know whether foreign firms also fall into the category of government-controlled firms, so double counting may be involved.

7. Quoted in Balls (2004).

8. Mr. Wood is quoted in Pocha (2006).

9. The data are from Urban Social and Economic Survey Team (1991; Urban Social and Economic Survey Team 1997, 2003, 2005).

10. It should be noted that official publications report a very high savings rate. There are two possibilities. One is that the government and businesses, rather than households, in Shanghai account for much of the savings. This is merely the asset side of the income approach of GDP. Because much of the income accrues to firms and the government, they have also accumulated the largest claims on the financial assets in the city. The other possibility is that some institutions may register their savings under individual names, a common practice in China.

11. This is documented in a study by OECD (2003).

12. Various issues of the Chinese statistical yearbooks provide employment. Also see NBS (2005a) for employment data broken down by regions.

13. This narrow measure has some advantages and disadvantages compared with our broad measure. The disadvantage is that it is too narrow and it fails to reflect what is going on in the private sector. The advantage is that it is a closer measure of urban employment and, therefore, we can use this measure to compare the city of Shanghai with other regions. The other advantage is that this narrow measure does not include private-sector employment. Because we know that Shanghai has an under-developed private sector, we can then use this measure as an indicator of a potential effect of suppressing private-sector development rather than as an indicator of this suppression.

14. See the website on the Pre-Qualified Medicines project, http://mednet3.who. int/prequal/, accessed on August 24, 2006.

15. See an interview on Xinhuanet, http://news.xinhuanet.com/fortune/2006– 08/07/content_4929294.htm, accessed on August 15, 2006.

16. The information on the NASDAQ-listed Chinese firms is culled from several websites. See http://tech.sina.com.cn/i/nasdaq_china.shtml and http://www. nasdaq.com/.

17. I have checked several sources on Chinese patents. Chinese patent data, unlike its economic data, are quite consistent across different sources and are clearly labeled and well defined. The annual patent application and grant data are published in the *Chinese Statistical Yearbook* from 1988 to 2006. In addition, I have drawn on two specialized publications on Chinese science and technology. These are the NBS and the Ministry of Science and Technology (1999 and 2002).

18. All the patent data that are presented in this section refer to patents granted to domestic residents. China's patent data also include patents filed by foreign residents – firms or individuals operating in China. I exclude these for the

purpose of illustrating the "newness" of the products or technologies. The inclusion of patents filed by foreigners would complicate the patent counts because Chinese law does not recognize patents registered outside of China and, therefore, foreign firms have to register their patents in China in order to receive patent protection. Thus, the high levels of FDI would automatically push up the patent counts, but it does not necessarily suggest inventions of new products or new technologies.

19. For a succinct description of the main features of the Chinese patent system, see Hu and Jefferson (2006).

20. The 1981 data are from NBS (1982, p. 443 and p. 454). The number of engineers and scientists refers only to those working in SOEs. In 1981, however, this likely exactly matched the total number of engineers and scientists. The number of college students does not begin to describe the full difference in terms of the level and quality of human capital. Shanghai is home to some of China's best-known universities, such as Fudan and Jiaotong. Zhejiang University, a historically strong academic institution, is usually ranked below these two Shanghai universities. Sun Yat-sen University in Guangdong is considered a second-tier institution.

21. See Li (2001).

22. For a very good account of the role of Shanghai industrialists in Hong Kong, see Wong (1988).

23. There is very little evidence that the policy had any real effects and there are even questions about the direction of the assistance. In one aid project, the Shanghai municipal government built a hotel in one of the most scenic areas of Yunnan province to attract tourists, but most of the profits were repatriated to Shanghai (Saich 2001, p. 151).

24. Batra, Kaufmann, and Stone (2003) provide an extensive discussion of the problems facing firms in the middle. Their findings are based on survey data of 10,000 firms in 81 countries. In the survey, middle-sized firms are found to be most constrained by a poor business environment.

25. Data are from NBS (2004a).

26. For example, the Soviet Union was competing head-to-head with and even led Western countries in steelmaking, machinery, synthetic materials, and microelectronics. The dynamics illustrated by Iacopetta is a familiar tale in centrally planned economies. Kogut and Zander (2000), studying Zeiss companies in East Germany and West Germany, found their products to be comparable in terms of technological sophistication. The difference was that Zeiss in East Germany was not self-funded and it soon collapsed during the economic transition as the new government withdrew the funding.

27. Although Shanghai's population (17 million) is much smaller than the total population of Zhejiang (45.7 million) and Guangdong (77.6 million), if we assume that patenting is primarily an urban activity, the gap in the urban population is not nearly as large. In 2004, Shanghai's urban population was 14 million, compared with 37.7 million in Zhejiang and 64.9 million in Guangdong. Thus, even if one controls for the population size, there is no question that Shanghai is substantially less innovative than Zhejiang and Guangdong. Basically, the urban population differential ranges between 0.37 – Shanghai to Zhejiang – and

0.22 – Shanghai to Zhejiang, and the individual patent grantee ratio ranges from 0.16 to 0.09. This is not to mention the analytical argument that population size may very well be irrelevant in this type of exercise, especially under the condition of the geographic mobility of talent. Those regions with a supportive and fostering environment may attract more capable and innovative individuals, and those regions with an inappropriate policy model may lose these people. The total number of patents granted is a superior measure, and by this measure, the gap between Shanghai and the two entrepreneurial regions in China is huge.

28. NBS (2005a) has detailed regional data on fixed asset investments.

29. The State Council report contains details about a number of individual businesses. The scale of their operations was substantial. One private entrepreneur successfully developed a demolition line of business and subcontracted work with the Shanghai Steel Factory. The long-term employment of her firm was 28 persons, and sometimes more than 100 persons during busy periods. In two years, the equity of her business grew from 2,000 to 440,000 yuan, a remarkable rate of growth. Another private entrepreneur with a successful construction business hired 120 workers. Sales in 1985 amounted to 160,000 yuan.

30. Both were trained as engineers and had spent long careers in technology before coming to Shanghai. Jiang had been minister of the electronics industry before moving to Shanghai and Zhu had worked in the State Economic Commission, the agency in charge of upgrading China's technology base.

31. Quoted in Pocha (2006).

32. This developmental vision for Shanghai was outlined in his inaugural speech after Jiang Zemin was appointed mayor of Shanghai. See Jiang Zemin (1988).

33. However, the effect of this change in the tax rule on private-sector development is ambiguous when private enterprises were not perceived of as part of a township's tax base, and this would tilt the incentives in favor of developing collective enterprises.

34. The Shanghai government justified this program as an effort to clear the "slum areas." But a commonsensical reasoning would refute this rationale. In 1997, Shanghai had about 4.8 million households. Displacing 541,400 households would suggest that 11 percent of Shanghai households lived in slums in the mid-1990s.

35. These interviews were conducted in 2007 with entrepreneurs, lawyers who specialize in registration regulations, and officials at the All-China Federation of Industry and Commerce, an organization representing private-sector businesses. In addition, I also visited several district offices of the Shanghai Bureau of Industry and Commerce, the agency in charge of registering and licensing firms.

36. The regional GDP are available from the NBS (2006c, pp. 63–64).

37. We do not report data for 1980 because the data for that year are not broken down by sectors. The NBS records the income data on a per capita basis and we use the income data valued on a cash basis. The NBS also collects data on total household income that includes the imputed market value of unsold products. Using the cash income minimizes potential variations in the valuation methodologies. I have deflated the Shanghai and China data to their 1978 price levels, using the Shanghai and China consumer price indexes. The national

consumer price index is available from the NBS (2006c). The Shanghai data were downloaded from the website of the Shanghai government, at http://www.stats-sh.gov.cn/2003shtj/tjnj/nj05.htm?d1=2005tjnj/C0901.htm. Using the nominal values would yield similar results in terms of the data trends.

38. See news.sohu.com/20070301/n248423843.shtml 86k, accessed on April 1, 2007.

39. Of all the private-sector surveys, SEBS1991 and PSS95 are the only two surveys that include both Shanghai and Shenzhen.

40. In the 1990s, Shanghai was a special economic zone in that it was a special recipient of the largesse of the central government, not that it had pioneered in economic liberalization. Pudong depended on handouts from the central government, whereas the four SEZs in the 1980s operated on a self-funded basis. In 1990, Zhu Rongji, then the mayor of Shanghai, revealed that the central government would earmark a special funding facility totaling 6.5 billion yuan to support Pudong development (Zhu Rongji 1990). This is the only explicit earmarking by the central government to support Shanghai. Shanghai is the venue of many SOEs directly managed by the central government. Until 2007, these SOEs did not pay dividends to the central government; instead, they plowed back their huge monopoly profits into reinvestments. Many of the reinvestments in Shanghai were essentially transfers from the rest of the country to Shanghai.

41. The Zhang Rongkun affair was covered extensively in the Chinese media, less so in Shanghai than elsewhere in the country. For coverage in the English media, see McGregor (2006a).

42. Since the downfall of Chen Liangyu, the Chinese media began to report more details on corruption cases in Shanghai. The magazine, *Caijing*, in particular has published a series of articles on the topic.

43. For one thing, the "rotten-deal" view is heavily colored by comparing Shanghai with Guangdong. Shirk (1982, p. 141) reported the following remark by Shanghai's mayor, Wang Daohan, "Of course we're behind Guangdong on reform. If the center gave us the same financial deal they gave Guangdong, we would be moving faster on reform." In the 1980s, Guangdong received a tax arrangement with the central government that allowed the province to keep much of what it collected, whereas Shanghai was required to remit most of its tax revenue to the central government (Oksenberg and Tong 1991).

44. The investment gap is even larger between Shanghai and Zhejiang. In 1986, Shanghai and Zhejiang had similar GDPs (41 billion yuan in Shanghai and 48.5 billion yuan in Zhejiang). But between 1986 and 1990, the central government invested in Shanghai 4.2 times more than what it invested in Zhejiang.

Chapter 5: Capitalism with Chinese Characteristics

1. This episode was reported extensively in the Chinese press. A number of prominent Chinese lawyers and legal scholars came out in defense of Mr. Cui. Mr. Cui received a lenient sentence, by Chinese standards. He was sentenced to a suspended death sentence. See the coverage in *Nanfang Daily*, at http%3A//www%2Enanfangdaily%2Ecom%2Ecn/zm/20070201/xw/fz/2007020100, accessed on June 16, 2007.

2. This account is from McMillan (2002). McMillan based his account on the work of Claire Robertson, a scholar on Africa.

3. There are numerous reports on this episode, including http://www. chinadaily.com.cn/english/doc/2004–06/23/, accessed on May 15, 2007.

4. These figures were reported by *China Youth Daily* on September 18, 2007, and transmitted by http://news.boxun.com/cgi-bin/news/gb_display/, accessed on September 19, 2007.

5. This view is widespread even though there is no systematic evidence in support of it. For a detailed discussion, see Rodrik (2007).

6. Sen (1999, p. 44) quotes from research by Anand and Ravallion (1993) that shows broadly defined human development is not solely a function of average income.

7. Nine-year compulsory education refers to schooling from primary to junior lower secondary levels. The 12-year system refers to schooling from primary to upper secondary levels.

8. See a recounting of a Xinhuanet story on the website on educational issues in Hebei province. See http://www.uedu.net/get/hebei/hebei_base/, accessed on November 20, 2005.

9. As far as I know, few have identified this issue. One exception is Naughton (2007, pp. 195–196), who discusses it in some detail.

10. The title of the article is unusually frank: "The ghost of illiteracy returns to haunt the country." Although the article garnered very little attention in the West, the Chinese Ministry of Education reacted strongly. It published a disclaimer saying that the 30 million figure is an estimate by academics rather than an official figure.

11. The 113.9 million is based on a sampling of 1.325 percent of the Chinese population.

12. See the statement by an official of the Ministry of Education confirming that the current illiteracy standard is still 1,500 Chinese characters.

13. Because rural households are also business units, we need to take out the expenditures on production inputs in order to accurately reflect the burdens on rural households from rising costs in health care and education. All the denominators used in the calculation of ratios refer to consumption expenditures.

14. Some of the findings of the study are summarized in www.chinahexie.org? Article_Show.asp?Artic, accessed on September 25, 2007.

15. Urban China fared slightly better but also faced immense problems. The collapse of the SOEs in the late 1990s contributed massively to the size of the problem. In Zhenjiang city, for example, it is estimated that more than half of the SOEs were not able to reimburse their employees the full cost of their medical care as of the late 1990s. (Zhenjiang city, which is located in prosperous Jiangsu province, probably has fared better than other regions of the country, such as the northeast region of the country where the SOEs have collapsed on a greater scale). Nationwide, as the World Bank points out (World Bank 2005b), China's overall reimbursement rate fell throughout the 1990s.

16. This is a government-sponsored program financed by the central government, county governments, and households in equal shares (10 yuan per participant) (World Bank 2005b).

17. In fact, Zhao Ziyang began to argue for the creation of a social protection system as early as 1984. In 1988, I participated in a World Bank study on the need and steps required for creating a social protection system in China. The project was initiated by the Chinese government.

18. Pei (2006, pp. 172–173) summarizes some of the research in this area.

19. Many of the standard indicators of development of a country's health sector reflect what is happening on the supply side rather than on the demand side. For example, the World Bank reports that China had 1.7 doctors per 1,000 persons and 2.4 hospital beds per 1,000 persons during 1995–2000. These figures put China in a favorable comparison with Malaysia (0.7 and 2.0), Thailand (0.4 and 2.0), and South Korea (1.3 and 6.1).

20. The data on the 1980s come from NBS (1993b, p. 802). Data for other years come from the respective *China Statistical Yearbooks*.

21. In this book, I am not concerned with some of the generic issues about GDP data, such as that they do not measure the subjective well-being of human beings or they do not sufficiently take into account the external effects of economic production such as pollution and resource depletion. I also do not discuss the issue of self-reporting, which China economists have identified as a problem. Local officials can over- or under-report GDP depending on their incentives. Some scholars (Rawski 2001b) have documented the rather substantial problems in Chinese GDP data.

22. Chinese construction of the CPI has already been questioned. After making some adjustments to the Chinese price indexes, Young (2003) used an alternative set of deflators and recalculated the GDP growth rates. He lowered the average annual GDP growth rate from 9.1 to 7.4 percent between 1978 and 1998. The main problem with the Chinese deflators identified by Young is the procedure used to collect the data. Most countries collect price data through sampling. But in China, the firms themselves report both nominal and constant values of output. Government statisticians then convert the data into price deflators. Some enterprises often assume equality between the nominal and constant values of their output, which means that the value of the reported deflators systematically understates the true inflation and thus systematically overstates the real growth.

23. The growth of household income as reported by the NBS is higher than that reported by Khan and Riskin (2005), who base their results on the 1995 and 2002 waves of the CHIP. Khan and Riskin themselves have noted this difference and attribute it to the different ways the NBS and CHIP define income.

24. In interpreting this finding, it is important to stress some data issues. This ratio is approximately the same ratio of employee compensation to GDP calculated on the basis of the income approach of GDP. We cannot show it here explicitly, but one may wish to argue that the declining ratio in the 1990s might reflect the increasing privatization of the Chinese economy if the household claims on corporate assets rose. This interpretation is not correct. For one thing, it is not possible to reconcile this rationale with the rising ratio in the 1980s when the private sector developed rapidly.

In fact, private-sector development should boost this ratio, as it did in the 1980s. This is because the household survey data on income include proprietors' income and capital gains (interest income and capital gains). So, theoretically at least, the declining income share of GDP has nothing to do with the possibility that Chinese households increasingly ran their own businesses or acquired claims on the corporate sector (through purchases of company shares). To the extent that these rising claims are important, they are already fully captured in the household income data.

25. Their finding that geographic factors account for 80 percent of the variance is generated without incorporating migrants into their data. When they do include migrants, the importance of geographic factors declined to only 21 percent in 2002. The problem is that the 1995 CHIP survey did not poll migrants, so we do not know what proportion of the explanation is due to migration in 1995. In any case, there is no econometric reason why geography should increase in explanatory importance even if the regressions do not explicitly incorporate migration.

26. For a good account on this topic, see Tanner (2004).

27. The details are from Pastor and Wise (1992) and Wise (1994).

28. The details of these measures are available from the NSB (2007a, p. 109 and pp. 378–381).

29. Data are from the National Bureau of Statistics (1990).

30. Some of these industrialists are household names in China. Rong Yiren, who ran the largest textile operation in China in the 1930s and 1940s, came from Suzhou. An Wang, who later founded Wang Computer in Massachusetts, came from Kunshan, a county in the vicinity of Suzhou. In politics, maybe as a sign of things to come, Zhou Enlai, Communist China's premier between 1949 and 1976, was born in Jiangsu. His nemesis, Generalissimo Chiang Kai-shek, the leader of the Nationalist government on the mainland and then on Taiwan, was born near Ningbo in Zhejiang.

31. Elsewhere I have provided statistical evidence linking these aspects of the two provinces. For now, let me concentrate on documenting this set of differences.

32. The adjustments are done to the Chinese GDP data rather than to the Indian GDP data because the official Chinese GDP data in the 1970s and 1980s were compiled according to different procedures from prevailing international practices.

33. The HDI data can be downloaded from the website of the UNDP at http://www.undp.org.

34. The data on social development in China and India can be accessed from the *World Development Indicators*, available at http://devdata.worldbank.org/dataonline.

35. The Chinese data are from various issues of the *China Statistical Yearbook*. A very useful data source on India is www.indiastat.com. The data on India's transportation facilities were accessed on May 1, 2006.

36. The data are available at http://devdata.worldbank.org/dataonline.

37. See World Bank (2001, pp. 60–61).

38. The output measures here refer to the ratios of output in labor-intensive (skill-intensive) industries to output in less labor-intensive (less skill-intensive) industries. High (low) labor-intensive industries are those industries above (below)

the median value of labor intensity. The skill-intensity measure is similarly derived. For details, see Kochhar et al. (2006).

39. The World Bank designed and implemented – with the cooperation of partner institutions – the WBES in 1999–2000. The survey was carried out in 81 countries and on more than 10,032 firms operating in these countries. The survey was designed to capture the firms' views on many aspects of the business environment pertaining to their operations. As far as this author is aware, there have been only two studies that have used this dataset. One study was conducted by a group of World Bank economists who focus on assessing the business environment around the world (Batra, Kaufmann, and Stone 2003). The other study focuses on differences in policy treatments between foreign and domestic firms (Huang 2004). An important feature of the WBES is its emphasis on entrepreneurial firms. The vast majority of the firms are owned privately. In the entire WBES sample, only 12 percent of the firms reported some government ownership.

40. It should be pointed out that in the same study, as compared to India, China fares much better when it comes to labor and licensing regulations.

41. India implemented meaningful financial reforms in part because of the way its reforms were triggered. The country experienced an *external* crisis in 1990 as its foreign exchange reserves were being drawn down and at one point were only sufficient to cover two months' worth of imports. The rupee crisis, as it is known, led to the involvement of the International Monetary Fund (IMF), which imposed financial reforms as a condition for providing bridge loans.

42. The history of Infosys has been reported extensively in business school cases. See Kuemmerle (2004).

43. For details, see http://www.gcr.weforum.org/.

44. Deng made this comment to Yang Shangkun, president of China at the time, on the eve of the declaration of martial law. The comment is recorded in Zhang, Nathan, and Link (2001, p. 218).

45. The data are provided by one of the best investigative journals in China. See http://www.nfcmag.com/list-2.html, accessed on February 2, 2008.

46. Pei (2006, pp. 28–29) summarizes the views of many insiders.

47. For example, Sachs, Varshney, and Bajpai (1999) and Ahluwalia (2002), after contrasting India's slower pace of export growth and FDI inflows with those in China, find India's rigid labor laws, substantially higher tariffs, restrictions on large firms, and exit barriers to be the sources of its lagging performance. Business analysts readily concur with the view that India's performance has been less impressive than China's. Two articles in *The Economist*, in 2003 and 2005, although inconsistent in their animal allegory – the tiger in the 2003 piece refers to India, whereas the tiger in the 2005 piece refers to China – are nevertheless consistent in their conclusion that China has substantially outperformed India. See *The Economist* ("The Tiger in Front: India and China" 2005; "A Tiger Falling Behind a Dragon" 2003). That said, business analysts have recently recognized that India has also performed well in an absolute sense but still not as impressively as China. Martin Wolf, a respected economic columnist for the *Financial Times*, summarizes this new "consensus" most succinctly

when he writes, "it will remain more China than India for some time." See Wolf (2005).

48. From World Bank (1989, p. 91).

49. For a detailed account of FDI in India during this era, see Encarnation (1989).

50. For example, see World Bank (1993), Stiglitz and Yusuf (2001), and Yusuf and Evenett (2002).

51. Naughton (2007, pp. 144–145) points out that China's investment to GDP ratio today is quite similar to that in Japan in the 1970s and that in Korea in the 1990s.

52. The data on East Asia in this section are based on Wade (1990), Lee (1996), and Campos and Root (1996).

53. Some analysts argue that Chinese GDP data undercount the service sector and, therefore, may overstate the investment/GDP ratio. All the figures cited in this text are based on revised GDP data that incorporate the previously under-reported private service sector.

54. The export share data for Taiwan come from Ranis and Schive (1985).

55. See World Bank (1993) and Campos and Root (1996).

56. See Yergin and Stanislaw (1998, p. 179). There is, to be sure, government ownership in Taiwan, but even according to an account normally sympathetic to the strong role of the state in the economy, government ownership in Taiwan seems to have been primarily confined to upstream, R&D sectors and not to the manufacturing stages of production. The role of the state was to jump-start businesses rather than to actively manage them (Amsden and Chu 2003, pp. 86–88).

57. Different studies and sources provide different Gini numbers, but they all converge on trend developments. See Haggard (1990), World Bank (1993), and Asian Development Bank (1995).

58. A report in http://finance.sina.com.cn/g/20011105/125514.html, accessed on October 5, 2007, summarizes these rounds of salary adjustments.

59. The poverty line is published by the NBS (2007b, p. 43). This is what the Chinese call the absolute poverty standard.

60. See http://news.sina.com.cn/c/2007–11-01/110414212069.shtml, accessed on November 4, 2007.

61. Li's findings are published in http://www.p5w.net/newfortune/index.htm, accessed on October 20, 2007.

62. Summarized in www.npr.org/templates/story/story.php?storyId=5411325, accessed on July 23, 2007, and by Dean (2006).

63. *China Digital Times* at http//chinadigitaltimes.net/ has a special section on forced evictions in China.

64. Quoted by Yergin and Stanislaw (1998), p. 130.

65. See some of the earlier studies on the TFP of the Chinese economy (Chen, Wang, Zheng, Jefferson, and Rawski 1988; Borensztein and Ostry 1996).

66. One exception to the findings reported here is Wang and Meng (2001), who report that TFP growth averaged 7.3 percent in the 1992–1997 period, but only 2.5 percent in the 1978–1991 period. However, the authors themselves dismiss this finding because they cannot locate the sources of this dramatic acceleration of TFP growth. A new factor in the 1990s, foreign investment, turns out to be

insignificantly correlated with TFP growth, leading the authors to conclude, "the extra 4.8 percentage points of industrial TFP growth during 1992–1997 appear to represent a statistical error."

67. The 17th Party Congress and Hu's speech are covered extensively at http://xinhuanet.org.

68. Greenspan's comment on the Chinese stock market was first reported by Bloomberg and transmitted by *China Daily*. See http://bbs.chinadaily.com.cn/redirect.php?gid=2&tid=583320&goto=lastpost, accessed on November 2, 2007.

Bibliography

Acemoglu, Daron, and Simon Johnson. 2005. "Unbundling Institutions." *Journal of Political Economy* 113 (5):949–95.

Acemoglu, Daron, Simon Johnson, and James A. *Robinson.* 2005. "Institutions as a Fundamental Cause of Long-Run Growth." In *Handbook of Economic Growth,* edited by Philippe Aghion and Steven N. Durlauf. Amsterdam: Elsevier B.V.

Agricultural Bank of China. 1984. "Guanyu 1984 Nian Shangbang Nian Nongcun Xindai Gongzuo Qingkuang [Situation of Rural Credit Work in the First Half of the Year]." In *Nongcun Jingrong Guizhang Zhidu Xuanbian [Selection of Rural Financial Regulations],* edited by The General Office of the Agricultural Bank of China. Beijing: Zhongguo jingrong chubanshe.

———. 1985 <1983>-a. *Guangyu Xingyongshe Dui Chengbaohu, Zhuanyehu (Zhongdianhu) Daikuan De Zhanxing Guiding [Provisional Regulations on Loans to Contract Households, Specialized Households (Designated Households) by Rural Credit Cooperatives].* Tianjin: Zhongguo jingrong chubanshe.

———. 1985 <1983>-b. *Guanyu Gaige Xingyongshe Guanli Dizhi De Shidian Yijian [Opinions on Pilot Programs to Reform the Supervision System of Credit Cooperatives].* Tianjin: Zhongguo jingrong chubanshe.

———. 1986 <1984>. "Nongcun Geti Gongshangye Daikuan Shixing Banfa [Provisional Regulations on Loans to Rural Individual Industrial and Commercial Businesses]." In *1984 Nian Nongcun Jingrong Guizhang Zhidu Xuanbian [Selection of Rural Financial Regulations in 1984],* edited by The General Office of the Agricultural Bank of China. Tianjin: Zhongguo jingrong chubanshe.

———. 1986 <1985>. *1985 Nongcun Jingrong Gongzuo Zongjian [Summary of Rural Financial Work in 1985].* Tianjin: Zhongguo jingrong chubanshe.

———. 1988a. "Geti Gongshanghu, Siying Qiye Daikuan Guanli Zhanxing Bangfa [Provisional Regulations on Loans to Individual Businesses and Private Enterprises]." In *Jingrong Guizhang Zhidu Xuanbian 1988 [Selection of Financial Regulations 1988],* edited by The General Office of the People's Bank of China. Beijing: Zhongguo jingrong chubanshe.

———. 1988b. "Nongcun Xinyong Hezuoshe Xiangzhen Qiye Daikuan Guanli Zhanxing Bangfa [Provisional Regulations on Loans to TVEs by Rural Credit Cooperatives] In *"Jingrong Guizhang Zhidu Xuanbian 1988 [Selection of Financial Regulations 1988],*

edited by The General Office of the People's Bank of China. Beijing: Zhongguo jingrong chubanshe.

———. 1988c. *Nongcun Xinyong Hezuoshe Zhigong Guanli Zhanxing Guiding [Pro-
visional Regulations on the Employment Practices of Rural Credit Cooperatives]* Beijing:
Zhongguo jingrong chubanshe.

———. 1992a. *Guanyu Jiakuai Nongcun Jingrong Gaige Kaifang De Yijian [An Opinion
to Speed up the Rural Financial Reforms and Opening]*. Beijing: Zhongguo jingrong
chubanshe.

———. 1992b. *Guanyu Jiaqiang Nongcun Xinyongshe Zhigong Duiwu Jianshe De Yijian
[Strengthening the Employment System at Rural Credit Cooperatives]*. Beijing: Zhongguo jingrong chubanshe.

———. 1994. *Guanyu Jinyibu Jiaqiang Nongcun Xinyongshe Xindai Guanli De Yijian
[Opinion to Strengthen the Supervision of Loans in Rural Credit Cooperatives]*. Beijing:
Zhongguo jingrong chubanshe.

———. 1995. *Nongcun Xinyong Hezuoshe Jihe Chufa Zhanxing Guiding [Provisional
Regulation on Auditing of Rural Credit Cooperatives and Punishment Measures]* Beijing:
Zhongguo jingrong chubanshe.

Ahluwalia, Montek S. 2002. "Economic Reforms in India since 1991: Has Gradualism
Worked?" *Journal of Economic Perspectives* 16 (3):67–88.

Allen, Franklin, Jun Qian, and Meijun Qian. 2005. "Law, Finance and Economic Growth
in China." *Journal of Financial Economics* 77 (1):57–116.

Amsden, Alice H., and Wan-Wen Chu. 2003. *Beyond Late Development: Taiwan's Upgrading Policies.* Cambridge: MIT Press.

Anand, Sudhir, and Martin Ravallion. 1993. "Human Development in Poor Countries:
On the Role of Private Incomes and Public Services." *Journal of Economic Perspectives*
7 (1):133–50.

Asian Development Bank. 1995. *Key Indicators of Developing Asian and Pacific Countries.*
Manila: Oxford University Press.

Bai, Chong-En, David D. Li, and Yijiang Wang. 2003. "Thriving on a Tilted Playing
Field." In *How Far across the River? Chinese Policy Reform at the Millennium*, edited by
Nicholas C. Hope, Dennis Tao Yang, and Mu Yang Li. Stanford: Stanford University
Press.

Ball, Andrew. 2004. "Focus Now on Logistics of Poverty Reduction." *Financial Times*,
May 25.

Banerjee, Abhijit V., Shawn Cole, and Esther Duflo. 2005. "Bank Competition in India."
Cambridge: Department of Economics.

"Bank Executive Arrested over $30 Million Fraud Scandal." 2004. *The Standard*,
August 20.

Barnett, A. Doak, and Ezra with Vogel. 1967 *Cadres, Bureaucracy, and Political Power in
Communist China.* New York: Columbia University Press.

Batra, Geeta, Daniel Kaufmann, and Andrew H. W. Stone. 2003. *Investment Climate
around the World: Voices of the Firms from the World Business Environment Survey.*
Washington, DC: World Bank.

Baumol, William, Robert E. Litan, and Carl J. Shramm. 2007. *Good Capitalism, Bad
Capitalism, and Economics of Growth and Prosperity.* New Haven, CT: Yale University
Press.

Borensztein, Eduardo, and Jonathan D. Ostry. 1996. "Accounting for China's Growth Performance." *American Economic Review* 86 (2):224–8.

Brandt, Loren, and Hongbin Li. 2002. "Bank Discrimination in Transition Economies: Ideology, Information or Incentives?" Ann Arbor: William Davidson Institute Working Paper No. 517.

Brandt, Loren, Hongbin Li, and Joanne Roberts. 2005. "Banks and Enterprise Privatization in China." *Journal of Law, Economics and Organization* 21 (2):524–46.

Bureau of Industry and Commerce Administration. 1990. *Gongshang Xingzheng Guanli Tongji Huibian 1989 [Statistical Collection of the Industry and Commerce Administration 1989]*. Beijing: Bureau of Industry and Commerce Administration.

Burns, John P. 1981. "Rural Guangdong's 'Second Economy,' 1962–74." *The China Quarterly* 88:629–44.

Byrd, William A. 1990. "Entrepreneurship, Capital, and Ownership." In *China's Rural Industry*, edited by William A. Byrd and Qingsong Lin. New York: Oxford University Press.

Byrd, William A., and Qingsong Lin. 1990. "China's Rural Industry: An Introduction." In *China's Rural Industry*, edited by William A. Byrd and Lin Qingsong. New York: Oxford University Press.

Cabral, Luis M. B., and Jose Mata. 2003. "On the Evolution of the Firm Size Distribution: Facts and Theory." *American Economic Review* 93 (4):1075–90.

Campos, Jose Edgardo, and Hilton L. Root. 1996. *The Key to the Asian Miracle*. Washington, DC: The Brookings Institution.

Carvey, Paul. 2006. "China Roe: Riding on the Edge." Hong Kong: Macquarie Research.

Central Committee. 1979. "Guanyu Jiakuai Nongye Fazhan Ruogan Wenti De Jueding [The Decision on Certain Questions Concerning the Acceleration of the Agricultural Development]." *People's Daily*, October 6, 1.

———. (1991 <1989>). "Guanyu jiaqiang dangde jieshede tongzhi [A circular on strengthening the construction of the Party]." In *Shisanda yilai zhongyao wenjian xuanbian [Selection of important documents since the Thirteenth Congress]*, edited by The Document Office of the CCP Central Committee. Beijing: Renmin chubanshe.

———. 1992 <1982>. "Quanguo Nongcun Gongzuo Huiyi Jiyao [Summary of the National Conference on Rural Work]." In *Xinshiqi Nongye He Nongcui Gongzuo Zhongyao Wenxian Xuanbian [Selections of Important Documents on Agriculture and Rural Sector During the New Age]*, edited by The Central Committee Document Office and The State Council Development Research Center. Beijing: The Central Committee Document Press.

———. 1992 <1983>. "Dangqian Nongcun Jingji Zhengce De Ruogan Wenti [A Few Questions on the Current Rural Economic Policies]." In *Xingshiqi Nongye He Nongcun Gongzuo Zhongyao Wenxian Xuanbian [Selection of Important Documents on Agriculture and Rural Sector Work in the New Period]*, edited by The Central Committee Document Office and The State Council Development Research Center. Beijing: The Central Committee Document Press.

———. 1992 <1984>. "1984 Nian Nongcun Gongzuo De Tongzhi [Circular on Rural Work for 1984]." In *Xingshiqi Nongye He Nongcun Gongzuo Zhongyao Wenxian Xuanbian [Selection of Important Documents on Agriculture and Rural Sector Work in the New Period]*, edited by The Central Committee Document Office and The State

Council Development Research Center. Beijing: The Central Committee Document Press.

Central Committee, and State Council. 1982 <1981>. "Guanyu Guangkai Menlu, Gao-huo Jingji, Jiejue Chengzhen Jiuye Wenti De Ruogan Jiuding [Expanding Chan-nels and Enlivening the Economy, and Solving Employment Problems in Cities and Townships]." In *Sanzhong Quanhui Yilai Zhongyao Wenxian Xuanbian [Selection of Important Documents since the Third Plenum]*, edited by The Document Office of the CCP Central Committee. Beijing: Renmin chubanshe.

———. 1992 <1985>. "Jinyibu Huoyue Nongcun Jingji De Shixiang Zhengce [Ten Policy Measures to Further Enliven the Rural Economy]." In *Xingshiqi Nongye He Nongcun Gongzuo Zhongyao Wenxian Xuanbian [Selections of Important Documents on Agriculture and Rural Sector Work in the New Period]*, edited by The Central Committee Document Office and The State Council Development Research Center. Beijing: The Central Committee Document Press.

Central Committee Policy Research Office, and Ministry of Agriculture. 2000. *National Rural Social-Economic Survey Data Collection*. Beijing: Zhongguo nongye chubanshe.

Chai Hongxia, Shi Bipo, and Gao Qing. 1997. *Hu Yaobang Moulue [The Wisdom of Hu Yaobang]*. Beijing: Hongqi chubanshe.

Chang, Chun, and Yijiang Wang. 1994. "The Nature of the Township Enterprise." *Journal of Comparative Economics* 19 (3):434–52.

Che, Jiahua, and Yingyi Qian. 1998a. "Insecure Property Rights and Government Own-ership of Firms." *Quarterly Journal of Economics* 113 (2):467–96.

———. 1998b. "Institutional Environment, Community Government, and Corporate Governance: Understanding China's Township-Village Enterprises." *Journal of Law, Economics, and Organization* 14 (1):1–23.

Chen, Kathy. 2006. "Zouguang" Huiyi Jiyao Xian Zhongguo Gaige Bianluan ["Leaked" Conference Minutes Revealing Debates on Chinese Reforms]." *Wall Street Journal Online (Chinese edition)*, April 6.

Chen, Kuan, Hongchang Wang, Yuxin Zheng, Gary H. Jefferson, and Thomas G. Rawski. 1988. "Productivity Change in Chinese Industry: 1953–1985." *Journal of Comparative Economics* 12 (4):570–91.

Chen, Muhua. 1987. *Zhongguo Muqian Jinrong Gongzuo [Current Chinese Monetary Work]*. Beijing: Zhongguo jinrong chubanshe.

China Finance Association. 1986. *Almanac of China's Finance and Banking*. Beijing: China Finance Press.

———. 1997. *Zhongguo Jinrong Nianjian 1997 [Chinese Financial Yearbook 1997]*. Beijing: Zhongguo jinrong nianjian bianjibu.

———. 2000. *Almanac of China's Finance and Banking 2000*. Beijing: China Finance Press.

Chua Chin Hon. 2007. "Hu's Grade in First-Term Report Card: 'Very Good' Analysts Give A for Growth and Political Stability, but Not for Reforms." *The Strait Times*, October 2.

Cui, Anban. 1983. "A Confession of Village Party Secretary." *Journal of Rural Work*:13.

Dai, Xianglong. 1997. "Ba Nongcun Xinyongshe Banzheng Hezuo Jingrong Zuzhi Genghao De Zhichi Nongye He Nongcun Jingji Fanzhan [Convert Rural Credit Unions into Cooperative Financial Organizations; Further Support Agriculture and Rural Economic Development]." In *Nongcun Xinyong Hezuoshe Wenjian Xuanbian*

1995–1997 [Selection of Documents on Rural Credit Cooperatives 1995–1997], edited by The People's Bank of China. Beijing: People's Bank of China.

De Soto, Hernando. 1989. *The Other Path: The Invisible Revolution in the Third World.* New York: Harper & Row.

Dean, Jason. 2006. "Land Seizures Rise Sharply in China." *The Wall Street Journal,* May 5.

Deng, Liqun. 2005. *Shier Ge Chunqiu (1975–1987) [Twenty Years (1975–1987)].* Hong Kong: Bozhi chubanshe.

Desai, Meghnad. 2003. India and China: An Essay in Comparative Political Economy. Paper read at IMF conference on India/China, November, at Delhi, India.

Donnithorne, Audrey. 1981. *China's Economic System.* London: Hurst.

Dougherty, Sean, and Richard Herd. 2005. "Fast-Falling Barriers and Growing Concentration: The Emergence of a Private Economy in China." Paris: Organisation for Economic Cooperation and Development.

Drèze, Jean, and Amartya Sen. 1999. *India: Economic Development and Social Opportunity.* New York: Oxford University Press.

Du, Lexun, Zhang Wenming, and Zhang Dawei, eds. 2004. *Zhongguo Yiliao Weisheng Chanye Fazhan Baogao [The Development Report of China's Health Industry].* Beijing: Social Science Documentation Publishing House.

Dyer, Geoff. 2006. "Income Gap in China Widens." *Financial Times,* December 27, 5.

Eckstein, Alexander 1977. *China's Economic Revolution.* Cambridge: Cambridge University Press.

Editorial Board of Zunyi Financial History. 1992. *Zunyi Xian Jingrong Zhi [Financial History of Zunyi County].* Guiyang: Guizhou renmin chubanshe.

Editorial Committee of Agricultural Yearbook. 1991. *Zhongguo Nongye Nianjian 1991 [China Agricultural Yearbook 1991].* Beijing: Zhongguo nongye chubanshe.

Editorial Committee of Contemporary China Series. 1989. *Dangdai Zhongguo De Guizhou [Guizhou in Contemporary China].* Beijing: Zhongguo shehui kexue chubanshe.

Editorial Committee of Guizhou Pan County Financial History. 1994. *Pan Xian Tequ Jingrong Zhi [Financial History of Pan County].* Guiyang: Guizhou renmin chubanshe.

Editorial Committee of Ten Years of Reforms in Guizhou. 1989. *Guizhou Gaige Kaifang De Shinian [Ten Years of Reforms in Guizhou].* Guiyang: Guizhou renmin chubanshe.

Editorial Committee of TVE Yearbook. 1989a. *Zhongguo Xiangzhen Qiye Nianjian 1989 [China TVE Yearbook 1989].* Beijing: Zhongguo nongye chubanshe.

———. 1989b. *Zhongguo Xiangzhen Qiye Nianjian (1978–1987) [China TVE Yearbook (1978–1987)].* Beijing: Zhongguo nongye chubanshe.

———. 1990. *Zhongguo Xiangzhen Qiye Nianjian 1990 [China TVE Yearbook 1990].* Beijing: Zhongguo nongye chubanshe.

———. 1991. *Zhongguo Xiangzhen Qiye Nianjian 1991 [China TVE Yearbook 1991].* Beijing: Zhongguo nongye chubanshe.

———. 1997. *Zhongguo Xiangzhen Qiye Nianjian 1997 [China TVE Yearbook 1997].* Beijing: Zhongguo Nongye Chubanshe.

Editorial Committee of Wenzhou Financial History. 1995. *Wenzhou Shi Jingrong Zhi [Wenzhou Financial History].* Shanghai: Shanghai kexun jishu wenxuan chubanshe.

Encarnation, Dennis J. 1989. *Dislodging Multinationals: India's Strategy in Comparative Perspective.* Ithaca: Cornell University Press.

Friedman, Thomas. 1999. "While We Were Sleeping: China's Post-Tiananmen Party Line." *New York Times*, March 26.

Frye, Timothy, and Andrei Shleifer. 1997. "The Invisible Hand and the Grabbing Hand." *American Economic Review* 87 (2):354–8.

Garnaut, Ross, and Guonan Ma. 1993 "How Rich Is China?: Evidence from the Food Economy." *The Australian Journal of Chinese Affairs* (30):121–48.

Garnaut, Ross, Ligang Song, Stoyan Tenev, and Yang Yao. 2005. *China's Ownership Transformation*. Washington, DC: International Finance Corporation.

Girardin, Eric. 1997. *Banking Sector Reform and Credit Control in China*. Paris: OECD.

Green, Stephen. 2003. *China's Stock Market: A Guide to Its Progress, Players and Prospects*. London: The Economist, in association with Profile Books.

Gregory, Neil F., Stoyan Tenev, and Dileep Wagle. 2000. *China's Emerging Private Enterprises: Prospects for the New Century*. Washington, DC: International Finance Corporation.

Gregory, Paul R., and Robert C. Stuart. *Soviet Economic Structure and Performance*. New York: Harper & Row, Publishers, Inc.

Groves, Theodore, Yongmiao Hong, John McMillan, and Barry Naughton. 1995. "China's Evolving Managerial Labor Market." *Journal of Political Economy* 103 (4):873–92.

Guthrie, Doug. 1999. *Dragon in a Three-Piece Suit*. Princeton, NJ: Princeton University Press.

Haggard, Stephan. 1990 *Pathways from the Periphery*. Ithaca, NY: Cornell University Press.

Haggard, Stephan, and Yasheng Huang. 2008. "The Political Economy of Private Sector Development in China." In *China's Economic Transition: Origins, Mechanisms, and Consequences*, edited by Loren Brandt and Thomas Rawski. New York: Cambridge University Press.

Han, Lei. 1984. "Zai Zhongguo Nongye Yinghang Quanguo Fenhang Hangzhang Zuotanhui Shang De Kaimuci [Opening Speech at the Conference of Branch Presidents of the Agricultural Bank of China]." In *Nongcun Jingrong Guizhang Zhidu Xuanbian [Selections of Regulations on Rural Finance]*, edited by The General Office of the Agricultural Bank of China. Beijing: Zhongguo jingrong chubanshe.

Hannum, Emily, Jere Behrman, and Meiyan Wang. 2008. "Human Capital in China." In *China's Economic Transition: Origins, Mechanisms, and Consequences*, edited by Loren Brandt and Thomas Rawski. New York: Cambridge University Press.

Harding, Harry. 1987. *China's Second Revolution*. Washington, DC: The Brookings Institution.

Hausmann, Ricardo, Lant Pritchett, and Dani Rodrik. 2004. "Growth Accelerations." NBER Working Paper No. 10566.

Hewett, Ed A. 1988. *Reforming the Soviet Economy*. Washington, DC: The Brookings Institution.

Heytens, Paul, and Harm Zebregs. 2003. "How Fast Can China Grow?" In *China: Competing in the Global Economy*, edited by Wanda Tseng and Markus Rodlauer. Washington, DC: International Monetary Fund.

Holz, Carsten A. 2005. "China's Economic Growth 1978–2025: What We Know Today About China's Economic Growth Tomorrow." Hong Kong: Hong Kong University of Science & Technology.

Hu, Albert Guangzhou, and Gary H. Jefferson. 2006. "A Great Wall of Patents: What Is Behind China's Recent Patent Explosion?" Singapore: Department of Economics, National University of Singapore.

Huang, Yasheng. 1996. *Inflation and Investment Controls in China*. New York: Cambridge University Press.

Huang, Yasheng. 2003. *Selling China: Foreign Direct Investment During the Reform Era*. New York: Cambridge University Press.

————. 2004. "Do Host Governments Favor Foreign Firms? Evidence from WBES." Cambridge: MIT Sloan School.

————. 2006. "Assessing Financing Constraints for Domestic Private Firms in China and India: Evidence from WBES." *Indian Journal of Economics & Business*, 69–92.

Huang, Yasheng, and David Lane. 2002. "Kelon: China's Corporate Dragon." Boston: Harvard Business School.

Huang, Yasheng, and Yi Qian (2008). *Is Entrepreneurship Missing in Shanghai*. Cambridge, paper prepared for the NBER conference on international differences in entrepreneurship, Savannah, Georgia, February 1-2.

Iacopetta, Maurizio. 2004. "Dissemination of Technology and Market and Planned Economics." *Contributions to Macroeconomics* 4 (1):1–30.

"Infatuation's End." 1999. *The Economist*, September 25, 71.

Institute of Industrial Economics. 2000. *Zhongguo Gongye Fazhan Baogao 2000 [Chinese Industrial Development Report 2000]*. Beijing: Jingji guanli chubanshe.

International Fund for Agricultural Development. 2002. *Rural Financial Services in China*.

Jiang Zemin. 1988. "Jishu Jingbu Shi Shanghai Jingji Xingeju De Jichu [Technological Progress Is the Foundation of Shanghai's New Economy]." *Jiefang Ribao [Liberation Daily]*, January 5, 1.

————. (1991 <1989>). Zai quanguo zuzhi buzhang huiyi shang de jianghua [Speech at national conference of chiefs of departments of organization]. *Shisanda yilai zhongyao wenjian xuanbian [Selection of important documents since the Thirteenth Congress]*. The Document Office of the CCP Central Committee. Beijing, Renmin chubanshe. 2: 578–87.

————. (2006 <2001>). *Jiang Zemin wenxuan [Selections of Jiang Zemin's works]*. Beijing, Renmin chubanshe.

Jiangsu Statistical Bureau. 1987. *1986 Nian Jiangsusheng Nongcun Zhuanyehu, Xinjingjiti Tongji Ziliao [The 1986 Statistics on Rural Specialized Households and New Economic Alliances in Jiangsu]*. Nanjing: Jiangsu Statistical Bureau.

————. 1988. *1987 Nian Jiangsusheng Nongcun Zhuanyehu, Xinjingjiti Tongji Ziliao [The 1987 Statistics on Rural Specialized Households and New Economic Alliances in Jiangsu]*. Nanjing: Jiangsu Statistical Bureau.

Jilin Branch of the People's Bank of China. 1987. *Jingrong Gaige Ziliao Huibian [Compilation of Materials on Financial Reforms]*. Changchun.

Johnson, Chalmers. 1987. "Political Institutions and Economic Performance: The Government-Business Relationship in Japan, South Korea, and Taiwan. In "The Political Economy of the New Asian Industrialism," edited by Frederic C. Deyo. Ithaca, NY: Cornell University Press.

Johnson, Simon, John McMillan, and Christopher Woodruff. 2000. "Entrepreneurs and the Ordering of Institutional Reform." *Economics of Transition* 8 (1):1–36.

Kahn, Joseph. 2007. "Political Moves in China: The More Things Change. . . ." *New York Times*, October 23.

Kelliher, Daniel. 1992. *Peasant Power in China: The Era of Rural Reforms, 1979–1989*. New Haven, CT: Yale University Press.

Khan, Azizur Rahman, and Carl Riskin. 2001. *Inequality and Poverty in China in the Age of Globalization*. Oxford: Oxford University Press.

Khan, Rahman Azizur, and Carl Riskin. 1998. "Income and Inequality in China: Composition, Distribution and Growth of Household Income, 1988 to 1995." *The China Quarterly* (154):221–53.

———. 2005. "China's Household Income and Its Distribution, 1995–2002." *The China Quarterly* (182):356–84.

King, Robert G., and Ross Levine. 1993. "Finance and Growth: Schumpeter Might Be Right." *Quarterly Journal of Economics* 108 (3):713–37.

Kirzner, Israel. 1979. *Perception, Opportunity and Profit: Studies in the Theory of Entrepreneurship*. Chicago: University of Chicago Press.

Knight, Frank. 1921. *Risk, Uncertainty and Profit*. Boston: Houghton Mifflin.

Kochhar, Kalpana, Utsav Kumar, Raghuram Rajan, Arvind Subramanian, and Ioannis Tokatlidis. 2006. "India's Pattern of Development: What Happened, What Follows?" Washington, DC: International Monetary Fund.

Kogut, Bruce, and Udo Zander. 2000. "Did Socialism Fail to Innovate? A Natural Experiment of the Two Zeiss Companies." *American Sociological Review* 65 (2):169–90.

Krugman, Paul. 2005. "The Chinese Challenge." *New York Times*, June 27, 15.

Krugman, Paul. 1994. "The Myth of Asia's Miracle." *Foreign Affairs* 73 (6):62–78.

Kuemmerle, Walter. 2004. "Financing Infosys." Boston: Harvard Business School Press.

Kuijs, Louis, and Tao Wang. 2005. "China's Pattern of Growth: Moving to Sustainability and Reducing Inequality." Washington, DC: World Bank.

Kumar, Krishna B., Raghuram G. Rajan, and Luigi Zingales. 1999. "What Determines Firm Size?" Cambridge, MA: NBER Working Paper Series No. 7208.

Kung, James Kai-Sing. 1999. "The Evolution of Property Rights in Village Enterprises." In *Property Rights and Economic Reform in China*, edited by Jean C. Oi and Andrew G. Walder. Stanford, CA: Stanford University Press.

Kuo, Shirley W. Y., Gustav Ranis, and John C. H. Fei. 1981. *The Taiwan Success Story – Rapid Growth with Improved Distribution in the Republic of China, 1952–1979*. Boulder, CO: Westview Press.

La Porta, Rafael, Florencio Lopez-De-Silanes, Andrei Shleifer, and Robert W. Vishny. 1997. "Law and Finance." *Journal of Political Economy* 106 (6):1113–55.

Lardy, Nicholas R. 1998. *China's Unfinished Economic Revolution*. Washington, DC: The Brookings Institution.

———. 2002. *Integrating China into the Global Economy*. Washington, DC: The Brookings Institution.

Lau, Lawrence J., Yingyi Qian, and Gerard Roland. 2000. "Reform without Losers: An Interpretation of China's Dual-Track Approach to Transition." *Journal of Political Economy*, 120–43.

Lee, Hyung-Koo. 1996. *The Korean Economy*. Albany, NY: State University of New York Press.

Lei Dian, and Hong Chen. 2004. *Sun Dawu: Wei Nongmin Er Sheng [Sun Dawu: Striving for the Livelihood of Peasants]*. Beijing: Zhongguo shehui kexue chubanshe.

Levine, Ross. 1997. "Financial Development and Economic Growth: Views and Agenda." *Journal of Economic Literature* 35 (2):688–726.

Li, Binqian. 1982. *A Few Points on Agricultural Procurement Policy*, Vol. IV. Beijing: Agricultural Publishing House.

Li, Changping. 2005. "Guojia Guihuan Renmin Quanli [The State Should Return the Rights to the People]."

Li, Cheng. 2001. *China's Leaders*. Lanham, MD: Rowman & Littlefield.

Li, David. 1996. "A Theory of Ambiguous Property Rights in Transition Economies." *Journal of Comparative Economics* 23 (1):1–19.

Li, Peng. 1989. "Zhengque Renshi Dangqian De Jinji Xingshi Jiyibu Gaohao Zhili Zhengdun [Correctly Understand the Current Economic Situation and Make Further Corrections and Adjustments]." In *State Council Bulletins*, edited. Beijing: State Council Office.

Lieberthal, Kenneth, and Michel Oksenberg. 1988. *Policy Making in China: Leaders, Structures and Processes*. Princeton, NJ: Princeton University Press.

Lin, Justin Yifu, Fang Cai, and Zhou Li. 1996. *The China Miracle*. Hong Kong: The Chinese University Press.

Lin, Qingsong. 1990. "Private Enterprises: Their Emergence, Rapid Growth, and Problems." In *China's Rural Industry*, edited by William A. Byrd Lin, Qingsong. New York: Oxford University Press.

Lin, Senmu. 1993. *Zhongguo Guding Zichan Touzi Touxi [An Analysis of China's Fixed Asset Investments]*. Beijing: Zhongguo Fazhan chubanshe.

Lin, Zili. 1983. *Lianchan Chengbao Zhi Jianghua [An Introduction to Responsibility System]*. Beijing: Jingji kexuan chubanshe.

Long, Simon. 2005. "The Tiger in Front." *The Economist*, March 3.

Lu, Qiwen. 2000. *China's Leap into the Information Age*. New York: Oxford University Press.

Luo, Xiaopeng. 1990. "Ownership and Status Stratification." In *China's Rural Industry*, edited by William A. Byrd and Qingsong Lin. New York: Oxford University Press.

Ma, Yongwei. 1987 <1986>. *Zai Nongye Yinhang Quanguo Fenhang Hangzhan Huibaohui Jiesushi De Jianghua [Speech at the National Conference of Branch Presidents of Agricultural Bank of China]*, Vol. 2. Tianjin: Zhongguo jingrong chubanshe.

Maddison, Angus. 1998. *Chinese Economic Performance in the Long Run*. Paris: OECD.

McGregor, Richard. 2004. "The World Should Be Braced for China's Expansion." *Financial Times*, December 22, 17.

———. 2006a. "Beijing Probes Shanghai Scandal." *Financial Times*, August 27.

———. 2006b. "China's Poorest Worse Off after Boom." *Financial Times*, November 21.

McMillan, John. 2002. *Reinventing the Bazaar: A Natural History of Markets*. New York: W. W. Norton.

McMillan, John, and Christopher Woodruff. 2002. "The Central Role of Entrepreneurs in Transitional Economies." *Journal of Economic Perspectives* 16 (3):153–70.

Meisner, Maurice. 1999. *Mao's China and After: A History of the People's Republic*. New York: The Free Press.

Ministry of Agriculture. 1985. *Zhongguo Nongye Nianjian 1985 [China Agricultural Statistical Yearbook 1985]*. Beijing: Nongye chubanshe.

————. 1995. "1994 Nian Quanguo Xiangzhen Qiye Jiben Qingkuang Ji Jingji Yunxing Fenxi [Analysis of Basic Situation and Economic Performance of China's TVEs in 1994]." Beijing: Bureau of Township and Village Enterprises, Ministry of Agriculture.

————. 1996. "1995 Nian Quanguo Xiangzhen Qiye Jiben Qingkuang Ji Jingji Yunxing Fenxi [An Analysis of the Basic Conditions and the Economic Performance of China's TVEs in 1995]." Beijing: Bureau of Township and Village Enterprises, Ministry of Agriculture.

————. 1997. "1996 Quanguo Xiangzhen Qiye Jiben Qingkuang Ji Jingji Yunxing Fenxi [An Analysis of Basic Conditions and the Economic Performance of TVEs in 1996]." Beijing: Bureau of Township and Village Enterprises, Ministry of Agriculture.

————. 2003. *Zhongguo Xiangzhen Qiye Tongji Ziliao (1978–2002) [Statistical Materials of Township and Village Enterprises in China 1978–2002].* Beijing: Zhongguo Nongye Chubanshe.

————. 2005. *Quanguo Xiangzhen Qiye Tongji Nianbiao Ji Caiwu Jiesuan Cailiao 2004 [Annual Reports and Budgetary Data of TVEs 1994].* Beijing: Bureau of Township and Village Enterprises, Ministry of Agriculture.

Ministry of Finance. 1989. *Zhongguo Caizheng Tongji (1950–1988) [Statistics on Chinese Finance (1950–1988)].* Beijing: Zhongguo caizheng jingji chubanshe.

Miyamoto, Katsuhiro, and Huangjin Liu. 2005. "An Analysis of the Determinants of Provincial-Level Performance in China's Economy." *Comparative Economic Studies*, September, 520–42.

Montinola, Gabriella, Yingyi Qian, and Barry Weingast. 1995. "Federalism, Chinese Style: The Political Basis for Economic Success in China." *World Politics* 48 (1):50–81.

National Bureau of Statistics. 1982. *Zhongguo Tongji Nianjian 1981 [China Statistical Yearbook 1981].* Beijing: Zhongguo tongji chubanshe.

————. 1986. *Zhongguo Tongji Nianjian 1986 [China Statistical Yearbook 1986].* Beijing: Zhongguo tongji chubanshe.

————. 1987. *Zhongguo Guding Zichan Touzi Tongji Ziliao (1950–1985) [Statistical Materials on Chinese Fixed-Asset Investment (1950–1985)].* Beijing: Zhongguo tonggi chubanshe.

————. 1988. *Zhongguo Tongji Nianjian 1988 [China Statistical Yearbook 1988].* Beijing: Zhongguo tongji chubanshe.

————. 1990. *Quanguo Gesheng, Zizhiqu, Zhixiashi Lishi Tongji Ziliao Huibian 1949–1989 [Collection of Historical Data of Chinese Provinces, Autonomous Regions, and Directly Administered Municipalities 1949–1989].* Beijing: Zhongguo tongji chubanshe.

————. 1991. *Zhongguo Guding Zichan Touzi Tongji Ziliao (1988–1989) [Statistical Materials on Fixed-Asset Investment in China (1988–1989)].* Beijing: Zhongguo tongji chubanshe.

————. 1992. *Zhongguo Guding Zichan Touzi Tongji Ziliao (1990–1991) [Statistics on Fixed-Asset Investment in China (1990–1991)].* Beijing: Zhongguo tongji chubanshe.

————. 1993a. *Zhongguo Guding Zichan Touzi Tongji Ziliao (1990–1991) [Statistics on Fixed-Asset Investment in China (1990–1991)].* Beijing: Zhongguo tongji chubanshe.

————. 1993b. *Zhongguo Tongji Nianjian 1993 [China Statistical Yearbook 1993].* Beijing: Zhongguo tongji chubanshe.

————. 1996. *China Regional Economy: A Profile of 17 Years of Reform and Opening-Up.* Beijing: Zhongguo tongji chubanshe.

———. 1997a. *Zhongguo Guding Zichan Touzi Tongji 1950–1995 [China Statistical Yearbook on Fixed Asset Investments 1950–1985].* Beijing: Zhongguo tongji chubanshe.

———. 1997b. *Zhongguo Tongji Nianjian 1997 [Chinese Statistical Yearbook 1997].* Beijing: Zhongguo tongji chubanshe.

———. 1998. *1998 Zhongguo Guding Zichan Touzi Tongji [China Statistical Yearbook on Fixed Asset Investments 1998].* Beijing: Zhongguo tongji chubanshe.

———. 1999a. *Guanyu Tongjishang Ruhe Fanying Suoyuzhi Jiegou Wenti De Yanjiu [Research on Statistical Reporting on Ownership Structures].* Beijing: Zhongguo tongji chubanshe.

———. 1999b. *Zhongguo Guding Zichan Touzi Tongji 1999 [China Statistical Yearbook on Fixed Asset Investments 1999].* Beijing: Zhongguo tongji chubanshe.

———. 2002. *Zhongguo Guding Zichan Touzi Tongji Nianjian (1950–2000) [Statistics on Investment in Fixed Assets of China (1950–2000)].* Beijing: China Statistics Press.

———. 2003a. *Zhongguo Gudingzichan Touzi Tongji Nianjian 2003 [China Fixed Asset Investment Yearbook 2003].* Beijing: China Statistics Press.

———. 2003b. *Zhongguo Tongji Nianjian 2003 [China Statistical Yearbook 2003].* Beijing: Zhongguo tongji chubanshe.

———. 2004a. *China Statistical Yearbook 2004.* Beijing: China Statistics Press.

———. 2004b. *Zhongguo Guding Zichan Touzi Tongji Nianjian 2004 [Statistical Yearbook of Chinese Investment in Fixed Assets 2004].* Beijing: Zhongguo jihua chubanshe.

———. 2005a. *China Compendium of Statistics 1949–2004.* Beijing: China Statistics Press.

———. 2005b. *China Statistical Yearbook 2005.* Beijing: China Statistics Press.

———. 2005c. *Zhongguo Guding Zichan Touzi Tongji Nianjian 2005 [Statistiscal Yearbook of Chinese Investment in Fixed Assets 2005].* Beijing: Zhongguo jihua chubanshe.

———. 2006a. *China Statistical Abstract 2006.* Beijing: China Statistics Press.

———. 2006b. *China Yearbook of Rural Household Survey.* Beijing: China Statistics Press.

———. 2006c. *Zhongguo Tongji Nianjian 2006 [China Statistical Yearbook 2006].* Beijing: Zhongguo tongji chubanshe.

———. 2007a. *China Statistical Yearbook 2007.* Beijing: China Statistical Press.

———. 2007b. *China Yearbook of Rural Household Survey 2007.* Beijing: China Statistics Press.

National Bureau of Statistics, and Ministry of Science and Technology. 1999. *China Statistical Yearbook on Science and Technology 1998.* Beijing: China Statistical Publishing House.

———. 2002. *China Statistical Yearbook on Science and Technology 2002.* Beijing: China Statistics Press.

Naughton, Barry. 1996. *Growing out of the Plan: Chinese Economic Reform, 1978–1993.* New York: Cambridge University Press.

Naughton, Barry 2007. *The Chinese Economy: Transitions and Growth.* Cambridge: The MIT Press.

North, Douglass. 2005. "The Chinese Menu (for Development)." *Wall Street Journal,* April 7, A14.

Nyberg, Albert, and Scott Rozelle. 1999. *Accelerating China's Rural Transformation.* Washington, DC: World Bank.

Oi, Jean C. 1999. *Rural China Takes Off.* Berkeley: University of California Press.

Oi, Jean C., and Scott Rozelle. 2000. "Elections and Power: The Locus of Decision-Making in Chinese Villages." *The China Quarterly*: 513–39.

Oksenberg, Michel, and James Tong. 1991. "The Evolution of Central-Provincial Fiscal Relations in China, 1971–1984: The Formal System." *The China Quarterly* (125): 1–32.

Organisation for Economic Co-Operation and Development. 2003 *China in the World Economy: An OECD Economic and Statistical Survey*. Paris: OECD.

Park, Albert, and Minggao Shen. 2000. "Joint Liability Lending and the Rise and Fall of China's Township and Village Enterprises." Ann Arbor: Department of Economics, University of Michigan.

———. 2001. "Decentralization in Financial Institutions: Theory and Evidence from China." Ann Arbor: Department of Economics, University of Michigan.

Pastor, Manuel Jr., and Carol Wise. 1992. "Peruvian Economic Policy in the 1980s: From Orthodoxy to Heterodoxy and Back." *Latin American Research Review* 27 (2):83–117.

Pei, Minxin. 2006. *China's Trapped Transition: The Limits of Developmental Autocracy*. Cambridge: Harvard University Press.

———. 2007. "Fighting Corruption: A Difficult Challenge for Chinese Leaders." Washington, DC: Carnegie Endowment of Peace.

People's Bank of China. 1987. *1986 Nian Jingrong Guizhang Zhidu Xuanbian [Selections of Financial Regulations in 1986]*. Tianjin: Zhongguo jingrong chubanshe.

———. 1999. "Guanyu Zuohao Dangqian Nongcun Xindai Gongzuo De Zhidao Yijian [Guidance on Improving Rural Lending Work]." In *Nongcun Xinyong Hezuoshe Wenjian Xuanbian 1998–1999.6. [Selection of Documents on Rural Credit Cooperatives 1998–July 1999]*, edited by The Monitoring Division of the People's Bank of China. Beijing: The People's Bank of China.

———. 1999 <1998>. "Nongcun Xinyong Hezuoshe He Nongcun Xinyong Hezuoshe Lianshe Zhuyao Fuzeren Renzhi Zige Guanli Shixing Banfa [Provisional Methods on Managing Appointment Qualifications of the Principals of the Rural Credit Cooperatives and the Associations of Rural Credit Cooperatives]." In *Nongcun Xinyong Hezuoshe Wenjian Xuanbian [Selection of Documents on Rural Credit Unions]*, edited by The General Office of the People's Bank of China. Beijing: The People's Bank of China.

———. 2000. *Zhongguo Jinrong Tongji 1997–1999 [Chinese Financial Statistics 1997–1999]*. Beijing: Zhongguo jinrong chubanshe.

———. 2001a. *Guanyu Jiaqiang Dui Nongcun Xinyongshe Jianguan Youguan Wenti De Tongzhi [Circular on Strengthening the Supervision of Rural Credit Cooperatives]*. Beijing: Zhongguo jingrong chubanshe.

———. 2001b. *Nongcun Xinyongshe Jianguan Gongzuo Zerenzhi Jiancha Kaohe Banfa [Evaluation System of the Responsibilities on the Part of Monitoring Staff in Charge of Rural Credit Cooperatives]*. Beijing: Zhongguo jingrong chubanshe.

———. 2003. *Zhongguo Jinrong Nianjian 2003 [Chinese Financial Yearbook 2003]*. Beijing: China Finance Press.

Pepper, Suzanne. 1990. *China's Education Reform in the 1980s: Policies, Issues, and Historical Perspectives*. Berkeley: Institute of East Asian Studies, Center for Chinese Studies, University of California.

Perkins, Dwight. 1986. *China: Asia's Next Economic Giant*. Seattle: University of Washington Press.

Perkins, Dwight, and Shahid Yusuf. 1984. *Rural Development in China*. Washington, DC: The World Bank.

Pink, Daniel H. 2005. "Why the World Is Flat." *Wired*.

Pocha, Jehangir S. 2006. "Shanghai Building Boom Pits Architects of East vs. West." *Boston Sunday Globe*, September, A16.

Putterman, Louis. 1995. "The Role of Ownership and Property Rights in China's Economic Transition." *The China Quarterly* (144):1049–64.

Qian, Yingyi. 1999. The Institutional Foundations of China's Market Transition. Paper read at The World Bank Annual Conference on Development Economics, April 28–30, Washington, DC.

———. 2003. "How Reform Worked in China." In *In Search of Prosperity: Analytic Narratives on Economic Growth*, edited by Dani Rodrik. Princeton, NJ: Princeton University Press.

Qian, Yingyi, and Joseph Stiglitz. 1996. "Institutional Innovations and the Role of Local Government in Transition Economies: The Case of Guangdong Province of China." In *Reforming Asian Socialism: The Growth of Market Institutions*, edited by John McMillan and Barry Naughton. Ann Arbor: University of Michigan Press.

Qu, Hongbin, and Sophia Ma Xiaoping. 2006. "China Economic Insight: Balancing Act." *Macro Economics* 25.

Rajan, Raghuram G., and Luigi Zingales. 1998. "Financial Dependence and Growth." *American Economic Review* 88:559–86.

Ranis, Gustav, and Chi Schive. 1985. "Direct Foreign Investment in Taiwan." In *Foreign Trade and Investment*, edited by Walter Galenson. Madison: University of Wisconsin Press.

Ravallion, Martin, and Shaohua Chen. 2007. "China's (Uneven) Progress against Poverty." *Journal of Development Economics* 82 (1): 1–42.

Rawski, Thomas G. 2001a. "China Reform Watch: Turning Point." *China Perspectives*, 28–35.

———. 2001b. "What Is Happening to China's GDP Statistics." *China Economic Review* 12 (4):347–54.

Ren, Ruoen, and Lin Lin Sun. 2006. "Total Factor Productivity Growth in Chinese Industries, 1981–2000." Beijing: Beihang University.

"A Report from the Shi Township." 1983. *Zhongguo nongmin bao [China's Peasants' Newspaper]*, August 16, 3.

Riskin, Carl. 1987. *China's Political Economy*. New York: Oxford University Press.

Roach, Stephen S. 2004. "Dateline India: From Mumbai to Pune." *The Globalist*.

Rodrik, Dani. 2007. *One Economics Many Recipes: Globalization, Institutions, and Economic Growth*. Princeton, NJ: Princeton University Press.

Roland, Gerard. 2000. *Transition and Economics: Politics, Markets, and Firms*. Cambridge: MIT Press.

Rozelle, Scott. 1996. "Stagnation without Equity: Patterns of Growth and Inequality in China's Rural Economy." *The China Journal* (35):63–93.

Rural Economy Research Team. 1998. "Zhongguo Nongcun Gaige Yu Shichang Jingji [China's Rural Reforms and Market Economy]." *State Council Development Research Center Research Report*, December 2, 1–16.

Rural Policy Research Office, and Rural Development Research Office. 1987. *Zhongguo Nongcun Shehui Jingji Dianxing Diaocha [A Representative Study of China's Rural Society and Economy]*. Beijing: Zhonguo shehui kexuan chubanshe.

Rural Work Leadership Team of Fujian Communist Party Committee. 1997. *Nong-cun Zhengce Fagui Huibian [Selections of Rural Policy Documents]*. Fuzhou: Fuzhou provincial government agricultural office.

Sachs, Jeffrey. 2006. *The End of Poverty*. New York: Penguin Books.

Sachs, Jeffrey, and Wing Thye Woo. 1994. "Structural Factors in the Economic Reforms of China, Eastern Europe, and the Former Soviet Union." *Economic Policy* (18):102–45.

Sachs, Jeffrey D. 2001. "Tropical Underdevelopment." Cambridge: National Bureau of Economic Research.

Sachs, Jeffrey D., Ashutosh Varshney, and Nirupam Bajpai. 1999. "Introduction." In *India in the Era of Economic Reforms*, edited by Jeffrey D. Sachs, Ashutosh Varshney, and Nirupam Bajpai. New Delhi: Oxford University Press.

Sáez, Lawrence. 2004. *Banking Reform in India and China*. New York: Palgrave Macmillan.

Saich, Tony. 2001. *Governance and Politics of China*. New York: Palgrave.

"Sayings of Deng Xiaoping." 1997. *New York Times*.

Schultz, Theodore W. 1953. *The Economic Organization of Agriculture*. New York: McGraw-Hill.

Sehrt, Kaja. 1998. "Banks vs. Budgets: Credit Allocation in the People's Republic of China, 1984–1997." Ann Arbor: Department of Political Science, University of Michigan.

Sen, Amartya. 1999. *Development as Freedom*. New York: Knopf.

Shandong Rural Social and Economic Survey Team. 1989. *Shandongsheng Nongcun Jingji Tiaocha Ziliao 1988 [Survey Materials of Shandong's Rural Economy 1988]*. N.P.: Shandong Rural Social and Economic Survey Team.

Shanghai Association of Industry and Commerce. 2006. *2006 Shanghai Minying Jingji [Shanghai's Private Economy in 2006]*. Shanghai: Shanghai Finance University Press.

Shanxi TVE Management Bureau. 1985. *Xiangzhen Qiye Guanli Jianmin Cidian [A Concise Dictionary of TVE Management]*. Taiyuan: Shanxi renmin chubanshe.

Shenkar, Oded. 2005. *The Chinese Century*. Upper Saddle River, NJ: Pearson Education.

———. 2006. "China's Economic Rise and the New Geopolitics." *International Journal* 61 (2):313–9.

Shi Jiliang. 1999. "Zai Quanguo Nongcun Xinyongshe Gongzuo Huiyi Shang De Zongjie Jianghua [Concluding Speech at the Work Conference of Rural Credit Unions]." In *Nongcun Xinyong Hezuoshe Wenjian Xuanbian [Selection of Documents on Rural Credit Unions]*, edited by The General Office of the People's Bank of China. Beijing: The People's Bank of China.

———. 1999 <1998>. "Shenhua Gaige Jiaqiang Guanli Fangfa Fengxian [Deepening Reforms, Strengthening Management, and Safeguarding Risks]." In *Nongcun Xinyong Hezuoshe Wenjian Xuanbian 1998–1999.6. [Selection of Documents on Rural Credit Unions 1998–July 1999]*, edited by The Monitoring Division of the People's Bank of China. Beijing: The People's Bank of China.

Shirk, Susan. 1982. *Competitive Comrades: Career Incentives and Student Strategies in China*. Berkeley: University of California Press.

Shirk, Susan L. 1993. *The Political Logic of Economic Reform in China*. Berkeley: University of California Press.

Sicular, Terry. 1988. "Agricultural Planning and Pricing in the Post-Mao Period." *The China Quarterly* (116):671–705.

Sicular, Terry, Ximing Yue, Bjorn Gustafsson, and Shi Li. 2007. "The Urban–Rural Income Gap and Inequality in China." *Review of Income and Wealth* 53 (1):93–126.

State Council. 1986. *Geti Jingji Tiaocha Yu Yanjiu [Investigations and Research on the Individual Economy]*. Beijing: Jingji kexuan chubanshe.

———. 1988. *Zhonghua Renmin Gongheguo 1985 Nian Gongye Pucha Ziliao [The Statistical Materials of the 1985 Industry Census]*, Vol. 3. Beijing: Zhongguo tongji chubanshe.

———. 1994 <1993>. *Guanyu Jingrong Tizhi Gaige De Jueding [Decision on Financial System Reform]*. Beijing: Zhongguo jingrong chubanshe.

———. 1996. "Guanyu Nongcun Jingrong Tizhi Gaige De Jiuding [Decision to Reform the Rural Financial System]." In *Nongcun Xinyong Hezuoshe Wenjian Xuanbian 1995–1997 [Selection of Documents on Rural Credit Cooperatives]*, edited by The People's Bank of China. Beijing: People's Bank of China.

———. 1998. *Feifa Jingrong Jigou He Feifa Jingrong Yewu Huodong Qudi Banfa [Procedures to Ban Illegal Financial Institutions and Illegal Financial Operations and Practices]*. Beijing: Zhongguo jingrong chubanshe.

State Development and Planning Commission. 1998. *Zhongguo Chanye Fazhan Baogao 1998 [Report on Chinese Industrial Development]*. Beijing: Zhongguo jingji chubanshe.

State System Reform Commission, Ministry of Commerce, and Husbandry Ministry of Agriculture and Fishing. 1992 <1984>. "Guangy Jinyibu Zuohao Nongcun Shangbin Liutong Gongzuo De Baogao [Report on Further Improving the Distribution of Agricultural Commodities]." In *Xingshiqi Nongye He Nongcun Gongzuo Zhongyao Wenxian Xuanbian [Selections of Important Documents on Agriculture and Rural Sector Work in the New Period]*, edited by The Central Committee Document Office and The State Council Development Research Center. Beijing: The Central Committee Document Press.

Stiglitz, Joseph E. 2006. "The Transition from Communism to Market: A Reappraisal after 15 Years." In *European Bank for Reconstruction and Development Annual Meeting*. London.

Stiglitz, Joseph E., and Shahid Yusuf, eds. 2001. *Rethinking the East Asian Miracle*. New York: Oxford University Press.

Sull, Donald N. 2005. *Made in China: What Western Managers Can Learn from Trailblazing Chinese Entrepreneurs*. Boston: Harvard Business School Press.

Sun, Yan. 2004. *Corruption and Market in Contemporary China*. Ithaca, NY: Cornell University Press.

Svejnar, Jan, and Josephine Woo. 1990. "Development Patterns in Four Countries." In *China's Rural Industry*, edited by William A. Byrd and Qingsong Lin. New York: Oxford University Press.

Tanner, Murray Scot. 2004. "China Rethinks Unrest." *The Washington Quarterly* 27 (3):137–56.

"Thousands of Ex-Soldiers Riot in China." 2007. *The Associated Press*, September 11.

"A Tiger Falling Behind a Dragon." 2003. *The Economist*: 9.

"The Tiger in Front: India and China." 2005. *The Economist*: 3–4.

Tsai, Kellee S. 2002. *Back Alley Banking: Private Entrepreneurs in China*. Ithaca, NY: Cornell University Press.

Urban Social and Economic Survey Team. 1991. *Zhongguo Chengshi Jumin Jiating Shouzhi Diaocha Ziliao 1991 [Statistical Materials on China Urban Household Income and Expenditure 1991]*. Beijing: China Statistics Press.

———. 1997. *Zhongguo Wujia Ji Chengshi Jumin Jiating Shouzhi Diaocha Tongji Nianjian 1997 [Statistical Book of Surveys on Price, Income and Expenditure of Chinese Urban Households 1997]*. Beijing: Zhongguo tongji chubanshe.

———. 2003. *Zhongguo Jiage Ji Chengshi Jumin Jiating Shouji Shouzhi Diaocha Tongji Nianjian 2003 [Statistical Yearbook of China's Prices and Urban Household Incomes and Expenditures 2003]*. Beijing: China Statistics Press.

———. 2005. *Zhongguo Jiage Ji Chengzhen Jumin Jiating Shouji Diaocha Tongji Nianjian 2005 [Statistical Yearbook of China's Prices and Urban Household Incomes and Expenditures]*. Beijing: China Statistics Press.

Vogel, Ezra F. 1989. *One Step Ahead in China: Guangdong under Reforms*. Cambridge: Harvard University Press.

Wade, Robert. 1990. *Governing the Market: Economic Theory and the Role of Government in East Asian Industrialization*. Princeton, NJ: Princeton University Press.

Walter, Carl E., and Fraser J.T. Howie (2003). *Privatizing China: The Stock Markets and Their Role in Corporate Reform*. Singapore: John Wiley & Sons (Asia) Pte Ltd.

Wan, Li. 1992 <1982>. "Jingyibu Fanzhan Rijing Kaizhuande Nongye Xingjumian [Further Developing Agriculture's New Situation]." In *Xingshiqi Nongye He Nongcun Gongzuo Zhongyao Wenxian Xuanbian [Selections of Important Documents on Agriculture and Rural Sector Work in the New Period]*, edited by The Central Committee Document Office and The State Council Development Research Center. Beijing: The Central Committee Document Press.

Wang, Kuicheng, Wei Daonan, and Chen Zi. 1981. "An Investigation on the Practice of Baochan Daohu in Anhui Province." In *Selection of Research Materials on Baochan Daohu*, edited by Chinese Agricultural Development Group. Beijing: Chinese Agricultural Development Group.

Wang, Xiaolu. 1990. "Capital Formation and Utilization." In *China's Rural Industry*, edited by William A. Byrd and Qingsong Lin. New York: Oxford University Press.

Wang, Xiaolu, and Lian Meng. 2001. "A Reevaluation of China's Economic Growth." *China Economic Review*, 338–46.

Wang, Yuanjiang. 2002. *Zhongguo Minyin Jingji Touzi Tizhi Yu Zhengce Huanjin [The Investment System and the Policy Enviroment for China's People-Run Economy]*. Beijing: Zhongguo jihua chubanshe.

Wang, Zhuoqiong. 2007. "The Ghost of Illiteracy Returns to Haunt Country." *China Daily*, April 2, 1.

Washburn, Dan. 2006. "Business China: How to Catch a Pirate." *Economist Intelligence Unit*.

Weingast, Barry R. 1995 "The Economic Role of Political Institutions." *Journal of Law, Economics and Organization* 11 (1):1–31.

Wessel, David, and Marcus Walker. 2004. "Good News for the Globe; Nobel Winners in Economics Are Upbeat About the Future as China and India Surge." *The Wall Street Journal*, September 3, A7.

Whiting, Susan. 2001. *Power and Wealth in Rural China: The Political Economy of Institutional Change*. Cambridge: Cambridge University Press.

Wise, Carol. 1994. "The Politics of Peruvian Economic Reform: Overcoming the Legacies of the State-Led Development." *Journal of International Studies and World Affairs* 32 (1):75–125.

Woetzel, Jonathan R. 2004. "China: The Best of All Possible Models." *The McKinsey Quarterly* (Special Issue):114–7.

Wolf, Martin. 2005. "Asia's Giants Take Different Routes." *Financial Times*, February 22.

Wong, Siu-Lun. 1988. *Emigrant Entrepreneurs: Shanghai Industrialists in Hong Kong.* Hong Kong: Oxford University Press.

Woo, Wing Thye. 2005. "China's Rural Enterprises in Crisis: The Role of Inadequate Financial Intermediation." In *Financial Sector Reform in China*, edited by Yasheng Huang, Tony Saich, and Edward S. Steinfeld. Cambridge: Harvard University Asia Center.

World Bank. 1983. *China: Socialist Economic Development.* Washington, DC: The World Bank.

———. 1989. *India: An Industrializing Economy in Transition.* Washington, DC: The World Bank.

———. 1993. *The East Asian Miracle.* New York: Oxford University Press.

———. 1995. *Bureaucrats in Business.* New York: Oxford University Press.

———. 1996. *World Development Report 1996: From Plan to Market.* New York: Oxford University Press.

———. 1999. *Strategic Goals for Chinese Education in the 21st Century.* Washington DC: World Bank.

———. 2001. *World Development Indicators 2001.* Washington, DC: The World Bank.

———. 2003. *China: Promoting Growth with Equity.* Washington DC: The World Bank.

———. 2005a. "China's Progress Towards the Health MDGs." *Briefing Note No. 2*, March.

———. 2005b. "Rural Health Insurance–Rising to the Challenge." *Briefing Note No. 6*, May.

———. 2006a. "China Governance, Investment Climate, and Harmonious Society: Competitiveness Enhancements for 120 Cities in China." Washington, DC: The World Bank Report No. 37759-CN.

———. 2006b. *Where Is the Wealth of Nations? Measuring Capital for the 21st Century.* Washington, DC: The World Bank.

Wu, Xiaobo. 2006. *Jidan Sanshi Nian [Significant Thirty Years].* Beijing: Zhongxin chubanshe.

———. 2007. *Dai Baiju Ii [Big Failures Ii].* Hangzhou: Zhejiang renmin chubanshe.

Wu, Yanrui. 2003. "Has Productivity Contributed to China's Growth?" *Pacific Economic Review* 8 (1):15–30.

———. 2004. "Productivity and Sustainable Growth." In *China: Is Rapid Growth Sustainable?*, edited by Ross Garnaut and Ligang Song. Canberra: Asia Pacific Press.

Xu, Xiaonian, and Yan Wang. 1997. "Ownership Structure, Corporate Governance, and Corporate Performance." Washington, DC: The World Bank.

Yang, Dongping. 2006. *2005 Nian Zhongguo Jiaoyu Fazhan Baogao [Transformation and Development of China's Education in 2005].* Beijing: Social Sciences Documentation Publishing House.

Yatsko, Pamela. 2004. *New Shanghai: The Rocky Rebirth of China's Legendary City.* New York: John Wiley & Sons.

Yergin, Daniel, and Joseph Stanislaw. 1998. *The Commanding Heights.* New York: Simon & Schuster.

Young, Alwyn. 1992. "A Tale of Two Cities: Factor Accumulation and Technical Change in Hong Kong and Singapore." In *Nber Macroeconomics Annual*, edited. Chicago: University of Chicago Press.

———. 1995. "The Tyranny of Numbers: Confronting the Statistical Realities of the East Asian Growth Experience." *Quarterly Journal of Economics*, August, 641–80.

———. 2003. "Gold into Base Metals: Productivity Growth in the People's Republic of China During the Reform Period." *Journal of Political Economy*, December, 1220–61.

Yusuf, Shahid, and Simon J. Evenett. 2002. *Can East Asia Compete?* New York: Oxford University Press.

Yusuf, Shahid, and Kaoru Nabeshima. 2006. *Postindustrial East Asian Cities.* Palo Alto, CA: Stanford University Press.

Yusuf, Shahid, Kaoru Nabeshima, and Dwight H. Perkins. 2006. *Under New Ownership: Privatizing China's State-Owned Enterprises.* Washington, DC: The World Bank.

Zhang Houyi, and Ming Lizhi, eds. 1999. *Zhongguo Siying Qiye Fazhan Baogao (1978–1998) [Report on Development of China's Private Enterprises (1978–1998)].* Beijing: Shehui kexue wenxian chubanshe.

Zhang, Liang, Andrew J. Nathan, and Perry Link, eds. 2001. *The Tiananmen Papers.* New York: Public Affairs.

Zhang, Lianjie, and Li Dingfu. 2001. *Zoujin Wenzhou [Walking into Wenzhou].* Beijing: Jingji ribao chubanshe.

Zhang, Tingwei. 2002. "Urban Development and a Socialist Pro-Growth Coalition in Shanghai." *Urban Affairs Review*, March, 475–99.

Zhang, Yi. 1990. *Zhongguo Xiangzhen Qiye Jianxin De Licheng [Chinese Township and Village Enterprises: A History of Hardship].* Beijing: Falu chubanshe.

Zhao, Shukai. 1999. "Cunmin Yu Fudan [Villagers and Burdens]." *State Council Investigation and Research Report* (168).

———. 2004a. "Bianju Zhong De Xiangzhen Jigou [Changing Township Organizations]." *State Council Investigation and Research Report* (119).

———. 2004b. "Xiangzhen Gaige Zhilu [Reforms of Townships]." *State Council Investigation and Research Report* (138).

———. 2005. "Xiangzhen Zhengfu De Cunji Guanli [Village Management by Township Governments]." *State Council Investigation and Research Report* (57).

Zhao, Ying. 1998. "Zhongguo Chanye Zhengce Shizheng Yanjiu Daocha Wenjuan Fenxi [Analysis of a Survey on Chinese Industrial Policy]." *Jingji Guanli [Economic Management]* (3):62–4.

Zhejiang Bureau of Statistics. 1985. *Zhejiang Jingji Tongji Nianjian 1985 [Zhejiang Economic Statistical Yearbook 1985].* Hangzhou: Zhejiang tongji ju.

Zheng, Jinghai, and Angang Hu. 2004. "An Empirical Analysis of Provincial Productivity in China (1979–2001)." Goteberg, Sweden: Department of Economics, Goteberg University.

Zhou, Kate Xiao. 1996. *How the Farmers Changed China.* Boulder, CO: Westview Press, 1996.

Zhou, Reli. 1979. "Luoshi Nongcun Jingji Zhengce De Jige Wenti [A Few Questions on the Implementation of the Agricultural Policy]." *Red Flag* (4):5.

Zhu, Rongji. 1990. *Zhu Rongji Tan Kaifa Pudong De Zijin Laiyuan [Zhu Rongji on the Sources of Funding for Pudong Development].* Shanghai: Shanghai Sanlian shudian.

Index